THE COMPLETE GREEK TRAGEDIES

VOLUME III

EURIPIDES

THE COMPLETE GREEK TRAGEDIES

Edited by David Grene and Richmond Lattimore

VOLUME III

EURIPIDES

THE  UNIVERSITY OF CHICAGO PRESS

Alcestis

© 1955 by The University of Chicago

The Medea

First published 1944, reprinted 1946 by John Lane,
The Bodley Head Limited, London, England

The Heracleidae

© 1955 by The University of Chicago

Hippolytus

© 1942 by The University of Chicago

*The Cyclops, Heracles, Iphigenia in Tauris, Helen,
Hecuba, Andromache, The Trojan Women*

© 1956 by The University of Chicago

Volume III published 1959. Second impression 1959
Composed and printed by The University of Chicago Press
Chicago, Illinois, U.S.A.

GENERAL INTRODUCTION

W<small>E ARE</small> told that Euripides, the son of Mnesarchus or Mnesarchides, was born at some time between 485 and 480 B.C., presented his first set of tragedies in 455, and won his first victory in 441, won only four victories during his lifetime, left Athens probably in 408 for the court of King Archelaus of Macedon, and died there late in 407 or early in 406. He wrote perhaps eighty-eight plays (twenty-two sets of four); nineteen survive under his name, though *Rhesus* may not be his.

Such seems to be the basic and believable vita (though I suspect that the dates for birth and first presentation are too early). We may ignore the fanciful gossip that passes for additional biography, but consider the critical opinions of the comic poets. The conclusion is that Euripides was only moderately successful in his own lifetime, though famous and influential after death. He won seldom but produced again and again. He was parodied and ridiculed by the comic poets more often and more brutally (and more intelligently, too) than any other literary man in Athens. This fact itself means that he made more of an impression than the now obscure competitors who must have beaten him again and again.

Plainly, he wrote shockers, and it is not enough to say that this was because he was an innovator. He was, but so were his predecessors. Aeschylus was more daring, drastic, and original; Sophocles was no serene and static classicist. Perhaps the most significant remark about Euripides and Sophocles is that supposed to have been made by Sophocles, that he himself showed men as they ought to be (or as one ought to show them) but Euripides showed them as they actually were. Whether or not Sophocles ever said this, it is true. Euripides was basically a realist, despite contrary tendencies toward fantasy and romance. The only materials available for his tragedies were the old heroic sagas. He used them as if they told the story not of characters heroic in all dimensions, but of real everyday people.

From the high legends of Jason and Heracles he chose to enact the moments of the heroes' decay and disintegration. What, he asks, does it feel like to have your wife die for you, and what kind of man will let her do it? What does it feel like to have murdered your mother? His Admetus fights hard to deceive himself, but we all see that he is a coward; his Orestes is a bad mental case with fits and seizures. Creusa, brutally violated by Apollo and then robbed of the baby she had guiltily borne, does not dance decorously out of the story like Pindar's Evadne in similar circumstances; the shame sticks with her, as if she were a real girl with a real experience; and Apollo, while managing that all comes well in the end, hides behind his temple and lets his sister speak for him.

Though the judges of Dionysus disapproved, there cannot be much doubt that the audience was fascinated even when it was not pleased. Was this enough, though? The sense of defeat and disappointment is constantly there in Euripides. It makes him bring to the fore those who are weak or oppressed, the despised and misunderstood: women, children, slaves, captives, strangers, barbarians. Women as chief characters outnumber men, and most of his choruses are female. It is not that he is "for" them or "against" them; he merely tries to present action from their point of view, and they fascinate him. So do children, but here his realism fails: obviously, he knew little about them. His servants are true to life, while his heroes who deliver the oppressed are wooden.

Euripides is sometimes perhaps more pathetic than tragic. The hero (or heroine) in Sophocles is prepared to fight stubbornly to the last; his Teucer, alone against an army full of warriors who could beat him singlehanded, acts as if he were the champion with an army at his back. Many characters of Euripides spend all their time trying to run away from something. Ion and Hippolytus are blissfully happy only while they lead do-nothing lives; then the real world with its entanglements catches up with them, and they are miserable. His choruses are not the first to long for the wings of the dove, but they do it oftenest; in him the drive to escape becomes an insistent, recurrent motive. Even his own invention, bright optimistic romantic comedy, becomes drama of escape. Usually, escape is impossible. He believed in a world he disliked. His gods represent this world.

With Euripides, tragedy is either transcending itself or going into a decline, in any case turning into something else. If Euripides is less of a master in his own medium than Aeschylus and Sophocles, it is partly because he was less happy in that medium. This shows in faults which his greatest admirers will concede. His pathos may degenerate into sentimentality. There are signs of haste, slovenliness, inconsequence, windiness, in most of his best plays. Some whole plays are mediocre. His most characteristic fault is to try to get too much into a single plot or character or situation. His Medea is several kinds of woman unsuccessfully assembled; his *Andromache* has two badly connected plots. He wrote some lovely lyrics, but often (as in *Helen*) they have nothing to do with what is going on in the play. And so on. His faults are obvious. Equally obvious is his genius. He is the father of the romantic comedy, the problem play. He has given us a series of unforgettable characters. There has never been anyone else like him.

RICHMOND LATTIMORE

BRYN MAWR COLLEGE

CONTENTS

ALCESTIS

Translated and with an Introduction by

RICHMOND LATTIMORE

INTRODUCTION TO *ALCESTIS*

The Legend

THE origins of the story as it is told by Euripides are difficult to trace. We hear of Admetus and of Alcestis, "loveliest of all the daughters of Pelias," in the *Iliad*, but only as parents of Eumelus, one of the Achaeans at Troy. There is an allusion to the story as Euripides tells it in the *skolion* or drinking catch attributed to the little-known poetess Praxilla:

> Mark the saying of Admetus, dear friend, and make friends with
>   the brave.
> Keep away from cowards, knowing that there is little grace in them.

We also know that Phrynichus, a dramatic poet of the early fifth century, used what seems to have been essentially the same version as that which Euripides followed. The best conclusion, though it is tentative, is that Euripides did not add any "facts" to the legend as he received it. The originality of the play would rather lie in the way in which he approached a known, though not particularly well-known, story from a new angle and with a new emphasis.

The Play

Grant, then, the basic outline of the plot: Alcestis voluntarily dying for her husband when his father and mother would not; Alcestis and Admetus delivered by Admetus' true friend, Heracles, who is guided by the remote hand of Apollo, also a true friend of Admetus. One may emphasize the heroism of Alcestis and the staunchness of Heracles, as against the way in which mother and father fail wretchedly in the crisis. This is as far as our *skolion* goes, for whether or not "the brave" designates both Alcestis and Heracles or only one, "cowards" means the mother and father, not Admetus himself. Admetus is merely the subject about whom these operations, of dying or refusing to die, revolve; his own character does not come into question.

Euripides took a different kind of interest. He gives Alcestis full honors. The beginning of the play is all hers, and she is the center of all memories throughout the play. If she appears cold and self-righteous, if she reserves her passion, on stage, for her children, and talks only business with Admetus, this is rather the embarrassment of being disappointed in him than coldness. Endearments addressed to Admetus at this time would be intolerable. Her true nature is brought out by what servants and others have to say about her. Pheres, the father, is effectively dealt with in his one scene. It is true he wins his argument, but all the justification in the world does not save him from being a horrible old man. But the principal character is Admetus. The theme of the drama is not "if a wife dies for her husband, how brave and devoted the wife," so much as "if a husband lets his wife die for him, what manner of man must that husband be?"

Admetus is drawn to the life, without mercy. He has all the superficial graces and sincerely loves his wife and children, but he lacks the courage to die as he ought instead of letting his wife die for him; and, further, he lacks the courage to admit, to himself or anyone else, that he ought to be dying but dare not do it. He has, however, one solid virtue. For if he and Alcestis are at last saved not by his own strength and resolution but by Heracles under authority of Apollo, yet there is good reason why these august persons should be so devoted to him. Admetus is the best of friends. The right treatment of guests is a passion, almost an obsession, with him, and in this matter his conviction makes him firm enough to override so great a man as Heracles, with a show of force quite different from his ungrounded violence against Pheres. We may call him hospitable. But if we do, we must understand that, while the lavish entertainment of visitors was a special tradition in Thessaly, the hospitality of Admetus goes far beyond this and is no merely sociable virtue. Rather, this is the old Homeric *xenia*. It is one of the steps by which society progresses from savagery to civilization, when strangers make a willing, immediate, and permanent agreement to be friends. In this sense, *xenia* also includes cases at least of the nonabuse of power against those over whom one has power. Apollo, for punishment, was put at the mercy of Admetus, and Admetus gave him fair and friendly treatment (ll. 8–10; 222–24; 568–79). A different king might have reveled in his power over such a subject and acted outrageously. This is what Laomedon, king of Troy, did to Apollo and Poseidon (*Iliad* xxi. 441–60), and Poseidon never forgave him or his people. So, too, with Heracles, generous hospitality for the tramping hero becomes more than just a matter of correctness or etiquette when one thinks of such "hosts" as Procrustes, Sciron, and Antaeus. Violation of the rights of *xenia* is an underlying theme which directs the action in both the story of Troy and the story of Odysseus. The sin of Laomedon provoked divine rage against Troy; then Paris doomed the city when, after being properly received in the house of Menelaus, he went off with his host's wife and most of his furniture. Decisive for the action of the *Odyssey* is that travesty of *xenia* performed by the suitors when they settle down and make themselves intolerably at home in the house of Odysseus.

If we adopt the admittedly somewhat hypothetical scheme according to which tragedy consists in the destruction or self-destruction of an otherwise great man through some fault or flaw in his character, then *Alcestis* might be viewed as a kind of inverted tragedy. For this hero, otherwise no better than ordinary, has one significant *virtue,* which *saves* him. Thus, again, the progress of the play is from ruin to safety, reversing what might be considered the normal course of tragedy. I would not press this view, although I think there is a little truth in it, because Euripides would have had to have a formula for tragedy before he could invert it, and we do not know that he had such a formula. At any rate, the "comic" qualities of *Alcestis* have puzzled critics since ancient times. It was played fourth in the set, in the position usually given to a satyr-play. But attempts to explain *Alcestis* as a modified satyr-play are not convincing, and the comic elements are not highly significant. Heracles may momentarily be a moderately funny drunk, but that is about all. The squabble between Admetus and Pheres, in which both really lose, is too humanly disagreeable to be funny; the squabble between Apollo and Death is grotesque, but scarcely uproarious. *Alcestis* is no satyr-play, but a tragicomedy which in part (loss, escape, reunion) anticipates the lighter escape-dramas (*Iphigeneia in Tauris, Helen*) still to come. But it goes deeper than these do.

Date and Circumstances

Alcestis was presented in 438 B.C. The first three plays in the set (all lost) were *The Women of Crete, Alcmaeon in Psophis,* and *Telephus.* Thus *Alcestis* is the earliest extant work of Euripides, with the possible exception of *The Cyclops* and (very doubtful) *Rhesus,* which are undated. Euripides won second place, being beaten by Sophocles.

Text

I have followed Murray's Oxford text, and used his line numbers, which are standard; except that I have adopted different readings which affect the translation of the following lines: 50, 124, 223, 943, 1140, 1153.

CHARACTERS

Apollo

Death

Chorus of citizens of Pherae

Maid, attendant of Alcestis

Alcestis, wife of Admetus

Admetus of Pherae, king of Thessaly

Boy (Eumelus), son of Admetus and Alcestis

Heracles

Pheres, father of Admetus

Servant of Admetus

Girl, daughter of Admetus and Alcestis (silent character)

Servants (silent)

ALCESTIS

SCENE: *Pherae, in Thessaly, before the house of Admetus. The front door of the house, or palace, is the center of the backdrop.*

(Enter Apollo from the house, armed with a bow.)

Apollo

House of Admetus, in which I, god though I am,
had patience to accept the table of the serfs!
Zeus was the cause. Zeus killed my son, Asclepius,
and drove the bolt of the hot lightning through his chest.
I, in my anger for this, killed the Cyclopes,   5
smiths of Zeus's fire, for which my father made me serve
a mortal man, in penance for my misdoings.
I came to this country, tended the oxen of this host
and friend, Admetus, son of Pheres. I have kept
his house from danger, cheated the Fates to save his life   10
until this day, for he revered my sacred rights
sacredly, and the fatal goddesses allowed
Admetus to escape the moment of his death
by giving the lower powers someone else to die
instead of him. He tried his loved ones all in turn,   15
father and aged mother who had given him birth,
and found not one, except his wife, who would consent
to die for him, and not see daylight any more.
She is in the house now, gathered in his arms and held
at the breaking point of life, because the destiny marks   20
this for her day of death and taking leave of life.
The stain of death in the house must not be on me. I
step therefore from these chambers dearest to my love.
And here is Death himself, I see him coming, Death
who dedicates the dying, who will lead her down   25
to the house of Hades. He has come on time. He has
been watching for this day on which her death falls due.

*(Enter Death, armed with a sword, from the wing. He sees
Apollo suddenly and shows surprise.)*

Death

  Ah!
You at this house, Phoebus? Why do you haunt
the place. It is unfair to take for your own   30
and spoil the death-spirits' privileges.
Was it not enough, then, that you blocked the death
of Admetus, and overthrew the Fates
by a shabby wrestler's trick? And now
your bow hand is armed to guard her too,   35
Alcestis, Pelias' daughter, though she
promised her life for her husband's.

Apollo

  Never fear. I have nothing but justice and fair words for you.

Death

  If you mean fairly, what are you doing with a bow?

Apollo

  It is my custom to carry it with me all the time.   40

Death

  It is your custom to help this house more than you ought.

Apollo

  But he is my friend, and his misfortunes trouble me.

Death

  You mean to take her body, too, away from me?

Apollo

  I never took *his* body away from you by force.

Death

  How is it, then, that he is above ground, not below?   45

Apollo

  He gave his wife instead, and you have come for her now.

Death

I have. And I shall take her down where the dead are.

Apollo

Take her and go. I am not sure you will listen to me.

Death

Tell me to kill whom I must kill. Such are my orders.

Apollo

No, only to put their death off. They must die in the end.   50

Death

I understand what you would say and what you want.

Apollo

Is there any way, then, for Alcestis to grow old?

Death

There is not. I insist on enjoying my rights too.

Apollo

You would not take more than one life, in any case.

Death

My privilege means more to me when they die young.   55

Apollo

If she dies old, she will have a lavish burial.

Death

What you propose, Phoebus, is to favor the rich.

Apollo

What is this? Have you unrecognized talents for debate?

Death

Those who could afford to buy a late death would buy it then.

Apollo

I see. Are you determined not to do this for me?   60

Death

I will not do it. And you know my character.

Apollo

I know it: hateful to mankind, loathed by the gods.

Death

You cannot always have your way where you should not.

Apollo

For all your brute ferocity you shall be stopped.
The man to do it is on the way to Pheres' house   65
now, on an errand from Eurystheus, sent to steal
a team of horses from the wintry lands of Thrace.
He shall be entertained here in Admetus' house
and he shall take the woman away from you by force,
nor will you have our gratitude, but you shall still   70
be forced to do it, and to have my hate beside.

Death

Much talk. Talking will win you nothing. All the same,
the woman goes with me to Hades' house. I go
to take her now, and dedicate her with my sword,
for all whose hair is cut in consecration   75
by this blade's edge are devoted to the gods below.

(*Death enters the house. Apollo leaves by the wing. The
Chorus enters and forms a group before the gates.*)

Chorus

It is quiet by the palace. What does it mean?
Why is the house of Admetus so still?
Is there none here of his family, none
who can tell us whether the queen is dead   80
and therefore to be mourned? Or does Pelias'
daughter Alcestis live still, still look
on daylight, she who in my mind appears
noble beyond
all women beside in a wife's duty?   85

(*Here they speak individually, not as a group.*)

First Citizen

Does someone hear anything?

The sound a hand's stroke would make,
or outcry, as if something were done
and over?

Second Citizen

       No. And there is no servant stationed
at the outer gates. O Paean,   90
healer, might you show in light
to still the storm of disaster.

Third Citizen

They would not be silent if she were dead.

Fourth Citizen

No, she is gone.

Fifth Citizen

They have not taken her yet from the house.

Sixth Citizen

So sure? I know nothing. Why are you certain?   95
And how could Admetus have buried his wife
with none by, and she so splendid?

Seventh Citizen

Here at the gates I do not see
the lustral spring water, approved
by custom for a house of death.   100

Eighth Citizen

Nor are there cut locks of hair at the forecourts
hanging, such as the stroke of sorrow
for the dead makes. I can hear no beating
of the hands of young women.

Ninth Citizen

Yet this is the day appointed.   105

Tenth Citizen

What do you mean? Speak.

Ninth Citizen

  On which she must pass to the world below.

Eleventh Citizen

  You touch me deep, my heart, where it hurts.

Twelfth Citizen

  Yes. He who from the first has claimed to be called
  a good man himself   110
  must grieve when good men are afflicted.

                         (Henceforward all the Chorus together.)
  Sailing the long sea, there is
  not any place on earth
  you could win, not Lycia,
  not the unwatered sands called   115
  of Ammon, not
  thus to approach and redeem the life
  of this unhappy woman. Her fate shows
  steep and near. There is no god's hearth
  I know you could reach and by sacrifice   120
  avail to save.

  There was only one. If the eyes
  of Phoebus' son were opened
  still, if he could have come
  and left the dark chambers,   125
  the gates of Hades.
  He upraised those who were stricken
  down, until from the hand of God
  the flown bolt of thunder hit him.
  Where is there any hope for life   130
  left for me any longer?

  For all has been done that can be done by our kings now,
  and there on all the gods' altars
  are blood sacrifices dripping in full,
  but no healing comes for the evil.   135

(Enter a maid from the house.)

Chorus

But here is a serving woman coming from the house.
The tears break from her. What will she say has taken place?
We must, of course, forgive your sorrow if something
has happened to your masters. We should like to know
whether the queen is dead or if she is still alive.   140

Maid

I could tell you that she is still alive or that she is dead.

Chorus

How could a person both be dead and live and see?

Maid

It has felled her, and the life is breaking from her now.

Chorus

Such a husband, to lose such a wife. I pity you.

Maid

The master does not see it and he will not see it   145
until it happens.

Chorus

           There is no hope left she will live?

Maid

None. This is the day of destiny. It is too strong.

Chorus

Surely, he must be doing all he can for her.

Maid

All is prepared so he can bury her in style.

Chorus

Let her be sure, at least, that as she dies, there dies   150
the noblest woman underneath the sun, by far.

Maid

Noblest? Of course the noblest, who will argue that?
What shall the wife be who surpasses her? And how

could any woman show that she loves her husband more
than herself better than by consent to die for him?   155
But all the city knows that well. You shall be told
now how she acted in the house, and be amazed
to hear. For when she understood the fatal day
was come, she bathed her white body with water drawn
from running streams, then opened the cedar chest and took   160
her clothes out, and dressed in all her finery
and stood before the Spirit in the Hearth, and prayed:
"Mistress, since I am going down beneath the ground,
I kneel before you in this last of all my prayers.
Take care of my children for me. Give the little girl   165
a husband; give the little boy a generous wife;
and do not let my children die like me, who gave
them birth, untimely. Let them live a happy life
through to the end and prosper here in their own land."
Afterward she approached the altars, all that stand   170
in the house of Admetus, made her prayers, and decked them all
with fresh sprays torn from living myrtle. And she wept
not at all, made no outcry. The advancing doom
made no change in the color and beauty of her face.
But then, in their room, she threw herself upon the bed,   175
and there she did cry, there she spoke: "O marriage bed,
it was here that I undressed my maidenhood and gave
myself up to this husband for whose sake I die.
Goodbye. I hold no grudge. But you have been my death
and mine alone. I could not bear to play him false.   180
I die. Some other woman will possess you now.
She will not be better, but she might be happier."
She fell on the bed and kissed it. All the coverings
were drenched in the unchecked outpouring of her tears;
but after much crying, when all her tears were shed,   185
she rolled from the couch and walked away with eyes cast down,
began to leave the room, but turned and turned again
to fling herself once more upon the bed. Meanwhile
the children clung upon their mother's dress, and cried,

until she gathered them into her arms, and kissed   190
first one and then the other, as in death's farewell.
And all the servants in the house were crying now
in sorrow for their mistress. Then she gave her hand
to each, and each one took it, there was none so mean
in station that she did not stop and talk with him.   195
This is what Admetus and the house are losing. Had
he died, he would have lost her, but in this escape
he will keep the pain. It will not ever go away.

Chorus

    Admetus surely must be grieving over this
    when such a wife must be taken away from him.   200

Maid

    Oh yes, he is crying. He holds his wife close in his arms,
    imploring her not to forsake him. What he wants
    is impossible. She is dying. The sickness fades her now.
    She has gone slack, just an inert weight on the arm.
    Still, though so little breath of life is left in her,   205
    she wants to look once more upon the light of the sun,
    since this will be the last time of all, and never again.
    She must see the sun's shining circle yet one more time.
    Now I must go announce your presence. It is not
    everyone who bears so much good will toward our kings   210
    as to stand by ready to help in their distress.
    But you have been my master's friends since long ago.

                                              (Exit.)

Chorus

    O Zeus, Zeus, what way out of this evil
    is there, what escape from this
    which is happening to our princes?
    A way, any way? Must I cut short my hair   215
    for grief, put upon me the black
    costume that means mourning?
    We must, friends, clearly we must; yet still

let us pray to the gods. The gods
have power beyond all power elsewhere.

Paean, my lord,   220
Apollo, make some way of escape for Admetus.
Grant it, oh grant it. Once you found
rescue in him. Be now
in turn his redeemer from death.
Oppose bloodthirsty Hades.   225

Admetus,
O son of Pheres, what a loss
to suffer, when such a wife goes.
A man could cut his throat for this, for this
and less he could bind the noose upon his neck
and hang himself. For this is   230
not only dear, but dearest of all,
this wife you will see dead
on this day before you.

*(Alcestis is carried from the house on a litter, supported by
Admetus and followed by her children and
servants of the household.)*

But see, see,
she is coming out of the house and her husband is with her.
Cry out aloud, mourn, you land
of Pherae for the bravest   235
of wives fading in sickness and doomed
to the Death God of the world below.

I will never again say that marriage brings
more pleasure than pain. I judge by what
I have known in the past, and by seeing now   240
what happens to our king, who is losing a wife
brave beyond all others, and must live a life
that will be no life for the rest of time.

Alcestis

Sun, and light of the day,
O turning wheel of the sky, clouds that fly.   245

Admetus

    The sun sees you and me, two people suffering,
    who never hurt the gods so they should make you die.

Alcestis

    My land, and palace arching my land,
    and marriage chambers of Iolcus, my own country.

Admetus

    Raise yourself, my Alcestis, do not leave me now.   250
    I implore the gods to pity you. They have the power.

Alcestis

    I see him there at the oars of his little boat in the lake,
    the ferryman of the dead,
    Charon, with his hand upon the oar,
    and he calls me now: "What keeps you?   255
    Hurry, you hold us back." He is urging me on
    in angry impatience.

Admetus

    The crossing you speak of is a bitter one for me;
    ill starred; it is unfair we should be treated so.

Alcestis

    Somebody has me, somebody takes me away, do you see,
    don't you see, to the courts   260
    of dead men. He frowns from under dark
    brows. He has wings. It is Death.
    Let me go, what are you doing, let go.
                        Such is the road
    most wretched I have to walk.

Admetus

    Sorrow for all who love you, most of all for me
    and for the children. All of us share in this grief.   265

Alcestis

    Let me go now, let me down,
    flat. I have no strength to stand.

Death is close to me.
The darkness creeps over my eyes. O children,
my children, you have no mother now,
not any longer. Daylight is yours,
my children. Look on it and be happy.

Admetus

Ah, a bitter word for me to hear,
heavier than any death of my own.
Before the gods, do not be so harsh
as to leave me, leave your children forlorn.
No, up, and fight it.
There would be nothing left of me if you died.
All rests in you, our life, our not
having life. Your love is our worship.

Alcestis

Admetus, you can see how it is with me. Therefore,
I wish to have some words with you before I die.
I put you first, and at the price of my own life
made certain you would live and see the daylight. So
I die, who did not have to die, because of you.
I could have taken any man in Thessaly
I wished and lived in queenly state here in this house.
But since I did not wish to live bereft of you
and with our children fatherless, I did not spare
my youth, although I had so much to live for. Yet
your father, and the mother who bore you, gave you up,
though they had reached an age when it was good to die
and good to save their son and end it honorably.
You were their only one, and they had no more hope
of having other children if you died. That way
I would be living and you would live the rest of our time,
and you would not be alone and mourning for your wife
and tending motherless children. No, but it must be
that some god has so wrought that things shall be this way.
So be it. But swear now to do, in recompense,

270

275

280

285

290

295

what I shall ask you—not enough, oh, never enough,　　300
since nothing is enough to make up for a life,
but fair, and you yourself will say so, since you love
these children as much as I do; or at least you should.
Keep them as masters in my house, and do not marry
again and give our children to a stepmother　　305
who will not be so kind as I, who will be jealous
and raise her hand to your children and mine. Oh no,
do not do that, do not. That is my charge to you.
For the new-come stepmother hates the children born
to a first wife, no viper could be deadlier.　　310
The little boy has his father for a tower of strength.
[He can talk with him and be spoken to in turn.]
But you, my darling, what will your girlhood be like,
how will your father's new wife like you? She must not
make shameful stories up about you, and contrive　　315
to spoil your chance of marriage in the blush of youth,
because your mother will not be there to help you
when you are married, not be there to give you strength
when your babies are born, when only a mother's help will do.
For I must die. It will not be tomorrow, not　　320
the next day, or this month, the horrible thing will come,
but now, at once, I shall be counted among the dead.
Goodbye, be happy, both of you. And you, my husband,
can boast the bride you took made you the bravest wife,
and you, children, can say, too, that your mother was brave.　　325

Chorus

Fear nothing; for I dare to speak for him. He will
do all you ask. If he does not, the fault is his.

Admetus

It shall be so, it shall be, do not fear, since you
were mine in life, you still shall be my bride in death
and you alone, no other girl in Thessaly　　330
shall ever be called wife of Admetus in your place.
There is none such, none so marked out in pride of birth

nor beauty's brilliance, nor in anything else. I have
these children, they are enough; I only pray the gods
grant me the bliss to keep them as we could not keep you.   335
I shall go into mourning for you, not for just
a year, but all my life while it still lasts, my dear,
and hate the woman who gave me birth always, detest
my father. These were called my own people. They were not.
You gave what was your own and dear to buy my life   340
and saved me. Am I not to lead a mourning life
when I have lost a wife like you? I shall make an end
of revelry and entertainment in my house,
the flowers and the music that were found here once.
No, I shall never touch the lutestrings ever again   345
nor have the heart to play music upon the flute
of Libya, for you took my joy in life with you.
I shall have the skilled hand of an artificer
make me an image of you to set in my room,
pay my devotions to it, hold it in my arms   350
and speak your name, and clasp it close against my heart,
and think I hold my wife again, though I do not,
cold consolation, I know it, and yet even so
I might drain the weight of sorrow. You could come
to see me in my dreams and comfort me. For they   355
who love find a time's sweetness in the visions of night.
Had I the lips of Orpheus and his melody
to charm the maiden daughter of Demeter and
her lord, and by my singing win you back from death,
I would have gone beneath the earth, and not the hound   360
of Pluto could have stayed me, not the ferryman
of ghosts, Charon at his oar. I would have brought you back
to life. Wait for me, then, in that place, till I die,
and make ready the room where you will live with me,
for I shall have them bury me in the same chest   365
as you, and lay me at your side, so that my heart
shall be against your heart, and never, even in death
shall I go from you. You alone were true to me.

Chorus

And I, because I am your friend and you
are mine, shall help you bear this sorrow, as I should.   370

Alcestis

Children, you now have heard your father promise me
that he will never marry again and not inflict
a new wife on you, but will keep my memory.

Admetus

I promise. I will keep my promise to the end.

Alcestis

On this condition, take the children. They are yours.   375

Admetus

I take them, a dear gift from a dear hand.

Alcestis

                                        And now
you must be our children's mother, too, instead of me.

Admetus

I must be such, since they will no longer have you.

Alcestis

O children, this was my time to live, and I must go.

Admetus

Ah me, what shall I do without you all alone.   380

Alcestis

Time will soften it. The dead count for nothing at all.

Admetus

Oh, take me with you, for God's love, take me there too.

Alcestis

No, I am dying in your place. That is enough.

Admetus

O God, what a wife you are taking away from me.

Alcestis

It is true. My eyes darken and the heaviness comes. 385

Admetus

But I am lost, dear, if you leave me.

Alcestis

There is no use
in talking to me any more. I am not there.

Admetus

No, lift your head up, do not leave your children thus.

Alcestis

I do not want to, but it is goodbye, children.

Admetus

Look at them, oh look at them.

Alcestis

No. There is nothing more. 390

Admetus

Are you really leaving us?

Alcestis

Goodbye.

Admetus

Oh, I am lost.

Chorus

It is over now. Admetus' wife is gone from us.

Boy

O wicked fortune. Mother has gone down there,
father, she is not here with us
in the sunshine any more. 395
She was cruel and went away
and left me to live all alone.
Look at her eyes, look at her hands, so still.
Hear me, mother, listen to me, oh please, 400
listen, it is I, mother,
I your little one lean and kiss
your lips, and cry out to you.

Admetus

She does not see, she does not hear you. You and I
both have a hard and heavy load to carry now.   405

Boy

Father, I am too small to be left alone
by the mother I loved so much. Oh,
it is hard for me to bear
all this that is happening,
and you, little sister, suffer   410
with me too. Oh, father,
your marriage was empty, empty, she did not live
to grow old with you.
She died too soon. Mother, with you gone away,
the whole house is ruined.   415

*(Alcestis is carried into the house, followed
by children and servants.)*

Chorus

Admetus, you must stand up to misfortune now.
You are not the first, and not the last of humankind
to lose a good wife. Therefore, you must understand
death is an obligation claimed from all of us.

Admetus

I understand it. And this evil which has struck   420
was no surprise. I knew about it long ago,
and knowledge was hard. But now, since we must bury our dead,
stay with me and stand by me, chant responsively
the hymn of the unsacrificed-to god below.
To all Thessalians over whom my rule extends   425
I ordain a public mourning for my wife, to be
observed with shaving of the head and with black robes.
The horses that you drive in chariots and those
you ride single shall have their manes cut short with steel,
and there shall be no sound of flutes within the city,   430
no sound of lyres, until twelve moons have filled and gone;
for I shall never bury any dearer dead

than she, nor any who loved me better. She deserves
my thanks. She died for me, which no one else would do.

(Exit into the house.)

Chorus

O daughter of Pelias   435
my wish for you is a happy life
in the sunless chambers of Hades.
Now let the dark-haired lord of Death himself, and the old man,
who sits at the steering oar   440
and ferries the corpses,
know that you are the bravest of wives, by far,
ever conveyed across the tarn
of Acheron in the rowboat.

Much shall be sung of you   445
by the men of music to the seven-strung mountain
lyre-shell, and in poems that have no music,
in Sparta when the season turns and the month Carneian
comes back, and the moon
rides all the night;   450
in Athens also, the shining and rich.
Such is the theme of song you left
in death, for the poets.

Oh that it were in my power   455
and that I had strength to bring you
back to light from the dark of death
with oars on the sunken river.
For you, O dearest among women, you only   460
had the hard courage
to give your life for your husband's and save
him from death. May the dust lie light
upon you, my lady. And should he now take
a new wife to his bed, he will win my horror and hatred,
mine, and your children's hatred too.   465

His mother would not endure
to have her body hidden in the ground

for him, nor the aged father.
He was theirs, but they had not courage to save him.
Oh shame, for the gray was upon them.   470
But you, in the pride
of youth, died for him and left the daylight.
May it only be mine to win
such wedded love as hers from a wife; for this
is given seldom to mortals; but were my wife such, I would
  have her
with me unhurt through her lifetime.   475

(*Enter Heracles from the road, travel-stained.*)

Heracles

My friends, people of Pherae and the villages
hereby, tell me, shall I find Admetus at home?

Chorus

Yes, Heracles, the son of Pheres is in the house.
But tell us, what is the errand that brings you here
to Thessaly and the city of Pherae once again?   480

Heracles

I have a piece of work to do for Eurystheus
of Tiryns.

Chorus

          Where does it take you? On what far journey?

Heracles

To Thrace, to take home Diomedes' chariot.

Chorus

How can you? Do you know the man you are to meet?

Heracles

No. I have never been where the Bistones live.   485

Chorus

You cannot master his horses. Not without a fight.

Heracles

It is my work, and I cannot refuse.

Chorus

                                      You must

kill him before you come back; or be killed and stay.

Heracles

If I must fight, it will not be for the first time.

Chorus

What good will it do you if you overpower their master?   490

Heracles

I will take the horses home to Tiryns and its king.

Chorus

It is not easy to put a bridle on their jaws.

Heracles

Easy enough, unless their nostrils are snorting fire.

Chorus

Not that, but they have teeth that tear a man apart.

Heracles

Oh no! Mountain beasts, not horses, feed like that.   495

Chorus

But you can see their mangers. They are caked with blood.

Heracles

And the man who raises them? Whose son does he claim he is?

Chorus

Ares'. And he is lord of the golden shield of Thrace.

Heracles

It sounds like my life and the kind of work I do.

It is a hard and steep way always that I go,   500

having to fight one after another all the sons

the war god ever got him, with Lycaon first,

again with Cycnus, and now here is a third fight

that I must have with the master of these horses. So—

I am Alcmene's son, and the man does not live   505
who will see me break before my enemy's attack.

Chorus

Here is the monarch of our country coming
from the house himself, Admetus.

(Enter Admetus.)

Admetus

Welcome and happiness
to you, O scion of Perseus' blood and child of Zeus.

Heracles

Happiness to you likewise, lord of Thessaly,   510
Admetus.

Admetus

I could wish it. I know you mean well.

Heracles

What is the matter? Why is there mourning and cut hair?

Admetus

There is one dead here whom I must bury today.

Heracles

Not one of your children! I pray God shield them from that.

Admetus

Not they. My children are well and living in their house.   515

Heracles

If it is your father who is gone, his time was ripe.

Admetus

No, he is still there, Heracles. My mother, too.

Heracles

Surely you have not lost your wife, Alcestis.

Admetus

Yes
and no. There are two ways that I could answer that.

Heracles

Did you say that she is dead or that she is still alive?   520

Admetus

She is, but she is gone away. It troubles me.

Heracles

I still do not know what you mean. You are being obscure.

Admetus

You know about her and what must happen, do you not?

Heracles

I know that she has undertaken to die for you.

Admetus

How can she really live, then, when she has promised that?   525

Heracles

Ah, do not mourn her before she dies. Wait for the time.

Admetus

The point of death is death, and the dead are lost and gone.

Heracles

Being and nonbeing are considered different things.

Admetus

That is your opinion, Heracles. It is not mine.

Heracles

Well, but whose is the mourning now? Is it in the family?   530

Admetus

A woman. We were speaking of a woman, were we not?

Heracles

Was she a blood relative or someone from outside?

Admetus

No relation by blood, but she meant much to us.

Heracles

How does it happen that she died here in your house?

Admetus

She lost her father and came here to live with us.   535

Heracles

I am sorry,
Admetus. I wish I had found you in a happier state.

Admetus

Why do you say that? What do you mean to do?

Heracles

                         I mean
to go on, and stay with another of my friends.

Admetus

No, my lord, no. The evil must not come to that.

Heracles

The friend who stays with friends in mourning is in the way.   540

Admetus

The dead are dead. Go on in.

Heracles

                   No. It is always wrong
for guests to revel in a house where others mourn.

Admetus

There are separate guest chambers. We can take you there.

Heracles

Let me go, and I will thank you a thousand times.

Admetus

You shall not go to stay with any other man.   545
You there: open the guest rooms which are across the court
from the house, and tell the people who are there to provide
plenty to eat, and make sure that you close the doors

facing the inside court. It is not right for guests
to have their pleasures interrupted by sounds of grief.   550

(Heracles is ushered inside.)

Chorus

Admetus, are you crazy? What are you thinking of
to entertain guests in a situation like this?

Admetus

And if I had driven from my city and my house
the guest and friend who came to me, would you have approved
of me more? Wrong. My misery would still have been   555
as great, and I should be inhospitable too,
and there would be one more misfortune added to those
I have, if my house is called unfriendly to its friends.
For this man is my best friend, and he is my host
whenever I go to Argos, which is a thirsty place.   560

Chorus

Yes, but then why did you hide what is happening here
if this visitor is, as you say, your best friend?

Admetus

He would not have been willing to come inside my house
if he had known what trouble I was in. I know.
There are some will think I show no sense in doing this.   565
They will not like it. But my house does not know how
to push its friends away and not treat them as it should.

(He goes inside.)

Chorus

O liberal and forever free-handed house of this man,
the Pythian himself, lyric Apollo,   570
was pleased to live with you
and had patience upon your lands
to work as a shepherd,
and on the hill-folds and the slopes   575
piped to the pasturing of your flocks
in their season of mating.

And even dappled lynxes for delight in his melody
joined him as shepherds. From the cleft of Othrys descended   580
a red troop of lions,
and there, Phoebus, to your lyre's strain
there danced the bright-coated
fawn, adventuring from the deep   585
bearded pines, lightfooted for joy
in your song, in its kindness.

Therefore, your house is beyond
all others for wealth of flocks by the sweet waters
of Lake Boebias. For spread of cornland   590
and pasturing range its boundary stands
only there where the sun
stalls his horses in dark air by the Molossians.
Eastward he sways all to the harborless   595
Pelian coast on the Aegaean main.

Now he has spread wide his doors
and taken the guest in, when his eyes were wet
and he wept still for a beloved wife who died
in the house so lately. The noble strain   600
comes out, in respect for others.
All that wisdom means is there in the noble. I stand
in awe, and good hope has come again to my heart
that for this godly man the end will be good.   605

(*Enter Admetus from the house, followed by
servants with a covered litter.*)

Admetus

Gentlemen of Pherae, I am grateful for your company.
My men are bearing to the burning place and grave
our dead, who now has all the state which is her due.
Will you then, as the custom is among us, say
farewell to the dead as she goes forth for the last time?   610

Chorus

Yes, but I see your father coming now. He walks

as old men do, and followers carry in their hands
gifts for your wife, to adorn her in the underworld.

(Enter Pheres, attended, from outside.)

Pheres

I have come to bear your sorrows with you, son. I know,
nobody will dispute it, you have lost a wife 615
both good and modest in her ways. Nevertheless,
you have to bear it, even though it is hard to bear.
Accept these gifts to deck her body, bury them
with her. Oh yes, she well deserves honor in death.
She died to save your life, my son. She would not let 620
me be a childless old man, would not let me waste
away in sorrowful age deprived of you. Thereby,
daring this generous action, she has made the life
of all women become a thing of better repute
than it was.

       O you who saved him, you who raised us up 625
when we were fallen, farewell, even in Hades' house
may good befall you.

       I say people ought to marry women
like this. Otherwise, better not to marry at all.

Admetus

I never invited you to come and see her buried,
nor do I count your company as that of a friend. 630
She shall not wear anything that you bring her.
She needs nothing from you to be buried in. Your time
to share my sorrow was when I was about to die.
But you stood out of the way and let youth take my place
in death, though you were old. Will you cry for her now? 635
It cannot be that my body ever came from you,
nor did the woman who claims she bore me and is called
my mother give me birth. I was got from some slave
and surreptitiously put to your wife to nurse.
You show it. Your nature in the crisis has come out. 640
I do not count myself as any child of yours.

Oh, you outpass the cowardice of all the world,
you at your age, come to the very last step of life
and would not, dared not, die for your own child. Oh, no,
you let this woman, married into our family,   645
do it instead, and therefore it is right for me
to call her all the father and mother that I have.
And yet you two should honorably have striven for
the right of dying for your child. The time of life
you had left for your living was short, in any case,   650
and she and I would still be living out our time
and I should not be hurt and grieving over her.
And yet, all that a man could have to bless his life
you have had. You had your youth in kingship. There was I
your son, ready to take it over, keep your house   655
in order, so you had no childless death to fear,
with the house left to be torn apart by other claims.
You cannot justify your leaving me to death
on grounds that I disrespected your old age. Always I
showed all consideration. See what thanks I get   660
from you and from the woman who gave me birth. Go on,
get you other children, you cannot do it too soon,
who will look after your old age, and lay you out
when you are dead, and see you buried properly.
I will not do it. This hand will never bury you.   665
I am dead as far as you are concerned, and if, because
I found another savior, I still look on the sun,
I count myself that person's child and fond support.
It is meaningless, the way the old men pray for death
and complain of age and the long time they have to live.   670
Let death only come close, not one of them still wants
to die. Their age is not a burden any more.

Chorus

Stop, stop. We have trouble enough already, child.
You will exasperate your father with this talk.

Pheres

My son, what do you take me for that you address me   675
like this? Some Lydian slave, some Phrygian that you bought?
I am a free Thessalian noble, nobly born
from a Thessalian. Are you forgetting that? You go
too far with your high-handedness. You volley brash
words at me, and fail to hit me, and then run away.   680
I gave you life, and made you master of my house,
and raised you. I am not obliged to die for you.
I do not acknowledge any tradition among us
that fathers should die for their sons. That is not Greek.
Your natural right is to find your own happiness   685
or unhappiness. All you deserve from me, you have.
You are lord of many. I have wide estates of land
to leave you, just as my father left them to me.
What harm have I done you then? What am I taking away
from you? Do not die for me, I will not die for you.   690
You like the sunlight. Don't you think your father does?
I count the time I have to spend down there as long,
and the time to live is little, but that little is sweet.
You fought shamelessly for a way to escape death,
and passed your proper moment, and are still alive   695
because you killed her. Then, you wretch, you dare to call
me coward, when you let your woman outdare you,
and die for her magnificent young man? I see.
You have found a clever scheme by which you *never* will die.
You will always persuade the wife you have at the time   700
to die for you instead. And you, so low, then dare
blame your own people for not wanting to do this.
Silence. I tell you, as you cherish your own life,
all other people cherish theirs. And if you call
us names, you will be called names, and the names are true.   705

Chorus

Too much evil has been said in this speech and in
that spoken before. Old sir, stop cursing your own son.

Admetus

    No, speak, and I will speak too. If it hurts to hear
    the truth, you should not have made a mistake with me.

Pheres

    I should have made a mistake if I had died for you.   710

Admetus

    Is it the same thing to die old and to die young?

Pheres

    Yes. We have only one life and not two to live.

Admetus

    I think you would like to live a longer time than Zeus.

Pheres

    Cursing your parents, when they have done nothing to you?

Admetus

    Yes, for I found you much in love with a long life.   715

Pheres

    Who is it you are burying? Did not someone die?

Admetus

    And that she died, you foul wretch, proves your cowardice.

Pheres

    You cannot say that we were involved in her death.

Admetus

    Ah.
    I hope that some day you will stand in need of me.   720

Pheres

    Go on, and court more women, so they all can die.

Admetus

    Your fault. You were not willing to.

Pheres

                      No, I was not.
    It is a sweet thing, this God's sunshine, sweet to see.

Admetus

    That is an abject spirit, not a man's.

Pheres

                                   You shall
    not mock an old man while you carry out your dead.

Admetus

    You will die in evil memory, when you do die.   725

Pheres

    I do not care what they say of me when I am dead.

Admetus

    How old age loses all the sense of shame.

Pheres

                                 She was
    not shameless, you found; she was only innocent.

Admetus

    Get out of here now and let me bury my dead.

Pheres

    I'll go. You murdered her, and you can bury her.   730
    But you will have her brothers still to face. You'll pay,
    for Acastus is no longer counted as a man
    unless he sees you punished for his sister's blood.

Admetus

    Go and be damned, you and that woman who lives with you.
    Grow old as you deserve, childless, although your son   735
    still lives. You shall not come again under the same roof
    with me. And if I had to proclaim by heralds that I
    disowned my father's house, I should have so proclaimed.

                               (Pheres goes off.)
    Now we, for we must bear the sorrow that is ours,
    shall go, and lay her body on the burning place.   740

Chorus

    Ah, cruel the price of your daring,

O generous one, O noble and brave,
farewell. May Hermes of the world below
and Hades welcome you. And if, even there,
the good fare best, may you have high honor   745
and sit by the bride of Hades.

(*The body is borne off, followed by Admetus, servants, and Chorus.
Thus the stage is empty. Then enter, from the house, the
servant who was put in charge of Heracles.*)

Servant

I have known all sorts of foreigners who have come in
from all over the world here to Admetus' house,
and I have served them dinner, but I never yet
have had a guest as bad as this to entertain.   750
In the first place, he could see the master was in mourning,
but inconsiderately came in anyway.
Then, he refused to understand the situation
and be content with anything we could provide,
but when we failed to bring him something, demanded it,   755
and took a cup with ivy on it in both hands
and drank the wine of our dark mother, straight, until
the flame of the wine went all through him, and heated him,
and then he wreathed branches of myrtle on his head
and howled, off key. There were two kinds of music now   760
to hear, for while he sang and never gave a thought
to the sorrows of Admetus, we servants were mourning
our mistress; but we could not show before our guest
with our eyes wet. Admetus had forbidden that.
So now I have to entertain this guest inside,   765
this ruffian thief, this highwayman, whatever he is,
while she is gone away from the house, and I could not
say goodbye, stretch my hand out to her in my grief
for a mistress who was like a mother to all the house
and me. She gentled her husband's rages, saved us all   770
from trouble after trouble. Am I not then right
to hate this guest who has come here in our miseries?

(Enter Heracles from the house, drunk, but not hopelessly so.)

Heracles

You there, with the sad and melancholy face, what is
the matter with you? The servant who looks after guests
should be polite and cheerful and not scowl at them.   775
But look at you. Here comes your master's dearest friend
to visit you, and you receive him with black looks
and frowns, all because of some trouble somewhere else.
Come here, I'll tell you something that will make you wise.
Do you really know what things are like, the way they are?   780
I don't think so. How could you? Well then, listen to me.
Death is an obligation which we all must pay.
There is not one man living who can truly say
if he will be alive or dead on the next day.
Fortune is dark; she moves, but we cannot see the way   785
nor can we pin her down by science and study her.
There, I have told you. Now you can understand. Go on,
enjoy yourself, drink, call the life you live today
your own, but only that, the rest belongs to chance.
Then, beyond all gods, pay your best attentions to   790
the Cyprian, man's sweetest. There's a god who's kind.
Let all this business go and do as I prescribe
for you, that is, if I seem to talk sense. Do I?
I think so. Well, then, get rid of this too-much grief,
put flowers on your head and drink with us, fight down   795
these present troubles; later, I know very well
that the wine splashing in the bowl will shake you loose
from these scowl-faced looks and the tension in your mind.
We are only human. Our thoughts should be human too,
since, for these solemn people and these people who scowl,   800
the whole parcel of them, if I am any judge,
life is not really life but a catastrophe.

Servant

I know all that. But we have troubles on our hands
now, that make revelry and laughter out of place.

Heracles

The dead woman is out of the family. Do not mourn   805
too hard. The master and the mistress are still alive.

Servant

What do you mean, alive? Do you not know what happened?

Heracles

Certainly, unless your master has lied to me.

Servant

He is too hospitable, too much.

Heracles

                  Should I not then
have enjoyed myself, because some outside woman was dead?   810

Servant

She was an outsider indeed. That is too true.

Heracles

Has something happened that he did not tell me about?

Servant

Never mind. Go. Our masters' sorrows are our own.

Heracles

These can be no outsiders' troubles.

Servant

                 If they were,
I should not have minded seeing you enjoy yourself.   815

Heracles

Have I been scandalously misled by my own friends?

Servant

You came here when we were not prepared to take in guests.
You see, we are in mourning. You can see our robes
of black, and how our hair is cut short.

Heracles

                 Who is dead?
The aged father? One of the children who is gone?   820

Servant

My lord, Admetus' wife is dead.

Heracles

What are you saying?
And all this time you were making me comfortable?

Servant

He could not bear to turn you from this house of his.

Heracles

My poor Admetus, what a helpmeet you have lost!

Servant

We are all dead and done for now, not only she.   825

Heracles

I really knew it when I saw the tears in his eyes,
his shorn hair and his face; but he persuaded me
with talk of burying someone who was not by blood
related. So, unwillingly, I came inside
and drank here in the house of this hospitable man   830
when he was in this trouble! Worse, I wreathed my head
with garlands, and drank freely. But you might have said
something about this great disaster in the house.
Now, where shall I find her? Where is the funeral being held?

Servant

Go straight along the Larisa road, and when you clear   835
the city you will see the monument and the mound.

(*He goes into the house, leaving Heracles alone on the stage.*)

Heracles

O heart of mine and hand of mine, who have endured
so much already, prove what kind of son it was
Alcmene, daughter of Electryon, bore to Zeus
in Tiryns. I must save this woman who has died   840
so lately, bring Alcestis back to live in this house,
and pay Admetus all the kindness that I owe.
I must go there and watch for Death of the black robes,
master of dead men, and I think I shall find him

drinking the blood of slaughtered beasts beside the grave.   845
Then, if I can break suddenly from my hiding place,
catch him, and hold him in the circle of these arms,
there is no way he will be able to break my hold
on his bruised ribs, until he gives the woman up
to me. But if I miss my quarry, if he does not come   850
to the clotted offering, I must go down, I must ask
the Maiden and the Master in the sunless homes
of those below; and I have confidence I shall bring
Alcestis back, and give her to the arms of my friend
who did not drive me off but took me into his house   855
and, though he staggered under the stroke of circumstance,
hid it, for he was noble and respected me.
Who in all Thessaly is a truer friend than this?
Who in all Greece? Therefore, he must not ever say
that, being noble, he befriended a worthless man.   860

(*He goes out. Presently Admetus comes on,*
followed by the Chorus.)

Admetus

Hateful is this
return, hateful the sight of this house
widowed, empty. Where shall I go?
Where shall I stay? What shall I say?
How can I die?
My mother bore me to a heavy fate.   865
I envy the dead. I long for those
who are gone, to live in their houses, with them.
There is no pleasure in the sunshine
nor the feel of the hard earth under my feet.
Such was the hostage Death has taken   870
from me, and given to Hades.

(*As they chant this, Admetus moans inarticulately.*)

Chorus

Go on, go on. Plunge in the deep of the house.
What you have suffered is enough for tears.
You have gone through pain, I know,

but you do no good to the woman who lies   875
below. Never again to look on the face
of the wife you loved hurts you.

Admetus

You have opened the wound torn in my heart.
What can be worse for a man than to lose
a faithful wife. I envy those   880
without wives, without children. I wish I had not
ever married her, lived with her in this house.
We have each one life. To grieve for this
is burden enough.
When we could live single all our days   885
without children, it is not to be endured
to see children sicken or married love
despoiled by death.

                                              (*As before.*)

Chorus

Chance comes. It is hard to wrestle against it.
There is no limit to set on your pain.   890
The weight is heavy. Yet still
bear up. You are not the first man to lose
his wife. Disaster appears, to crush
one man now, but afterward another.

Admetus

How long my sorrows, the pain for my loves   895
down under the earth.
Why did you stop me from throwing myself
in the hollow cut of the grave, there to lie
dead beside her, who was best on earth?
Then Hades would have held fast two lives,   900
not one, and the truest of all, who crossed
the lake of the dead together.

Chorus

There was a man
of my people, who lost a boy

any house would mourn for,   905
the only child. But still
he carried it well enough, though childless,
and he stricken with age
and the hair gray on him,
well on through his lifetime.   910

Admetus

O builded house, how shall I enter you?
How live, with this turn
of my fortune? How different now and then.
Then it was with Pelian pine torches,   915
with marriage songs, that I entered my house,
with the hand of a sweet bride on my arm,
with loud rout of revelers following
to bless her who now is dead, and me,
for our high birth, for nobilities   920
from either side which were joined in us.
Now the bridal chorus has changed for a dirge,
and for white robes the costumed black
goes with me inside
to where her room stands deserted.   925

Chorus

Your luck had been
good, so you were inexperienced when
grief came. Still you saved
your own life and substance.
Your wife is dead, your love forsaken.   930
What is new in this? Before
now death has parted
many from their wives.

Admetus

Friends, I believe my wife is happier than I   935
although I know she does not seem to be. For her,
there will be no more pain to touch her ever again.

She has her glory and is free from much distress.
But I, who should not be alive, who have passed by
my moment, shall lead a sorry life. I see it now.　　　　940
How can I bear to go inside this house again?
Whom shall I speak to, who will speak to me, to give
me any pleasure in coming home? Where shall I turn?
The desolation in my house will drive me out
when I see my wife's bed empty, when I see the chairs　　945
she used to sit in, and all about the house the floor
unwashed and dirty, while the children at my knees
huddle and cry for their mother and the servants mourn
their mistress and remember what the house has lost.
So it will be at home, but if I go outside　　　　　　　950
meeting my married friends in Thessaly, the sight
of their wives will drive me back, for I cannot endure
to look at my wife's agemates and the friends of her youth.
And anyone who hates me will say this of me:
"Look at the man, disgracefully alive, who dared　　　　955
not die, but like a coward gave his wife instead
and so escaped death. Do you call him a man at all?
He turns on his own parents, but he would not die
himself." Besides my other troubles, they will speak
about me thus. What have I gained by living, friends,　　960
when reputation, life, and action all are bad?

Chorus

I myself, in the transports
of mystic verses, as in study
of history and science, have found
nothing so strong as Compulsion,　　　　　　　　965
nor any means to combat her,
not in the Thracian books set down
in verse by the school of Orpheus,
not in all the remedies Phoebus has given the heirs　　970
of Asclepius to fight the many afflictions of man.

She alone is a goddess
without altar or image to pray

before. She heeds no sacrifice.   975
Majesty, bear no harder
on me than you have in my life before!
All Zeus even ordains
only with you is accomplished.
By strength you fold and crumple the steel of the Chalybes.   980
There is no pity in the sheer barrier of your will.

> (*They turn and speak directly to Admetus, who*
> *remains in the background.*)

Now she has caught your wife in the breakless grip of her hands.
Take it. You will never bring back, by crying,   985
the dead into the light again.
Even the sons of the gods fade
and go in death's shadow.   990
She was loved when she was with us.
She shall be loved still, now she is dead.
It was the best of all women to whom you were joined in
  marriage.

The monument of your wife must not be counted among the
  graves   995
of the dead, but it must be given its honors
as gods are, worship of wayfarers.
And as they turn the bend of the road   1000
and see it, men shall say:
"She died for the sake of her husband.
Now she is a blessed spirit.
Hail, majesty, be gracious to us." Thus will men speak in her
  presence.   1005

But here is someone who looks like Alcmene's son,
Admetus. He seems on his way to visit you.

> (*Heracles enters, leading a veiled woman by the hand.*)

Heracles

A man, Admetus, should be allowed to speak his mind
to a friend, instead of keeping his complaints suppressed
inside him. Now, I thought I had the right to stand   1010

beside you and endure what you endured, so prove
my friendship. But you never told me that she, who lay
dead, was your wife, but entertained me in your house
as if your mourning were for some outsider's death.
And so I wreathed my head and poured libations out   1015
to the gods, in your house, though your house had suffered so.
This was wrong, wrong I tell you, to have treated me
thus, though I have no wish to hurt you in your grief.
Now, as for the matter of why I have come back again,
I will tell you. Take this woman, keep her safe for me,   1020
until I have killed the master of the Bistones
and come back, bringing with me the horses of Thrace.
If I have bad luck—I hope not, I hope to come
back home—I give her to the service of your house.
It cost a struggle for her to come into my hands.   1025
You see, I came on people who were holding games
for all comers, with prizes which an athlete might
well spend an effort winning.

                                               (Points to the woman.)
                         Here is the prize I won
and bring you. For the winners in the minor events
were given horses to take away, while those who won   1030
the heavier stuff, boxing and wrestling, got oxen,
and a woman was thrown in with them. Since I happened
to be there, it seemed wrong to let this splendid prize
go by. As I said, the woman is for you to keep.
She is not stolen. It cost me hard work to bring   1035
her here. Some day, perhaps, you will say I have done well.

Admetus

I did not mean to dishonor nor belittle you
when I concealed the fate of my unhappy wife,
but it would have added pain to pain already there
if you had been driven to shelter with some other host.   1040
This sorrow is mine. It is enough for me to weep.
As for the woman, if it can be done, my lord,

I beg you, have some other Thessalian, who has not
suffered as I have, keep her. You have many friends
in Pherae. Do not bring my sorrows back to me.   1045
I would not have strength to see her in my house and keep
my eyes dry. I am weak now. Do not add weakness
to my weakness. I have sorrow enough to weigh me down.
And where could a young woman live in this house? For
she is young, I can see it in her dress, her style.   1050
Am I to put her in the same quarters with the men?
And how, circulating among young men, shall she be kept
from harm? Not easy, Heracles, to hold in check
a young strong man. I am thinking of your interests.
Or shall I put her in my lost wife's chamber, keep   1055
her there? How can I take her to Alcestis' bed?
I fear blame from two quarters, from my countrymen
who might accuse me of betraying her who helped
me most, by running to the bed of another girl,
and from the dead herself. Her honor has its claim   1060
on me. I must be very careful. You, lady,
whoever you are, I tell you that you have the form
of my Alcestis; all your body is like hers.
Too much. Oh, for God's pity, take this woman away
out of my sight. I am beaten already, do not beat   1065
me again. For as I look on her, I think I see
my wife. It churns my heart to tumult, and the tears
break streaming from my eyes. How much must I endure
the bitter taste of sorrow which is still so fresh?

Chorus

I cannot put a good name to your fortune; yet   1070
whoever you are, you must endure what the god gives.

Heracles

I only wish that my strength had been great enough
for me to bring your wife back from the chambered deep
into the light. I would have done that grace for you.

Admetus

    I know you would have wanted to. Why speak of it?   1075
    There is no way for the dead to come back to the light.

Heracles

    Then do not push your sorrow. Bear it as you must.

Admetus

    Easier to comfort than to suffer and be strong.

Heracles

    But if you wish to mourn for always, what will you gain?

Admetus

    Nothing. I know it. But some impulse of my love   1080
    makes me.

Heracles

              Why, surely. Love for the dead is cause for tears.

Admetus

    Her death destroyed me, even more than I can say.

Heracles

    You have lost a fine wife. Who will say you have not?

Admetus

                                 So fine
    that I, whom you see, never shall be happy again.

Heracles

    Time will soften it. The evil still is young and strong.   1085

Admetus

    You can say time will soften it, if time means death.

Heracles

    A wife, love, your new marriage will put an end to this.

Admetus

    Silence! I never thought you would say a thing like that.

Heracles

    What? You will not remarry but keep an empty bed?

Admetus

No woman ever shall sleep in my arms again.   1090

Heracles

Do you believe you help the dead by doing this?

Admetus

Wherever she may be, she deserves my honors still.

Heracles

Praiseworthy, yes, praiseworthy. And yet foolish, too.

Admetus

Call me so, then, but never call me a bridegroom.

Heracles

I admire you for your faith and love you bear your wife.   1095

Admetus

Let me die if I betray her, though she is gone.

Heracles

                                        Well then,
receive this woman into your most generous house.

Admetus

Please, in the name of Zeus your father, no!

Heracles

                              And yet
you will be making a mistake if you do not;

Admetus

and eaten at the heart with anguish if I do.   1100

Heracles

Obey. The grace of this may come where you need grace.

Admetus

Ah.
I wish you had never won her in those games of yours.

Heracles

Where I am winner, you are winner along with me.

Admetus

Honorably said. But let the woman go away.

Heracles

She will go, if she should. First look. See if she should.   1105

Admetus

She should, unless it means you will be angry with me.

Heracles

Something I know of makes me so insistent with you.

Admetus

So, have your way. But what you do does not please me.

Heracles

The time will come when you will thank me. Only obey.

Admetus (to attendants)

Escort her in, if she must be taken into this house.   1110

Heracles

I will not hand this lady over to attendants.

Admetus

You yourself lead her into the house then, if you wish.

Heracles

I will put her into your hands and into yours alone.

Admetus

I will not touch her. But she is free to come inside.

Heracles

No, I have faith in your right hand, and only yours.   1115

Admetus

My lord, you are forcing me to act against my wish.

Heracles

Be brave. Reach out your hand and take the stranger's.

Admetus

So.

Here is my hand; I feel like Perseus killing the gorgon.

Heracles

You have her?

Admetus

Yes, I have her.

Heracles

Keep her, then. Some day
you will say the son of Zeus came as your generous guest.   1120
But look at her. See if she does not seem most like
your wife. Your grief is over now. Your luck is back.

Admetus

Gods, what shall I think! Amazement beyond hope, as I
look on this woman, this wife. Is she really mine,
or some sweet mockery for God to stun me with?   1125

Heracles

Not so. This is your own wife you see. She is here.

Admetus

Be careful she is not some phantom from the depths.

Heracles

The guest and friend you took was no necromancer.

Admetus

Do I see my wife, whom I was laying in the grave?

Heracles

Surely. But I do not wonder at your unbelief.   1130

Admetus

May I touch her, and speak to her, as my living wife?

Heracles

Speak to her. All that you desired is yours.

Admetus

Oh, eyes
and body of my dearest wife, I have you now
beyond all hope. I never thought to see you again.

Heracles

You have her. May no god hate you for your happiness.   1135

Admetus

> O nobly sprung child of all-highest Zeus, may good
> fortune go with you. May the father who gave you birth
> keep you. You alone raised me up when I was down.
> How did you bring her back from down there to the light?

Heracles

> I fought a certain deity who had charge of her.   1140

Admetus

> Where do you say you fought this match with Death?

Heracles

>   Beside
> the tomb itself. I sprang and caught him in my hands.

Admetus

> But why is my wife standing here, and does not speak?

Heracles

> You are not allowed to hear her speak to you until
> her obligations to the gods who live below   1145
> are washed away. Until the third morning comes. So now
> take her and lead her inside, and for the rest of time,
> Admetus, be just. Treat your guests as they deserve.
> And now goodbye. I have my work that I must do,
> and go to face the lordly son of Sthenelus.   1150

Admetus

> No, stay with us and be the guest of our hearth.

Heracles

>   There still
> will be a time for that, but I must press on now.

Admetus

> Success go with you. May you find your way back here.
>   *(Heracles goes.)*
> I proclaim to all the people of my tetrarchy
> that, for these blessed happenings, they shall set up
> dances, and the altars smoke with sacrifice offered.   1155

For now we shall make our life again, and it will be
a better one.
                    I was lucky. That I cannot deny.

(He takes Alcestis by the hand and leads
her inside the house.)

Chorus (going)

Many are the forms of what is unknown.
Much that the gods achieve is surprise.   1160
What we look for does not come to pass;
God finds a way for what none foresaw.
Such was the end of this story.

THE
MEDEA

Translated and with an Introduction by

REX WARNER

INTRODUCTION TO *THE MEDEA*

THE Athenian audience who saw the first performance of Euripides' *Medea* at the state dramatic contest in 431 B.C. and who awarded the third prize to Euripides would have been familiar with the whole story of the chief characters, and we, twenty-three centuries later, are handicapped in our understanding of the play if we have not at least some knowledge of the same story.

The Athenians would have known Medea as a barbarian princess and as a sorceress, related to the gods. She came from the faraway land of Colchis at the eastern extremity of the Black Sea, where her father, King Aeetes, a sorcerer himself and the son of Helius, god of the sun, kept the Golden Fleece. Here Jason had come with the Argonauts, the first expedition of western Greeks against the eastern barbarians. Medea had fallen in love with him, and by her aid he was able to avoid the traps laid for him by Aeetes, to regain the Golden Fleece, and to escape, taking Medea with him. She, to assist the escape, had murdered her own brother, strewing the pieces of his body over the water so that her father's fleet, while collecting the fragments for burial, might lose time in the pursuit of the fugitives.

Medea and Jason then settled in Jason's hereditary kingdom of Iolcus, where Pelias, his uncle, still cheated him of his rights. Medea, hoping to do Jason a favor, persuaded the daughters of Pelias to attempt, under her guidance, a magic rejuvenation of their father. The old man was to be killed, cut in pieces, and then, with the aid of herbs and incantations, restored to his first youth. The unsuspecting daughters did as they were told, and Medea left them with their father's blood upon their hands. However, the result of this crime was no advancement for Jason but rather exile for him, Medea, and their two children.

From Iolcus they came to Corinth, the scene of Euripides' play. Here Jason, either, as he says himself, wishing to strengthen his own economic position, or, as Medea thinks, because he was tired of his

dangerous foreign wife, put her aside and married the daughter of
Creon, king of Corinth. It is at this point that the action of the play
begins; but the Athenian audience would know well enough what
the plot would be. They would know that Medea, in her jealous
rage, would destroy both Creon and his daughter by means of a
poisoned robe which clung to the flesh and burned it; that, despair-
ing of her children's safety and wishing through them to injure
Jason in every way, she would kill them with her own hands; and
that, finally, by supernatural means, she would escape to their own
city and take refuge with the old King Aegeus.

CHARACTERS

Medea, princess of Colchis and wife of

Jason, son of Aeson, king of Iolcus

Two children of Medea and Jason

Creon, king of Corinth

Aegeus, king of Athens

Nurse to Medea

Tutor to Medea's children

Messenger

Chorus of Corinthian Women

THE MEDEA

Nurse

How I wish the Argo never had reached the land
Of Colchis, skimming through the blue Symplegades,
Nor ever had fallen in the glades of Pelion
The smitten fir-tree to furnish oars for the hands
Of heroes who in Pelias' name attempted   5
The Golden Fleece! For then my mistress Medea
Would not have sailed for the towers of the land of Iolcus,
Her heart on fire with passionate love for Jason;
Nor would she have persuaded the daughters of Pelias
To kill their father, and now be living here   10
In Corinth with her husband and children. She gave
Pleasure to the people of her land of exile,
And she herself helped Jason in every way.
This is indeed the greatest salvation of all—
For the wife not to stand apart from the husband.   15
But now there's hatred everywhere, Love is diseased.
For, deserting his own children and my mistress,
Jason has taken a royal wife to his bed,
The daughter of the ruler of this land, Creon.
And poor Medea is slighted, and cries aloud on the   20
Vows they made to each other, the right hands clasped
In eternal promise. She calls upon the gods to witness
What sort of return Jason has made to her love.
She lies without food and gives herself up to suffering,
Wasting away every moment of the day in tears.   25
So it has gone since she knew herself slighted by him.
Not stirring an eye, not moving her face from the ground,
No more than either a rock or surging sea water

She listens when she is given friendly advice.
Except that sometimes she twists back her white neck and   30
Moans to herself, calling out on her father's name,
And her land, and her home betrayed when she came away with
A man who now is determined to dishonor her.
Poor creature, she has discovered by her sufferings
What it means to one not to have lost one's own country.   35
She has turned from the children and does not like to see them.
I am afraid she may think of some dreadful thing,
For her heart is violent. She will never put up with
The treatment she is getting. I know and fear her
Lest she may sharpen a sword and thrust to the heart,   40
Stealing into the palace where the bed is made,
Or even kill the king and the new-wedded groom,
And thus bring a greater misfortune on herself.
She's a strange woman. I know it won't be easy
To make an enemy of her and come off best.   45
But here the children come. They have finished playing.
They have no thought at all of their mother's trouble.
Indeed it is not usual for the young to grieve.

> (*Enter from the right the slave who is the tutor to Medea's
> two small children. The children follow him.*)

Tutor

You old retainer of my mistress' household,
Why are you standing here all alone in front of the   50
Gates and moaning to yourself over your misfortune?
Medea could not wish you to leave her alone.

Nurse

Old man, and guardian of the children of Jason,
If one is a good servant, it's a terrible thing
When one's master's luck is out; it goes to one's heart.   55
So I myself have got into such a state of grief
That a longing stole over me to come outside here
And tell the earth and air of my mistress' sorrows.

Tutor

Has the poor lady not yet given up her crying?

Nurse

Given up? She's at the start, not halfway through her tears.   60

Tutor

Poor fool—if I may call my mistress such a name—
How ignorant she is of trouble more to come.

Nurse

What do you mean, old man? You needn't fear to speak.

Tutor

Nothing. I take back the words which I used just now.

Nurse

Don't, by your beard, hide this from me, your fellow-servant.   65
If need be, I'll keep quiet about what you tell me.

Tutor

I heard a person saying, while I myself seemed
Not to be paying attention, when I was at the place
Where the old draught-players sit, by the holy fountain,
That Creon, ruler of the land, intends to drive   70
These children and their mother in exile from Corinth.
But whether what he said is really true or not
I do not know. I pray that it may not be true.

Nurse

And will Jason put up with it that his children
Should suffer so, though he's no friend to their mother?   75

Tutor

Old ties give place to new ones. As for Jason, he
No longer has a feeling for this house of ours.

Nurse

It's black indeed for us, when we add new to old
Sorrows before even the present sky has cleared.

Tutor

But you be silent, and keep all this to yourself.   80
It is not the right time to tell our mistress of it.

Nurse

Do you hear, children, what a father he is to you?
I wish he were dead—but no, he is still my master.
Yet certainly he has proved unkind to his dear ones.

Tutor

What's strange in that? Have you only just discovered   85
That everyone loves himself more than his neighbor?
Some have good reason, others get something out of it.
So Jason neglects his children for the new bride.

Nurse

Go indoors, children. That will be the best thing.
And you, keep them to themselves as much as possible.   90
Don't bring them near their mother in her angry mood.
For I've seen her already blazing her eyes at them
As though she meant some mischief and I am sure that
She'll not stop raging until she has struck at someone.
May it be an enemy and not a friend she hurts!   95

(*Medea is heard inside the house.*)

Medea

Ah, wretch! Ah, lost in my sufferings,
I wish, I wish I might die.

Nurse

What did I say, dear children? Your mother
Frets her heart and frets it to anger.
Run away quickly into the house,   100
And keep well out of her sight.
Don't go anywhere near, but be careful
Of the wildness and bitter nature
Of that proud mind.
Go now! Run quickly indoors.   105
It is clear that she soon will put lightning

In that cloud of her cries that is rising
With a passion increasing. O, what will she do,
Proud-hearted and not to be checked on her course,
A soul bitten into with wrong?   110

(The Tutor takes the children into the house.)

Medea

Ah, I have suffered
What should be wept for bitterly. I hate you,
Children of a hateful mother. I curse you
And your father. Let the whole house crash.

Nurse

Ah, I pity you, you poor creature.   115
How can your children share in their father's
Wickedness? Why do you hate them? Oh children,
How much I fear that something may happen!
Great people's tempers are terrible, always
Having their own way, seldom checked,   120
Dangerous they shift from mood to mood.
How much better to have been accustomed
To live on equal terms with one's neighbors.
I would like to be safe and grow old in a   125
Humble way. What is moderate sounds best,
Also in practice *is* best for everyone.
Greatness brings no profit to people.
God indeed, when in anger, brings
Greater ruin to great men's houses.   130

*(Enter, on the right, a Chorus of Corinthian women. They have
come to inquire about Medea and to attempt to console her.)*

Chorus

I heard the voice, I heard the cry
Of Colchis' wretched daughter.
Tell me, mother, is she not yet
At rest? Within the double gates   135
Of the court I heard her cry. I am sorry
For the sorrow of this home. O, say, what has happened?

Nurse

>There is no home. It's over and done with.   140
>Her husband holds fast to his royal wedding,
>While she, my mistress, cries out her eyes
>There in her room, and takes no warmth from
>Any word of any friend.

Medea

>Oh, I wish
>That lightning from heaven would split my head open.
>Oh, what use have I now for life?   145
>I would find my release in death
>And leave hateful existence behind me.

Chorus

>O God and Earth and Heaven!
>Did you hear what a cry was that
>Which the sad wife sings?   150
>Poor foolish one, why should you long.
>For that appalling rest?
>The final end of death comes fast.
>No need to pray for that.
>Suppose your man gives honor   155
>To another woman's bed.
>It often happens. Don't be hurt.
>God will be your friend in this.
>You must not waste away
>Grieving too much for him who shared your bed.

Medea

>Great Themis, lady Artemis, behold   160
>The things I suffer, though I made him promise,
>My hateful husband. I pray that I may see him,
>Him and his bride and all their palace shattered
>For the wrong they dare to do me without cause.   165
>Oh, my father! Oh, my country! In what dishonor
>I left you, killing my own brother for it.

Nurse

> Do you hear what she says, and how she cries
> On Themis, the goddess of Promises, and on Zeus,
> Whom we believe to be the Keeper of Oaths? 170
> Of this I am sure, that no small thing
> Will appease my mistress' anger.

Chorus

> Will she come into our presence?
> Will she listen when we are speaking
> To the words we say? 175
> I wish she might relax her rage
> And temper of her heart.
> My willingness to help will never
> Be wanting to my friends.
> But go inside and bring her 180
> Out of the house to us,
> And speak kindly to her: hurry,
> Before she wrongs her own.
> This passion of hers moves to something great.

Nurse

> I will, but I doubt if I'll manage
> To win my mistress over. 185
> But still I'll attempt it to please you.
> Such a look she will flash on her servants
> If any comes near with a message,
> Like a lioness guarding her cubs.
> It is right, I think, to consider 190
> Both stupid and lacking in foresight
> Those poets of old who wrote songs
> For revels and dinners and banquets,
> Pleasant sounds for men living at ease;
> But none of them all has discovered 195
> How to put to an end with their singing
> Or musical instruments grief,
> Bitter grief, from which death and disaster

Cheat the hopes of a house. Yet how good
If music could cure men of this! But why raise   200
To no purpose the voice at a banquet? For *there* is
Already abundance of pleasure for men
With a joy of its own.

                            (The Nurse goes into the house.)

Chorus

I heard a shriek that is laden with sorrow.
Shrilling out her hard grief she cries out   205
Upon him who betrayed both her bed and her marriage.
Wronged, she calls on the gods,
On the justice of Zeus, the oath sworn,
Which brought her away
To the opposite shore of the Greeks   210
Through the gloomy salt straits to the gateway
Of the salty unlimited sea.

              (Medea, attended by servants, comes out of the house.)

Medea

Women of Corinth, I have come outside to you
Lest you should be indignant with me; for I know   215
That many people are overproud, some when alone,
And others when in company. And those who live
Quietly, as I do, get a bad reputation.
For a just judgment is not evident in the eyes
When a man at first sight hates another, before   220
Learning his character, being in no way injured;
And a foreigner especially must adapt himself.
I'd not approve of even a fellow-countryman
Who by pride and want of manners offends his neighbors.
But on me this thing has fallen so unexpectedly,   225
It has broken my heart. I am finished. I let go
All my life's joy. My friends, I only want to die.
It was everything to me to think well of one man,
And he, my own husband, has turned out wholly vile.
Of all things which are living and can form a judgment   230

We women are the most unfortunate creatures.
Firstly, with an excess of wealth it is required
For us to buy a husband and take for our bodies
A master; for not to take one is even worse.
And now the question is serious whether we take   235
A good or bad one; for there is no easy escape
For a woman, nor can she say no to her marriage.
She arrives among new modes of behavior and manners,
And needs prophetic power, unless she has learned at home,
How best to manage him who shares the bed with her.   240
And if we work out all this well and carefully,
And the husband lives with us and lightly bears his yoke,
Then life is enviable. If not, I'd rather die.
A man, when he's tired of the company in his home,
Goes out of the house and puts an end to his boredom   245
And turns to a friend or companion of his own age.
But we are forced to keep our eyes on one alone.
What they say of us is that we have a peaceful time
Living at home, while they do the fighting in war.
How wrong they are! I would very much rather stand   250
Three times in the front of battle than bear one child.
Yet what applies to me does not apply to you.
You have a country. Your family home is here.
You enjoy life and the company of your friends.
But I am deserted, a refugee, thought nothing of   255
By my husband—something he won in a foreign land.
I have no mother or brother, nor any relation
With whom I can take refuge in this sea of woe.
This much then is the service I would beg from you:
If I can find the means or devise any scheme   260
To pay my husband back for what he has done to me—
Him and his father-in-law and the girl who married him—
Just to keep silent. For in other ways a woman
Is full of fear, defenseless, dreads the sight of cold
Steel; but, when once she is wronged in the matter of love, 265
No other soul can hold so many thoughts of blood.

Chorus

> This I will promise. You are in the right, Medea,
> In paying your husband back. I am not surprised at you
> For being sad.
>
> But look! I see our King Creon
> Approaching. He will tell us of some new plan.   270

> *(Enter, from the right, Creon, with attendants.)*

Creon

> You, with that angry look, so set against your husband,
> Medea, I order you to leave my territories
> An exile, and take along with you your two children,
> And not to waste time doing it. It is my decree,
> And I will see it done. I will not return home   275
> Until you are cast from the boundaries of my land.

Medea

> Oh, this is the end for me. I am utterly lost.
> Now I am in the full force of the storm of hate
> And have no harbor from ruin to reach easily.
> Yet still, in spite of it all, I'll ask the question: 280
> What is your reason, Creon, for banishing me?

Creon

> I am afraid of you—why should I dissemble it?—
> Afraid that you may injure my daughter mortally.
> Many things accumulate to support my feeling.
> You are a clever woman, versed in evil arts,   285
> And are angry at having lost your husband's love.
> I hear that you are threatening, so they tell me,
> To do something against my daughter and Jason
> And me, too. I shall take my precautions first.
> I tell you, I prefer to earn your hatred now   290
> Than to be soft-hearted and afterward regret it.

Medea

> This is not the first time, Creon. Often previously
> Through being considered clever I have suffered much.

A person of sense ought never to have his children
Brought up to be more clever than the average.   295
For, apart from cleverness bringing them no profit,
It will make them objects of envy and ill-will.
If you put new ideas before the eyes of fools
They'll think you foolish and worthless into the bargain;
And if you are thought superior to those who have   300
Some reputation for learning, you will become hated.
I have some knowledge myself of how this happens;
For being clever, I find that some will envy me,
Others object to me. Yet all my cleverness
Is not so much.   305
                   Well, then, are you frightened, Creon,
That I should harm you? There is no need. It is not
My way to transgress the authority of a king.
How have you injured me? You gave your daughter away
To the man you wanted. Oh, certainly I hate   310
My husband, but you, I think, have acted wisely;
Nor do I grudge it you that your affairs go well.
May the marriage be a lucky one! Only let me
Live in this land. For even though I have been wronged,
I will not raise my voice, but submit to my betters.   315

Creon
  What you say sounds gentle enough. Still in my heart
  I greatly dread that you are plotting some evil,
  And therefore I trust you even less than before.
  A sharp-tempered woman, or, for that matter, a man,
  Is easier to deal with than the clever type   320
  Who holds her tongue. No. You must go. No need for more
  Speeches. The thing is fixed. By no manner of means
  Shall you, an enemy of mine, stay in my country.

Medea
  I beg you. By your knees, by your new-wedded girl.

Creon
  Your words are wasted. You will never persuade me.   325

Medea

Will you drive me out, and give no heed to my prayers?

Creon

I will, for I love my family more than you.

Medea

O my country! How bitterly now I remember you!

Creon

I love my country too—next after my children.

Medea

Oh what an evil to men is passionate love!   330

Creon

That would depend on the luck that goes along with it.

Medea

O God, do not forget who is the cause of this!

Creon

Go. It is no use. Spare me the pain of forcing you.

Medea

I'm spared no pain. I lack no pain to be spared me.

Creon

Then you'll be removed by force by one of my men.   335

Medea

No, Creon, not that! But do listen, I beg you.

Creon

Woman, you seem to want to create a disturbance.

Medea

I *will* go into exile. *This* is not what I beg for.

Creon

Why then this violence and clinging to my hand?

Medea

Allow me to remain here just for this one day,   340
So I may consider where to live in my exile,

And look for support for my children, since their father
Chooses to make no kind of provision for them.
Have pity on them! You have children of your own.
It is natural for you to look kindly on them.   345
For myself I do not mind if I go into exile.
It is the children being in trouble that I mind.

Creon

There is nothing tyrannical about my nature,
And by showing mercy I have often been the loser.
Even now I know that I am making a mistake.   350
All the same you shall have your will. But this I tell you,
That if the light of heaven tomorrow shall see you,
You and your children in the confines of my land,
You die. This word I have spoken is firmly fixed.
But now, if you must stay, stay for this day alone.   355
For in it you can do none of the things I fear.

(Exit Creon with his attendants.)

Chorus

Oh, unfortunate one! Oh, cruel!
Where will you turn? Who will help you?
What house or what land to preserve you   360
From ill can you find?
Medea, a god has thrown suffering
Upon you in waves of despair.

Medea

Things have gone badly every way. No doubt of that
But not these things this far, and don't imagine so.   365
There are still trials to come for the new-wedded pair,
And for their relations pain that will mean something.
Do you think that I would ever have fawned on that man
Unless I had some end to gain or profit in it?
I would not even have spoken or touched him with my hands.   370
But he has got to such a pitch of foolishness
That, though he could have made nothing of all my plans
By exiling me, he has given me this one day

To stay here, and in this I will make dead bodies
Of three of my enemies—father, the girl, and my husband.   375
I have many ways of death which I might suit to them,
And do not know, friends, which one to take in hand;
Whether to set fire underneath their bridal mansion,
Or sharpen a sword and thrust it to the heart,
Stealing into the palace where the bed is made.   380
There is just one obstacle to this. If I am caught
Breaking into the house and scheming against it,
I shall die, and give my enemies cause for laughter.
It is best to go by the straight road, the one in which
I am most skilled, and make away with them by poison.   385
So be it then.
And now suppose them dead. What town will receive me?
What friend will offer me a refuge in his land,
Or the guaranty of his house and save my own life?
There is none. So I must wait a little time yet,
And if some sure defense should then appear for me,   390
In craft and silence I will set about this murder.
But if my fate should drive me on without help,
Even though death is certain, I will take the sword
Myself and kill, and steadfastly advance to crime.
It shall not be—I swear it by her, my mistress,   395
Whom most I honor and have chosen as partner,
Hecate, who dwells in the recesses of my hearth—
That any man shall be glad to have injured me.
Bitter I will make their marriage for them and mournful,
Bitter the alliance and the driving me out of the land.   400
Ah, come, Medea, in your plotting and scheming
Leave nothing untried of all those things which you know.
Go forward to the dreadful act. The test has come
For resolution. You see how you are treated. Never
Shall you be mocked by Jason's Corinthian wedding,   405
Whose father was noble, whose grandfather Helius.
You have the skill. What is more, you were born a woman,
And women, though most helpless in doing good deeds,
Are of every evil the cleverest of contrivers.

Chorus

Flow backward to your sources, sacred rivers,   410
And let the world's great order be reversed.
It is the thoughts of *men* that are deceitful,
Their pledges that are loose.   415
Story shall now turn my condition to a fair one,
Women are paid their due.
No more shall evil-sounding fame be theirs.   420

Cease now, you muses of the ancient singers,
To tell the tale of my unfaithfulness;
For not on us did Phoebus, lord of music,
Bestow the lyre's divine   425
Power, for otherwise I should have sung an answer
To the other sex. Long time
Has much to tell of us, and much of them.   430

You sailed away from your father's home,
With a heart on fire you passed
The double rocks of the sea.
And now in a foreign country   435
You have lost your rest in a widowed bed,
And are driven forth, a refugee
In dishonor from the land.

Good faith has gone, and no more remains
In great Greece a sense of shame.   440
It has flown away to the sky.
No father's house for a haven
Is at hand for you now, and another queen
Of your bed has dispossessed you and
Is mistress of your home.   445

                              (Enter Jason, with attendants.)

Jason

This is not the first occasion that I have noticed
How hopeless it is to deal with a stubborn temper.
For, with reasonable submission to our ruler's will,
You might have lived in this land and kept your home.
As it is you are going to be exiled for your loose speaking.   450

Not that I mind myself. You are free to continue
Telling everyone that Jason is a worthless man.
But as to your talk about the king, consider
Yourself most lucky that exile is your punishment.
I, for my part, have always tried to calm down   455
The anger of the king, and wished you to remain.
But you will not give up your folly, continually
Speaking ill of him, and so you are going to be banished.
All the same, and in spite of your conduct, I'll not desert
My friends, but have come to make some provision for you,   460
So that you and the children may not be penniless
Or in need of anything in exile. Certainly
Exile brings many troubles with it. And even
If you hate me, I cannot think badly of you.

Medea

O coward in every way—that is what I call you,   465
With bitterest reproach for your lack of manliness,
You have come, you, my worst enemy, have come to me!
It is not an example of overconfidence
Or of boldness thus to look your friends in the face,   470
Friends you have injured—no, it is the worst of all
Human diseases, shamelessness. But you did well
To come, for I can speak ill of you and lighten
My heart, and you will suffer while you are listening.
And first I will begin from what happened first.   475
I saved your life, and every Greek knows I saved it,
Who was a shipmate of yours aboard the Argo,
When you were sent to control the bulls that breathed fire
And yoke them, and when you would sow that deadly field.
Also that snake, who encircled with his many folds   480
The Golden Fleece and guarded it and never slept,
I killed, and so gave you the safety of the light.
And I myself betrayed my father and my home,
And came with you to Pelias' land of Iolcus.
And then, showing more willingness to help than wisdom,   485
I killed him, Pelias, with a most dreadful death

At his own daughters' hands, and took away your fear.
This is how I behaved to you, you wretched man,
And you forsook me, took another bride to bed,
Though you had children; for, if that had not been,   490
You would have had an excuse for another wedding.
Faith in your word has gone. Indeed, I cannot tell
Whether you think the gods whose names you swore by then
Have ceased to rule and that new standards are set up,
Since you must know you have broken your word to me.   495
O my right hand, and the knees which you often clasped
In supplication, how senselessly I am treated
By this bad man, and how my hopes have missed their mark!
Come, I will share my thoughts as though you were a friend—
You! Can I think that you would ever treat me well?   500
But I will do it, and these questions will make you
Appear the baser. Where am I to go? To my father's?
Him I betrayed and his land when I came with you.
To Pelias' wretched daughters? What a fine welcome
They would prepare for me who murdered their father!   505
For this is my position—hated by my friends
At home, I have, in kindness to you, made enemies
Of others whom there was no need to have injured.
And how happy among Greek women you have made me
On your side for all this! A distinguished husband   510
I have—for breaking promises. When in misery
I am cast out of the land and go into exile,
Quite without friends and all alone with my children,
That will be a fine shame for the new-wedded groom,
For his children to wander as beggars and she who saved him.   515
O God, you have given to mortals a sure method
Of telling the gold that is pure from the counterfeit;
Why is there no mark engraved upon men's bodies,
By which we could know the true ones from the false ones?

Chorus

It is a strange form of anger, difficult to cure,   520
When two friends turn upon each other in hatred.

Jason

As for me, it seems I must be no bad speaker.
But, like a man who has a good grip of the tiller,
Reef up his sail, and so run away from under
This mouthing tempest, woman, of your bitter tongue.   525
Since you insist on building up your kindness to me,
My view is that Cypris was alone responsible
Of men and gods for the preserving of my life.
You are clever enough—but really I need not enter
Into the story of how it was love's inescapable   530
Power that compelled you to keep my person safe.
On this I will not go into too much detail.
In so far as you helped me, you did well enough.
But on this question of saving me, I can prove
You have certainly got from me more than you gave.   535
Firstly, instead of living among barbarians,
You inhabit a Greek land and understand our ways,
How to live by law instead of the sweet will of force.
And all the Greeks considered you a clever woman.
You were honored for it; while, if you were living at   540
The ends of the earth, nobody would have heard of you.
For my part, rather than stores of gold in my house
Or power to sing even sweeter songs than Orpheus,
I'd choose the fate that made me a distinguished man.
There is my reply to your story of my labors.   545
Remember it was you who started the argument.
Next for your attack on my wedding with the princess:
Here I will prove that, first, it was a clever move,
Secondly, a wise one, and, finally, that I made it
In your best interests and the children's. Please keep calm.   550
When I arrived here from the land of Iolcus,
Involved, as I was, in every kind of difficulty,
What luckier chance could I have come across than this,
An exile to marry the daughter of the king?
It was not—the point that seems to upset you—that I   555
Grew tired of your bed and felt the need of a new bride;

Nor with any wish to outdo your number of children.
We have enough already. I am quite content.
But—this was the main reason—that we might live well,
And not be short of anything. I know that all   560
A man's friends leave him stone-cold if he becomes poor.
Also that I might bring my children up worthily
Of my position, and, by producing more of them
To be brothers of yours, we would draw the families
Together and all be happy. You need no children.   565
And it pays me to do good to those I have now
By having others. Do you think this a bad plan?
You wouldn't if the love question hadn't upset you.
But you women have got into such a state of mind
That, if your life at night is good, you think you have   570
Everything; but, if in that quarter things go wrong,
You will consider your best and truest interests
Most hateful. It would have been better far for men
To have got their children in some other way, and women
Not to have existed. Then life would have been good.   575

Chorus

Jason, though you have made this speech of yours look well,
Still I think, even though others do not agree,
You have betrayed your wife and are acting badly.

Medea

Surely in many ways I hold different views
From others, for I think that the plausible speaker   580
Who is a villain deserves the greatest punishment.
Confident in his tongue's power to adorn evil,
He stops at nothing. Yet he is not really wise.
As in your case. There is no need to put on the airs
Of a clever speaker, for one word will lay you flat.   585
If you were not a coward, you would not have married
Behind my back, but discussed it with me first.

Jason

And you, no doubt, would have furthered the proposal,

If I had told you of it, you who even now
Are incapable of controlling your bitter temper.   590

Medea

It was not that. No, you thought it was not respectable
As you got on in years to have a foreign wife.

Jason

Make sure of this: it was not because of a woman
I made the royal alliance in which I now live,
But, as I said before, I wished to preserve you   595
And breed a royal progeny to be brothers
To the children I have now, a sure defense to us.

Medea

Let me have no happy fortune that brings pain with it,
Or prosperity which is upsetting to the mind!

Jason

Change your ideas of what you want, and show more sense.   600
Do not consider painful what is good for you,
Nor, when you are lucky, think yourself unfortunate.

Medea

You can insult me. You have somewhere to turn to.
But I shall go from this land into exile, friendless.

Jason

It was what you chose yourself. Don't blame others for it.   605

Medea

And how did I choose it? Did I betray my husband?

Jason

You called down wicked curses on the king's family.

Medea

A curse, that is what I am become to your house too.

Jason

I do not propose to go into all the rest of it;
But, if you wish for the children or for yourself   610

In exile to have some of my money to help you,
Say so, for I am prepared to give with open hand,
Or to provide you with introductions to my friends
Who will treat you well. You are a fool if you do not
Accept this. Cease your anger and you will profit.   615

Medea

I shall never accept the favors of friends of yours,
Nor take a thing from you, so you need not offer it.
There is no benefit in the gifts of a bad man.

Jason

Then, in any case, I call the gods to witness that
I wish to help you and the children in every way,   620
But you refuse what is good for you. Obstinately
You push away your friends. You are sure to suffer for it.

Medea

Go! No doubt you hanker for your virginal bride,
And are guilty of lingering too long out of her house.
Enjoy your wedding. But perhaps—with the help of God—   625
You will make the kind of marriage that you will regret.

                              (*Jason goes out with his attendants.*)

Chorus

When love is in excess
It brings a man no honor
Nor any worthiness.
But if in moderation Cypris comes,   630
There is no other power at all so gracious.
O goddess, never on me let loose the unerring
Shaft of your bow in the poison of desire.

Let my heart be wise.   635
It is the gods' best gift.
On me let mighty Cypris
Inflict no wordy wars or restless anger
To urge my passion to a different love.

But with discernment may she guide women's weddings,   640
Honoring most what is peaceful in the bed.

O country and home,
Never, never may I be without you,
Living the hopeless life,   645
Hard to pass through and painful,
Most pitiable of all.
Let death first lay me low and death
Free me from this daylight.
There is no sorrow above   650
The loss of a native land.

I have seen it myself,
Do not tell of a secondhand story.
Neither city nor friend   655
Pitied you when you suffered
The worst of sufferings.
O let him die ungraced whose heart
Will not reward his friends,   660
Who cannot open an honest mind
No friend will he be of mine.

(*Enter Aegeus, king of Athens, an old friend of Medea.*)

Aegeus

Medea, greeting! This is the best introduction
Of which men know for conversation between friends.

Medea

Greeting to you too, Aegeus, son of King Pandion.   665
Where have you come from to visit this country's soil?

Aegeus

I have just left the ancient oracle of Phoebus.

Medea

And why did you go to earth's prophetic center?

Aegeus

I went to inquire how children might be born to me.

Medea

Is it so? Your life still up to this point is childless?   670

Aegeus

Yes. By the fate of some power we have no children.

Medea

Have you a wife, or is there none to share your bed?

Aegeus

There is. Yes, I am joined to my wife in marriage.

Medea

And what did Phoebus say to you about children?

Aegeus

Words too wise for a mere man to guess their meaning.   675

Medea

It is proper for me to be told the god's reply?

Aegeus

It is. For sure what is needed is cleverness.

Medea

Then what was his message? Tell me, if I may hear.

Aegeus

I am not to loosen the hanging foot of the wine-skin . . .

Medea

Until you have done something, or reached some country?   680

Aegeus

Until I return again to my hearth and house.

Medea

And for what purpose have you journeyed to this land?

Aegeus

There is a man called Pittheus, king of Troezen.

Medea

A son of Pelops, they say, a most righteous man.

Aegeus

With him I wish to discuss the reply of the god.   685

Medea

Yes. He is wise and experienced in such matters.

Aegeus

And to me also the dearest of all my spear-friends.

Medea

Well, I hope you have good luck, and achieve your will.

Aegeus

But why this downcast eye of yours, and this pale cheek?

Medea

O Aegeus, my husband has been the worst of all to me.   690

Aegeus

What do you mean? Say clearly what has caused this grief.

Medea

Jason wrongs me, though I have never injured him.

Aegeus

What has he done? Tell me about it in clearer words.

Medea

He has taken a wife to his house, supplanting me.

Aegeus

Surely he would not dare to do a thing like that.   695

Medea

Be sure he has. Once dear, I now am slighted by him.

Aegeus

Did he fall in love? Or is he tired of your love?

Medea

He was greatly in love, this traitor to his friends.

Aegeus

Then let him go, if, as you say, he is so bad.

Medea

A passionate love—for an alliance with the king.   700

Aegeus

And who gave him his wife? Tell me the rest of it.

Medea

It was Creon, he who rules this land of Corinth.

Aegeus

Indeed, Medea, your grief was understandable.

Medea

I am ruined. And there is more to come: I am banished.

Aegeus

Banished? By whom? Here you tell me of a new wrong.   705

Medea

Creon drives me an exile from the land of Corinth.

Aegeus

Does Jason consent? I cannot approve of this.

Medea

He pretends not to, but he will put up with it.
Ah, Aegeus, I beg and beseech you, by your beard
And by your knees I am making myself your suppliant,   710
Have pity on me, have pity on your poor friend,
And do not let me go into exile desolate,
But receive me in your land and at your very hearth.
So may your love, with God's help, lead to the bearing
Of children, and so may you yourself die happy.   715
You do not know what a chance you have come on here.
I will end your childlessness, and I will make you able
To beget children. The drugs I know can do this.

Aegeus

For many reasons, woman, I am anxious to do
This favor for you. First, for the sake of the gods,   720
And then for the birth of children which you promise,

For in that respect I am entirely at my wits' end.
But this is my position: if you reach my land,
I, being in my rights, will try to befriend you.
But this much I must warn you of beforehand: 725
I shall not agree to take you out of this country;
But if you by yourself can reach my house, then you
Shall stay there safely. To none will I give you up
But from this land you must make your escape yourself,
For I do not wish to incur blame from my friends.   730

Medea

It shall be so. But, if I might have a pledge from you
For this, then I would have from you all I desire.

Aegeus

Do you not trust me? What is it rankles with you?

Medea

I trust you, yes. But the house of Pelias hates me,
And so does Creon. If you are bound by this oath,   735
When they try to drag me from your land, you will not
Abandon me; but if our pact is only words,
With no oath to the gods, you will be lightly armed,
Unable to resist their summons. I am weak,
While they have wealth to help them and a royal house. 740

Aegeus

You show much foresight for such negotiations.
Well, if you will have it so, I will not refuse.
For, both on my side this will be the safest way
To have some excuse to put forward to your enemies,
And for you it is more certain. You may name the gods. 745

Medea

Swear by the plain of Earth, and Helius, father
Of my father, and name together all the gods. . .

Aegeus

That I will act or not act in what way? Speak.

Medea

That you yourself will never cast me from your land,
Nor, if any of my enemies should demand me,   750
Will you, in your life, willingly hand me over.

Aegeus

I swear by the Earth, by the holy light of Helius,
By all the gods, I will abide by this you say.

Medea

Enough. And, if you fail, what shall happen to you?

Aegeus

What comes to those who have no regard for heaven.   755

Medea

Go on your way. Farewell. For I am satisfied.
And I will reach your city as soon as I can,
Having done the deed I have to do and gained my end.

                                        (*Aegeus goes out.*)

Chorus

May Hermes, god of travelers,
Escort you, Aegeus, to your home!   760
And may you have the things you wish
So eagerly; for you
Appear to me to be a generous man.

Medea

God, and God's daughter, justice, and light of Helius!
Now, friends, has come the time of my triumph over   765
My enemies, and now my foot is on the road.
Now I am confident they will pay the penalty.
For this man, Aegeus, has been like a harbor to me
In all my plans just where I was most distressed.
To him I can fasten the cable of my safety   770
When I have reached the town and fortress of Pallas.
And now I shall tell to you the whole of my plan.
Listen to these words that are not spoken idly.
I shall send one of my servants to find Jason

And request him to come once more into my sight.   775
And when he comes, the words I'll say will be soft ones.
I'll say that I agree with him, that I approve
The royal wedding he has made, betraying me.
I'll say it was profitable, an excellent idea.
But I shall beg that my children may remain here: 78c
Not that I would leave in a country that hates me
Children of mine to feel their enemies' insults,
But that by a trick I may kill the king's daughter.
For I will send the children with gifts in their hands
To carry to the bride, so as not to be banished—   785
A finely woven dress and a golden diadem.
And if she takes them and wears them upon her skin
She and all who touch the girl will die in agony;
Such poison will I lay upon the gifts I send.
But there, however, I must leave that account paid.   790
I weep to think of what a deed I have to do
Next after that; for I shall kill my own children.
My children, there is none who can give them safety.
And when I have ruined the whole of Jason's house,
I shall leave the land and flee from the murder of my   795
Dear children, and I shall have done a dreadful deed.
For it is not bearable to be mocked by enemies.
So it must happen. What profit have I in life?
I have no land, no home, no refuge from my pain.
My mistake was made the time I left behind me   800
My father's house, and trusted the words of a Greek,
Who, with heaven's help, will pay me the price for that.
For those children he had from me he will never
See alive again, nor will he on his new bride
Beget another child, for she is to be forced   805
To die a most terrible death by these my poisons.
Let no one think me a weak one, feeble-spirited,
A stay-at-home, but rather just the opposite,
One who can hurt my enemies and help my friends;
For the lives of such persons are most remembered.   810

Chorus

   Since you have shared the knowledge of your plan with us,
   I both wish to help you and support the normal
   Ways of mankind, and tell you not to do this thing.

Medea

   I can do no other thing. It is understandable
   For you to speak thus. You have not suffered as I have.   815

Chorus

   But can you have the heart to kill your flesh and blood?

Medea

   Yes, for this is the best way to wound my husband.

Chorus

   And you, too. Of women you will be most unhappy.

Medea

   So it must be. No compromise is possible.

                                (She turns to the Nurse.)

   Go, you, at once, and tell Jason to come to me.   820
   You I employ on all affairs of greatest trust.
   Say nothing of these decisions which I have made,
   If you love your mistress, if you were born a woman.

Chorus

   From of old the children of Erechtheus are
   Splendid, the sons of blessed gods. They dwell   825
   In Athens' holy and unconquered land,
   Where famous Wisdom feeds them and they pass gaily
   Always through that most brilliant air where once, they say,   830
   That golden Harmony gave birth to the nine
   Pure Muses of Pieria.

   And beside the sweet flow of Cephisus' stream,   835
   Where Cypris sailed, they say, to draw the water,
   And mild soft breezes breathed along her path,
   And on her hair were flung the sweet-smelling garlands   840

Of flowers of roses by the Lovers, the companions
Of Wisdom, her escort, the helpers of men
In every kind of excellence. 845

How then can these holy rivers
Or this holy land love you,
Or the city find you a home,
You, who will kill your children,
You, not pure with the rest? 850
O think of the blow at your children
And think of the blood that you shed.
O, over and over I beg you,
By your knees I beg you do not
Be the murderess of your babes! 855

O where will you find the courage
Or the skill of hand and heart,
When you set yourself to attempt
A deed so dreadful to do?
How, when you look upon them, 860
Can you tearlessly hold the decision
For murder? You will not be able,
When your children fall down and implore you,
You will not be able to dip
Steadfast your hand in their blood. 865

(Enter Jason with attendants.)

Jason

I have come at your request. Indeed, although you are
Bitter against me, this you shall have: I will listen
To what new thing you want, woman, to get from me.

Medea

Jason, I beg you to be forgiving toward me
For what I said. It is natural for you to bear with 870
My temper, since we have had much love together.
I have talked with myself about this and I have
Reproached myself. "Fool" I said, "why am I so mad?

Why am I set against those who have planned wisely?
Why make myself an enemy of the authorities   875
And of my husband, who does the best thing for me
By marrying royalty and having children who
Will be as brothers to my own? What is wrong with me?
Let me give up anger, for the gods are kind to me.
Have I not children, and do I not know that we   880
In exile from our country must be short of friends?"
When I considered this I saw that I had shown
Great lack of sense, and that my anger was foolish.
Now I agree with you. I think that you are wise
In having this other wife as well as me, and I   885
Was mad. I should have helped you in these plans of yours,
Have joined in the wedding, stood by the marriage bed,
Have taken pleasure in attendance on your bride.
But we women are what we are—perhaps a little
Worthless; and you men must not be like us in this,   890
Nor be foolish in return when we are foolish.
Now, I give in, and admit that then I was wrong.
I have come to a better understanding now.

                                        (*She turns toward the house.*)

Children, come here, my children, come outdoors to us!
Welcome your father with me, and say goodbye to him,   895
And with your mother, who just now was his enemy,
Join again in making friends with him who loves us.

                        (*Enter the children, attended by the Tutor.*)

We have made peace, and all our anger is over.
Take hold of his right hand—O God, I am thinking
Of something which may happen in the secret future.   900
O children, will you just so, after a long life,
Hold out your loving arms at the grave? O children,
How ready to cry I am, how full of foreboding!
I am ending at last this quarrel with your father,
And, look my soft eyes have suddenly filled with tears.   905

Chorus

> And the pale tears have started also in my eyes.
> O may the trouble not grow worse than now it is!

Jason

> I approve of what you say. And I cannot blame you
> Even for what you said before. It is natural
> For a woman to be wild with her husband when he   910
> Goes in for secret love. But now your mind has turned
> To better reasoning. In the end you have come to
> The right decision, like the clever woman you are.
> And of you, children, your father is taking care.
> He has made, with God's help, ample provision for you.   915
> For I think that a time will come when you will be
> The leading people in Corinth with your brothers.
> You must grow up. As to the future, your father
> And those of the gods who love him will deal with that.
> I want to see you, when you have become young men,   920
> Healthy and strong, better men than my enemies.
> Medea, why are your eyes all wet with pale tears?
> Why is your cheek so white and turned away from me?
> Are not these words of mine pleasing for you to hear?

Medea

> It is nothing. I was thinking about these children.   925

Jason

> You must be cheerful. I shall look after them well.

Medea

> I will be. It is not that I distrust your words,
> But a woman is a frail thing, prone to crying.

Jason

> But why then should you grieve so much for these children?

Medea

> I am their mother. When you prayed that they might live   930
> I felt unhappy to think that these things will be.

But come, I have said something of the things I meant
To say to you, and now I will tell you the rest.
Since it is the king's will to banish me from here—
And for me, too, I know that this is the best thing,   935
Not to be in your way by living here or in
The king's way, since they think me ill-disposed to them—
I then am going into exile from this land;
But do you, so that you may have the care of them,
Beg Creon that the children may not be banished.   940

Jason

I doubt if I'll succeed, but still I'll attempt it.

Medea

Then you must tell your wife to beg from her father
That the children may be reprieved from banishment.

Jason

I will, and with her I shall certainly succeed.

Medea

If she is like the rest of us women, you will.   945
And I, too, will take a hand with you in this business,
For I will send her some gifts which are far fairer,
I am sure of it, than those which now are in fashion,
A finely woven dress and a golden diadem,
And the children shall present them. Quick, let one of you   950
Servants bring here to me that beautiful dress.

(*One of her attendants goes into the house.*)

She will be happy not in one way, but in a hundred,
Having so fine a man as you to share her bed,
And with this beautiful dress which Helius of old,
My father's father, bestowed on his descendants.   955

(*Enter attendant carrying the poisoned dress and diadem.*)

There, children, take these wedding presents in your hands.
Take them to the royal princess, the happy bride,
And give them to her. She will not think little of them.

Jason

    No, don't be foolish, and empty your hands of these.
    Do you think the palace is short of dresses to wear?   960
    Do you think there is no gold there? Keep them, don't give them
    Away. If my wife considers me of any value,
    She will think more of me than money, I am sure of it.

Medea

    No, let me have my way. They say the gods themselves
    Are moved by gifts, and gold does more with men than words.   965
    Hers is the luck, her fortune that which god blesses;
    She is young and a princess; but for my children's reprieve
    I would give my very life, and not gold only.
    Go children, go together to that rich palace,
    Be suppliants to the new wife of your father,   970
    My lady, beg her not to let you be banished.
    And give her the dress—for this is of great importance,
    That she should take the gift into her hand from yours.
    Go, quick as you can. And bring your mother good news
    By your success of those things which she longs to gain.   975

            (*Jason goes out with his attendants, followed by the Tutor
            and the children carrying the poisoned gifts.*)

Chorus

    Now there is no hope left for the children's lives.
    Now there is none. They are walking already to murder.
    The bride, poor bride, will accept the curse of the gold,
    Will accept the bright diadem.
    Around her yellow hair she will set that dress   980
    Of death with her own hands.

    The grace and the perfume and glow of the golden robe
    Will charm her to put them upon her and wear the wreath,
    And now her wedding will be with the dead below,   985
    Into such a trap she will fall,
    Poor thing, into such a fate of death and never
    Escape from under that curse.

You, too, O wretched bridegroom, making your match with   990
   kings,
You do not see that you bring
Destruction on your children and on her,
Your wife, a fearful death.
Poor soul, what a fall is yours!   995

In your grief, too, I weep, mother of little children,
You who will murder your own,
In vengeance for the loss of married love
Which Jason has betrayed   1000
As he lives with another wife.

                    (*Enter the Tutor with the children.*)

Tutor

Mistress, I tell you that these children are reprieved,
And the royal bride has been pleased to take in her hands
Your gifts. In that quarter the children are secure.
But come,
Why do you stand confused when you are fortunate?   1005
Why have you turned round with your cheek away from me?
Are not these words of mine pleasing for you to hear?

Medea

Oh! I am lost!

Tutor

That word is not in harmony with my tidings.

Medea

I am lost, I am lost!

Tutor

             Am I in ignorance telling you
Of some disaster, and not the good news I thought?   1010

Medea

You have told what you have told. I do not blame you.

Tutor

Why then this downcast eye, and this weeping of tears?

Medea

Oh, I am forced to weep, old man. The gods and I,
I in a kind of madness, have contrived all this.

Tutor

Courage! You, too, will be brought home by your children.   1015

Medea

Ah, before that happens I shall bring others home.

Tutor

Others before you have been parted from their children.
Mortals must bear in resignation their ill luck.

Medea

That is what I shall do. But go inside the house,
And do for the children your usual daily work.   1020

(*The Tutor goes into the house. Medea turns to her children.*)

O children, O my children, you have a city,
You have a home, and you can leave me behind you,
And without your mother you may live there forever.
But I am going in exile to another land
Before I have seen you happy and taken pleasure in you,   1025
Before I have dressed your brides and made your marriage beds
And held up the torch at the ceremony of wedding.
Oh, what a wretch I am in this my self-willed thought!
What was the purpose, children, for which I reared you?
For all my travail and wearing myself away?   1030
They were sterile, those pains I had in the bearing of you.
Oh surely once the hopes in you I had, poor me,
Were high ones: you would look after me in old age,
And when I died would deck me well with your own hands;
A thing which all would have done. Oh but now it is gone,   1035
That lovely thought. For, once I am left without you,
Sad will be the life I'll lead and sorrowful for me.
And you will never see your mother again with
Your dear eyes, gone to another mode of living.
Why, children, do you look upon me with your eyes?   1040

Why do you smile so sweetly that last smile of all?
Oh, Oh, what can I do? My spirit has gone from me,
Friends, when I saw that bright look in the children's eyes.
I cannot bear to do it. I renounce my plans
I had before. I'll take my children away from   1045
This land. Why should I hurt their father with the pain
They feel, and suffer twice as much of pain myself?
No, no, I will not do it. I renounce my plans.
Ah, what is wrong with me? Do I want to let go
My enemies unhurt and be laughed at for it?   1050
I must face this thing. Oh, but what a weak woman
Even to admit to my mind these soft arguments.
Children, go into the house. And he whom law forbids
To stand in attendance at my sacrifices,
Let him see to it. I shall not mar my handiwork.   1055
Oh! Oh!
Do not, O my heart, you must not do these things!
Poor heart, let them go, have pity upon the children.
If they live with you in Athens they will cheer you.
No! By Hell's avenging furies it shall not be—
This shall never be, that I should suffer my children   1060
To be the prey of my enemies' insolence.
Every way is it fixed. The bride will not escape.
No, the diadem is now upon her head, and she,   1065
The royal princess, is dying in the dress, I know it.
But—for it is the most dreadful of roads for me
To tread, and them I shall send on a more dreadful still—
I wish to speak to the children.
                              (*She calls the children to her.*)
                              Come, children, give
Me your hands, give your mother your hands to kiss them.   1070
Oh the dear hands, and O how dear are these lips to me,
And the generous eyes and the bearing of my children!
I wish you happiness, but not here in this world.
What is here your father took. Oh how good to hold you!
How delicate the skin, how sweet the breath of children!   1075

Go, go! I am no longer able, no longer
To look upon you. I am overcome by sorrow.

(*The children go into the house.*)

I know indeed what evil I intend to do,
But stronger than all my afterthoughts is my fury,
Fury that brings upon mortals the greatest evils.   1080

(*She goes out to the right, toward the royal palace.*)

Chorus

Often before
I have gone through more subtle reasons,
And have come upon questionings greater
Than a woman should strive to search out.
But we too have a goddess to help us   1085
And accompany us into wisdom.
Not all of us. Still you will find
Among many women a few,
And our sex is not without learning.
This I say, that those who have never   1090
Had children, who know nothing of it,
In happiness have the advantage
Over those who are parents.
The childless, who never discover
Whether children turn out as a good thing   1095
Or as something to cause pain, are spared
Many troubles in lacking this knowledge.
And those who have in their homes
The sweet presence of children, I see that their lives
Are all wasted away by their worries.   1100
First they must think how to bring them up well and
How to leave them something to live on.
And then after this whether all their toil
Is for those who will turn out good or bad,
Is still an unanswered question.
And of one more trouble, the last of all,   1105
That is common to mortals I tell.

For suppose you have found them enough for their living,
Suppose that the children have grown into youth
And have turned out good, still, if God so wills it,
Death will away with your children's bodies,
And carry them off into Hades.   1110
What is our profit, then, that for the sake of
Children the gods should pile upon mortals
After all else
This most terrible grief of all?   1115

(Enter Medea, from the spectators' right.)

Medea

Friends, I can tell you that for long I have waited
For the event. I stare toward the place from where
The news will come. And now, see one of Jason's servants
Is on his way here, and that labored breath of his
Shows he has tidings for us, and evil tidings.   1120

(Enter, also from the right, the Messenger.)

Messenger

Medea, you who have done such a dreadful thing,
So outrageous, run for your life, take what you can,
A ship to bear you hence or chariot on land.

Medea

And what is the reason deserves such flight as this?

Messenger

She is dead, only just now, the royal princess,   1125
And Creon dead, too, her father, by your poisons.

Medea

The finest words you have spoken. Now and hereafter
I shall count you among my benefactors and friends.

Messenger

What! Are you right in the mind? Are you not mad,
Woman? The house of the king is outraged by you.   1130
Do you enjoy it? Not afraid of such doings?

Medea

> To what you say I on my side have something too
> To say in answer. Do not be in a hurry, friend,
> But speak. How did they die? You will delight me twice
> As much again if you say they died in agony.   1135

Messenger

> When those two children, born of you, had entered in,
> Their father with them, and passed into the bride's house,
> We were pleased, we slaves who were distressed by your wrongs.
> All through the house we were talking of but one thing,
> How you and your husband had made up your quarrel.   1140
> Some kissed the children's hands and some their yellow hair,
> And I myself was so full of my joy that I
> Followed the children into the women's quarters.
> Our mistress, whom we honor now instead of you,
> Before she noticed that your two children were there,   1145
> Was keeping her eye fixed eagerly on Jason.
> Afterwards, however, she covered up her eyes,
> Her cheek paled, and she turned herself away from him,
> So disgusted was she at the children's coming there.
> But your husband tried to end the girl's bad temper,   1150
> And said "You must not look unkindly on your friends.
> Cease to be angry. Turn your head to me again.
> Have as your friends the same ones as your husband has.
> And take these gifts, and beg your father to reprieve
> These children from their exile. Do it for my sake."   1155
> She, when she saw the dress, could not restrain herself.
> She agreed with all her husband said, and before
> He and the children had gone far from the palace,
> She took the gorgeous robe and dressed herself in it,
> And put the golden crown around her curly locks,   1160
> And arranged the set of the hair in a shining mirror,
> And smiled at the lifeless image of herself in it.
> Then she rose from her chair and walked about the room,
> With her gleaming feet stepping most soft and delicate,

All overjoyed with the present. Often and often   1165
She would stretch her foot out straight and look along it.
But after that it was a fearful thing to see.
The color of her face changed, and she staggered back,
She ran, and her legs trembled, and she only just
Managed to reach a chair without falling flat down.   1170
An aged woman servant who, I take it, thought
This was some seizure of Pan or another god,
Cried out "God bless us," but that was before she saw
The white foam breaking through her lips and her rolling
The pupils of her eyes and her face all bloodless.   1175
Then she raised a different cry from that "God bless us,"
A huge shriek, and the women ran, one to the king,
One to the newly wedded husband to tell him
What had happened to his bride; and with frequent sound
The whole of the palace rang as they went running.   1180
One walking quickly round the course of a race-track
Would now have turned the bend and be close to the goal,
When she, poor girl, opened her shut and speechless eye,
And with a terrible groan she came to herself.
For a twofold pain was moving up against her.   1185
The wreath of gold that was resting around her head
Let forth a fearful stream of all-devouring fire,
And the finely woven dress your children gave to her,
Was fastening on the unhappy girl's fine flesh.
She leapt up from the chair, and all on fire she ran,   1190
Shaking her hair now this way and now that, trying
To hurl the diadem away; but fixedly
The gold preserved its grip, and, when she shook her hair,
Then more and twice as fiercely the fire blazed out.
Till, beaten by her fate, she fell down to the ground,   1195
Hard to be recognized except by a parent.
Neither the setting of her eyes was plain to see,
Nor the shapeliness of her face. From the top of
Her head there oozed out blood and fire mixed together.
Like the drops on pine-bark, so the flesh from her bones   1200

Dropped away, torn by the hidden fang of the poison.
It was a fearful sight; and terror held us all
From touching the corpse. We had learned from what had
    happened.
But her wretched father, knowing nothing of the event,
Came suddenly to the house, and fell upon the corpse,   1205
And at once cried out and folded his arms about her,
And kissed her and spoke to her, saying, "O my poor child,
What heavenly power has so shamefully destroyed you?
And who has set me here like an ancient sepulcher,
Deprived of you? O let me die with you, my child!"   1210
And when he had made an end of his wailing and crying,
Then the old man wished to raise himself to his feet;
But, as the ivy clings to the twigs of the laurel,
So he stuck to the fine dress, and he struggled fearfully.
For he was trying to lift himself to his knee,   1215
And she was pulling him down, and when he tugged hard
He would be ripping his aged flesh from his bones.
At last his life was quenched, and the unhappy man
Gave up the ghost, no longer could hold up his head.
There they lie close, the daughter and the old father,   1220
Dead bodies, an event he prayed for in his tears.
As for your interests, I will say nothing of them,
For you will find your own escape from punishment.
Our human life I think and have thought a shadow,
And I do not fear to say that those who are held   1225
Wise among men and who search the reasons of things
Are those who bring the most sorrow on themselves.
For of mortals there is no one who is happy.
If wealth flows in upon one, one may be perhaps
Luckier than one's neighbor, but still not happy.   1230

                                                (Exit.)

Chorus

    Heaven, it seems, on this day has fastened many
    Evils on Jason, and Jason has deserved them.
    Poor girl, the daughter of Creon, how I pity you

And your misfortunes, you who have gone quite away
To the house of Hades because of marrying Jason.   1235

Medea

Women, my task is fixed: as quickly as I may
To kill my children, and start away from this land,
And not, by wasting time, to suffer my children
To be slain by another hand less kindly to them.
Force every way will have it they must die, and since   1240
This must be so, then I, their mother, shall kill them.
Oh, arm yourself in steel, my heart! Do not hang back
From doing this fearful and necessary wrong.
Oh, come, my hand, poor wretched hand, and take the sword,
Take it, step forward to this bitter starting point,   1245
And do not be a coward, do not think of them,
How sweet they are, and how you are their mother. Just for
This one short day be forgetful of your children,
Afterward weep; for even though you will kill them,
They were very dear—Oh, I am an unhappy woman!   1250

(*With a cry she rushes into the house.*)

Chorus

O Earth, and the far shining
Ray of the Sun, look down, look down upon
This poor lost woman, look, before she raises
The hand of murder against her flesh and blood.
Yours was the golden birth from which   1255
She sprang, and now I fear divine
Blood may be shed by men.
O heavenly light, hold back her hand,
Check her, and drive from out the house
The bloody Fury raised by fiends of Hell.   1260

Vain waste, your care of children;
Was it in vain you bore the babes you loved,
After you passed the inhospitable strait
Between the dark blue rocks, Symplegades?

O wretched one, how has it come, 1265
This heavy anger on your heart,
This cruel bloody mind?
For God from mortals asks a stern
Price for the stain of kindred blood
In like disaster falling on their homes. 1270

(A cry from one of the children is heard.)

Chorus

Do you hear the cry, do you hear the children's cry?
O you hard heart, O woman fated for evil!

One of the children (from within)

What can I do and how escape my mother's hands?

Another child (from within)

O my dear brother, I cannot tell. We are lost.

Chorus

Shall I enter the house? Oh, surely I should 1275
Defend the children from murder.

A child (from within)

O help us, in God's name, for now we need your help.
Now, now we are close to it. We are trapped by the sword.

Chorus

O your heart must have been made of rock or steel,
You who can kill 1280
With your own hand the fruit of your own womb.
Of one alone I have heard, one woman alone
Of those of old who laid her hands on her children,
Ino, sent mad by heaven when the wife of Zeus
Drove her out from her home and made her wander; 1285
And because of the wicked shedding of blood
Of her own children she threw
Herself, poor wretch, into the sea and stepped away
Over the sea-cliff to die with her two children.
What horror more can be? O women's love, 1290

So full of trouble,
How many evils have you caused already!

(*Enter Jason, with attendants.*)

Jason

You women, standing close in front of this dwelling,
Is she, Medea, she who did this dreadful deed,
Still in the house, or has she run away in flight?   1295
For she will have to hide herself beneath the earth,
Or raise herself on wings into the height of air,
If she wishes to escape the royal vengeance.
Does she imagine that, having killed our rulers,
She will herself escape uninjured from this house?   1300
But I am thinking not so much of her as for
The children—her the king's friends will make to suffer
For what she did. So I have come to save the lives
Of my boys, in case the royal house should harm them
While taking vengeance for their mother's wicked deed.   1305

Chorus

O Jason, if you but knew how deeply you are
Involved in sorrow, you would not have spoken so.

Jason

What is it? That she is planning to kill me also?

Chorus

Your children are dead, and by their own mother's hand.

Jason

What! That is it? O woman, you have destroyed me!   1310

Chorus

You must make up your mind your children are no more.

Jason

Where did she kill them? Was it here or in the house?

Chorus

Open the gates and there you will see them murdered.

Jason

Quick as you can unlock the doors, men, and undo
The fastenings and let me see this double evil,   1315
My children dead and her—Oh her I will repay.

(*His attendants rush to the door. Medea appears above the house in
a chariot drawn by dragons. She has the dead bodies
of the children with her.*)

Medea

Why do you batter these gates and try to unbar them,
Seeking the corpses and for me who did the deed?
You may cease your trouble, and, if you have need of me,
Speak, if you wish. You will never touch me with your hand,   1320
Such a chariot has Helius, my father's father,
Given me to defend me from my enemies.

Jason

You hateful thing, you woman most utterly loathed
By the gods and me and by all the race of mankind,
You who have had the heart to raise a sword against   1325
Your children, you, their mother, and left me childless—
You have done this, and do you still look at the sun
And at the earth, after these most fearful doings?
I wish you dead. Now I see it plain, though at that time
I did not, when I took you from your foreign home   1330
And brought you to a Greek house, you, an evil thing,
A traitress to your father and your native land.
The gods hurled the avenging curse of yours on me.
For your own brother you slew at your own hearthside,
And then came aboard that beautiful ship, the Argo.   1335
And that was your beginning. When you were married
To me, your husband, and had borne children to me,
For the sake of pleasure in the bed you killed them.
There is no Greek woman who would have dared such deeds,
Out of all those whom I passed over and chose you   1340
To marry instead, a bitter destructive match,
A monster, not a woman, having a nature

Wilder than that of Scylla in the Tuscan sea.
Ah! no, not if I had ten thousand words of shame
Could I sting you. You are naturally so brazen.   1345
Go, worker in evil, stained with your children's blood.
For me remains to cry aloud upon my fate,
Who will get no pleasure from my newly wedded love,
And the boys whom I begot and brought up, never
Shall I speak to them alive. Oh, my life is over!   1350

Medea

Long would be the answer which I might have made to
These words of yours, if Zeus the father did not know
How I have treated you and what you did to me.
No, it was not to be that you should scorn my love,
And pleasantly live your life through, laughing at me;   1355
Nor would the princess, nor he who offered the match,
Creon, drive me away without paying for it.
So now you may call me a monster, if you wish,
A Scylla housed in the caves of the Tuscan sea.
I too, as I had to, have taken hold of your heart.   1360

Jason

You feel the pain yourself. You share in my sorrow.

Medea

Yes, and my grief is gain when you cannot mock it.

Jason

O children, what a wicked mother she was to you!

Medea

They died from a disease they caught from their father.

Jason

I tell you it was not my hand that destroyed them.   1365

Medea

But it was your insolence, and your virgin wedding.

Jason

And just for the sake of that you chose to kill them.

Medea

Is love so small a pain, do you think, for a woman?

Jason

For a wise one, certainly. But you are wholly evil.

Medea

The children are dead. I say this to make you suffer. 1370

Jason

The children, I think, will bring down curses on you.

Medea

The gods know who was the author of this sorrow.

Jason

Yes, the gods know indeed, they know your loathsome heart.

Medea

Hate me. But I tire of your barking bitterness.

Jason

And I of yours. It is easier to leave you. 1375

Medea

How then? What shall I do? I long to leave you too.

Jason

Give me the bodies to bury and to mourn them.

Medea

No, that I will not. I will bury them myself,
Bearing them to Hera's temple on the promontory;
So that no enemy may evilly treat them 1380
By tearing up their grave. In this land of Corinth
I shall establish a holy feast and sacrifice
Each year for ever to atone for the blood guilt.
And I myself go to the land of Erechtheus
To dwell in Aegeus' house, the son of Pandion. 1385
While you, as is right, will die without distinction,
Struck on the head by a piece of the Argo's timber,
And you will have seen the bitter end of my love.

Jason

    May a Fury for the children's sake destroy you,
    And justice, Requitor of blood.   1390

Medea

    What heavenly power lends an ear
    To a breaker of oaths, a deceiver?

Jason

    Oh, I hate you, murderess of children.

Medea

    Go to your palace. Bury your bride.

Jason

    I go, with two children to mourn for.   1395

Medea

    Not yet do you feel it. Wait for the future.

Jason

    Oh, children I loved!

Medea

                     I loved them, you did not.

Jason

    You loved them, and killed them.

Medea

                            To make you feel pain.

Jason

    Oh, wretch that I am, how I long
    To kiss the dear lips of my children!   1400

Medea

    Now you would speak to them, now you would kiss them.
    Then you rejected them.

Jason

                  Let me, I beg you,
    Touch my boys' delicate flesh.

Medea

I will not. Your words are all wasted.

Jason

O God, do you hear it, this persecution,   1405
These my sufferings from this hateful
Woman, this monster, murderess of children?
Still what I can do that I will do:
I will lament and cry upon heaven,
Calling the gods to bear me witness   1410
How you have killed my boys and prevent me from
Touching their bodies or giving them burial.
I wish I had never begot them to see them
Afterward slaughtered by you.

Chorus

Zeus in Olympus is the overseer   1415
Of many doings. Many things the gods
Achieve beyond our judgment. What we thought
Is not confirmed and what we thought not god
Contrives. And so it happens in this story.

(Curtain.)

THE
HERACLEIDAE

Translated and with an Introduction by

RALPH GLADSTONE

INTRODUCTION TO *THE HERACLEIDAE*

The Legend

EURYSTHEUS, king of Argos, was given control over his cousin Heracles through the contrivance of Hera. He persecuted Heracles throughout that hero's life, sending him on the famous and perilous "Labors." After Heracles had died and been transformed into a god, Eurystheus continued to persecute the family. Wherever these disinherited refugees went, he would send his herald to demand that they be denied sanctuary. He was the most powerful king in Greece, and none dared resist him. But in Attica the Heracleidae finally found a state which was willing to defend their rights; and when Eurystheus invaded Attica to claim them by force, he was defeated and killed.

Such were the main outlines of the legend, at least the Athenian legend (there was a Theban variant as well). Aeschylus had written a tragedy on the subject, and Athenian playwrights loved to glorify an ancient Athens which had stood up for the weak and the oppressed (Aeschylus, *The Eumenides;* Sophocles, *Oedipus at Colonos;* Euripides, *The Suppliants, Medea, Heracles*). There are certain details which Euripides either invented or chose to emphasize. He is the first, as far as we know, to bring in the self-immolation of a daughter of Heracles. He also makes a major character out of Iolaus, Heracles' nephew and old companion-in-arms, at the expense of Hyllus, the eldest of the Heracleidae. Some said Hyllus killed Eurystheus, others that Iolaus did. Euripides makes Hyllus a son who is of fighting age, and the messenger's account of the battle gives him an honorable part, but Hyllus never appears on stage. The leader of the Heracleidae is Iolaus, a decrepit but indomitable warrior who is rejuvenated in the course of battle and becomes the hero of the day. Finally, instead of having Eurystheus killed in battle (all other authorities do, as far as we know), Euripides makes Iolaus take him prisoner and have him handed over to Alcmene, who puts him to death over the protests of the Athenians. This last feature may have a bearing on the date and occasion of the play.

The Date

No date for this play has been given by ancient authorities. The versification has technical qualities which find a parallel in three early-dated tragedies: *Alcestis* (438 B.C.), *Medea* (431 B.C.), and *Hippolytus* (428 B.C.). The dating and interpretation may be further helped if we consider an event which took place between autumn of 430 and winter or early spring of 429 B.C. At that time Athens was at war with the Peloponnesian League. Five Peloponnesian envoys, on their way to the king of Persia, were treacherously seized by friends of the Athenians in Thrace, brought to Athens, and there "put to death on the day of their arrival, without trial and without permission to say some things they wished to say" (Thucydides ii. 67. 4; also mentioned by Herodotus vii. 137. 3). Since our play deals with the summary execution of an unarmed prisoner and was written at some date not far from 430, we can hardly ignore this event. Of course, *The Heracleidae* may have been written and produced earlier; but if we date it just after the execution of the envoys, we may understand why Euripides chose to end the play with the execution of Eurystheus instead of his death in battle.

This abruptly changes the whole direction of the play and reverses our sympathies. From the beginning, we have been made to take the side of the innocent Heracleidae and their gallant protectors against the wicked king, who, not content with his abuse of the father, insists on hunting the children and their feeble guardians to death. It is as simple as that, sheer white against black. The outrageousness of the Argive king is aggravated by a truculent herald; the virtue of the afflicted by the self-sacrifice of a virgin martyr. But when at last Eurystheus appears, he is nothing like his herald; he frankly admits his past misdeeds, neither extenuating nor boasting, and faces death with calm dignity. It is Alcmene who turns horrible in her insistence on revenge, while the Athenians (represented by the chorus) appear, though Euripides does his best for them, as nothing much better than weak well-meaners.

Why has this been done, when following the accepted (so we presume) legend and having Eurystheus killed in battle would have meant an acceptable "straight" play? Euripides knew that brutality brutalizes; people who have been injured or abused too long become worse than their tormentors (Medea, Hecuba, Creusa, Electra, Orestes, Dionysus). But this reversal is uncommonly sudden and lacks the careful and convincing motivation which we find in *Medea, Ion, Orestes,* and elsewhere. I would hazard a guess that the envoys were executed in the winter, not very long before the spring productions; that Euripides was still at work on *The Heracleidae,* and the event made him change the end of the play to suit the occasion. There are certain signs of haste in the writing. Euripides obviously could and did write iambics at breakneck speed, but *The Heracleidae* has a smaller proportion of the far more difficult choral lyric than any other Euripidean play. If the manuscript is sound (but it may not be) the end of the play is carelessly composed. One other point is the more than usual emphasis on woman's place in a modest, but determined, maiden's apology for public appearance; it recalls the pronouncement of Pericles in the winter of 431–430 to the effect that women should not even be seen, much less heard (Thucydides ii. 45. 2).

My guess, then, is spring 429 B.C. for this play. The execution was a horror, the worse because just retaliation was pleaded, as if two wrongs were to make a right. But both Athens and Sparta were to do far worse still. This play has an Athens still unbrutalized, though acquiescent; it is the wronged and rescued suppliants who turn beastly; and who are these but the ancestors of the Lacedaemonians, after all? The Argives (neutral in 429; but one Argive *was* executed at Athens) are not so bad as we thought, though all heralds grow arrogant on their sacred immunity. There is plenty of "glorious Athens," and "liberty" is a key word. But Athens has slipped, this once. Euripides' faith in his city is not to be broken for a long time, but here is reproof and warning.

The Play

It is rapid, with little lyric or high poetry, not profound but, despite the melodrama, often shrewd. The young king is really a democrat in disguise; will do nothing without the people's consent; and therefore, while ready to protect the afflicted, cannot help wishing (like the king in *The Suppliants* of Aeschylus) that these particular suppliants had never come his way. Macaria seems a mere abstraction of virtue, until her outburst at Iolaus, when he offers to spoil her act, shows her as human after all. The most challenging piece of treatment is that accorded to Iolaus. Why must he be so old? We are not to press legendary ages, but, after all, Iolaus was of the generation of Hyllus, not of Alcmene; he was the nephew of Heracles, not his uncle. Probably, for one thing, for the story. The point is that the Heracleidae are helpless until helped by Athens and cannot be protected by two strong fighters of their own. So Hyllus comes in as an afterthought and is kept (with his army) off stage, while Iolaus is superannuated. Therefore, also, Demophon is king of Athens instead of Good King Theseus, as in other versions; Demophon can be more plausibly represented as a younger man. But also the theme of resolute old age and of rejuvenation seems to fascinate the tragedian. The prototype is Laertes in the 24th book of the *Odyssey*. But it has been suggested that Aeschylus in his lost play rejuvenated Iolaus, and, if so, Euripides is (as elsewhere) having his fun with Aeschylus. For there is irony, at least, in the treatment of Iolaus. As to whether the miracle ever took place at all, the messenger prefaces his account in the best manner of Herodotus, the scientific historian of the day: "Up to this point [the prayer of Iolaus] I am telling you what I saw; for what followed, I am telling you what they tell me." Note that no rejuvenated Iolaus returns to the stage. The going forth to battle of Iolaus is indisputably comic, though it is that tragic funniness that makes old age so cruel (Aeschylus with Cilissa in *The Libation Bearers,* the Prophetess in *The Eumenides*). As so often, Euripides has tried to cram too much into one play, to move in too many directions at once; but he has made livelier what started as a most conventional piece.

One feature of the play is the supernumerary male children of Heracles. They are on stage, presumably, from start to finish, though they say nothing. The play is named from them, not, as usually, from the chorus or a principal character. Neither the daughter of Heracles nor the herald is named in the text. The names Macaria and Copreus are in the ancient *dramatis personae*. The latter comes from the *Iliad*. The scene is at Marathon, on the coast of Attica.

THE HERACLEIDAE

CHARACTERS

Iolaus, an old man and friend of Heracles

Copreus, herald of Eurystheus

Chorus of old men of Marathon

Demophon, son of Theseus and king of Athens

Macaria, daughter of Heracles

Alcmene, mother of Heracles

Attendants

Eurystheus, king of Argos and Mycenae

Small children of Heracles, guards, townspeople

THE HERACLEIDAE

(Iolaus, accompanied by small children of Heracles, enters.)

Iolaus

For years I've known that anyone who's just
Is born to serve his neighbors, but the man
Who will persist in feathering his nest
Has got no public spirit and is hard
To deal with, as I've found out to my cost.   5
And though I could have lived respectably
In Argos, with my family and in peace,
As right-hand man of Heracles, I served
Through his worst trials, while he still was alive.
Now he's in heaven, and as guardian of   10
His children, I could use a guard myself.
When he was dead and gone, Eurystheus
Decided to eliminate us, too.
We got away, and, though we saved our skins,
Our home is gone; and now we stand condemned   15
To keep on wandering from state to state,
Because this king, whose record is as black
As sin, has had the front to lay on us
A new humiliation. Anywhere
We go, when he finds out, he sends someone   20
To bully them into expelling us,
And claims his town's too strong and he's too rich
To risk offending. When our hosts recall
That *these* are orphans, that *I've* no support,
They cringe and end by sending us away.   25
With displaced children I displace myself
To share with those who have more than their share
Of sorrows. If I left them, men might say,

"He failed to do his duty by them, once
  Their father died, in spite of family ties."   30
And since the rest of Greece is banned to us,
We've reached the neighborhood of Marathon
To throw ourselves upon the mercy of
The gods and seek their help. Two kings, I'm told,
Of Pandion's and Theseus' line have here   35
Come into power, both our relatives.
That's why we've come to the world-famous state
Of Athens, on a trip conceived and planned
By two old strategists. So I, for one,
Am seeing to the safety of these boys.   40
Meanwhile Alcmene minds the girls and keeps
Them all inside the temple. It would look
Highly improper if we let them stand
In front of it, exposed to people's eyes.
Then Hyllus and the older boys have gone   45
To find another refuge, just in case
We ever should be forced to leave this town.
Quick, children! Come back! Hold on tight!
That's Eurystheus' herald coming here,
The one that has us chased from place to place,   50

                                    (Enter Copreus.)

And made us homeless refugees. Scum!
I'll see you damned and your employer too.
Why, you're the selfsame man who used to bring
Bad news repeatedly to Heracles.

Copreus

Oh come now, do you really think you've found   55
A refuge and protection? Are you mad
Enough to think that anyone would choose
Your helplessness in preference to our strength?
Why don't you stop this fuss? You're bound to come
Right back to Argos and a stony end.   60

Iolaus

Not on your life! I'm well protected by
God's temple and this free and sovereign state.

Copreus

Oh, then you'll give my muscles exercise?

Iolaus

You wouldn't dare to take us out by force.

Copreus

You'll soon see how wrong that prediction is.   65
                              (*Tries to seize children.*)

Iolaus

Then over my dead body, if you do.

Copreus

Keep out of this. I need no leave from you
To take away my master's property.
                              (*Throws Iolaus down.*)

Iolaus

Help! Men of this historic town, though we're
Protected by Zeus's temple in the square,   70
We've been assaulted and our wreaths defiled,
Which outrages the city and the gods!

Chorus

You there! Just what's the meaning of all this
Ungodly noise, and by the altar too?
Oh! This poor old man is lying   75
On the ground. What a shameful thing!
Who was it handled you so brutally?

Iolaus

This man here dragged me from the altar by
Main force, and showed contempt for all your gods.

Chorus

What country are you coming from, old man?   80
Have you reached these federated states

By the blade of the oar in the sea? Were you
Rowed over here from some Euboean port?

Iolaus

No, we're no islanders. We've made our way
To Athens from Mycenae.   85

Chorus

And what name did you go by
Among the Mycenaean citizens?

Iolaus

You've heard of me, I think. I'm Iolaus,
Known as the right-hand man of Heracles.

Chorus

The name has a familiar ring. But please,   90
Why don't you tell us whose young children these
Are, whom you're leading by the hand?

Iolaus

These are the sons of Heracles, who've come
To ask protection here from you and yours.

Chorus

Just what is it you want of us? Are you   95
Applying for a hearing here?

Iolaus

We ask you to stand by us and to keep
The Argives from abducting us by force.

Copreus

That's hardly good enough. Your betters here
Have found you and will have the final say.   100

Chorus

The rights of those the gods protect
Are bound to be respected. To go off
And leave an altar desecrated makes
A mockery of justice.

Copreus

    Who spoke of such a thing? I'm asking you   105
    To drive my master's subjects from the land.

Chorus

    That would be sacrilegious,
    Rejecting people who demand our help.

Copreus

    It would be healthier to change your minds
    And keep your city out of trouble's way.   110

Chorus

    Instead of kidnapping these refugees
    So brazenly, you should have seen the king
    And shown respect for Athens' sovereign rights.

Copreus

    Now that you menion it, who is the king?

Chorus

    Demophon, son of the great Theseus.   115

Copreus

    Oh, then my business lies with him! All this
    Is just a waste of breath and nothing more.

Chorus

    Look! There he comes, and his brother Acamas.
    They're hurrying to judge this whole affair.

                  (Enter Demophon, with Acamas.)

Demophon

    Since you old men rushed here upon the scene,   120
    Before the young ones helped or reached the shrine,
    Suppose you tell us just what's drawn this crowd?

Chorus

    These children, who have hung the altar with
    The wreaths you see, are Heracles' sons.
    Iolaus was their father's right-hand man.   125

Demophon

But why were there such awful cries for help?

Chorus

That man just tried to drag them all away,
Which caused the cries we heard. The way he threw
That poor old man down touched me to the heart.

Demophon

Although he looks and dresses like a Greek,   130
It needs a savage to behave like that.
Stranger, it's up to you. Be quick and let
Me know what sort of country you come from.

Copreus

Well, since you ask, I come from Argos. Now
I'll tell who sent me and just why I'm here.   135
It was Eurystheus of Mycenae told
Me to come here and bring these back. I have
Authority for all I do or say;
Since, as an Argive, I'm recovering
These Argive nationals who've run away,   140
Though legally condemned to death at home.
We have a perfect right to carry out
The laws we make for our own sovereign land.
I've often made this point, each time I reached
A new "protector." Not a single one   145
Was ever rash enough to play with fire.
Now they've come here. Why, they must take you for
Colossal fools, or else they want to take
One reckless chance and get it over with.
They can't think seriously that you alone   150
Of all the Greeks they've seen would feel for them
In their sad state, unless you'd lost your minds;
Consider what you stand to gain if you
Should let them in or let us take them out.
For our part we can offer to you all   155

The weight of power; our king's great influence
Will be behind your town in all you do.
But if their artful talk and wailing move
Your pity, that can only mean one thing.
A total war! Don't you believe that we'll   160
Give up our fight and bring no steel into play.
But why should you provoke us? Have we seized
What's yours? Are we aggressors? Or is your
Allies' security at stake? What kind
Of cause is this to die for? Your own men   165
Will surely curse your name if you insist
On scuttling everything so recklessly
For these young brats and this half-dead old man.
You may believe the long view bears you out,
But that will hardly help you now, my friend.   170
These boys would never stand against our arms,
Not even as grown men, as you may hope.
Well, anyhow that day's far off, and you'll
Be dealt with in the meantime; take my word
For that. We're asking nothing, but we want   175
To take back what is ours. I know that you
Are in the habit of declaring for
The underdog by choice. I warn you. Don't.

Chorus

It's very hard to judge or understand
A case like this until we've heard both sides.   180

Iolaus

I'll say in your land's favor, Majesty,
I'm not being driven out of *here* at least
Until I've listened and have had my say.
This man is nothing to us, and we want
No part of Argos. That's been so since they   185
Passed sentence on us; we're expatriates.
What earthly right has he to drag us all
Back to the town that drove us out, as though

They still had claims on us. We're aliens now.
Must Argive exiles leave the rest of Greece?   190
You can't intimidate Athenians
And make them drive out Heracles' own sons.
This isn't an Achaean town, you know,
Or Trachis, so your heavy handed ways
Of getting temples to evict us and   195
Your saber-rattling will not work here.
If I were wrong, and you should have your way,
This wouldn't be the free state that I know.
But I *do* know what stuff they're made of here.
They'd sooner die. Like all right-thinking men   200
They're sure that death is better than disgrace.
So much for Athens. It's a bad mistake
To overpraise, and I myself have been
Annoyed at getting more than was my due.
But, I'll explain why you're in duty bound   205
To save these boys, as ruler of this land.
Pittheus was Pelops' son and in his turn
Sired Aethra, who gave birth to Theseus,
Your father. Now, to come back to these boys,
Their father springs from Zeus and Alcmene,   210
And she was Pelops' daughter, which would make
Near cousins of your father and of theirs.
So much for ties of blood, and now I'll tell
What else obliges you to stand up for them.
I carried Heracles' own shield upon   215
The bloody expedition to bring back
For Theseus the Amazon queen's belt.
And Heracles, as every Greek knows, saved
Your father from the moated depths of hell.
And in return, what they now ask of you   220
Is not to be betrayed, not to be torn
By force from altars and from your frontiers.
It would be a disgrace for you, for all
Of Athens to let refugees—and those

Your cousins, too—be dragged off. Oh, my God!   225
Just look at them! On my knees I beg of you!
For pity's sake! Oh please don't let them go!
The sons of Heracles are in your hands.
Then prove yourself their cousin and their friend,
Their father, brother, ruler, all in one,   230
Rather than throw them to their enemies.

Chorus

This story touches all our hearts. We've seen
Now for the first time what it is to be
Well-born, yet in distress. Nobility
Can suffer, and through no fault of its own.   235

Demophon

Three factors have decided me against
Expelling, Iolaus, friends and guests.
For, first and foremost, you took refuge at
God's altar, with these children at your side.
Then family ties, and for our father's sake,   240
A debt of honor to be kind to them.
Last, but not least, concern for my prestige.
If I let strangers break the temple bounds,
Then everyone will say we gave these up
To Argos out of fear and that we're not   245
Our own real masters here. I'd sooner die.
Don't be afraid. I wish you could have come
In better days, but nobody would dare
To touch you or the children while you're here.

                                        (*To Herald.*)   250

Go back home, and there say to your king
He'll have a hearing if he likes, but you
Won't take these refugees away with you.

Copreus

Not even if my claim is right and wins?

Demophon

What? Right to drag off refugees by force?

Copreus

If I get a bad name, it won't hurt you.   255

Demophon

But I will too, if I let you drag them home.

Copreus

Just banish them, I'll do the rest myself.

Demophon

You fool! To think you can outwit the god!

Copreus

This is a nest for outlaws, I can see.

Demophon

The temple gives protection to all men.   260

Copreus

My countrymen may not agree with you.

Demophon

But I'm the master when in my own house.

Copreus

If you behave yourself and don't harm us.

Demophon

I'll chance that rather than outrage the gods.

Copreus

I wouldn't want to see you fighting us.   265

Demophon

No more would I, but still I'll stand by these.

Copreus

I'll take what's mine back with me, just the same.

Demophon

You think so? Well, you won't get very far.

Copreus

In any case I'll try the thing and see.

(Tries to seize children again.)

Demophon

You'll lay a hand on them at your own risk!   270

(Makes threatening motion.)

Chorus

For heaven's sake, don't hit a diplomat.

Demophon

Then let the diplomat behave himself.

Chorus

Yes, go away. Don't touch him, Majesty!

Copreus

I'm going, since I'm quite outnumbered here.
But I'll return with armies at my back.   275
There's an enormous army waiting for
Me with Eurystheus at the head. He's at
The boundaries of Alcathus' own state
And stands on the alert. So when he hears
Of this disgrace, he'll strike you like a flash,   280
You and your land and every living thing.
What are our soldiers for if not to fight
And punish you, who give us ample cause?

Demophon

To hell with you! Your Argos won't make me
Give in an inch, and you won't drag these off   285
And shame us, since we take no orders here
From Argos, but we do just as we like.

(Exit Copreus.)

Chorus

Time to think about defense
Before their army strikes our soil.
Argives were always bloodthirsty, but now   290

« 127 »

What they'll soon learn will make them twice as fierce.
Since diplomats are all alike and will
Distort and magnify what they've gone through.
I know he'll tell his lord he was so
Mistreated here that, all in all,   295
He barely got his skin away.

Iolaus

There's nothing better for a boy than to
Have had a good and noble father and
To marry well. I can't approve of those
Who go below their station out of love   300
And compromise their sons through their own lust.
Since noble people stand adversity
Much better than the mob; for instance, we
Were at our last gasp, till we found these friends
And relatives. Alone of all the Greeks,   305
They've dared to stand up and defend our rights.
There, children, go and give your hand to them,
And you give your hand too. Now, go ahead!
O children, these are really friends in need.
If you should ever see your native land   310
And home again and there receive your due,
Remember them as friends who saved your lives.
With this in mind, don't ever fight with them
At all, but treat them as your best allies.
They've earned your full respect by taking on   315
A formidable enemy on our
Account. Though we'd no place to lay our heads,
They didn't drive us out or let us go
For all of that. And I for one must say
That while I live and breathe—and after, too—   320
I'll honor you like Theseus and I'll sing
Your praises everywhere and tell the world
How well you treated and protected these
Young children. You've kept up your father's name
In Greece. You're living up to the high standard   325

Set by your great family in every way.
That's most unusual. You'll find, I think,
That very few men match their fathers now.

Chorus

We've always felt it was the decent thing
To succor men who couldn't help themselves.   330
We've fought for others many times before,
And now we see a new war coming up.

Demophon

Thank you. I'm sure of your sincerity,
Old man, and that you're grateful, as you say.
And now I've got to mobilize my men   335
And station them so that the enemy
Will get a hot reception. First my scouts
Will go to see we're not caught by surprise.
The Argives waste no time in their attacks.
Meanwhile I'll sacrifice with seers, but   340
You take the children from this altar and
Go to my palace. You'll be in good hands
While this keeps me away. Why, go ahead.

Iolaus

No, I'll stay at the altar. We'll sit down
And wait and pray until you've won the fight.   345
And when your triumph is complete, we'll go
Home with you. I think that the gods
On our side are more than a match for theirs.
Hera may be their patron but we have
Athena; and what counts in the long run   350
Is having stronger gods upon your side.
Pallas will never let the others win.

                                              (*Exit Demophon.*)

Chorus

STROPHE

Then brag away until you're hoarse.
But know that Argive bluster can't

Affect our minds, nor can it force   355
Us to turn tail. Not for such rant
As this of yours to bring our great
And lovely city down so low
And leave her prey to such a fate.
To think you and your king are so   360
Crack-brained as that!

ANTISTROPHE

To kidnap refugees, and those
The wards of both our gods and men,
Is bad enough, for one who knows
Our state's as good as yours; and then   365
To have a stranger treat our king
Like dirt, without a single claim
To right and justice is a thing
That only fools and men past shame
Can well defend.   370

EPODE

We're peaceful men, but in advance
We warn a king who's gone berserk
To keep away. He'll have no chance
To carry out his dirty work.
Though butchery's his special field,   375
We'll hold our own if it should come
To handling a spear or shield.
He'd better keep his creatures from
Attacking Athens, hold his hand,
And not pollute our lovely land.   380

                                              (Re-enter Demophon.)

Iolaus

My son, why are you looking so depressed?
Bad news about the Argive movements? Don't
Keep us all guessing. Is all quiet or
Are they advancing? What their herald said
Is worth attention, as their king will come   385

Here as the pet of chance and of the gods,
And cordially detests this city, to boot.
Still, in the end, Zeus sees to it that no
One can afford such high and mighty airs.

Demophon

The Argives and their king are on the way.
I've reconnoitered, since a man who sets   390
Up for a decent general has got
To see these things himself, not second-hand.
They haven't reached the plain; their leader keeps
Them on the rocky cliff. He's looking for
A way to bring his army to the heart   395
Of Attica, and camp there, I should think,
Without unnecessary risk. And our
Own preparations are complete; the town
Is on a battle footing. We're about
To offer all the things up to the gods   400
Required to save us and to win the fight.
While priests are sacrificing everywhere,
I've had all oracles, all old and well-known
Or confidential forecasts analyzed
To find out what to do. In most respects   405
They varied a great deal, but in one thing
They tally every one: we have to give
Up to Demeter's child as victim a
Young lady of respectable descent.
Now you'll admit, I've done my best for you.   410
But I can hardly kill my child, or force
Another citizen to such a point.
Only a lunatic would let his child
Be killed that way, and angry groups in all
The streets are thrashing out the question now.   415
Some say we're bound to fight for refugees;
While others claim I've acted like a fool.
So if I did this for you, I would have

A full-scale civil war upon my hands.
However, maybe you can find a way   420
To save yourselves and us as well without
My losing face upon this issue. As
I'm not a tyrant over savages,
Good government must be both give and take.

Chorus

We're anxious to defend you, but the gods   425
Now seem determined not to let us fight.

Iolaus

O children, we're like sailors who've set through
A hurricane and almost reached the shore,
Only to have the wind veer round and blow
Us back to sea. And we ourselves are forced   430
Out of the harbor in that same way, although
We'd thought that we were safe inside the port.
O God! How terrible to have a hope
That charms and cheats you. Still, I know that you
Are not to blame. I can't expect you to   435
Kill off your subjects' children. This whole state
Has done its best. Although the gods see fit
To treat us this way, still I won't forget.
I don't know what to do, boys, since we've no
More refuges to try, and no more gods   440
To pray to, no more countries in the world
To emigrate to. We're as good as gone.
The game is up. I don't care for myself,
Although I hate to let the Argives have
The joy of killing me; it's you that drive   445
Me frantic, and your poor old grandmother,
Brought down so low at such a time of life!
But all I've gone through doesn't count at all;
We're absolutely destined from the start
To fall and be cut down like animals.   450
Yet maybe you can think of something. I

Still think there may be some way out; why don't
You give me up instead of these young boys
And save their lives without risk to yourself?
That's it! I've got no cause to hang onto   455
My life, and their king would be very pleased
To catch and torture Heracles' good friend.
The man's quite low enough. A man with brains
Had better fight with someone of his class,
And so get decent treatment when he's down.   460

Chorus

Oh please don't put the blame on us. To hear
Ourselves accused of giving you away
Sounds ugly, even though it's not deserved.

Demophon

Said like a gentleman, but it won't do.
      (*To Iolaus. Macaria enters while he speaks.*)
The king's not marching here for you; an old   465
Man's not worth bothering about. It's these
He wants to put out of the way, since, as
He's very well aware, young nobles with
A family score to settle can, when they
Grow up, make matters awkward for him then.   470
If you've another plan, let's hear it, since,
I don't mind telling you, these oracles
Have got me worried and at my wit's end.

Macaria

Strangers, before all else, I hope you won't
Think it was brazen of me to come out.   475
I know a woman should be quiet and
Discreet, and that her place is in the home.
Yet I came out because I heard your cries. (*Speaking to Iolaus.*)
Although I'm not the family head, I have
A right to be concerned about the fate   480
Of my own brothers, and I'd like to know,

For my sake too, what new thing has turned up
To plague you—as if this were not enough.

Iolaus

I've always thought your family contains
No cooler head than yours, Macaria.   485
The fact is, just when things were going well,
We suddenly fell downward with a crash,
Back where we were. The king's priests say he has
To sacrifice—not just a bull or calf—
A real live girl, of noble stock, to please   490
Persephone, if any of us here
Values his life. And that's our quandary.
The king won't kill a stranger's child, much less
His own, and hinted pretty plainly that
If we see no way out, we'll have to find   495
Another refuge. As for him, he's bound
To think of his own country's safety first.

Macaria

And on that issue, then, we stand or fall?

Iolaus

All other matters being equal, yes.

Macaria

Then all your Argive fears are over, since   500
This volunteer is quite prepared to die,
And let herself be led off to the slaughter.
What could we say if Athens were to court
This frightful danger just for us, and we
Left all the brunt to them, and wouldn't help   505
Ourselves because we couldn't bear the thought
Of death. To keep on sniveling like this
At altars while we show to all the world
Our cowardice would admirably fit
Our father's name, or is it like the brave   510
To make fools of themselves? I'd sooner see

This city taken—God forbid—and let
Myself be caught and have worst come to worst
To Heracles' own child, and die that way.
If I give in and leave here, then how shall   515
I look when people ask why trembling slaves
Like us have come to ask protection there.
They'll turn us out and say they're not disposed
To lift a finger for such spineless things.
Why, even if I did survive the deaths   520
Of my own brothers, I'd have no hope left
(Though people have been known to sell their friends
Upon that chance). But who would marry me,
Or want this friendless girl as mother of
His sons? To end things now is much to be   525
Preferred to *that* shame, even though a girl
Not so well-known might well make the other choice.
Come, lead me to the place where I'm to die.
Then wreathe me and begin whenever you like;
And go and win the fight. I hereby put   530
Myself on record that of my free will
I volunteer to die for these and for
Myself. The brave have found no finer prize
Than leaving life the way it should be done.

Chorus

A girl who gives her own life to save these   535
And says such things leaves nothing unsaid.
No words could be compared to hers; no acts
Of flesh and blood rank higher than her own.

Iolaus

There speaks the hero's daughter, Heracles'
Own child. At any rate, there's no way to   540
Mistake *your* family tree. But, though I'm proud
Of what you've said, your plight goes to my heart.
Yet there's a better way. You ought to call
Your sisters and draw lots to choose the one

Who'll die to save us all. Why, otherwise,   545
It isn't fair for you to die this way.

Macaria

I *won't* be butchered as a gambling debt.
No, it won't do; there's nothing fine in that.
But if you'll take me and consent to use
Me of yourselves, I offer up my life   550
For them of my own accord, but won't be forced.

Iolaus

Wonder of wonders!
That answer was more splendid than the fine
One that you made before, if anything;
And you outdo yourself in pluck and sense.   555
I can't tell you to die or not to die,
Although your death will save your brothers' lives.

Macaria

Well put. Don't worry, no guilt can attach
To you, since I myself elect to die.
Come on; I'd like to have you hold me when   560
I die, and cover me up afterward,
Since now it's time to go to meet the knife,
If I'm my father's daughter, as I claim.

Iolaus

Oh, no, I couldn't bear to watch you die.

Macaria

Then ask the king to let me end my days   565
In women's hands, and not the hands of men.

Demophon

Poor girl! Of course, I never could forgive
Myself if I forgot the honors due
You, and God knows I've cause enough not to:
Your grit, your honest heart, such courage as   570
I've never known a woman show before.

Well, go ahead and speak to the old man
And children here, if you've a last request.

Macaria

This is goodbye. Please bring my brothers up
To be as wise as you, no more, no less,   575
In all, and I'll be satisfied. I count
On you to do your loyal best to save
Them, since we're your brood in a way, and raised
By your hands, and I'm giving up my prime
And chance for marriage just to die for them.   580
And now I wish to all my brothers here
The best of everything, and may you win
The things for which I'm staking my own life.
Be sure to pay respect to this old man
And your old grandmother inside as well,   585
And these good people. If the gods will let
You find relief and see your home again,
Remember to give the girl that saved your lives
The kind of funeral that she deserves,
Since she played fair with you and gave hers up.   590
These values will sustain me afterward
As spinster, childless. . . . Afterward: is there
An afterward? I hope not. If there's *then*
No end to all our troubles, where do we
Go on from there—since death itself, they say,   595
Supplies the cure for everything that ails?

Iolaus

As bravest of your sex, be sure that we
Would never think of failing to pay you
The highest honors, here and when you're gone.
And so Godspeed, saving the pardon of   600
The goddess in whose hands your life is placed.

(Exit Macaria.)

This shock's too much for me, and everything

(Totters.)

Is going black. Quick, children, prop me up!
Let me sit down and cover me with these.
To flout the oracle would be the end of all   605
Of us; though this alternative is sad,
Still, it's the lesser evil of the two.

Chorus

STROPHE

In all our ups and downs a wise
Man knows the gods have final say,
Nor can one house monopolize   610
Destiny, but from day to day
Luck pirouettes, and people who
Had conquered stoop, while drudges make
Their fortunes overnight. But you
Cannot get out of it or break   615
Through by chicanery. You'll find
To try's a waste, time out of mind.

ANTISTROPHE

Don't take God's orders lying down
Or fret because Macaria's won   620
A high and durable renown
For kin and country. She's undone,
For doing what will send her through
The ages. A stout heart commands
Its way through pain. In that she's true   625
To everything her father stands
For and her birthright, true as steel.
The brave are gone; the quick must feel.

                                      (Enter Attendant.)

Attendant

Come, children, can you tell where Iolaus   630
And your own grandmother have gone from here?

Iolaus

Why here I am, as far as that's concerned.

Attendant

Reclining, with your head bowed down! What for?

Iolaus

The troubles of those near to me strike home.

Attendant

Well, now you can get up. Look at me, man.   635

Iolaus

I'm old and these old bones have got no strength.

Attendant

But I have news for you, and what news too!

Iolaus

Who are you? Where have I seen you before?

Attendant

I'm Hyllus' servant. Don't you know me yet?

Iolaus

You're a real friend! You're here to save us all?   640

Attendant

Yes, everything is going to be all right.

Iolaus

Alcmene, come on out. It's you I want
To hear the wonderful news this man's brought.
You've worried yourself sick for so long now
About your grandsons' trip. They're back at last.   645
                              (Enter Alcmene.)

Alcmene

What's wrong? What's causing all this noise that fills
The house? Another Argive to assault
You? Stranger, I warn you. I'm weak, God knows
But I'll fight kidnappers till my last breath,
Or Heracles was not his mother's son.   650
If you so much as lay a hand upon

These children, then you'll have the glory of
Attacking two defenseless oldsters first.

Iolaus

Cheer up. There's nothing of the sort. This man
Is not an Argive come to threaten us.   655

Alcmene

Then why cry out and give the sign of fright?

Iolaus

I only cried out to bring you out here.

Alcmene

That's quite another thing. Who is this man?

Iolaus

He's come to tell you that your grandson's here.

Alcmene

Your glad news makes you welcome, as he is.   660
But if he *has* arrived, where is he now?
What kept him from accompanying you
And gladdening his old grandmother's heart?

Attendant

He's halted, and is drawing up his troops.

Alcmene

Well that, of course, is no concern of mine.   665

Iolaus

It is, though I'm the one to ask details.

Attendant

Well, just what is it that you want to know?

Iolaus

How many men did Hyllus bring with him?

Attendant

Plenty. I couldn't tell you more than that.

Iolaus

And Athens' leaders have been notified?   670

Attendant

Yes, and he's stationed to the left of them.

Iolaus

Why they must be about to start the fight?

Attendant

Yes, victims have been brought forth to be killed.

Iolaus

How far from your lines are the enemy?

Attendant

I saw the Argive king plain as could be.   675

Iolaus

Yes? What's he up to? Drawing up his men?

Attendant

Yes, I should think so, though I heard no news.
I'm off to my own chiefs; when action starts
I don't intend to leave them in the lurch.

Iolaus

Well, wait for me! That's just the thing! I want   680
To go and join my friends and help them out.

Attendant

Come now, don't talk such rot. It's not like you.

Iolaus

Not like me, is it, to fight for my friends?

Attendant

You'd do no good, unless your looks could kill.

Iolaus

What? I could smash a shield in just like that!   685

Attendant

You might, if you could keep from falling first.

Iolaus

There's not a one that will stand up to me.

Attendant

There, easy now; you're not the man you were.

Iolaus

I'll take on just as many as I did.

Attendant

Your help won't turn the tide in any case.   690

Iolaus

Don't keep me from a thing I'm set to do.

Attendant

To do? You mean to want it done, don't you?

Iolaus

Say what you please, but still I go along.

Attendant

But you're unarmed. How can you face a fight?

Iolaus

I'll use the captured arms which happen to   695
Be hanging in the temple here. The god
Will get them back if I survive; if not,
He'll never dun me. Go and take them down.
Quick! Bring the gear out here! A stay-at-home
Is a disgrace, that's what he is. He keeps   700
Out of harm's way and shakes, while others fight.

                            (*Exit Attendant.*)

Chorus

The years have left your spirit just
As fiery, in your faded body.
But why must you try so hard to hurt yourself?
It does *our* state no good, if you can't bring   705
Yourself to act your age and not go off

On useless tangents. No one
Can bring you back your prime again.

Alcmene

What lunacy is this? Do you propose
To leave me and the children here alone?   710

Iolaus

War is a man's job. Your work's minding these.

Alcmene

What's to become of me if you should die?

Iolaus

The grandsons who are left will tend you then.

Alcmene

Suppose worse comes to worst—my God!—for them?

Iolaus

These others will stand by you, never fear.   715

Alcmene

Then here I put my trust, my last resort.

Iolaus

I'm sure that Zeus is also on your side.

Alcmene

Hm!
It's not for me to criticize Zeus, but
Still he knows best if he's played fair with me.   720
                              (*Re-enter Attendant.*)

Attendant

Here is a full and fitting battle outfit;
Be quick and put it on. The fight's at hand.
For above everything the God of Battles
Detests a slacker. If the gear's too heavy,
Go on without it. Once inside the ranks   725
You can encase yourself; till then I'll carry it.

Iolaus

    All right, come on; but keep my things all ready.
    Now put the spear-shaft into my left hand
    And take my right arm so, to guide my steps.

Attendant

    Ye gods! Am I to nursemaid you to war?   730

Iolaus

    No, but we'll watch our step. To fall's bad luck.

Attendant

    If only you could do what you can dream.

Iolaus

    Hurry! I can't afford to miss the fight.

Attendant

    You are the dawdler, though you think it's I.

Iolaus

    But don't you see how very fast I'm walking?   735

Attendant

    I see the speed is largely in your mind.

Iolaus

    You'll change your tune as soon as I get there.

Attendant

    What will you do? I want to see you win.

Iolaus

    You'll see me smash clean through somebody's shield.

Attendant

    If ever we arrive there, which I doubt.   740

Iolaus

    I wish, oh arm of mine, that you could help
    Me as you used to, when with Heracles
    I ravaged Sparta, in my youth and power.

Then how we'd thrash this king, Eurystheus, now,
Who hasn't got the pluck to face a fight.   745
But fortune always will confer an aura
Of worth, unworthily; and in this world
The lucky person passes for a genius.

                                              (*Exeunt.*)

Chorus

STROPHE

We call earth and the all-night span
Owned by the moon, and on the sun,
The god that radiates to man,   750
To send the word down here. With one
Voice make the whole sky ring like mad
To Zeus's own throne, and all the way
Out to Athena with the glad
News. As for us, we say: 755
For Athens, home, and for the right
Of refugees, we mean to fight
With naked steel.

ANTISTROPHE

A dreadful and appalling thing
It is, to think that such a great   760
Town like Mycenae, threatening,
Should store up spite against our state.
But we'd have thoroughly deserved
Our ample fill of shame and curses
If, with guest-rights unobserved,   765
We gave to Argos' tender mercies
Their fugitives. Our champion Zeus
Prizes us, nor will I reduce
The gods beneath ourselves.

STROPHE

Mother of our state and Queen!   770
Defender and Mistress as well!

Smash the false attackers' spleen.
Send their serried spears to hell!
Our cause is good, and I refuse
To think that we deserve to lose   775
Our native city.

ANTISTROPHE

We honor the abundant rite
Of yours, and when the month is done,
In sequent song the young and light
Of foot can dance and chant, as one.   780
While night brings to the windy hill
The pulse of dance, and girls that fill
The dark with reveling.

                              (Enter another Attendant.)

Attendant

Madam, the news I bring is short and sweet,
Short in the telling, and yet sweet to hear.   785
We've won and set up a memorial
Hung with a full display of captured arms.

Alcmene

How wonderful! This lucky day has set
You free for all time, since you bring such news.
Yet I'm not free myself of one nightmare: 790
Are all my near and dear ones still alive?

Attendant

Alive and well and heroes every one.

Alcmene

And is old Iolaus all right, too?

Attendant

Covered with glory, too, with heaven's help.

Alcmene

What? Has he something to his credit too?   795

Attendant

He's been changed back to a young man again.

Alcmene

Well, of all things! But, first of all, please tell
Us how our soldiers won this victory.

Attendant

I'll give you the whole story here and now.
When we had drawn our own troops up and stood   800
Directly opposite the enemy,
Hyllus dismounted from his chariot.
Standing in no-man's land between the two,
He called to Eurystheus, "What's the use
Of hurting Athens, king? Why not expose   805
Just one man's life, instead of harming your
Land too? I challenge you to fight it out
With me alone. If you win, you can take
The sons of Heracles, and if I do
I'll win my family seat and honor back."   810
And all the army madly cheered the thought
Of Hyllus' pluck and of their own relief.
But not the audience nor sheer concern
For his prestige as leader proved enough
To shame the king there into showing fight.   815
He didn't dare. And that's the kind of man
Who wants to capture Heracles' own sons.
Then Hyllus took his place back in the ranks.
And when the seers realized that there was
No hope of ending matters with a duel,   820
They sacrificed at once, and let the blood
Flow down the victims' throats, in augury.
The chiefs got in their chariots; the rest
Hid ribs with shield-ribs; Demophon cheered on
His troops in language worthy of his birth.   825
"Athenians, this earth that bore and raised

You all, needs you to fight for her today."
Meantime, the other king implored his men
Not to shame Argos' or Mycenae's name,
Until the trumpet call came high and clear. 830
And then both sides closed in. The sound of all
Those shields colliding came in one great crash,
And shrieks and pandemonium broke loose.
At first their spearmen proved too much for us
And drove us back; then they gave ground again, 835
And it was touch and go. We buckled down
To fighting at close quarters, hand to hand.
Men dropped all round as war-cries swept the field.
"Athens, come on." Then "Men of Argos, strike;
Don't let the enemy make fools of us." 840
And we had all that we could do, but with
Great trouble, in the end we broke their ranks.
Then Iolaus, seeing Hyllus rush
By him begged hard to be allowed to get
Up on a chariot. Once there, he took 845
The reins himself and set his course straight for
The Argive king. That much I saw myself.
I'll tell the rest as it was told to me.
Passing Pallene and Athena's hill
He saw Eurystheus' car, and so he prayed 850
To Zeus and Hebe, to get back his youth
For just a day, and take a full revenge.
Then came the most astounding thing of all!
Two stars shone on the yoke. They threw a dark
Cloud over the whole car, and people who 855
Should know say they were Hebe and your own
Great son. Then the haze lifted to disclose
A young fellow with husky biceps, and,
Like a true hero, Iolaus caught
The king's own chariot at Sciron's rocks. 860
He's brought that chief who used to be so high

And mighty back with him, a prisoner
Of war with hands tied up. The lesson of
The thing is very plain. Don't envy men
Because they seem to have a run of luck,   865
Since luck's a nine days' wonder. Wait their end.

Chorus

Give thanks to Zeus, who fought for us. At last
A day on which our worries are removed.

Alcmene

Hail Zeus! You took your time in helping me,
But I'm not less obliged to you for that.   870
And now I know my son is really with
The gods, although I had my doubts before.
Children, just think! You're safe from danger now!
Safe from the king, who's going to die like
A dog. You'll soon set eyes upon your own   875
Country and have the soil that's yours by right
Beneath your feet. At last you'll worship those
Gods of your fathers who were banned for you
While you were poor and homeless. Tell me, though,
Why didn't Iolaus kill the king?   880
What's back of it? To me there is no point
In being kind to captured enemies.

Attendant

But it was done for you, so you could see
Eurystheus in his glory, in our hands.
It was brute force that brought him in, and not   885
His own accord, since he'd no heart to see
Your face, or pay the price for what he'd done.
And now goodbye. Please don't forget what you
First said when I began, that you would set
Me free; since I should think it's best to keep   890
Faith in these things. *Noblesse oblige,* you know.

(Exit Attendant.)

Chorus

STROPHE

There's nothing like the flute's sound when
We dance and sing and eat our fill
And love in all its sweetness. Then
I feel too glad for words and thrill   895
To see the happy ending for
Those near my heart, in brief, to see
Poor devils had good luck in store
For themselves, thanks to Destiny
And Change and Time.   900

ANTISTROPHE

I hope we keep along the right
Road. Up to now we've paid the high
Gods all their due; it takes a quite
Unbalanced person to deny
It in the face of all the facts,   905
And Zeus himself has verified
It very clearly in his acts
Today, in taking down the pride
Of callous brutes.

STROPHE

Your son, Alcmene, never died.   910
He rules above, and never set
His foot in Hades, or inside
The crematory fire, but met
The wedding-god and fell in love
With Hebe, and the two were paid   915
The honors due to children of
Zeus. It was a marriage made
In heaven's gilded halls.

ANTISTROPHE

How small a world it is. They say
That Pallas helped the father in   920

The nick of time, and now today
The children's lives have also been
Saved by the goddess' own town.
The pride of that tormentor who
Ill-used them so was taken down,   925
And we'll have nothing more to do
With ruthlessness and greed.

(*Enter Attendant with Guards bringing in*
Eurystheus in chains.)

Attendant

Madame, we're bringing in, as you can see,
Eurystheus, which must surprise you and
Was the last thing that *he* expected too.   930
He hadn't bargained for this capture at
Your hands, when he set out from home with such
A force, in his insufferable conceit,
To smash this state. But fate arranged affairs
Quite otherwise and turned the tables here.   935
Hyllus and Iolaus, who were at
Work raising a memorial to Zeus,
Told me to bring this man to you and make
You happy, since there's nothing like the sight
Of an old enemy down on his luck.   940

Alcmene

You brute! So God has punished you at last.
Come, turn this way! Or haven't you the nerve
To look your enemies straight in the eye?
By God, you'll take the orders that you used
To give us, if you really are the man   945
Who piled humiliations upon my
Poor son. You filthy scum! You made him go
To hell before he died; you sent him out
To kill off hydras, lions, not to speak
Of all the other horrors—it would take   950
Too long to tell it all. But as though this

Were not enough for you; you drove me and
The children out of temples throughout Greece
Where we had taken refuge, hounding old   955
People and babes in arms until you found
A country that was free and wouldn't scare.
And now you'll get what's coming to you, though
Killing is much too good for you. To pay
For what you've done would take a thousand deaths.   960

Chorus

Wait! You can't put a man to death like that.

Attendant

What was the use of capturing him then?

Alcmene

Show me a law against his being killed!

Chorus

But the authorities won't stand for it.

Alcmene

You mean they don't like killing enemies?   965

Chorus

Not prisoners of war, at any rate.

Alcmene

And Hyllus, too, agreed with that idea?

Chorus

Do you expect him to defy our laws?

Alcmene

Why, then, we should have killed the man at once.

Chorus

That's when the wrong was done, since he's survived.   970

Alcmene

Why, what's the difference? We'll correct it now.

Chorus

No one will lay a hand upon this man.

Alcmene

No one? Suppose I do. Or don't I count?

Chorus

There'll be a strong reaction if you do.

Alcmene

No one can say that I don't love this city,   975
But just let someone try to take away
This man from me, now I've got hold of him.
Call me a reckless fool as often as
You like, and say I don't behave the way
A woman should. I'll kill him all the same.   980

Chorus

We feel for you. God knows that you have cause
Enough to hate this man so terribly.

Eurystheus

Don't think I'm going to grovel to you or
Show the white feather here and beg to save
My skin. In any case, I didn't start   985
This feud of my accord. I knew quite well
That you're my cousin and that Heracles
Was consequently my own flesh and blood.
I couldn't help myself when heaven took
A hand, and Hera saddled me with this   990
Scourge in the first place. Once I had estranged
Your son for good and knew the fight was on,
I racked my brains to make things hard for him
And sat up nights to think of ways to beat
And finish off my enemies, and end   995
The fear that never left me day and night.
I didn't underrate your son and knew
His caliber, to give the man his due

For courage, though he was no friend of mine.
But though he'd died, the others kept alive   1000
The spite. I knew the feud was handed down.
That's why I had to try so hard to get
Them killed or exiled, and to plot and plan;
Those tactics meant the only hope for me.
And in my own place, you'd have beaten off   1005
The snarling cubs left by the lion who
Had hated you. Don't try to tell me that
You'd let them stay at peace, in Argos too.
You missed your chance to kill me at the time
When I was willing, so by all Greek laws   1010
My death pollutes the one who strikes me down.
Athens has let me live and knows enough
To think of piety before revenge.
I rest my case. Remember I was not
Afraid to go, and I'll have blood for blood.   1015
I don't particularly want to die
Or mind it either, and that's how things stand.

Chorus

Take my advice, Alcmene. Let this man
Go, since that's what this city would prefer.

Alcmene

Suppose we kill him—but respect their words?   1020

Chorus

That's fine, but how would you bring that about?

Alcmene

It's simple. All you have to do is let me kill
And let friends call for the body. Far be it
For me to cheat this city of his corpse.
He'll settle his account with me first, though.   1025

Eurystheus

Go on, I won't complain. But since your state
Here wouldn't stoop to kill me, I'll tell you

Of an old oracle of Loxias which
Will help you some day more than you may think.
You'll bury me, just as it stipulates,   1030
Before Athena's own Pallenian shrine,
And as the guest of Athens' soil I'll guard
You and preserve you till the end of time.
But when these children's children march on you
In force, then I'll be their arch-enemy.   1035
That's their idea of thanks, and that's the kind
Of people that you saved. You'll ask why I
Ignored the god and came in the first place.
Because I trusted Hera more and thought
That she'd keep faith. Don't let this woman pour   1040
Libations and blood-offerings on my tomb.
But in revenge I'll spoil the homecoming
Of these, and so my end will do two things
At once; it helps you, and it will hurt these.

Alcmene

What are you waiting for, to put this man   1045
Out of the way, since as you've heard, it makes
Your city safe from us? He's pointed out
Your wisest course, since your worst enemy
Becomes your best friend, once he's underground.
Take him away, and when you've killed him, throw   1050
                                        (To Guards.)
Him to the dogs, to scotch his last hope that
He can come back and exile me again.

Chorus

That's the solution. Take away this man.
I want to make sure that our kings are cleared
Of all responsibility in this.   1055
                                        (Exeunt.)

HIPPOLYTUS

Translated and with an Introduction by

DAVID GRENE

INTRODUCTION TO *HIPPOLYTUS*

IF IT is necessary that I say anything about a woman's excellence," says Pericles in the history of Thucydides, "I could sum it up in the words: great is her renown whose name is least upon the lips of men either for good or for ill." This has sometimes been taken as the general view of women in Athenian society of the fifth century B.C. However, we have only to look at the tragic stage to realize that the audience at least was immensely interested in women and in their place in human society. Aristophanes attacks Euripides as the author in whose plays the perverse, violent, or monstrous woman has a leading place, and he cites Medea, Sthenoboea, and Phaedra in support of the justice of his charge. As far as the importance of feminine roles goes, Euripides' two predecessors are as guilty as he is. Clytemnestra, Cassandra, Queen Atossa, Electra, Tecmessa, Antigone, and Deianeira are among the most crucial and carefully worked characters in the plays of Aeschylus and Sophocles.

But it *is* probably true that the Athenian audience noticed with special interest, either with delight or with repulsion, Euripides' gallery of bad women. Medea, Sthenoboea, and Phaedra are the three singled out by Aristophanes. Both Sthenoboea and Phaedra are examples of incestuous love; in the *Hippolytus*, Euripides apparently had to revise an early version of the play in which Phaedra makes her proposal of love direct to her stepson. In the second version the nurse was invented to act as a go-between, and Phaedra's conscious responsibility for the address to Hippolytus is left in doubt. But Phaedra's passion for Hippolytus is still the center of the piece. It is not necessary to debate whether, to the fifth-century Greek, sexual relations between stepmother and stepson would be technically incestuous or not. It is enough that we can be sure that they involved an extreme violation of the trust and affection between father and son, and something worse than that, even if the evil cannot be exactly charted.

The play is framed by a Prologue and an Epilogue, each spoken by a goddess. When these goddesses are identified as Aphrodite and Artemis, it becomes all too easy to allegorize them and see the play as a conflict between Lust and Continence with Phaedra and Hippolytus as the appropriate human representatives. But if this view were correct, surely the point of issue would have to be a conflict where the moral really emerged, where, that is, it was dramatically stated with a fair chance of an outcome in either direction. Hippolytus should be tempted where an ordinary man might fall, and Phaedra yield to a passion which, if blameworthy, is comprehensible. Instead, the monstrousness of the relationship is the hinge on which everything turns. Phaedra, when rejected, must kill herself for shame. Theseus, when he learns of it, is ready to murder his son; Hippolytus, in his defense before his father, says that he is accused of a crime from which even an ordinarily unchaste man would shrink. The truth seems to be that Euripides used a story with an almost Homeric flavor, of rival goddesses and their favorites, to write of the absolute power of passion over the human animal. The more horrible the crime of which she is guilty, the more clear it is that Phaedra is being driven far out of her natural course. The perversity of Hippolytus' ostentatious purity—for so the Greeks certainly regarded it—is the cynical foil to Phaedra's guilty lust. She must fall in love with the one man who is a very monk for continence!

This is certainly the right way to see the play, but the explanation also shows some of the play's weaknesses. The author is deeply concerned with Phaedra—Aristophanes is quite right to see that she is the principal character—and much less with Hippolytus. Consequently, when Phaedra dies, only halfway through the play, Euripides is left to deal with a denouement in which he is only professionally interested, because he must properly tidy up the ends of the story. He does this somewhat mechanically and with a flavor of rhetorical commonplace in the argument between Hippolytus and his father. After the disappearance of Phaedra, he enjoyed himself, one feels, only in writing the messenger's speech, with its exciting account of the young man's death. But the figure of Phaedra and

even the nurse's intervention—that dramatist's second thought—
and the flimsy ambiguity of motive all remain with us to illustrate
what is meant by the statement that Euripides marks the beginning
of modern psychological tragedy.

The play was first performed in 428 B.C.

HIPPOLYTUS

Theseus

Hippolytus, his son by the queen of the Amazons

Phaedra, Theseus' wife, stepmother to Hippolytus

A Servant

A Messenger

The Nurse

The Chorus of Palace women, natives of Troezen

A Chorus of huntsmen, in attendance on Hippolytus

The Goddess Aphrodite

The Goddess Artemis

HIPPOLYTUS

SCENE: *Troezen, in front of the house of Theseus.*

PROLOGUE

Aphrodite

I am called the Goddess Cypris:
I am mighty among men and they honor me by many names.
All those that live and see the light of sun
from Atlas' Pillars to the tide of Pontus
are mine to rule.   5
Such as worship my power in all humility,
I exalt in honor.
But those whose pride is stiff-necked against me
I lay by the heels.
There is joy in the heart of a God also
when honored by men.

Now I will quickly tell you the truth of this story.

Hippolytus, son of Theseus by the Amazon,   10
pupil of holy Pittheus,
alone among the folk of this land of Troezen has blasphemed me
counting me vilest of the Gods in Heaven.
He will none of the bed of love nor marriage,
but honors Artemis, Zeus's daughter,   15
counting her greatest of the Gods in Heaven
he is with her continually, this Maiden Goddess, in the greenwood.
They hunt with hounds and clear the land of wild things,
mortal with immortal in companionship.
I do not grudge him such privileges: why should I?   20
But for his sins against me
I shall punish Hippolytus this day.
I have no need to toil to win my end:
much of the task has been already done.

Once he came from Pittheus' house[1] to the country of Pandion
that he might see and be initiate in the holy mysteries.   25
Phaedra saw him
and her heart was filled with the longings of love.
This was my work.
So before ever she came to Troezen
close to the rock of Pallas in view of this land,   30
she dedicated a temple to Cypris.
For her love, too, dwelt in a foreign land.
Ages to come will call this temple after him,
the temple of the Goddess established here.
When Theseus left the land of Cecrops,
flying from the guilty stain of the murder of the Pallantids,   35
condemning himself to a year's exile
he sailed with his wife to this land.
Phaedra groans in bitterness of heart
and the goads of love prick her cruelly,
and she is like to die.
But she breathes not a word of her secret and none of the servants   40
know of the sickness that afflicts her.
But her love shall not remain thus aimless and unknown.
I will reveal the matter to Theseus and all shall come out.
Father shall slay son with curses—
this son that is hateful to me.
For once the Lord Poseidon, Ruler of the Sea,
granted this favor to Theseus   45
that three of his prayers to the God should find answer.

1. "Pittheus' house": The historian Pausanias, relating the legend of Hippolytus,
says: "King Theseus, when he married Phaedra, daughter of the king of Crete, was in
a quandary what to do with Hippolytus, his son by his former mistress, Antiope the
Amazon. He did not wish that after his own death Hippolytus should rule the children
of his legitimate marriage, nor yet that Hippolytus should be ruled by them, for he
loved him. So he sent the boy to be brought up by his grandfather Pittheus, who lived
in Troezen and ruled there. Theseus hoped that when Pittheus died, Hippolytus might
inherit the kingdom, and thus peace within the family be preserved, Hippolytus gov-
erning Troezen, and Phaedra's children holding sway in Athens." "Pandion's country"
and "land of Cecrops" both signify Attica. Pandion and Cecrops were early legendary
heroes of Attica.

Renowned shall Phaedra be in her death, but none the less
die she must.
Her suffering does not weigh in the scale so much
that I should let my enemies go untouched
escaping payment of that retribution
that honor demands that I have.   50
Look, here is the son of Theseus, Hippolytus!
He has just left his hunting.
I must go away.
See the great crowd that throngs upon his heels
and shouts the praise of Artemis in hymns!   55
He does not know
that the doors of death are open for him,
that he is looking on his last sun.

SCENE I

(Enter Hippolytus, attended by friends and servants carrying
nets, hunting spears, etc.)

Hippolytus

Follow me singing
the praises of Artemis,
Heavenly One, Child of Zeus,
Artemis!
We are the wards of your care.   60

(The Chorus of huntsmen chant.)

Hail, Holy and Gracious!
Hail, Daughter of Zeus!
Hail, Maiden Daughter of Zeus and Leto!   65
Dweller in the spacious sky!
Maid of the Mighty Father!
Maid of the Golden Glistening House!
Hail!
Maiden Goddess most beautiful of all the Heavenly Host that
   lives in Olympus!   70

(Hippolytus advances to the altar of Artemis and
lays a garland on it, praying.)

My Goddess Mistress, I bring you ready woven
this garland. It was I that plucked and wove it,
plucked it for you in your inviolate Meadow.
No shepherd dares to feed his flock within it: 75
no reaper plies a busy scythe within it:
only the bees in springtime haunt the inviolate Meadow.
Its gardener is the spirit Reverence who
refreshes it with water from the river.
Not those who by instruction have profited
to learn, but in whose very soul the seed   80
of Chastity toward all things alike
nature has deeply rooted, they alone
may gather flowers there! the wicked may not.

Loved mistress, here I offer you this coronal;
it is a true worshipper's hand that gives it you
to crown the golden glory of your hair.
With no man else I share this privilege
that I am with you and to your words   85
can answer words. True, I may only hear:
I may not see God face to face.
So may I turn the post set at life's end
even as I began the race.

Servant

King—for I will not call you "Master," that belongs
to the Gods only—will you take good advice?

Hippolytus

Certainly I will take good advice. I am not a fool.   90

Servant

In men's communities one rule holds good,
do you know it, King?

Hippolytus

           Not I. What is this rule?

Servant

Men hate the haughty of heart who will not be
the friend of every man.

Hippolytus

And rightly too:
For haughty heart breeds arrogant demeanor.

Servant

And affability wins favor, then?   95

Hippolytus

Abundant favor. Aye, and profit, too,
at little cost of trouble.

Servant

Do you think
that it's the same among the Gods in Heaven?

Hippolytus

If we in our world and the Gods in theirs
know the same usages—Yes.

Servant

Then, King, how comes it
that for a holy Goddess you have not even
a word of salutation?

Hippolytus

Which Goddess?
Be careful, or you will find that tongue of yours   100
may make a serious mistake.

Servant

This Goddess here
who stands before your gates, the Goddess Cypris.

Hippolytus

I worship her—but from a long way off,
for I am chaste.

Servant

Yet she's a holy Goddess,
and fair is her renown throughout the world.

Hippolytus

Men make their choice: one man honors one God,
and one another.

Servant
Well, good fortune guard you!

if you have the mind you should have.   105

Hippolytus

God of nocturnal prowess is not my God.

Servant

The honors of the Gods you must not scant, my son.

Hippolytus

Go, men, into the house and look to supper.
A plentiful table is an excellent thing
after the hunt. And you (*singling out two*) rub down my horses.   110
When I have eaten I shall exercise them.
For your Cypris here—a long goodbye to her!

> (*The old man is left standing alone on the stage.*
> *He prays before the statue of Aphrodite.*)

O Cypris Mistress, we must not imitate
the young men when they have such thoughts as these.
As fits a slave to speak, here at your image   115
I bow and worship. You should grant forgiveness
when one that has a young tempestuous heart
speaks foolish words. Seem not to hear them.
You should be wiser than mortals, being Gods.   120

> (*Enter Chorus of women, servants in Phaedra's house.*)

Chorus

STROPHE

There is a rock streaming with water,
whose source, men say, is Ocean,
and it pours from the heart of its stone a spring
where pitchers may dip and be filled.
My friend was there and in the river water   125
she dipped and washed the royal purple robes,
and spread them on the rock's warm back
where the sunbeams played.

It was from her I heard at first
of the news of my mistress' sorrow.   130

ANTISTROPHE

She lies on her bed within the house,
within the house and fever wracks her
and she hides her golden head in fine-spun robes.
This is the third day   135
she has eaten no bread
and her body is pure and fasting.
For she would willingly bring her life to anchor
at the end of its voyage
the gloomy harbor of death.   140

STROPHE

Is it Pan's frenzy that possesses you
or is Hecate's madness upon you, maid?
Can it be the holy Corybantes,
or the mighty Mother who rules the mountains?
Are you wasted in suffering thus,   145
for a sin against Dictynna, Queen of hunters?
Are you perhaps unhallowed, having offered
no sacrifice to her from taken victims?
For she goes through the waters of the Lake[2]
can travel on dry land beyond the sea,
the eddying salt sea.   150

ANTISTROPHE

Can it be that some other woman's love,
a secret love that hides itself from you,
has beguiled your husband
the son of Erechtheus
our sovran lord, that prince of noble birth?
Or has some sailor from the shores of Crete   155

2. Limnae, the Lake, a district in Laconia, was the center of the worship of Artemis
in the Peloponnese. From it she is sometimes called Limnaios, or Lady of the Lake.

put in at this harbor hospitable to sailors,
bearing a message for our queen,
and so because he told her some calamity
her spirit is bound in chains of grief
and she lies on her bed in sorrow?   160

EPODE

Unhappy is the compound of woman's nature;
the torturing misery of helplessness,
the helplessness of childbirth and its madness
are linked to it for ever.
My body, too, has felt this thrill of pain,   165
and I called on Artemis, Queen of the Bow;
she has my reverence always
as she goes in the company of the Gods.

But here is the old woman, the queen's nurse   170
here at the door. She is bringing her mistress out.
There is a gathering cloud upon her face.
What is the matter? my soul is eager to know.
What can have made the queen so pale?
What can have wasted her body so?   175

SCENE II

(*Enter the Nurse, supporting Phaedra.*)

Nurse

A weary thing is sickness and its pains!
What must I do now?
Here is light and air, the brightness of the sky.
I have brought out the couch on which you tossed
in fever—here clear of the house.   180
Your every word has been to bring you out,
but when you're here, you hurry in again.
You find no constant pleasure anywhere
for when your joy is upon you, suddenly
you're foiled and cheated.
There's no content for you in what you have
for you're forever finding something dearer,

some other thing—because you have it not.   185
It's better to be sick than nurse the sick.
Sickness is single trouble for the sufferer:
but nursing means vexation of the mind,
and hard work for the hands besides.
The life of man entire is misery:
he finds no resting place, no haven from calamity.   190
But something other dearer still than life
the darkness hides and mist encompasses;
we are proved luckless lovers of this thing
that glitters in the underworld: no man
can tell us of the stuff of it, expounding   195
what is, and what is not: we know nothing of it.
Idly we drift, on idle stories carried.

Phaedra (to the servants)

Lift me up! Lift my head up! All the muscles
are slack and useless. Here, you, take my hands.
They're beautiful, my hands and arms!   200
Take away this hat! It is too heavy to wear.
Take it away! Let my hair fall free on my shoulders.

Nurse

Quiet, child, quiet! Do not so restlessly
keep tossing to and fro! It's easier
to bear an illness if you have some patience   205
and the spirit of good breeding.
We all must suffer sometimes: we are mortal.

Phaedra

O,
if I could only draw from the dewy spring
a draught of fresh spring water!
If I could only lie beneath the poplars,   210
in the tufted meadow and find my rest there!

Nurse

Child, why do you rave so? There are others here.

Cease tossing out these wild demented words
whose driver is madness.

Phaedra

Bring me to the mountains! I *will* go to the mountains!   215
Among the pine trees where the huntsmen's pack
trails spotted stags and hangs upon their heels.
God, how I long to set the hounds on, shouting!
And poise the Thessalian javelin drawing it back—
here where my fair hair hangs above the ear—   220
I would hold in my hand a spear with a steel point.

Nurse

What ails you, child? What is this love of hunting,
and you a lady! Draught of fresh spring water!
Here, beside the tower there is a sloping ridge   225
with springs enough to satisfy your thirst.

Phaedra

Artemis, mistress of the Salty Lake,
mistress of the ring echoing to the racers' hoofs,
if only I could gallop your level stretches,   230
and break Venetian colts!

Nurse

This is sheer madness,
that prompts such whirling, frenzied, senseless words.
Here at one moment you're afire with longing
to hunt wild beasts and you'd go to the hills,
and then again all your desire is horses,
horses on the sands beyond the reach of the breakers.   235
Indeed, it would need to be a mighty prophet
to tell which of the Gods mischievously
jerks you from your true course and thwarts your wits!

Phaedra

O, I am miserable! What is this I've done?
Where have I strayed from the highway of good sense?   240
I was mad. It was the madness sent from some God

that caused my fall.
I am unhappy, so unhappy! Nurse,
cover my face again. I am ashamed   245
of what I said. Cover me up. The tears
are flowing, and my face is turned to shame.
Rightness of judgment is bitterness to the heart.
Madness is terrible. It is better then
that I should die and know no more of anything.

Nurse

There, now, you are covered up. But my own body   250
when will death cover that? I have learned much
from my long life. The mixing bowl of friendship,
the love of one for the other, must be tempered.
Love must not touch the marrow of the soul.   255
Our affections must be breakable chains that we
can cast them off or tighten them.
That one soul so for two should be in travail
as I for her, that is a heavy burden.   260
The ways of life that are most fanatical
trip us up more, they say, than bring us joy.
They're enemies to health. So I praise less
the extreme than temperance in everything.   265
The wise will bear me out.

Chorus Leader

Old woman, you are Phaedra's faithful nurse.
We can see that she is in trouble but the cause
that ails her is black mystery to us.
We would like to hear you tell us what is the matter.   270

Nurse

I have asked and know no more. She will not tell me.

Chorus Leader

Not even what began it?

Nurse

          And my answer
is still the same: of all this she will not speak.

Chorus Leader

But see how ill she is, and how her body
is wracked and wasted!

Nurse

                    Yes, she has eaten nothing
for two days now.   275

Chorus Leader

               Is this the scourge of madness?
Or can it be . . . that death is what she seeks?

Nurse

Aye, death. She is starving herself to death.

Chorus Leader

I wonder that her husband suffers this.

Nurse

She hides her troubles, swears that she isn't sick.

Chorus Leader

But does he not look into her face and see   280
a witness that disproves her?

Nurse

                   No, he is gone.
He is away from home, in foreign lands.

Chorus Leader

Why, you must force her then to find the cause
of this mind-wandering sickness!

Nurse

                  Every means
I have tried and still have won no foot of ground.
But I'll not give up trying, even now.   285
You are here and can in person bear me witness
that I am loyal to my masters always,
even in misfortune's hour.
Dear child, let us both forget our former words.
Be kinder, you: unknit that ugly frown.

For my part I will leave this track of thought: 290
I cannot understand you there. I'll take
another and a better argument.

If you are sick and it is some secret sickness,
here are women standing at your side to help.
But if your troubles may be told to men,   295
speak, that a doctor may pronounce upon it.
So, not a word! Oh, why will you not speak?
There is no remedy in silence, child.
Either I am wrong and then you should correct me:
or right, and you should yield to what I say.
Say something! Look at me!   300

Women, I have tried and tried and all for nothing.
We are as far as ever from our goal.
It was the same before. She was not melted
by anything I said. She would not obey me.

But this you shall know, though to my reasoning
you are more dumbly obstinate than the sea:
If you die, you will be a traitor to your children.   305
They will never know their share in a father's palace.
No, by the Amazon Queen, the mighty rider
who bore a master for your children, one
bastard in birth but true-born son in mind,
you know him well—Hippolytus. . . .
                    So that has touched you?   310

Phaedra

You have killed me, nurse. For God's sake, I entreat you,
never again speak that man's name to me.

Nurse

You see? You have come to your senses, yet despite that,
you will not make your children happy nor
save your own life besides.

Phaedra

I love my children.
It is another storm of fate that batters me.   315

Nurse

There is no stain of blood upon your hands?

Phaedra

My hands are clean: the stain is in my heart.

Nurse

The hurt comes from outside? Some enemy?

Phaedra

One I love destroys me. Neither of us wills it.

Nurse

Has Theseus sinned a sin against you then?   320

Phaedra

God keep me equally guiltless in his sight!

Nurse

What is this terror urging you to death?

Phaedra

Leave me to my sins. My sins are not against you.

Nurse

Not of my will, but yours, you cast me off.

Phaedra

Would you force confession, my hand-clasping suppliant?   325

Nurse

Your knees too—and my hands will never free you.

Phaedra

Sorrow, nurse, sorrow, you will find my secret.

Nurse

Can I know greater sorrow than losing you?

Phaedra

You will kill me. My honor lies in silence.

Nurse

And then you will hide this honor, though I beseech you?   330

Phaedra

Yes, for I seek to win good out of shame.

Nurse

Where honor is, speech will make you more honorable.

Phaedra

O God, let go my hand and go away!

Nurse

No, for you have not given me what you should.

Phaedra

I yield. Your suppliant hand compels my reverence.   335

Nurse

I will say no more. Yours is the word from now.

Phaedra

Unhappy mother, what a love was yours!

Nurse

It is her love for the bull you mean, dear child?

Phaedra

Unhappy sister, bride of Dionysus!

Nurse

Why these ill-boding words about your kin?   340

Phaedra

And I the unlucky third, see how I end!

Nurse

Your words are wounds. Where will your tale conclude?

Phaedra

Mine is an inherited curse. It is not new.

Nurse

I have not yet heard what I most want to know.

Phaedra

If you could say for me what I must say for myself.   345

Nurse

I am no prophet to know your hidden secrets.

Phaedra

What is this thing, this love, of which they speak?

Nurse

Sweetest and bitterest, both in one, at once.

Phaedra

One of the two, the bitterness, I've known.

Nurse

Are you in love, my child? And who is he?   350

Phaedra

There is a man, . . . his mother was an Amazon. . . .

Nurse

You mean Hippolytus?

Phaedra
                            You
have spoken it, not I.

Nurse

What do you mean? This is my death.
Women, this is past bearing. I'll not bear
life after this. A curse upon the daylight!
A curse upon this shining sun above us!   355
I'll throw myself from a cliff, throw myself headlong!
I'll be rid of life somehow, I'll die somehow!
Farewell to all of you! This is the end for me.

The chaste, they love not vice of their own will,
but yet they love it. Cypris, you are no God.

You are something stronger than God if that can be.   360
You have ruined her and me and all this house.

(*The Nurse goes off. The Chorus forms into two half-choruses.*)

First Half-chorus

Did you hear, did you hear
the queen crying aloud,
telling of a calamity
which no ear should hear?

Second Half-chorus

I would rather die
than think such thoughts as hers.   365

First Half-chorus

I am sorry for her trouble.

Second Half-chorus

Alas for troubles, man-besetting.

First Half-chorus (turning to Phaedra)

You are dead, you yourself
have dragged your ruin to the light.
What can happen now in the long
dragging stretch of the rest of your days?
Some new thing will befall the house.   370

Chorus (united)

We know now, we know now
how your love will end,
poor unhappy Cretan girl!

Phaedra

Hear me, you women of Troezen who live
in this extremity of land this anteroom to Argos.
Many a time in night's long empty spaces   375
I have pondered on the causes of a life's shipwreck.
I think that our lives are worse than the mind's quality
would warrant. There are many who know virtue.

We know the good, we apprehend it clearly.   380
But we can't bring it to achievement. Some
are betrayed by their own laziness, and others
value some other pleasure above virtue.
There are many pleasures in a woman's life—
long gossiping talks and leisure, that sweet curse.
Then there is shame that thwarts us. Shame is of two kinds.   385
The one is harmless, but the other a plague.
For clarity's sake, we should not talk of "shame,"
a single word for two quite different things.
These then are my thoughts. Nothing now can seduce me   390
to the opposite opinion. I will tell you
in my own case the track which my mind followed.
At first when love had struck me, I reflected
how best to bear it. Silence was my first plan.
Silence and concealment. For the tongue
is not to be trusted: it can criticize   395
another's faults, but on its own possessor
it brings a thousand troubles.
Then I believed that I could conquer love,
conquer it with discretion and good sense.
And when that too failed me, I resolved to die.   400
And death is the best plan of them all. Let none of you
dispute that.
It would always be my choice
to have my virtues known and honored. So
when I do wrong I could not endure to see
a circle of condemning witnesses.
I know what I have done: I know the scandal: 405
and all too well I know that I am a woman,
object of hate to all. Destruction light
upon the wife who herself plays the tempter
and strains her loyalty to her husband's bed
by dalliance with strangers. In the wives   410
of noble houses first this taint begins:
when wickedness approves itself to those

of noble birth, it will surely be approved
by their inferiors. Truly, too, I hate
lip-worshippers of chastity who own
a lecherous daring when they have privacy.
O Cypris, Sea-Born Goddess, how can they   415
look frankly in the faces of their husbands
and never shiver with fear lest their accomplice,
the darkness, and the rafters of the house
take voice and cry aloud?
This then, my friends, is my destruction:
I cannot bear that I should be discovered   420
a traitor to my husband and my children.
God grant them rich and glorious life in Athens—
famous Athens—freedom in word and deed,
and from their mother an honorable name.
It makes the stoutest-hearted man a slave
if in his soul he knows his parents' shame.   425

The proverb runs: "There is one thing alone
that stands the brunt of life throughout its course,
a quiet conscience," . . . a just and quiet conscience
whoever can attain it.
Time holds a mirror, as for a young girl,
and sometimes as occasion falls, he shows us
the ugly rogues of the world. I would not wish
that I should be seen among them.   430

Chorus Leader

How virtue is held lovely everywhere,
and harvests a good name among mankind!

(*The Nurse returns.*)

Nurse

Mistress, the trouble you have lately told me,
coming on me so suddenly, frightened me;
but now I realize that I was foolish.   435
In this world second thoughts, it seems, are best.
Your case is not so extraordinary,

beyond thought or reason. The Goddess in her anger
has smitten you, and you are in love. What wonder
is this? There are many thousands suffer with you.
So, you will die for love! And all the others,   440
who love, and who will love, must they die, too?
How will that profit them? The tide of love,
at its full surge, is not withstandable.
Upon the yielding spirit she comes gently,
but to the proud and the fanatic heart   445
she is a torturer with the brand of shame.
She wings her way through the air; she is in the sea,
in its foaming billows; from her everything,
that is, is born. For she engenders us
and sows the seed of desire whereof we're born,   450
all we her children, living on the earth.
He who has read the writings of the ancients
and has lived much in books, he knows
that Zeus once loved the lovely Semele;
he knows that Dawn, the bright light of the world,
once ravished Cephalus hence to the God's company   455
for love's sake. Yet all these dwell in heaven.
They are content, I am sure, to be subdued
by the stroke of love.
But you, you won't submit! Why, you should certainly
have had your father beget you on fixed terms   460
or with other Gods for masters, if you don't like
the laws that rule this world. Tell me, how many
of the wise ones of the earth do you suppose
see with averted eyes their wives turned faithless;
how many erring sons have fathers helped
with secret loves? It is the wise man's part   465
to leave in darkness everything that is ugly.

We should not in the conduct of our lives
be too exacting. Look, see this roof here—
these overarching beams that span your house—

could builders with all their skill lay them dead straight?
You've fallen into the great sea of love
and with your puny swimming would escape!   470
If in the sum you have more good luck than ill,
count yourself fortunate—for you are mortal.

Come, dear, give up your discontented mood.
Give up your railing. It's only insolent pride
to wish to be superior to the Gods.   475
Endure your love. The Gods have willed it so.
You are sick. Then try to find some subtle means
to turn your sickness into health again.
There are magic love charms, spells of enchantment;
we'll find some remedy for your love-sickness.
Men would take long to hunt devices out,   480
if we the women did not find them first.

Chorus Leader

Phaedra, indeed she speaks more usefully
for today's troubles. But it is you I praise.
And yet my praise brings with it more discomfort
than her words: it is bitterer to the ear.   485

Phaedra

This is the deadly thing which devastates
well-ordered cities and the homes of men—
that's it, this art of oversubtle words.
It's not the words ringing delight in the ear
that one should speak, but those that have the power
to save their hearer's honorable name.

Nurse

This is high moralizing! What you want   490
is not fine words, but the man! Come, let's be done.
And tell your story frankly and directly.
For if there were no danger to your life,
as now there is—or if you could be prudent,
I never would have led you on so far,   495

merely to please your fancy or your lust.
But now a great prize hangs on our endeavors,
and that's the saving of a life—yours, Phaedra,
there's none can blame us for our actions now.

Phaedra

What you say is wicked, wicked! Hold your tongue!
I will not hear such shameful words again.

Nurse

O, they are shameful! But they are better than   500
your noble-sounding moral sentiments.
"The deed" is better if it saves your life:
than your "good name" in which you die exulting.

Phaedra

For God's sake, do not press me any further!
What you say is true, but terrible!
My very soul is subdued by my love
and if you plead the cause of wrong so well   505
I shall fall into the abyss
from which I now am flying.

Nurse

If that is what you think, you should be virtuous.
But if you are not, obey me: that is next best.
It has just come to my mind, I have at home   510
some magic love charms. They will end your trouble;
they'll neither harm your honor nor your mind.
They'll end your trouble, . . . only you must be brave.   515

Phaedra

Is this a poison ointment or a drink?

Nurse

I don't know. Don't be overanxious, child,
to find out what it is. Accept its benefits.

Phaedra

I am afraid of you: I am afraid
that you will be too clever for my good.

Nurse

You are afraid of everything. What is it?

Phaedra

You surely will not tell this to Hippolytus?   520

Nurse

Come, let that be: I will arrange all well.
Only, my lady Cypris of the Sea,
be my helper you. The other plans I have
I'll tell to those we love within the house;
that will suffice.

(*The Nurse goes off.*)

Chorus

STROPHE

Love distills desire upon the eyes,   525
love brings bewitching grace into the heart
of those he would destroy.
I pray that love may never come to me
with murderous intent,
in rhythms measureless and wild.
Not fire nor stars have stronger bolts   530
than those of Aphrodite sent
by the hand of Eros, Zeus's child.

ANTISTROPHE

In vain by Alpheus' stream,   535
in vain in the halls of Phoebus' Pythian shrine
the land of Greece increases sacrifice.
But Love the King of Men they honor not,   540
although he keeps the keys
of the temple of desire,
although he goes destroying through the world,
author of dread calamities
and ruin when he enters human hearts.

STROPHE

The Oechalian maiden who had never known   545
the bed of love, known neither man nor marriage,

the Goddess Cypris gave to Heracles.
She took her from the home of Eurytus,
maiden unhappy in her marriage song,
wild as a Naiad or a Bacchanal,
with blood and fire, a murderous hymenaeal!   550

ANTISTROPHE

O holy walls of Thebes and Dirce's fountain   555
bear witness you, to Love's grim journeying:
once you saw Love bring Semele to bed,
lull her to sleep, clasped in the arms of Death,
pregnant with Dionysus by the thunder king.   560
Love is like a flitting bee in the world's garden
and for its flowers, destruction is in his breath.

SCENE III

(Phaedra is standing listening near the central door of the palace.)

Phaedra

Women, be silent!

(She listens and then recoils.)

Oh, I am destroyed forever.   565

Chorus Leader

What is there terrible within the house?

Phaedra

Hush, let me hear the voices within!

Chorus Leader

And I obey. But this is sorrow's prelude.

Phaedra (cries out)

Oh, I am the most miserable of women!   570

*(The Chorus Leader and the Chorus babble
excitedly among themselves.)*

What does she mean by her cries?
Why does she scream?
Tell us the fear-winged word, Mistress, the fear-winged word,
rushing upon the heart.

Phaedra

    I am lost. Go, women, stand and listen there yourselves   575
    and hear the tumult that falls on the house.

Chorus Leader

    Mistress, you stand at the door.
    It is you who can tell us best
    what happens within the house.   580

Phaedra

    Only the son of the horse-loving Amazon,
    Hippolytus, cursing a servant maid.

Chorus Leader

    My ears can catch a sound,   585
    but I can hear nothing clear.
    I can only hear a voice
    scolding in anger.

Phaedra

    It is plain enough. He cries aloud against
    the mischievous bawd who betrays her mistress' love.   590

Chorus Leader

    Lady, you are betrayed!
    How can I help you?
    What is hidden is revealed.
    You are destroyed.
    Those you love have betrayed you.   595

Phaedra

    She loved me and she told him of my troubles,
    and so has ruined me. She was my doctor,
    but her cure has made my illness mortal now.

Chorus Leader

    What will you do? There is no cure.

Phaedra

    I know of one, and only one—quick death.
    That is the only cure for my disease.   600

(She retires into the palace through one of the side doors just as Hippolytus issues through the central door, dogged by the Nurse. Phaedra is conceived of as listening from behind her door during the entire conversation between the Nurse and Hippolytus.)

Hippolytus

O Mother Earth! O Sun and open sky!
What words I have heard from this accursed tongue!

Nurse

Hush, son! Someone may hear you.

Hippolytus

You cannot
expect that I hear horror and stay silent.

Nurse

I beg of you, entreat you by your right hand,
your strong right hand, . . . don't speak of this!   605

Hippolytus

Don't lay your hand on me! Let go my cloak!

Nurse

By your knees then, . . . don't destroy me!

Hippolytus

What is this?
Don't you declare that you have done nothing wrong?

Nurse

Yes, but the story, son, is not for everyone.

Hippolytus

Why not? A pleasant tale makes pleasanter telling,
when there are many listeners.   610

Nurse

You will not break your oath to me, surely you will not?

Hippolytus

My tongue swore, but my mind was still unpledged.

Nurse

Son, what would you do?
You'll not destroy your friends?

Hippolytus

"Friends" you say!
I spit the word away. None of the wicked
are friends of mine.

Nurse

Then pardon, son. It's natural
that we should sin, being human.   615

Hippolytus

Women! This coin which men find counterfeit!
Why, why, Lord Zeus, did you put them in the world,
in the light of the sun? If you were so determined
to breed the race of man, the source of it
should not have been women. Men might have dedicated
in your own temples images of gold,   620
silver, or weight of bronze, and thus have bought
the seed of progeny, . . . to each been given
his worth in sons according to the assessment
of his gift's value. So we might have lived
in houses free of the taint of women's presence.
But now, to bring this plague into our homes   625
we drain the fortunes of our homes. In this
we have a proof how great a curse is woman.
For the father who begets her, rears her up,
must add a dowry gift to pack her off
to another's house and thus be rid of the load.
And he again that takes the cursed creature   630
rejoices and enriches his heart's jewel
with dear adornment, beauty heaped on vileness.
With lovely clothes the poor wretch tricks her out
spending the wealth that underprops his house.   635
That husband has the easiest life whose wife
is a mere nothingness, a simple fool,

uselessly sitting by the fireside.
I hate a clever woman—God forbid   640
that I should ever have a wife at home
with more than woman's wits! Lust breeds mischief
in the clever ones. The limits of their minds
deny the stupid lecherous delights.
We should not suffer servants to approach them,   645
but give them as companions voiceless beasts,
dumb, . . . but with teeth, that they might not converse,
and hear another voice in answer.
But now at home the mistress plots the mischief,
and the maid carries it abroad. So you, vile woman,   650
came here to me to bargain and to traffic
in the sanctity of my father's marriage bed.
I'll go to a running stream and pour its waters
into my ear to purge away the filth.
Shall I who cannot even hear such impurity,
and feel myself untouched, . . . shall I turn sinner?   655
Woman, know this. It is my piety saves you.
Had you not caught me off my guard and bound
my lips with an oath, by heaven I would not refrain
from telling this to my father.
Now I will go and leave this house until
Theseus returns from his foreign wanderings,
and I'll be silent. But I'll watch you close.   660
I'll walk with my father step by step and see
how you look at him, . . . you and your mistress both.
I have tasted of the daring of your infamy.
I'll know it for the future. Curses on you!
I'll hate you women, hate and hate and hate you,
and never have enough of hating. . . .
                                        Some
say that I talk of this eternally,   665
yes, but eternal, too, is woman's wickedness.
Either let someone teach them to be chaste,
or suffer me to trample on them forever.

(Phaedra comes out from behind the door. Exit Hippolytus.)

Phaedra

Bitter indeed is woman's destiny!
I have failed. What trick is there now, what cunning plea   670
to loose the knot around my neck?
I have had justice. O earth and the sunlight!
Where shall I escape from my fate?
How shall I hide my trouble?
What God or man would appear
to bear hand or part in my crime?   675
There is a limit to all suffering and I have reached it.
I am the unhappiest of women.

Chorus

Alas, mistress, all is over now   680
your servant's schemes have failed and you are ruined.

(Enter the Nurse.)

Phaedra

This is fine service you have rendered me,
corrupted, damned seducer of your friends!
May Zeus, the father of my fathers' line,
blot you out utterly, raze you from the world
with thunderbolts! Did I not see your purpose,   685
did I not say to you, "Breathe not a word of this"
which now overwhelms me with shame? But you,
you did not hold back. And therefore I must die
and die dishonored.
Enough of this. We have a new theme now.
The anger of Hippolytus is whetted.
He will tell his father all the story of your sin   690
to my disparagement. He will tell old Pittheus, too.
He will fill all the land with my dishonor.
May my curse
light upon you, on you and all the others
who eagerly help unwilling friends to ruin.

Nurse

Mistress, you may well blame my ill-success,   695
for sorrow's bite is master of your judgment.
But I have an answer to make if you will listen.
I reared you up. I am your loyal servant.
I sought a remedy for your love's sickness,
and found, . . . not what I sought.
Had I succeeded, I had been a wise one.   700
Our wisdom varies in proportion to
our failure or achievement.

Phaedra

                              So, that's enough
for me? Do I have justice if you deal me
my death blow and then say "I was wrong: I grant it."

Nurse

We talk too long. True I was not wise then.
But even from this desperate plight, my child,   705
you can escape.

Phaedra

                    You, speak no more to me.
You have given me dishonorable advice.
What you have tried has brought dishonor too.
Away with you!
Think of yourself. For me and my concerns
I will arrange all well.

                                        (*Exit Nurse.*)

You noble ladies of Troezen, grant me this,   710
this one request, that what you have heard here
you wrap in silence.

Chorus Leader

I swear by holy Artemis, child of Zeus,
never to bring your troubles to the daylight.

Phaedra

I thank you. I have found one single blessing   715
in this unhappy business, one alone,

that I can pass on to my children after me
life with an uncontaminated name,
and myself profit by the present throw
of Fortune's dice. For I will never shame you,
my Cretan home, nor will I go to face   720
Theseus, defendant on an ugly charge,
never—for one life's sake.

Chorus Leader

What is the desperate deed you mean to do,
the deed past cure?

Phaedra

            Death. But the way of it, that
is what I now must plan.

Chorus Leader

               Oh, do not speak of it!

Phaedra

No, I'll not speak of it. But on this day
when I shake off the burden of this life   725
I shall delight the Goddess who destroys me,
the Goddess Cypris.
Bitter will have been the love that conquers me,
but in my death I shall at least bring sorrow,
upon another, too, that his high heart
may know no arrogant joy at my life's shipwreck;
he will have his share in this my mortal sickness   730
and learn of chastity in moderation.

Chorus

STROPHE

Would that I were under the cliffs, in the secret hiding-places of
    the rocks,
that Zeus might change me to a winged bird
and set me among the feathered flocks.
I would rise and fly to where the sea   735
washes the Adriatic coast,
and to the waters of Eridanus. .

Into that deep-blue tide,
where their father, the Sun, goes down,
the unhappy maidens weep
tears from their amber-gleaming eyes   740
in pity for Phaethon.

ANTISTROPHE

I would win my way to the coast,
apple-bearing Hesperian coast,
of which the minstrels sing.
Where the Lord of the Ocean
denies the voyager further sailing,   745
and fixes the solemn limit of Heaven
which Giant Atlas upholds.
There the streams flow with ambrosia
by Zeus's bed of love,
and holy earth, the giver of life,   750
yields to the Gods rich blessedness.

STROPHE

O Cretan ship with the white sails,
from a happy home you brought her,
my mistress over the tossing foam, over the salty sea,   755
to bless her with a marriage unblest.
Black was the omen that sped her here,
black was the omen for both her lands,
for glorious Athens and her Cretan home,
as they bound to Munychia's pier   760
the cables' ends with their twisted strands
and stepped ashore on the continent.

ANTISTROPHE

The presage of the omen was true;   765
Aphrodite has broken her spirit
with the terrible sickness of impious love.
The waves of destruction are over her head,
from the roof of her room with its marriage bed,

she is tying the twisted noose.   770
And now it is around her fair white neck!
The shame of her cruel fate has conquered.
She has chosen good name rather than life:
she is easing her heart of its bitter load of love.   775

Nurse (*within*)

Ho, there, help!
You who are near the palace, help!
My mistress, Theseus' wife, has hanged herself.

Chorus Leader

It is done, she is hanged in the dangling rope.
Our Queen is dead.

Nurse (*within*)

Quick! Someone bring a knife!   780
Help me cut the knot around her neck.

                                        (*The Chorus talks among itself.*)

First Woman

What shall we do, friends? Shall we cross the threshold,
and take the Queen from the grip of the tight-drawn cords?

Second Woman

Why should we? There are servants enough within
for that. Where hands are overbusy,
there is no safety.   785

Nurse (*within*)

Lay her out straight, poor lady.
Bitter shall my lord find her housekeeping.

Third Woman

From what I hear, the queen is dead.
They are already laying out the corpse.

                               Scene IV
                                        (*Theseus enters.*)

Theseus

Women, what is this crying in the house?   790

I heard heavy wailing on the wind,
as it were servants, mourning. And my house
deigns me no kindly welcome, though I come
crowned with good luck from Delphi.
The doors are shut against me. Can it be
something has happened to my father. He is old.   795
His life has traveled a great journey,
but bitter would be his passing from our house.

Chorus Leader

King, it is not the old who claim your sorrow.
Young is the dead and bitterly you'll grieve.

Theseus

My children . . . has death snatched a life away?

Chorus Leader

Your children live—but sorrowfully, King.   800
Their mother is dead.

Theseus

           It cannot be true, it cannot.
My wife! How could she be dead?

Chorus Leader

She herself tied the rope around her neck.

Theseus

Was it grief and numbing loneliness drove her to it,
or has there been some violence at work?

Chorus Leader

I know no more than this. I, too, came lately
to mourn for you and yours, King Theseus.   805

Theseus

Oh,
Why did I plait this coronal of leaves,
and crown my head with garlands, I the envoy
who find my journey end in misery.

(To the servants within.)

Open the doors! Unbar the fastenings,
that I may see this bitter sight, my wife
who killed me in her own death.   810

*(The doors are opened, and Theseus goes inside. The Chorus in
the Orchestra divide again into half-choruses and chant.)*

First Half-chorus

Woman unhappy, tortured,
your suffering, your death,
has shaken this house to its foundations.

Second Half-chorus

You were daring, you who died
in violence and guilt.
Here was a wrestling: your own hand against your life.   815

Chorus (united)

Who can have cast a shadow on your life?

SCENE V

(Enter Theseus.)

Theseus

O city, city! Bitterness of sorrow!
Extremest sorrow that a man can suffer!
Fate, you have ground me and my house to dust,
fate in the form of some ineffable
pollution, some grim spirit of revenge.   820
The file has whittled away my life until
it is a life no more.
I am like a swimmer that falls into a great sea:
I cannot cross this towering wave I see before me.   825

My wife! I cannot think
of anything said or done to drive you to this horrible death.
You are like a bird that has vanished out of my hand.
You have made a quick leap out of my arms
into the land of Death.

It must be the sin of some of my ancestors in the dim past   830
God in his vengeance makes me pay now.

Chorus Leader

You are not the only one, King.
Many another as well as you
has lost a noble wife.   835

Theseus

Darkness beneath the earth, darkness beneath the earth!
How good to lie there and be dead,
now that I have lost you, my dearest comrade.
Your death is no less mine.   840
Will any of you
tell me what happened?
Or does the palace keep a flock of you for nothing?

God, the pain I saw in the house!
I cannot speak of it, I cannot bear it.   845
I cannot speak of it, I cannot bear it. I am a dead man.
My house is empty and my children orphaned.
You have left them, you
my loving wife—
the best of wives   850
of all the sun looks down on or the blazing stars of the night.

Chorus

Woe for the house! Such storms of ill assail it.
My eyes are wells of tears and overrun,
and still I fear the evil that shall come.   855

Theseus

Let her be, let her be:
What is this tablet fastened to her dear hand?
What can she wish to tell me of news?
Have you written begging me to care
for our children or, in entreaty,
about another woman? Sad one, rest confident.   860
There is no woman in the world who shall come to this house

and sleep by my side.
Look, the familiar signet ring,
hers who was once my wife!
Come, I will break the seals,
and see what this letter has to tell me.   865

(The Chorus of women speak singly.)

First Woman

   Surely some God
   brings sorrow upon sorrow in succession.

Second Woman

   The house of our lords is destroyed: it is no more.   870

Third Woman

   God, if it so may be, hear my prayer.
   Do not destroy this house utterly. I am a prophet:
   I can see the omen of coming trouble.

Theseus

   Alas, here is endless sorrow upon sorrow.
   It passes speech, passes endurance.   875

Chorus Leader

   What is it? Tell us if we may share the story.

Theseus

   It cries aloud, this tablet, cries aloud,
   and Death is its song!   880

Chorus Leader

   Prelude of ruin!

Theseus

   I shall no longer hold this secret prisoner
   in the gates of my mouth. It is horrible,
   yet I will speak.
   Citizens,
   Hippolytus has dared to rape my wife.   885
   He has dishonored God's holy sunlight.

(He turns in the direction of the sea.)

Father Poseidon, once you gave to me
three curses. . . . Now with one of these, I pray,
kill my son. Suffer him not to escape,
this very day, if you have promised truly.   890

Chorus Leader

Call back your curses, King, call back your curses.
Else you will realize that you were wrong
another day, too late. I pray you, trust me.

Theseus

I will not. And I now make this addition:
I banish him from this land's boundaries.
So fate shall strike him, one way or the other,
either Poseidon will respect my curse,   895
and send him dead into the House of Hades,
or exiled from this land, a beggar wandering,
on foreign soil, his life shall suck the dregs
of sorrow's cup.

Chorus Leader

Here comes your son, and seasonably, King Theseus.
Give over your deadly anger. You will best   900
determine for the welfare of your house.

> (*Enter Hippolytus with companions.*)

Hippolytus

I heard you crying, father, and came quickly.
I know no cause why you should mourn.
Tell me.

> (*Suddenly he sees the body of Phaedra.*)

O father, father—Phaedra! Dead! She's dead!   905
I cannot believe it. But a few moments since
I left her. . . . And she is still so young.
But what could it be? How did she die, father?
I *must* hear the truth from you. You say nothing to me?   910

When you are in trouble is no time for silence
The heart that would hear everything

is proved most greedy in misfortune's hour.
You should not hide your troubles from your friends,
and, father, those who are closer than your friends. 915

Theseus

What fools men are! You work and work for nothing,
you teach ten thousand tasks to one another,
invent, discover everything. One thing only
you do not know: one thing you never hunt for—
a way to teach fools wisdom. 920

Hippolytus

Clever indeed
would be the teacher able to compel
the stupid to be wise! This is no time
for such fine logic chopping.
                              I am afraid
your tongue runs wild through sorrow.

Theseus

                                        If there were
some token now, some mark to make the division 925
clear between friend and friend, the true and the false!
All men should have two voices, one the just voice,
and one as chance would have it. In this way
the treacherous scheming voice would be confuted 930
by the just, and we should never be deceived.

Hippolytus

Some friend has poisoned your ear with slanderous tales.
Am I suspected, then, for all my innocence?
I am amazed. I am amazed to hear
your words. They are distraught. They go indeed
far wide of the mark! 935

Theseus

The mind of man—how far will it advance?
Where will its daring impudence find limits?
If human villainy and human life

shall wax in due proportion, if the son
shall always grow in wickedness past his father,
the Gods must add another world to this   940
that all the sinners may have space enough.

Look at this man! He was my son and he
dishonors my wife's bed! By the dead's testimony
he's clearly proved the vilest, falsest wretch.   945
Come—you could stain your conscience with the impurity—
show me your face; show it to me, your father.

You are the veritable holy man!
You walked with Gods in chastity immaculate!
I'll not believe your boasts of God's companionship: 950
the Gods are not so simple nor so ignorant.
Go, boast that you eat no meat, that you have Orpheus
for your king. Read until you are demented
your great thick books whose substance is as smoke.
For I have found you out. I tell you all,   955
avoid such men as he. They hunt their prey
with holy-seeming words, but their designs
are black and ugly. "She is dead," you thought,
"and that will save me." Fool, it is chiefly that
which proves your guilt. What oath that you can swear,   960
what speech that you can make for your acquittal,
outweighs this letter of hers? You'll say, to be sure,
she was your enemy and that the bastard son
is always hateful to the legitimate line.
Your words would argue her a foolish merchant
whose stock of merchandise was her own life
if she should throw away what she held dearest
to gratify her enmity for you.   965

Or you will tell me that this frantic folly
is inborn in a woman's nature; man
is different: but I know that young men
are no more to be trusted than a woman

when love disturbs the youthful blood in them.
The very male in them will make them false. 970
But why should I debate against you in words?
Here is the dead, surest of witnesses.
Get from this land with all the speed you can
to exile—may you rot there! Never again
come to our city, God-built Athens, nor
to countries over which my spear is king. 975

If I should take this injury at your hands
and pardon you, then Sinis of the Isthmus,
whom once I killed, would vow I never killed him,
but only bragged of the deed. And Sciron's rocks
washed by the sea would call me liar when
I swore I was a terror to ill-doers. 980

Chorus Leader

I cannot say of any man: he is happy.
See here how former happiness lies uprooted!

Hippolytus

Your mind and intellect are subtle, father:
here you have a subject dressed in eloquent words;
but if you lay the matter bare of words, 985
the matter is not eloquent. I am
no man to speak with vapid, precious skill
before a mob, although among my equals
and in a narrow circle I am held
not unaccomplished in the eloquent art.
That is as it should be. The demagogue
who charms a crowd is scorned by cultured experts.
But here in this necessity I must speak. 990
First I shall take the argument you first
urged as so irrefutable and deadly.
You see the earth and air about you, father?
In all of that there lives no man more chaste
than I, though you deny it. 995

It is my rule to honor the Gods first
and then to have as friends only such men
as do no sin, nor offer wicked service,
nor will consent to sin to serve a friend
as a return for kindness. I am no railer
at my companions. Those who are my friends   1000
find me as much their friends when they are absent
as when we are together.

There is one thing that I have never done, the thing
of which you think that you convict me, father,
I am a virgin to this very day.
Save what I have heard or what I have seen in pictures,   1005
I'm ignorant of the deed. Nor do I wish
to see such things, for I've a maiden soul.
But say you disbelieve my chastity.
Then tell me how it was *your* wife seduced me:
was it because she was more beautiful
than all the other women in the world?   1010
Or did I think, when I had taken her,
to win your place and kingdom for a dowry
and live in your own house? I would have been
a fool, a senseless fool, if I had dreamed it.
Was rule so sweet? Never, I tell you, Theseus,
for the wise. A man whom power has so enchanted
must be demented. I would wish to be   1015
first in the contests of the Greeks,
but in the city I'd take second place
and an enduring happy life among
the best society who are my friends.
So one has time to work, and danger's absence
has charms above the royal diadem.   1020
But a word more and my defense is finished.
If I had one more witness to my character,
if I were tried when *she* still saw the light,
deeds would have helped you as you scanned your friends

to know the true from the false. But now I swear,
I swear to you by Zeus, the God of oaths,   1025
by this deep-rooted fundament of earth,
I never sinned against you with your wife
nor would have wished or thought of it.
If I have been a villain, may I die
unfamed, unknown, a homeless stateless beggar,
an exile! May the earth and sea refuse   1030
to give my body rest when I am dead!
Whether your wife took her own life because
she was afraid, I do not know. I may not speak
further than this.
Virtuous she was in deed, although not virtuous:
I that have virtue used it to my ruin.   1035

Chorus Leader

You have rebutted the charge enough by your oath:
it is a great pledge you took in the God's name.

Theseus

Why, here's a spell-binding magician for you!
He wrongs his father and then trusts his craft,
his smooth beguiling craft to lull my anger.   1040

Hippolytus

Father, I must wonder at this in you.
If I were father now, and you were son,
I would not have banished you to exile! I
would have killed you if I thought you touched my wife.

Theseus

This speech is worthy of you: but you'll not die so.   1045
A quick death is the easiest of ends
for miserable men. No, you'll go wandering
far from your fatherland and beg your way.
This is the payment of the impious man.   1050

Hippolytus

What will you do? You will not wait until

time's pointing finger proves me innocent.
Must I go at once to banishment?

Theseus

                        Yes, and had I the power,
your place of banishment would be beyond
the limits of the world, the encircling sea
and the Atlantic Pillars.
That is the measure of my hate, my son.

Hippolytus

Pledges, oaths, and oracles—you will not test them?   1055
You will banish me from the kingdom without trial?

Theseus

This letter here is proof without lot-casting.
The ominous birds may fly above my head:
they do not trouble me.

Hippolytus

                Eternal Gods!
Dare I speak out, since I am ruined now   1060
through loyalty to the oath I took by you?
No, he would not believe who should believe
and I should be false to my oath for nothing.

Theseus

This is more of your holy juggling!
I cannot stomach it. Away with you!
Get from this country—and go quickly!   1065

Hippolytus

Where shall I turn? What friend will take me in,
when I am banished on a charge like this?

Theseus

Doubtless some man who loves to entertain
his wife's seducers welcoming them at the hearth.

Hippolytus

That blow went home.   1070

I am near crying when I think that I
am judged to be guilty and that it is you who are judge.

Theseus

You might have sobbed and snivelled long ago,
and thought of that before when you resolved
to rape your father's wife.

Hippolytus

House, speak for me!
Take voice and bear me witness if I have sinned.   1075

Theseus

You have a clever trick of citing witnesses,
whose testimony is dumb. Here is your handiwork.

(Points to the body.)

It, too, can't speak—but it convicts you.

Hippolytus

If I could only find
another *me* to look me in the face
and see my tears and all that I am suffering!

Theseus

Yes, in self-worship you are certainly practiced.   1080
You are more at home there than in the other virtues,
justice, for instance, and duty toward a father.

Hippolytus

Unhappy mother mine, and bitter birth-pangs,
when you gave me to the world! I would not wish
on any of my friends a bastard's birth.

Theseus (to the servants)

Drag him away!
Did you not hear me, men, a long time since
proclaiming his decree of banishment?   1085

Hippolytus

Let one of them touch me at his peril! But you,
you drive me out yourself—if you have the heart!

Theseus

    I'll do it, too, unless you go at once.
    No, there is no chance that pity for your exile
    will steal on my hard heart and make me change.

                          (Theseus goes out.)

Hippolytus

    So, I'm condemned and there is no release.   1090
    I know the truth and dare not tell the truth.

               (He turns to the statue of Artemis.)

    Daughter of Leto, dearest of the Gods to me,
    comrade and partner in the hunt, behold me,
    banished from famous Athens.
    Farewell, city! Farewell Erechtheus' land!   1095
    Troezen, farewell! So many happy times
    you knew to give a young man, growing up.
    This is the last time I shall look upon you,
    the last time I shall greet you.

                     (To his companions.)

    Come friends, you are of my age and of this country,
    say your farewells and set me on my way.
    You will not see a man more innocent—   1100
    innocent despite my judge!—condemned to banishment.

                  (Hippolytus goes out.)

Chorus

               STROPHE

    The care of God for us is a great thing,
    if a man believe it at heart:
    it plucks the burden of sorrow from him.
    So I have a secret hope   1105
    of someone, a God, who is wise and plans;
    but my hopes grow dim when I see
    the deeds of men and their destinies.

    For fortune is ever veering, and the currents of life are shifting
    shifting, wandering forever.   1110

ANTISTROPHE

This is the lot in life I seek
and I pray that God may grant it me,
luck and prosperity
and a heart untroubled by anguish.
And a mind that is neither false clipped coin,
nor too clear-eyed in sincerity,   1115
that I may lightly change my ways,
my ways of today when tomorrow comes,
and so be happy all my life long.

STROPHE

My heart is no longer clear: 1120
I have seen what I never dreamed,
I have seen the brightest star of Athens,
stricken by a father's wrath,
banished to an alien land.   1125

Sands of the seashore!
Thicket of the mountain!
Where with his pacing hounds
he hunted wild beasts and killed
to the honor of holy Dictynna.   1130

ANTISTROPHE

He will never again mount his car
with its span of Venetian mares,
nor fill the ring of Limnae with the sound of horses' hoofs.
The music which never slept
on the strings of his lyre, shall be dumb,   1135
shall be dumb in his father's house.
The haunts of the Goddess Maid
in the deep rich meadow shall want their crowns.
You are banished: there's an end   1140
of the rivalry of maids for your love.

But my sorrow shall not die,
still my eyes shall be wet with tears
for your heartless doom.
Sad mother, you bore him in vain: 1145
I am angry against the Gods.
Sister Graces, why did you let him go
guiltless, out of his native land,
out of his father's house?   1150

But here I see Hippolytus' servant,
in haste making for the house, his face sorrowful.

SCENE VI

(Enter a Messenger.)

Messenger

Where shall I go to find King Theseus, women?
If you know, tell me. Is he within doors?   1155

Chorus

Here he is coming out.

Messenger

King Theseus,
I bring you news worthy of much thought
for you and all the citizens who live
in Athens' walls and boundaries of Troezen.

Theseus

What is it? Has some still newer disaster   1160
seized my two neighboring cities?

Messenger

Hippolytus is dead: I may almost say dead:
he sees the light of day still, though the balance
that holds him in this world is slight indeed.

Theseus

Who killed him? I can guess that someone hated him,
whose wife he raped, as he did mine, his father's.   1165

Messenger

It was the horses of his own car that killed him,
they, and the curses of your lips,
the curses you invoked against your son,
and prayed the Lord of Ocean to fulfil them.

Theseus

O Gods—Poseidon, you are then truly
my father! You have heard my prayers.   1170
How did he die? Tell me. How did the beam
of Justice's dead-fall strike him, my dishonorer?

Messenger

We were combing our horses' coats beside the sea,
where the waves came crashing to the shore. And we were crying
for one had come and told us that our master,   1175
Hippolytus, should walk this land no more,
since you had laid hard banishment upon him.
Then he came himself down to the shore to us,
with the same refrain of tears,
and with him walked a countless company
of friends and young men his own age.   1180

But at last he gave over crying and said:
Why do I rave like this? It is my father
who has commanded and I must obey him.
Prepare my horses, men, and harness them.
There is no longer a city of mine.
Then every man made haste. Before you could say the words, 1185
there was the chariot ready before our master.
He put his feet into the driver's rings,
and took the reins from the rail into his hands.
But first he folded his hands like this and prayed: 1190
Zeus, let me die now, if I have been guilty!
Let my father know that he has done me wrong,
whether I live to see the day or not.

With that, he took the goad and touched the horses.
And we his servants followed our master's car,   1195

close by the horses' heads, on the straight road
that leads to Argos and to Epidaurus.
When we were entering the lonely country
the other side of the border, where the shore   1200
goes down to the Saronic Gulf, a rumbling
deep in the earth, terrible to hear,
growled like the thunder of Father Zeus.
The horses raised their heads, pricked up their ears,
and gusty fear was on us all to know,
whence came the sound. As we looked toward the shore,   1205
where the waves were beating, we saw a wave appear,
a miracle wave, lifting its crest to the sky,
so high that Sciron's coast was blotted out
from my eye's vision. And it hid the Isthmus
and the Asclepius Rock. To the shore it came,   1210
swelling, boiling, crashing, casting its surf around,
to where the chariot stood.
But at the very moment when it broke,
the wave threw up a monstrous savage bull.
Its bellowing filled the land, and the land echoed it,   1215
with shuddering emphasis. And sudden panic
fell on the horses in the car. But the master—
he was used to horses' ways—all his life long
he had been with horses—took a firm grip of the reins   1220
and lashed the ends behind his back and pulled
like a sailor at the oar. The horses bolted:
their teeth were clenched upon the fire-forged bit.
They heeded neither the driver's hand nor harness
nor the jointed car. As often as he would turn them   1225
with guiding hand to the soft sand of the shore,
the bull appeared in front to head them off,
maddening the team with terror.
But when in frenzy they charged toward the cliffs,   1230
the bull came galloping beside the rail,
silently following until he brought disaster,
capsizing the car, striking the wheel on a rock.

Then all was in confusion. Axles of wheels,
and lynch-pins flew up into the air,   1235
and he the unlucky driver, tangled in the reins,
was dragged along in an inextricable
knot, and his dear head pounded on the rocks,
his body bruised. He cried aloud and terrible
his voice rang in our ears: Stand, horses, stand!   1240
You were fed in my stables. Do not kill me!
My father's curse! His curse! Will none of you
save me? I am innocent. Save me!

Many of us had will enough, but all
were left behind in the race. Getting free of the reins,
somehow he fell. There was still life in him.   1245
But the horses vanished and that ill-omened monster,
somewhere, I know not where, in the rough cliffs.

I am only a slave in your household, King Theseus,
but I shall never be able to believe   1250
that your son was guilty, not though the tribe of women
were hanged for it, not though the weight of tablets
of a high pine of Ida, filled with writing,
accused him—for I know that he was good.

Chorus Leader

It has been fulfilled, this bitter, new disaster,   1255
for what is doomed and fated there is no quittance.

Theseus

For hatred of the sufferer I was glad
at what you told me. Still, he was my son.
As such I have reverence for him and the Gods:
I neither rejoice nor sorrow at this thing.   1260

Messenger

What is your pleasure that we do with him?
Would you have him brought to you? If I might counsel,
you would not be harsh with your son—now he is unfortunate.

Theseus

Bring him to me that I may see his face.   1265
He swore that he had never wronged my wife.
I will refute him with God's punishing stroke.

Chorus

Cypris, you guide men's hearts
and the inflexible
hearts of the Gods and with you
comes Love with the flashing wings,   1270
comes Love with the swiftest of wings.
Over the earth he flies
and the loud-echoing salt-sea.
He bewitches and maddens the heart
of the victim he swoops upon.   1275
He bewitches the race of the mountain-hunting
lions and beasts of the sea,
and all the creatures that earth feeds,
and the blazing sun sees—
and man, too—
over all you hold kingly power,   1280
Love, you are only ruler
over all these.

Epilogue

Artemis

I call on the noble king, the son of Aegeus,
to hear me! It is I, Artemis, child of Leto.   1285

Miserable man, what joy have you in this?
You have murdered a son, you have broken nature's laws.
Dark indeed was the conclusion
you drew from your wife's lying accusations,
but plain for all to see is the destruction
to which they led you.
There is a hell beneath the earth: haste to it,   1290
and hide your head there! Or will you take wings,

and choosing the life of a bird instead of man
keep your feet from destruction's path in which they tread?
Among good men, at least, you have no share in life.   1295
Hear me tell you, Theseus, how these things came to pass.
I shall not better them, but I will give you pain.
I have come here for this—to show you that your son's heart
was always just, so just that for his good name
he endured to die. I will show you, too,
the frenzied love that seized your wife, or I may call it,   1300
a noble innocence. For that most hated Goddess,
hated by all of us whose joy is virginity,
drove her with love's sharp prickings to desire
your son. She tried to overcome her love
with the mind's power, but at last against her will,
she fell by the nurse's strategems,   1305
the nurse, who told your son under oath her mistress loved him.
But he, just man, did not fall in with her
counsels, and even when reviled by you
refused to break the oath he had pledged.
Such was his piety. But your wife fearing
lest she be proved the sinner wrote a letter,   1310
a letter full of lies; and so she killed
your son by treachery; but she convinced you.

Theseus

Alas!

Artemis

This is a bitter story, Theseus. Stay,
hear more that you may groan the more.
You know you had three curses from your father,   1315
three, clear for you to use? One you have launched,
vile wretch, at your own son, when you might have
spent it upon an enemy. Your father,
King of the Sea, in loving kindness to you
gave you, by his bequest, all that he ought.
But you've been proved at fault both in his eyes   1320

and mine in that you did not stay for oaths
nor voice of oracles, nor gave a thought
to what time might have shown; only too quickly
you hurled the curses at your son and killed him.

Theseus

Mistress, I am destroyed.

Artemis

You have sinned indeed, but yet you may win pardon.   1325
For it was Cypris managed the thing this way
to gratify her anger against Hippolytus.
This is the settled custom of the Gods:
No one may fly in the face of another's wish:
we remain aloof and neutral. Else, I assure you,   1330
had I not feared Zeus, I never would have endured
such shame as this—my best friend among men
killed, and I could do nothing.
As for you, in the first place ignorance acquits you,
and then your wife, by her death, destroyed the proofs,   1335
the verbal proofs which might have still convinced you.
You and I are the chief sufferers, Theseus.
Misfortune for you, grief for me.
The Gods do not rejoice when pious worshippers die: 1340
the wicked we destroy, children, house and all.

Chorus

Here comes the suffering Hippolytus,
his fair young body and his golden head,
a battered wreck. O trouble of the house,
what double sorrow from the hand of God   1345
has been fulfilled for this our royal palace!

Hippolytus

A battered wreck of body! Unjust father,
and oracle unjust—this is your work.
Woe for my fate!   1350
My head is filled with shooting agony,

and in my brain there is a leaping fire.
Let me be!
For I would rest my weary frame awhile.
Curse on my team! How often have I fed you   1355
from my own hand, you who have murdered me!
O, O!
In God's name touch my wounded body gently.
Who is this standing on the right of me?   1360
Come lift me carefully, bear me easily,
a man unlucky, cursed by my own father
in bitter error. Zeus, do you see this,
see me that worshipped God in piety,   1365
me that excelled all men in chastity,
see me now go to death which gapes before me;
all my life lost, and all for nothing now
labors of piety in the face of men?

O the pain, the pain that comes upon me!   1370
Let me be, let me be, you wretches!
May death the healer come for me at last!
You kill me ten times over with this pain.
O for a spear with a keen cutting edge   1375
to shear me apart—and give me my last sleep!
Father, your deadly curse!
This evil comes from some manslaying of old,   1380
some ancient tale of murder among my kin.
But why should it strike me, who am clear of guilt?
What is there to say? How can I shake from me   1385
this pitiless pain? O death, black night of death,
resistless death, come to me now the miserable,
and give me sleep!

Artemis
Unhappy boy! You are yoked to a cruel fate.
The nobility of your soul has proved your ruin.   1390

Hippolytus
O divine fragrance! Even in my pain

I sense it, and the suffering is lightened.
The Goddess Artemis is near this place.

Artemis

She is, the dearest of the Gods to you.

Hippolytus

You see my suffering, mistress?   1395

Artemis

I see it. Heavenly law forbids my tears.

Hippolytus

Gone is your huntsman, gone your servant now.

Artemis

Yes, truly: but you die beloved by me.

Hippolytus

Gone is your groom, gone your shrine's guardian.

Artemis

Cypris, the worker of mischief, so contrived.   1400

Hippolytus

Alas, I know the Goddess who destroyed me!

Artemis

She blamed your disrespect, hated your chastity.

Hippolytus

She claimed us three as victims then, did Cypris?

Artemis

Your father, you, and me to make a third.

Hippolytus

Yes, I am sorry for my father's suffering.   1405

Artemis

Cypris deceived him by her cunning snares.

Hippolytus

O father, this is sorrow for you indeed!

Theseus

I, too, am dead now. I have no more joy in life.

Hippolytus

I sorrow for you in this more than myself.

Theseus

Would that it was I who was dying instead of you! 1410

Hippolytus

Bitter were Poseidon's gifts, my father, bitter.

Theseus

Would that they had never come into my mouth.

Hippolytus

Even without them, you would have killed me—
you were so angry.

Theseus

A God tripped up my judgment.

Hippolytus

O, if only men might be a curse to Gods! 1415

Artemis

Hush, that is enough! You shall not be unavenged,
Cypris shall find the angry shafts she hurled
against you for your piety and innocence
shall cost her dear.
I'll wait until she loves a mortal next time, 1420
and with this hand—with these unerring arrows
I'll punish him.

To you, unfortunate Hippolytus,
by way of compensation for these ills,
I will give the greatest honors of Troezen.
Unwedded maids before the day of marriage 1425
will cut their hair in your honor. You will reap
through the long cycle of time, a rich reward in tears.
And when young girls sing songs, they will not forget you,

your name will not be left unmentioned,
nor Phaedra's love for you remain unsung. 1430

(*To Theseus.*)

Son of old Aegeus, take your son
to your embrace. Draw him to you. Unknowing
you killed him. It is natural for men
to err when they are blinded by the Gods.

(*To Hippolytus.*)

Do not bear a grudge against your father. 1435
It was fate that you should die so.
Farewell, I must not look upon the dead.
My eye must not be polluted by the last
gaspings for breath. I see you are near this.

Hippolytus

Farewell to you, too holy maiden! Go in peace. 1440
You can lightly leave a long companionship.
You bid me end my quarrel with my father,
and I obey. In the past, too, I obeyed you.

The darkness is upon my eyes already.

Father, lay hold on me and lift me up. 1445

Theseus

Alas, what are you doing to me, my son?

Hippolytus

I am dying. I can see the gates of death.

Theseus

And so you leave me, my hands stained with murder.

Hippolytus

No, for I free you from all guilt in this.

Theseus

You will acquit me of blood guiltiness? 1450

Hippolytus

So help me Artemis of the conquering bow!

Theseus

  Dear son, how noble you have proved to me!

Hippolytus

  Yes, pray to heaven for such legitimate sons.

Theseus

  Woe for your goodness, piety, and virtue.

Hippolytus

  Farewell to you, too, father, a long farewell!   1455

Theseus

  Dear son, bear up. Do not forsake me.

Hippolytus

  This is the end of what I have to bear.
  I'm gone. Cover my face up quickly.

Theseus

  Pallas Athene's famous city,
  what a man you have lost! Alas for me!   1460
  Cypris, how many of your injuries
  I shall remember.

Chorus

  This is a common grief for all the city;
  it came unlooked for. There shall be
  a storm of multitudinous tears for this;
  the lamentable stories of great men   1465
  prevail more than of humble folk.

THE

CYCLOPS

Translated and with an Introduction by

WILLIAM ARROWSMITH

INTRODUCTION TO *CYCLOPS**

Interest in Euripides' *Cyclops* is generally justified historically: other than a chunk of Sophocles' *Ichneutae*, it is the only example of a satyr-play, that ribald piece which in the dramatic festivals crowned a group of three tragedies or a tragic trilogy. But the *Cyclops* is more than historically interesting; it is, by modern standards, good fast farce, clearly stageworthy, with a fine dramatic intelligence behind it. The movement is typically Euripidean, not merely in the sharp reversal of roles and sympathies, the crisp dialogue and the consistent anachronization, but in formal structure and underlying idea as well. Moreover, despite the play's sportive obscenity and knockabout humor, its underlying idea is essentially serious. The *Cyclops*, that is, may be clearly a farce, but it is primarily a farce of ideas, a gay and ironic flirtation with the problem of civilized brutality. As such, it lies within the main stream of Euripides' tragic thought, and, if its treatment and tone differ from that of tragedy, the difference is less a difference of dramatic quality or genius than a difference of genre.

We should like to know a great deal more about satyr-drama as a genre than we do, and we should especially like to know what in fifth-century practice was the formal connection between a satyr-play and the three tragedies which preceded it. But unfortunately the *Cyclops* is undated and cannot, with any degree of certainty, be assigned to one of the extant tragedies.[1] In the absence of that crucial

* This play first appeared in the *Hudson Review* (Spring, 1952), Vol. I, No. 1, and is reprinted here by permission.

1. The most tempting suggestion has been, I think, that the *Cyclops* should be assigned to a group of three tragedies of which the extant *Hecuba* was one. (The *Hecuba* is dated, on very good grounds, almost certainly to 425 B.C.) The assignment is strengthened not merely by topical considerations (cf. E. Delebecque, *Euripide et la guerre du Péloponnèse*) but by very close formal resemblances between the two plays. Thus the blinding of Polyphemus parallels the blinding of Polymnestor, and Polyphemus' final appearance from the cave vividly recalls Polymnestor's emergence from the tent. In both plays again, the guiding idea is that of civilized brutality, and in both cases a barbaric vengeance is taken upon a barbarian (Polymnestor,

information, it becomes difficult to speak with assurance of the formal nature of the play or to generalize from it to the formal definition of fifth-century satyr-drama. Indeed, even if we possessed the requisite information, the very distance which separates the tragedy of Euripides from that of Aeschylus and Sophocles would tend by analogy to preclude a generalization about satyr-plays. One ancient writer, it is true, speaks of satyr-drama as being "tragedy-at-play" or "joking tragedy."[2] But this is hardly helpful, since it may mean either that satyr-drama was mock tragedy, or tragedy *buffa*, or pure farce, or simply a sportive treatment of the subject matter of tragedy. All of these are possibilities applicable to the *Cyclops*, but we have no evidence which might allow us to decide among them.

In point of origins the satyr-play, like both comedy and tragedy, was closely bound up with Dionysiac fertility ritual. Even in the fifth century satyr-drama in its frequent obscenity, its conventional use of Silenus as "nurse" and companion of Dionysus, and its chorus of satyrs with their *phalloi* preserves more vividly than tragedy the memory of its origins. What the original connection between tragedy and comedy and "satyr" may have been, we do not know, though Aristotle in a much disputed passage asserts that the satyr-play was one of the early stages of tragedy;[3] but the value of the testimony appears doubtful.[4] On the whole, scholars have preferred to believe that both satyr-drama and tragedy are independent developments of Dionysiac ritual and that satyr-drama was probably adopted by the dramatist Pratinas from a Peloponnesian source and attached to the Attic festivals. Alternatively, it is held that the double aspect of Dionysiac ritual—the mourning for the dead god and the

---

Polyphemus) by a "civilized" person (Hecuba, Odysseus). The final prophecies again closely parallel each other, and the portrayal of Odysseus in the *Hecuba* is given a great deal of point if we have in mind the sequel in *Cyclops*. In the dovetailing of actions and the reversal of roles, the two plays are strikingly similar.

2. Demetrius of Phalerum *De interp.* 169; cf. Horace *Ars poetica* 231–33.

3. *Poetics* 1449[a] 9 ff.

4. Cf. A. W. Pickard-Cambridge, *Dithyramb, Tragedy and Comedy* (Oxford, 1927), p. 124.

joyous celebration at his resurrection—accounts for the connection between tragedy and the satyr-play. On this theory tragedy contains the *agon* of the dying god, while the satyr-play, like comedy, exhibits the happy celebration for the reborn god and the ritual of the sacred marriage and rounds off the complete drama of the rite in a sportive coda. The presence in the *Cyclops* of an attenuated *komos* and a hinted mock (male) marriage between Silenus and Polyphemus offers some slight evidence for the theory. But it is this very attenuation of the ritual element in the play that reminds us that a theory of formal origins does not really explain what we need to know—the *literary* use and the meaning of the developed form. An account of origins may perhaps explain the conventions of a given form, but it will seldom explain the conscious literary deployment of those conventions.

For the rest our information is tantalizingly slight. Thus we know that the satyr-plays were briefer than the tragedies (the *Cyclops* is the shortest of extant plays); they had their own peculiar choral dance, the *sikinnis*, and they allowed, in prosody and diction, a very slight relaxation from tragic standards in the direction of colloquial speech. For its material satyr-drama drew upon the same sources in myth and *epos* as tragedy. Thus the *Oresteia* appears to have been followed by the *Proteus*, a satyr-play dealing with Menelaus' Egyptian adventure with the Old Man of the Sea, while the *Cyclops* is a conflation of the Polyphemus episode from the ninth book of the *Odyssey* with the story of the capture of Dionysus by Lydian pirates.[5] Both the chorus of satyrs and its "father" Silenus form a standard part of satyric convention, and their characters are accordingly stylized: the satyrs are boisterous, childlike "horse-men" (*not* "goat-men") with a strong streak of cowardice, while Silenus is at every point the ancestor of Falstaff—lewd, fat, bald, drunken, boastful, knavish, and foolish. Finally, it needs to be stressed that, however comic a satyr-play may seem, it is not to be confounded with Greek comedy, which differs from it not only in its material (usually free invention or mythological burlesque), but in structure, conventions, and the degree of topicality and license.

5. Cf. *Homeric Hymn to Dionysus*.

In plot and detail Euripides' adaptation of his Homeric material is remarkably close. If Odysseus here does not escape from the cave by clinging to a ram's belly, and if the immense boulder which in Homer blocked the cave has here been rolled away, these are clearly alterations demanded by the necessities of theatrical presentation. In Euripides the Cyclops is still the creature of his belly, a barking barbarian, and Odysseus is still in some sense the shrewd and civilized man who manages by exercise of mother wit to mutilate the man-eating monster and escape. Or so, at least, it might seem if we possessed only the first half of the play. But the *Cyclops* is not merely a dramatic retelling of Homer; rather, it is Homer's parable of the civilized man and the savage systematically anachronized into its fifth-century equivalent, an altogether different parable.

Neither Odysseus nor Polyphemus is really Homeric at all. Odysseus is not the type of the civilized man, and the Euripidean Cyclops, like the United States in Wilde's epigram, has passed directly from barbarism to decadence without pause for civilization. Both manifest late fifth-century types of corruption: Odysseus' Homeric heroism in its new context is systematically undercut, less heroism than a transparent vainglory and depraved eloquence; Polyphemus is less Caliban than Callicles, an outright exponent of philosophical egoism and the immoralist equation of might and right. Euripides has taken considerable pains, moreover, to indicate to his audience that this is no longer Homer's world, but their own. Thus, when Odysseus first appears, he is greeted by Silenus as a "glib sharper" and "son of Sisyphus." Now, whatever Odysseus may be in Homer, he is never merely a "glib sharper," and his father is Laertes, not Sisyphus. To an audience bred on Homer the distinction is revealing: at one blow Euripides deprives Odysseus of his Homeric paternity in order to attach him to Sisyphus, the proverbial type of cheat and thief, and thereby warns his audience of what they may expect. Odysseus is in fact the familiar depraved politician of the *Hecuba*, the *Trojan Women*, and the *Iphigeneia at Aulis;* he stands, as he almost always does in tragedy, for that refinement of intellect and eloquence which makes civilized brutality so much more terrible than mere savagery. In the *Cyclops*, however, he is on the defensive, and there is irony in the reversal of roles as the man who refused mercy and *nomos* to Hecuba must now himself plead for it. If we sympathize with Odysseus at first, this initial sympathy is nonetheless quickly alienated by the sheer, otiose brutality of his revenge and by Polyphemus' transformation into a drunken, almost lovable, buffoon. The gory description of the Cyclops' cannibalism may perhaps justify Odysseus' revenge, but it does not thereby redeem its barbaric cruelty. Just as the full action of the *Hecuba* consists in reducing both Hecuba and the barbarian Polymnestor to a common subhuman cruelty, so the *Cyclops* shows, not the distinction, but the identity, between Odysseus and Polyphemus.

Odysseus' speech for *nomos* and mercy is the crux of the play. As Silenus recognizes, the speech is pure sophistry, but the sophistry has important consequences that we need to examine. The difficulty lies in the thoroughness of the anachronization and the allusions to the sanctions and background of the Peloponnesian War.

It opens with a disclaimer of responsibility for the Trojan War: "A god was responsible; don't blame men." Such disclaimers in Euripides normally operate to damn those who make them, as, for instance, Helen's disavowal of responsibility in the *Trojan Women.* The next argument sounds very strange indeed. The Greeks, Odysseus argues, have preserved the temples of Poseidon (father of Cyclops) and saved Hellas; therefore the Cyclops, who is Greek because he lives in Greek Sicily (another anachronism), should spare Odysseus and his men. What we have here is a covert but unmistakable allusion to the Persian Wars, when Athens claimed to have saved Hellas and the ancestral gods from the Persians. There is irony in the claim that it was piety which saved the silver-mines of Laurium on Cape Sunium (where there happened to be a shrine to Poseidon), but the larger irony is somewhat more complex.

What Odysseus is urging here is nothing more or less than the argument which Athens had used to acquire her empire: Athens had saved Hellas and should have the rewards of her deed. This sanction for empire was employed down to the time of the Peloponnesian War to coerce neutrals and unwilling states into the Athenian orbit, and the sanction was as loathsome to most Greeks as the Athenian

Empire. Herodotus, writing in the forties, is so much aware of the unpopularity of Athens and her sanction that he is reluctant to state the real truth which underlies the sanction—Athens *did* save Hellas. In 432 B.C., just before the outbreak of the Peloponnesian War, the unofficial Athenian envoys at Sparta could say of their empire:

We have a fair claim to our possessions. . . . We need not refer to remote antiquity . . . but to the Persian War and contemporary history we must refer, although we are rather tired of continually bringing this subject forward.[6]

By 416, the Athenian generals at Melos could argue naked imperialism; the empire had outgrown its sanction:

We shall not trouble you with specious pretences . . . either of how we have a right to our empire because we overthrew the Persians, or are now attacking you because of wrong that you have done us . . . since you know as well as we do that right, as the world goes, is only in question between equals in power, while the strong do what they can and the weak suffer what they must.[7]

This, then, is the sanction Odysseus urges, and it is one whose irony it would be difficult for his audience to miss. The irony lies in the fact that an argument normally used to deny mercy to others is here being used to obtain it. When it fails before the Cyclops' massive egoism, Odysseus resorts to the ultimate argument of the weak, law and civilized custom (*nomos*). In so doing he joins Thucydides' Plataeans and Melians, as well as his own victim Hecuba. And, like Hecuba, failing to receive *nomos*, he finally resorts to a revenge utterly unsanctioned by any civilized standards, *anomos*. The speech closes on an overt reference to the cost of human suffering in the Peloponnesian War. And here, as so often in Euripides, the really serious argument is put in the mouth of a man who is not qualified to make it, or who contradicts it in his actions. The contradiction lies in the inverted use of the imperialistic sanction and the implied indifference to human suffering in other circumstances.

If Odysseus speaks in part the language of the Athenian im-

6. Thuc. i. 73. 2 ff.
7. *Ibid.* v. 89.

perialists and in part the language of the Melians, the Cyclops out-distances him by far. Devoid of respect for the gods, his religion is his belly and his right his desires. He speaks exactly the language of Plato's Thrasymachus and Callicles, a straightforward egoism rest-ing on an appeal to Nature for the disregard of morality. *Nomos*, so far as he is concerned, is a mere convention of the weak to elude the strong. In the contrast, then, of Polyphemus and Odysseus we have no Homeric contrast of barbarism and cool, civilized intelligence, but a juxtaposition of two related types of civilized brutality whose difference is merely that of circumstance, one being weak, the other strong. It is because neither Cyclops nor Odysseus has any genuine moral dignity, because both of them are shown as effectively brutal and corrupt, that the bloody blinding of Polyphemus can come as close to pathos as it does without becoming any less comic.

The ending is in fact superbly controlled. As usual in Euripides, the sympathy invoked for one character is suddenly alienated and shifted to another; the victim and the oppressor change places. Polyphemus, from being first a Homeric cannibal and then a Euripidean Callicles, is suddenly turned into a decadent, rather lik-able buffoon who loathes war, understands generosity, and tipsily "rapes" Silenus. Odysseus makes his bid for glory by blinding this cannibal oaf while he sleeps drunkenly. The shift in sympathy is not decisive, because no real principle is involved; but it is not therefore illusory. Odysseus' action is contemptible, but not quite criminal; Polyphemus gets what he deserves, but we pity him. That we are meant to view the action in this way seems clear both in Poly-phemus' final prophecy of trouble for Odysseus and in Odysseus' statement that he would have done wrong had he burned Troy but not avenged his men. Whatever his rights in avenging his men may be, they are not sanctioned by the burning of Troy, an action which the Cyclops condemns, and with him Euripides. The truth is that Odysseus and the Cyclops deserve, not justice, but each other. The *Cyclops* in its seriousness and its humor plays about a struggle for justice between two men who either distort justice or deny its existence and who cannot therefore meaningfully claim it when wronged. And yet they get it.

THE CYCLOPS

CHARACTERS

Silenus

Chorus of satyrs

Coryphaeus, or chorus-leader

Odysseus

Cyclops, called Polyphemus

Members of Odysseus' crew

Slaves

THE CYCLOPS

SCENE: *An enormous cave at the foot of Mt. Etna. In the foreground, a slope of pasture; on the right, a small brook. Silenus comes out of the cave to speak the prologue. He is old, fat, and bald. A horse's tail hangs down his legs. He wears a filthy tunic and carries a rake.*

Silenus

O Bromios,
thanks to you, my troubles are as many now
as in my youth when my body still was strong!
First I remember when Hera drove you mad
and you left your nurses, the mountain nymphs.
And then there was that war with the Giants: 5
there I stood, on your right, covering your flank
with my spear. And I hit Enceladus
square on the button of his shield and killed him.
Or wait: was that in a dream? No, by Zeus,
for I showed the very spoils to Bacchus.
And now I must bail against a wilder wave   10
of trouble. For when I heard that Hera
had pricked on those Lydian pirates to sell you
as a slave abroad, I hoisted sail with my sons
to search for you. Right on the stern I stood,
the tiller in my hands, steering the ship.   15
And my boys strained at the oars, churning white
the green sea in our search for you, my king!
And then we had almost made Malea
when an east wind cracked down and drove us here,
to rocky Etna, where the one-eyed sons   20
of the sea-god, the murderous Cyclopes,
live in their desolate caves. One of them—
they call him Polyphemus—captured us
and made us slaves in his house. So now,
instead of dancing in the feasts of Bacchus,   25

we herd the flocks of this godless Cyclops.
Down at the foot of the mountain, my sons—
young men all of them—watch the youngling herd.
I am assigned to stay and fill the troughs
and clean the quarters and play the chef 30
for the loathsome dinners of the Cyclops.
And now I must scour the cave with this rake—
these are my orders—to welcome back home
my absent master and his flock of sheep. 35

> (*He halts suddenly, turns to the left and looks. A confused*
> *hubbub, mingled with singing, offstage.*)

But I see my sons shepherding their sheep
this way. What? (*Shouts.*) How can you dance like that?
Do you think you're mustered at Bacchus' feast
and mincing your lewd way with lyre-music
to the halls of Althaea? 40

> (*Preceded by a flute-player and driving their herds before them, the*
> *chorus of satyrs bounds into the orchestra. Except for short goat-*
> *skin jerkins, they are naked. About their waists they wear belts—*
> *skin-colored—to each of which is fixed, in front, a phallus, and in*
> *the rear, a horse's tail. They do a series of fast and intricate steps*
> *as they push the stubborn rams, coax the ewes,*
> *and round up the strays.*)

Chorus

> (*To a ewe who dashes for the slope.*)

STROPHE

You there, with the fine pedigree
on both sides, dam and sire,
  why run for the rocks?
Haven't you here a quiet breeze,
  green grass for the grazing?
Look: the water from the brook 45
  beside the cave
  swirls through your troughs
  and the small lambs bleat.

(To an obstinate ram.)

Hey, you too? Are you off as well
to crop on the dew on the hill?   50
Move, or I'll pelt you with stones!
In with you, horny-head, move along
into the fold of Shepherd Cyclops!

(To a stubborn ewe.)

ANTISTROPHE

Relieve your swollen teats!   55
Come, suckle your young whom you left
    all alone in the lamb-pens!
Asleep all day, your new-born lambs
    bleat that they want you.
Leave your cropping and into the fold,   60
    into the rocks of Etna!

[Hey, you too? Are you off as well
to crop on the dew on the hill?
Move, or I'll pelt you with stones!
In with you, horny-head, move along
into the fold of Shepherd Cyclops!]

EPODE

No Bacchus here! Not here the dance,
or the women whirling the *thyrsos*,
or the timbrels shaken,   65
where the springs rill up!
Not here the gleam of wine,
and no more at Nysa with nymphs,
crying *Iacchos! Iacchos!*
Where is Aphrodite? . . .   70
she that I used to fly after
along with the bare-footed Bacchae!
Dear lord Bacchus, where do you run,
tossing your auburn hair?   75
For I, your servant, am a wretched slave,
tricked out in dirty goatskin   80

to serve a one-eyed Cyclops,
and out of the way, lord, of your love.

> (*Silenus, who has been scanning anxiously the horizon on the
> right, turns suddenly, his finger on his lips.*)

Silenus

Be quiet, my sons. Quick, order the slaves
to corral the flocks into the rock-fold.

Coryphaeus

Move along there.

> (*Slaves appear and hustle the animals into the cave.*)

But why this hurry, father?

Silenus

I see a Greek ship drawn up on the shore   85
and oarsman led by a captain coming
toward our cave. They carry water-pitchers
and empty containers about their necks:
they'll want supplies. Poor strangers, who are they?
They can't know our master Polyphemus,   90
coming like this to the maneater's cave
and looking for a welcome in his maw.
But hush, so we can learn from where they've come,
and why, to Sicily and Mt. Etna.   95

> (*Odysseus appears on the right. He carries a sword. A wine-flask
> made of skin is suspended from his neck; a cup is attached to the
> cord. He is followed by crew-members carrying pitchers and jugs.*)

Odysseus

Strangers, could you tell us where we might find
running water? We have nothing to drink.
Would some one of you like to sell some food
to hungry sailors? *What?* Do I see right?
We must have come to the city of Bacchus.
These are satyrs I see around the cave.   100
Let me greet the oldest among you first.

Silenus

 Greeting, stranger. Who are you, and from where?

Odysseus

 I am Odysseus of Ithaca, king of the Cephallenians.

Silenus

 I've heard of you: a glib sharper, Sisyphus' bastard.

Odysseus

 I am he. Keep your abuse to yourself.   105

Silenus

 From what port did you set sail for Sicily?

Odysseus

 We come from Troy and from the war there.

Silenus

 What? Couldn't you chart your passage home?

Odysseus

 We were driven here by wind and storm.

Silenus

 Too bad. I had the same misfortune.   110

Odysseus

 You too were driven from your course by storm?

Silenus

 We were chasing the pirates who captured Bacchus.

Odysseus

 What is this place? Is it inhabited?

Silenus

 This is Etna, the highest peak in Sicily.

Odysseus

 Where are the walls and the city-towers?   115

Silenus

 This is no city. No man inhabits here.

Odysseus
  Who does inhabit it? Wild animals?

Silenus
  The Cyclopes. They live in caves, not houses.

Odysseus
  Who governs them? Or do the people rule?

Silenus
  They are savages. There is no government.   120

Odysseus
  How do they live? Do they till the fields?

Silenus
  Their whole diet is milk, cheese, and meat.

Odysseus
  Do they grow grapes and make the vine give wine?

Silenus
  No. The land is sullen. There is no dance.

Odysseus
  Are they hospitable to strangers here?   125

Silenus
  Strangers, they say, make excellent eating.

Odysseus
  What? You say they feast on human flesh?

Silenus
  Here every visitor is devoured.

Odysseus
  Where is this Cyclops now? In the . . . house?

Silenus
  Gone hunting on Mt. Etna with his packs.   130

Odysseus
  What should we do to make our escape?

Silenus
  I don't know, Odysseus. We'll do what we can.

Odysseus

Then sell us some bread. We have none left.

Silenus

There is nothing to eat, I said, except meat.

Odysseus

Meat is good, and it will stop our hunger.   135

Silenus

We do have fig-cheese. And there is milk.

Odysseus

Bring it out. The buyer should see what he buys.

Silenus

Tell me, how much are you willing to pay?

Odysseus

In money, nothing. But I have some . . . wine.

Silenus

Delicious word! How long since I've heard it.   140

Odysseus

Maron, son of a god, gave me this wine.

Silenus

Not the same lad I once reared in these arms?

Odysseus

The son of Bacchus himself, to be brief.

Silenus

Where is the wine? on board ship? you have it?

Odysseus

In this flask, old man. Look for yourself.   145

Silenus

That? That wouldn't make one swallow for me.

Odysseus

No? For each swallow you take, the flask gives two.

Silenus

A fountain among fountains, that! I *like* it.

Odysseus

Will you have it unwatered to start with?

Silenus

That's fair. The buyer should have a sample.   150

Odysseus

I have a cup here to go with the flask.

Silenus

Pour away. A drink will joggle my memory.

Odysseus

                    (*Unstoppers the flask, pours out a cup and
                    waves it under Silenus' nose.*)

There you are.

Silenus

            Mmmmmm. Gods, what a bouquet!

Odysseus

Can you *see* it?

Silenus

            No, by Zeus, but I can whiff it.

Odysseus

Have another. Then you'll *sing* its praises.   155

Silenus

Mmmmmmaa. A dance for Bacchus! La de da.

Odysseus

Did that purl down your gullet sweetly?

Silenus

Right down to the tips of my toenails.

Odysseus

Besides the wine, we'll give you money.   160

Silenus

Money be damned! Just pour out the wine.

Odysseus

Then bring out your cheese, or some lambs.

Silenus
                        Right away.
I don't give a hoot for any master.
I would go mad for one cup of that wine!
I'd give away the herds of all the Cyclopes.   165
Once I get drunk and happy, I'd go jump
in the sea off the Leucadian rock!
The man who doesn't like to drink is mad.
Why, when you're drunk, you stand up stiff down here

                        (Gestures.)

and then get yourself a fistful of breast   170
and browse on the soft field ready to your hands.
You dance, and goodbye to troubles. Well then,
why shouldn't I adore a drink like that
and be damned to the stupid Cyclops
with his eye in the middle?
                        (He enters the cave.)

Coryphaeus
Listen, Odysseus, we'd like a word with you.   175

Odysseus
By all means. We are all friends here.

Coryphaeus
Did you take Helen when you took Troy?

Odysseus
We rooted out the whole race of Priam.

Coryphaeus
When you took that woman, did you all take turns
and bang her? She liked variety in men,   180
the fickle bitch! Why, the sight of a man
with embroidered pants and a golden chain
so fluttered her, she left Menelaus,
a fine little man. I wish there were   185
no women in the world—except for me.

        *(Silenus reappears from the cave, his arms loaded with wicker
                panniers of cheese; he leads some lambs.)*

Silenus

    King Odysseus, here are some lambs for you,
    the fat of the flock, and here, a good stock
    of creamed cheeses. Take them and leave the cave   190
    as fast as you can. But first give me a drink
    of that blessed wine to seal our bargain.
    Help us! Here comes the Cyclops! What shall we do?

Odysseus

    We're finished now, old man. Where can we run?

Silenus

    Into the cave. You can hide in there.   195

Odysseus

    Are you mad? Run right into the trap?

Silenus

    No danger. The rocks are full of hiding-places.

Odysseus

                                  (*Grandiloquently.*)

    Never. Why, Troy itself would groan aloud
    if we ran from one man. Many's the time
    I stood off ten thousand Phrygians with my shield.   200
    If die we must, we must die with honor.
    If we live, we live with our old glory!

      (*The satyrs run pell-mell around the orchestra; Silenus slinks into*
            the cave. On the left appears a bearded man of great
                height. He holds a club and is followed by dogs.)

Cyclops

    Here. Here. What's going on? What's this uproar?
    Why this Bacchic hubbub? There's no Bacchus here,
    no bronze clackers or rattling castanets!   205
    How are my newborn lambs in the cave?
    Are they at the teat, nuzzling their mothers?
    Are the wicker presses filled with fresh cheese?
    Well? What do you say? Answer, or my club   210
    will drub the tears out of you! Look up, not down.

Coryphaeus
There. We're looking right up at Zeus himself.
I can see Orion and all the stars.

Cyclops
Is my dinner cooked and ready to eat?

Coryphaeus
Ready and waiting. You have only to bolt it.   215

Cyclops
And are the vats filled up, brimming with milk?

Coryphaeus
You can swill a whole hogshead, if you like.

Cyclops
Cow's milk, or sheep's milk, or mixed?

Coryphaeus
Whatever you like. Just don't swallow me.

Cyclops
You least. I'd soon be dead if I had you   220
jumping through your capers in my belly.
          (*He suddenly sees the Greeks standing near the cave.*)
Hey! what's that crowd I see over by the cave?
Have pirates or thieves taken the country?
Look: sheep from my fold tied up with withies!   225
And cheese-presses all around! And the old man
with his bald head swollen red with bruises!
          (*Silenus emerges from the cave, groaning; he is red-faced
                                        from the wine.*)

Silenus
Ohhh. I'm all on fire. They've beaten me up.

Cyclops
Who did? Who's been beating your head, old man?

Silenus
                              (*Indicating the Greeks.*)
They did, Cyclops. I wouldn't let them rob you.   230

Cyclops

Didn't they know that I am a god?
Didn't they know my ancestors were gods?

Silenus

I tried to tell them. But they went on robbing.
I tried to stop them from stealing your lambs
and eating your cheeses. What's more, they said
they would yoke you to a three-foot collar   235
and squeeze out your bowels through your one eye,
and scourge your backsides with a whip,
and then they were going to tie you up
and throw you on a ship and give you away
for lifting rocks or for work at a mill.   240

Cyclops

Is that so? Run and sharpen my cleavers.
Take a big bunch of faggots and light it.
I'll murder them right now and stuff my maw
with their meat hot from the coals. Why wait   245
to carve? I'm fed up with mountain food:
too many lions and stags and too long
since I've had a good meal of manmeat.

Silenus

And quite right, master. A change in diet   250
is very pleasant. It's been a long time
since we've had visitors here at the cave.

Odysseus

Cyclops, let your visitors have their say.
We came here to your cave from our ship
because we needed food. This fellow here   255
sold us some lambs in exchange for wine—
all quite voluntary, no coercion.
There's not a healthy word in what he says;
the fact is he was caught peddling your goods.   260

Silenus

I? Why, damn your soul.

Odysseus

If I'm lying. . . .

Silenus

I swear, Cyclops, by your father Poseidon,
by Triton the great, I swear by Nereus,
by Calypso and by Nereus' daughters,
by the holy waves and every species of fish,   265
I swear, dear master, sweet little Cyclops,
I did not sell your goods to the strangers!
If I did, then let my dear children die for it.

Coryphaeus

And the same to you. With these very eyes
I saw you selling goods to the strangers.   270
And if I'm lying, then let my father
die for it. But don't do wrong to strangers.

Cyclops

You're lying. I would rather believe him

                            (*He indicates Silenus.*)

than Rhadamanthus himself. And I say
that he's right. But I want to question you.
Where have you come from, strangers? where to?   275
And tell me in what city you grew up.

Odysseus

We are from Ithaca. After we sacked
the city of Troy, sea-winds drove us here,
safe and sound, to your country, Cyclops.

Cyclops

Was it you who sacked Troy-on-Scamander   280
because that foul Helen was carried off?

Odysseus

We did. Our terrible task is done.

Cyclops

You ought to die for shame: to go to war
with the Phrygians for a single woman!

Odysseus

A god was responsible; don't blame men.   285
But we ask as free men, we implore you,
do not, O noble son of the sea-god,
murder men who come to your cave as friends.
Do not profane your mouth by eating us.

(*He waxes rhetorical.*)

For it is we, my lord, who everywhere
in Hellas preserved your father Poseidon   290
in the tenure of his temples. Thanks to us,
Taenarus' sacred harbor is inviolate;
the peak of Sunium with its silver-lodes
sacred to Athena, is still untouched;
and safe, the sanctuaries of Geraestus!   295
We did not betray Greece—perish the thought!—
to Phrygians. And you have a share in this:
for this whole land, under volcanic Etna
in whose depths you live, is part of Hellas.

(*The Cyclops shows disapproval.*)

In any case—and if you disagree—
all men honor that custom whereby   300
shipwrecked sailors are clothed and protected.
Above all, they should not gorge your mouth and paunch,
nor be spitted as men might spit an ox.
The land of Priam has exhausted Greece,
soaked up the blood of thousands killed in war: 305
wives made widows, women without their sons,
old men turned snow-white. If you roast the rest
for your ungodly meal, where will Hellas turn?
Change your mind, Cyclops! Forget your hunger!   310
Forget this sacrilege and do what is right.
Many have paid the price for base profits.

Silenus

A word of advice, Cyclops. If you eat
all of his flesh and chew on his tongue,
you'll become eloquent and very glib.   315

Cyclops
　　Money's the wise man's religion, little man.
　　The rest is mere bluff and purple patches.
　　I don't give a damn for my father's shrines
　　along the coast! Why did you think I would?
　　And I'm not afraid of Zeus's thunder;　　　　　　　320
　　in fact, I don't believe Zeus is stronger
　　than I am. And anyway I don't care,
　　and I'll tell you why I don't care. When Zeus
　　pours down rain, I take shelter in this cave
　　and feast myself on roast lamb or venison.　　　　　325
　　Then I stretch myself and wash down the meal,
　　flooding my belly with a vat of milk.
　　Then, louder than ever Zeus can thunder,
　　I fart through the blankets. When the wind sweeps down
　　with snow from Thrace, I wrap myself in furs　　　　330
　　and light up the fire. Then let it snow
　　for all I care! Whether it wants or not,
　　the earth must grow the grass that feeds my flocks.
　　And as for sacrifices, I make mine,
　　not to the gods, but the greatest god of all,　　　　335
　　this belly of mine! To eat, to drink
　　from day to day, to have no worries—
　　that's the real Zeus for your clever man!
　　As for those who embroider human life
　　with their little laws—damn the lot of them!　　　　340
　　I shall go right on indulging myself—
　　by eating you. But, to be in the clear,
　　I'll be hospitable and give you fire
　　and my father's water—plus a cauldron.
　　Once it starts to boil, it will render down　　　　　345
　　your flesh very nicely. So, inside with you,
　　and gather round the altar to the god
　　of the cave, and wish him hearty eating.
　　　　　(*Cyclops enters the cave, driving Odysseus' crew before him.*)

Odysseus

    Gods! Have I escaped our hardships at Troy
    and on the seas only to be cast up
    and wrecked on the reef of this savage heart?
    O Pallas, lady, daughter of Zeus, now   350
    if ever, help me! Worse than war at Troy,
    I have come to my danger's deepest place.
    O Zeus, god of strangers, look down on me
    from where you sit, throned among the bright stars!
    If you do not look down upon me now,
    you are no Zeus, but a nothing at all!   355

              (He disappears into the cave; Silenus follows him.)

Chorus

    Open the vast O of your jaws, Cyclops!
    Dinner is served: the limbs of your guests,
    boiled, roasted, or broiled, ready for you
       to gnaw, rend, and chew
    while you loll on your shaggy goatskin.   360

    Don't ask me to dinner. Stow that cargo
    on your own. Let me keep clear of this cave,
    well clear of the Cyclops of Etna,
       this loathsome glutton,   365
    who gorges himself on the guts of his guests!

    Savage! Stranger to mercy! A monster
    who butchers his guests on his hearth,
    who boils up their flesh and bolts it,   370
       whose foul mouth munches
    on human meat plucked from the sizzling coals!

                (Odysseus appears from the cave.)

Odysseus

    Zeus, how can I say what I saw in that cave?   375
    Unbelievable horrors, the kind of things
    men do in myths and plays, not in real life!

Coryphaeus
  Has that god-forsaken Cyclops butchered
  your crew? Tell us what happened, Odysseus.

Odysseus
  He snatched up two of my men, the soundest
  and heaviest. He weighed them in his hands.   380

Coryphaeus
  How horrible! How could you stand to watch?

Odysseus
  First, after we had entered the cave,
  he lit a fire and tossed down on the huge hearth
  logs from a vast oak—you would have needed
  three wagons merely to carry the load.   385
  Then he pulled his pallet of pine-needles
  close to the fire. After he milked the sheep,
  he filled a hundred-gallon vat with milk.
  By his side, he put an ivy-wood box,
  nearly four feet in width and six feet deep.   390
  Next he put a cauldron of brass to boil
  on the fire, and beside it thorn-wood spits
  whose points had been sharpened in the coals
  and the rest trimmed down with an axe. There were
  bowls for catching blood, big as Etna,
  and set flush against the blade of the axe.   395
  Well, when this damned cook of Hades was ready,
  he snatched up two of my men. With one blow
  he slit the throat of one over the lip
  of the brass cauldron. Holding the other
  by the heels, he slammed him against a rock   400
  and bashed out his brains. Then he hacked away
  the flesh with his terrible cleaver
  and put the pieces to roast on the coals.
  The leftovers he tossed in the pot to boil.
  With the tears streaming down, I went up close   405
  and waited on the Cyclops. The others,

their faces ashen, huddled up like birds
in the crannies of the rocks. Then he leaned back,
bloated with his awful meal on my men,
and let out a staggering belch. Just then   410
some god sent me a marvelous idea!
I filled a cup and gave him Maron's wine
to drink. "Cyclops," I said, "son of the sea-god,
see what a heavenly drink yield the grapes
of Greece, the gladness of Dionysus!"   415
Glutted with his dreadful meal, he took it
and drained it off at one gulp, then lifted
his hands in thanks: "You are the best of guests!
You have given me a noble drink to crown
a noble meal." When I saw how pleased he was,   420
I poured him another, knowing the wine
would quickly fuddle him and pay him back.
Then he started to sing. I poured one drink
after another and warmed his belly.
So there he is, inside, singing away   425
while my crew wails; you can hear the uproar.
I slipped quietly out. Now, if you agree,
I'd like to save myself and you as well.
So tell me, yes or no, whether you want
to escape this monster and live with the nymphs   430
in the halls of Bacchus. Your father in there
agrees, but he's weak and loves his liquor.
He's stuck to the cup as though it were glue,
and can't fly. But you are young, so follow me
and save yourselves; find again your old friend,   435
Dionysus, so different from this Cyclops!

Coryphaeus
My good friend, if only we might see that day
when we escape at last this godless Cyclops!

                                    (*Showing his phallus.*)
This poor hose has been a bachelor
a long time now. But we can't eat the Cyclops *back!*   440

Odysseus

  Listen to my plan for setting you free
  and our revenge upon this loathsome beast.

Coryphaeus

  Tell on. I would rather hear tell of his death
  than hear all the harps in Asia play.

Odysseus

  He is so delighted with Bacchus' drink   445
  he wants to carouse with his relatives.

Coryphaeus

  I see. You'll set an ambush in the woods
  and kill him—or push him over a cliff.

Odysseus

  No, I had something more subtle in mind.

Coryphaeus

  I thought from the first you were sly. What then?   450

Odysseus

  I hope to stop his going on this spree
  by saying he shouldn't give his wine away,
  but keep it for himself and live in bliss.
  Then, as soon as the wine puts him to sleep,
  I'll take my sword and sharpen up the trunk   455
  of an olive tree I saw inside the cave.
  I'll put it in the coals and when it's caught,
  I'll shove it home, dead in the Cyclops' eye,
  and blind him. Just like a timber-fitter
  whirling his auger around with a belt,   460
  I'll screw the brand in his eye, round and round,
  scorch out his eyeball and blind him for good.

Coryphaeus

  Bravo! I'm for your plan with all my heart.   465

Odysseus

And finally, my friends, I'll embark you
and your old father aboard my black ship
and sail full speed away from this place.

Coryphaeus

May I lend a hand at this ritual?
Help hold the pole when you put out his eye?   470
This is one sacrifice I want to share.

Odysseus

You must. The brand is huge. You all must lift.

Coryphaeus

I could shoulder a hundred wagon-loads
so long as Cyclops died a wretched death!
We'll smoke out his eye like a hornets' nest.   475

Odysseus

Be quiet now. You know my stratagem.
When I give the word, obey your leaders.
I refuse to save myself and leave my men
trapped inside. I could, of course, escape:
here I am, outside. But I have no right   480
to abandon my crew and save myself alone.

> (*He enters the cave.*)

Chorus

Who'll be first along the brand? Who next?
We'll shove it square in the Cyclops' eye!
We'll rip away his sight.   485
> Quiet.
> Shhhh.

> (*Polyphemus appears from the cave flanked by Odysseus and
> Silenus. Odysseus carries the flask and cup, while Silenus
> holds a pitcher and a mixing-bowl.*)

Here he comes, flat, off-key drunkard,
reeling out of his home in the rock,   490

braying some wretched tune. Ha!
We'll give him lessons in carousing!

(*Polyphemus stumbles blindly about.*)

A little while: then, perfect blindness!

First semichorus

Happy the man who cries *Evohé!* 495
stretched out full length and making merry,
for whom the wine keeps flowing,
whose arms are open to his friend!
Lucky man, upon whose bed there blows
the soft bloom of a lovely girl 500
with gleaming hair, sweet with oil!
who cries: "Who'll open me the door?"

Cyclops

Mamama. Am I crammed with wine!
How I love the fun of a feast!
The hold of my little dory 505
is stuffed right up to the gunwales!
This marvelous meal reminds me:
I should go feast in the soft spring
with my brothers, the Cyclopes.
Here, here, my friend, hand me the flask. 510

Second semichorus

O the flash of a handsome Eye!
Handsome himself comes from his house,
Handsome the groom, Handsome the lover!
A soft bride burns for this groom; 515
she burns in the cool of the cave!
And soon we shall wreathe his head
with a wreath of reddest flowers!

Odysseus

Listen, Cyclops. I've spent a lot of time
with this drink of Bacchus I gave you. 520

Cyclops
 What sort of god is this Bacchus held to be?

Odysseus
 Best of all in blessing the lives of men.

Cyclops

(*Belching.*)

 At least he makes very tasty belching.

Odysseus
 That's the kind of god he is: hurts no one.

Cyclops
 How can a god bear to live in a flask?   525

Odysseus
 Wherever you put him, he's quite content.

Cyclops
 Gods shouldn't shut themselves up in wine-skins.

Odysseus
 What matter, if you like him? Does the flask irk you?

Cyclops
 I loathe the flask. The wine is what I like.

Odysseus
 Then you should stay here and enjoy yourself.   530

Cyclops
 Shouldn't I share the wine with my brothers?

Odysseus
 Keep it to yourself; you'll be more esteemed.

Cyclops
 But I'd be more useful if I shared it.

Odysseus
 Yes, but carousing often ends in fights.

Cyclops
 I'm so drunk nothing could hurt me now.   535

Odysseus
My dear man, drunkards ought to stay at home.

Cyclops
But the man's a fool who drinks by himself.

Odysseus
It's the wise man who stays home when he's drunk.

Cyclops
What should we do, Silenus? Should I stay home?

Silenus
I would. Why do we want more drinkers, Cyclops?   540

Cyclops
                                        (*Yawning.*)
Anyway, the ground is soft and the flowers. . . .

Silenus
There's nothing like a drink when the sun is hot.
Lie down there; stretch yourself out on the ground.
            (*Cyclops obediently lies down, and furtively Silenus
                        puts the bowl behind his back.*)

Cyclops
There. Why did you put the bowl behind my back?   545

Silenus
Someone might tip it over.

Cyclops
                    You wanted
to steal a drink. Put it in the middle.
You there, stranger, tell me what your name is.

Odysseus
"Nobody" is my name. But how will you reward me?

Cyclops
I will eat you the last of all your crew.   550

Silenus
That's a fine gift to give your guest, Cyclops.
                            (*He quickly drains cup.*)

Cyclops

    What are you doing? Drinking on the sly?

Silenus

    The wine kissed me—for my beautiful eyes.

Cyclops

    Watch out. You love the wine; it doesn't love you.

Silenus

    Yes, by Zeus, it has a passion for my good looks.   555

Cyclops

    Here, pour me a cupful. But just *pour* it.

Silenus

    How is it mixed? Let me taste and see.

                            (He takes a quick pull.)

Cyclops

    Damnation! give it here.

Silenus

                  By Zeus, not before

    I see you crowned—

                (He offers Cyclops a wreath of flowers.)

    and have another drink.

                          (He empties the cup.)

Cyclops

    This wine-pourer is a cheat!   560

Silenus

                  Not at all.

    The wine's so good it slides down by itself.

    Now wipe yourself off before you drink again.

Cyclops

                  (Wiping his face and beard.)

    There. My mouth is clean and so is my beard.

Silenus

    Then crook your arm—gracefully now—and drink,

    just as you see me drink—and now you don't.

                            (He drains cup.)

Cyclops
    Here! What are you doing?   565

Silenus
                        Guzzling sweetly.

Cyclops
                (Snatching away the cup and handing it to Odysseus.)
    Here, stranger. Take the flask and pour for me.

Odysseus
    At least the wine feels at home in my hand.

Cyclops
    Come on, *pour!*

Odysseus
                    I *am* pouring. Just be still.

Cyclops
    That's not so easy when you're in your cups.

Odysseus
    There, take it up and drink down every drop,   570
    and don't say die until the wine is gone.

Cyclops
    Mama. What a wizard the vine must be!

Odysseus
    If you drench yourself on a full stomach
    and swill your belly full, you'll sleep deep.
    If you leave any, Bacchus will shrivel you up.   575

Cyclops
                                        (Reeling.)

    Whoosh! I can scarcely swim out of this flood.
    Pure pleasure! Ohhh. Earth and sky going round,
    all mixed up together! Look: I can see
    'the throne of Zeus and the holy glory   580
    of the gods.
                    (The satyrs dance around him suggestively.)
            No, I couldn't make love to you!
    The Graces tempt me! My Ganymede here
                            (He grabs Silenus.)

is good enough for me. With him I'll sleep
magnificently. By these Graces, I will!
And anyway, I prefer boys to girls.

Silenus

Am I Zeus' little Ganymede, Cyclops?   585

Cyclops

You are, by Zeus! The boy I stole from Dardanos!

Silenus

I'm done for, children. Foul things await me.

Cyclops

Sneer at your lover, do you, because he's drunk?

Silenus

It's a bitter wine I'll have to drink now.

(*Cyclops drags off Silenus protesting into the cave.*)

Odysseus

To work, you noble sons of Dionysus!   590
Our man's inside the cave. In a short while
his belly will heave its foul meal of flesh.
Look, the brand has begun to smoke inside.
We prepared it for just this: to smoke out
the Cyclops' eye. Now you must act like men.   595

Coryphaeus

Our will is made of unbreakable rock.
But hurry inside before *that* happens
to my father. All is ready out here.

Odysseus

(*Prays.*)

O Hephaestus, ruler over Etna,
free yourself from this vile neighbor of yours!
Sear out his bright eye at one blow! O Sleep,   600
child of black Night, leap with all your might
on this god-detested beast! And do not,
after our glorious trials at Troy,

betray Odysseus and his crew to death
from a man who cares for neither man nor god.   605
If you do, we will make a goddess of Chance,
and count her higher than all the other gods!

                  (*He disappears into the cave.*)

Chorus

Grim tongs shall clutch by the throat
this beast who bolts down his guests.
Fire shall quench the fire of his eye.   610
The brand, big as a tree, already waits,
waits in the coals.   615

            On, wine, to your work!
Rip out the eye of this raving Cyclops!
Make him regret the day he drank you!
What I want with all my soul to see
is Bacchus, the god who loves the ivy!   620
Shall I ever see that day?

              (*Odysseus reappears from the cave.*)

Odysseus

Quiet, you dogs! By the gods, be quiet!
Hold your tongues. I don't want a man of you
to wink or clear his throat or even breathe.   625
If we wake up that scourge of evil,
we won't be able to sear out his eye.

        (*The satyrs freeze into silence. The following dialogue*
                is conducted entirely in whispers.)

Coryphaeus

We *are* quiet. Our mouths are locked up tight.

Odysseus

To work then. And grab the brand with both hands   630
when you enter the cave. The point is red-hot.

Coryphaeus

You should tell us our stations. Who'll be first
on the blazing pole? And then we can all
take our part in searing out the Cyclops' eye.

First parastate

Where we stand, over here by the entrance,
we're too far away to reach his eye.   635

Second parastate

(*Limping in pain.*)

And just this minute we've gone lame.

First parastate

And we have too. While we were standing here
we sprained our ankles, I don't know how.

Odysseus

Sprained your ankles, standing still?   640

Second parastate

And my eyes
are full of dust and ashes from somewhere.

Odysseus

What cowards! I won't get any help from you.

Coryphaeus

And because I feel for my back and spine
and don't want to have my teeth knocked out,
I'm a coward, am I? But I can say   645
a fine Orphic spell that will make the brand
fly of its own accord into the skull
of this one-eyed whelp of Earth and scorch him up.

Odysseus

I knew from that first what sort you were,
and now I know it better. If you're too weak   650
to lend a hand, at least cheer on my men
and put some heart in them by shouting.

(*He enters the cave.*)

Coryphaeus

We'll shout and this "Nobody" will run the risks.
We'll fuddle the Cyclops with our shouting.   655

Chorus

> *(Dancing excitedly, shouting at the top of its lungs, and*
> *imitating the action taking place in the cave.)*

Go! Go! As hard as you can!
Push! Thrust! Faster! Burn off
the lashes of the guest-eater!
Smoke him out, burn him out,
the shepherd of Etna! 660
Twist it! Turn! Careful:
he is hurt and desperate.

> *(A great shriek from within the cave.)*

Cyclops

Owwooooo! My eye is scorched to ashes! 665

Coryphaeus

Oh song of songs! Sing it for me, Cyclops!

Cyclops

Owwoo! They've murdered me! I'm finished!
But you won't escape this cave to enjoy
your triumph, you contemptible nothings.
I'll stand at the entrance and block it—so.

> *(Polyphemus appears at the threshold of the cave and stretches*
> *his arms across it; his face streams with blood.)*

Coryphaeus

What's the matter, Cyclops?

Cyclops

　　　　　　　　I'm dying.

Coryphaeus

You look terrible.

Cyclops

　　　　　　　　I feel terrible. 670

Coryphaeus

Were you so drunk you fell in the fire?

Cyclops

"Nobody" wounded me.

Coryphaeus

Then you're not hurt.

Cyclops
  "Nobody" blinded me.

Coryphaeus

Then you're not blind.

Cyclops
  Blind as you.

Coryphaeus

How could nobody make you blind?

Cyclops
  You mock me. Where is "Nobody"?   675

Coryphaeus

Nowhere.

Cyclops
  It's the stranger I mean, you fool, the one
  who stuffed me full of wine and did me in.

Coryphaeus

(Sententiously.)

  Wine is tricky; very hard to wrestle with.

Cyclops
  By the gods, has he escaped or is he inside?

Coryphaeus
  There they are, standing quiet over there,   680
  under cover of the rock.

Cyclops

On which side?

Coryphaeus
  On your right.

  *(Cyclops leaves the entrance and stumbles with outstretched
              hands toward the right. Meanwhile the Greeks
                          steal out of the cave.)*

Cyclops

Where?

Coryphaeus
>   Over against the rock.

Do you have them?

Cyclops
>   (*Running into a jutting rock.*)
>   Ouf! Trouble on trouble.

I've split my head.

Coryphaeus
>   And now they've escaped you.

Cyclops
  This way, did you say?

Coryphaeus
>   No, the other way.

Cyclops
  Which way?

Coryphaeus
>   Turn around. There. On your left.   685

Cyclops
  You're laughing at me in my misery.

Coryphaeus
  Not now. There he is in front of you.

Cyclops
  Where are you, demon?
>   (*The Greeks stand at the entrance on the right, a whole
>   length of the stage away from Cyclops.*)

Odysseus
>   Out of your reach,

  Looking after the safety of Odysseus.   690

Cyclops
  What? A new name? Have you changed your name?

Odysseus
  Odysseus: the name my father gave me.
  You have had to pay for your unholy meal.

I would have done wrong to have fired Troy
but not revenge the murder of my men.   695

Cyclops

Ah! The old oracle has been fulfilled.
It said that after you had come from Troy,
you would blind me. But you would pay for this,
it said, and wander the seas for many years.   700

Odysseus

Much I care! What's done is done. As for me,
I'm off to the shore where I'll launch my ship
on the Sicilian shore and sail for home.

(Exit.)

Cyclops

Not yet. I'll rip a boulder from this cliff
and crush you and all your crew beneath it.   705
Blind I may be, but I'll reach the mountain-top
soon enough through the tunnel in the cave.

(Exits into cave.)

Chorus

We'll enlist in the crew of Odysseus.
From now our orders come from Bacchus.

HERACLES

Translated and with an Introduction by

WILLIAM ARROWSMITH

INTRODUCTION TO *HERACLES*

THE *Heracles* of Euripides is seldom assigned a high place in the corpus of extant tragedy. If no one any longer quite accepts Swinburne's description of the play as a "grotesque abortion," the reason is less real disagreement than a habit of respect for the author, supported by a cautious intuition of the play's extraordinary power. Of caution there should be no question. However dislocated in structure the *Heracles* may be, its dramatic power and technical virtuosity are unmistakable. With the possible exception of the *Bacchae*, there is no play into which Euripides has put more of himself and his mature poetic skills than this one. In scene after scene one senses that sureness of movement and precise control of passion which come only with the dramatist's full mastery of his medium. One thinks first of the staggering brutality and shock which erupts in the madness scene, a brutality made all the more terrible by the tenderness which precedes it; or of the great dirge which celebrates the labors of Heracles, and then the confrontation of that ode with the hero's simple "Farewell, my labors"; or, again, of the exquisite ode in praise of youth and the service of the Muses, poetry tense with the full pressure of the poet's life behind it; and, last of all, that anguished exchange between Theseus and Heracles in which the hero, broken by his suffering, weak, reduced to his final humanity, comes on his greatest heroism, surely one of the most poignant codas in Greek tragedy.

Technically, at least, it is a brilliant performance, boldness of dramatic stroke and vigor of invention everywhere visible, but particularly in the brisk counterpoint of peripeties on which the tragedy turns, wheeling over and over as one action pivots to its opposite, or, juxtaposed against a sudden illumination, is as suddenly shattered and annulled. Through theme after theme, with perfect tact of tempo and placing, the reversals crowd, taking each motif a further turn of the wheel. Thus the first action of the play, slow, conventional, overwhelmed by the weakness of its characters, creates out of desperation a sudden and time-honored theodicy. The wheel turns, and a violent irruption of the irrational smashes all theodicy; then, in the last swing, both irrational and theodicy are alike undone in the hero's enormous leap to an illusion of order in divinity, an assertion which he maintains squarely in the teeth of his experience. The savior who suddenly turns destroyer is in turn saved from self-destruction by the man he had earlier saved from Hades. The hero is reduced to his humanity as the condition of his heroism. Throughout the tragedy, gathering momentum by contrast, runs the rhythm of its minor terms: first despair, then hope, then again despair, and finally an endurance deeper than either; age and youth, weakness and strength, both pairs resolved in the condition that makes them one. Schematic, brilliant, savagely broken, the *Heracles* is a play of great power and, with the exception of the *Orestes*, the most violent structural tour-de-force in Greek tragedy.

It is this very dislocation, this virtuosity and violence in the play's structure, which more than anything else has injured its reputation and hindered reappraisal. Given Aristotelian standards of judgment (and Aristotle even today affects dramatic criticism at a profound level), the play's dislocation could not but appear either pointless or gratuitous; for at almost every conceivable point the play is in flat contradiction to the principles of the *Poetics*. Thus Heracles has no visible *hamartia;* if he falls, he falls for no flaw of his own nature or failure of judgment, but as the innocent victim of divine brutality. And still worse, the play exhibits not at all that deep, necessitous *propter hoc* connection between its parts, which for Aristotle constituted the right structure of tragedy.[1] With almost one voice both critics and scholars from Aristotle to the present have reported the dislocation of the play as an insuperable blemish. The *Heracles*, they say, is "broken-backed,"[2] a tragedy that "falls so clearly into two parts that we cannot view it as a work of art."[3] But in so saying, they report, I think, as much their own outraged Aristotelianism as the obvious facts of the play's structure.

1. *Poetics* 1452ᵃ. 20.
2. Gilbert Murray, *Greek Studies*, p. 112.
3. Gilbert Norwood, *Greek Tragedy*, p. 229.

Beyond question the play falls starkly into two discrete but continuous actions, and between these two actions there is neither
causal necessity nor even probability: the second action follows but
by no means arises out of the first. Through the close of the chorus
which celebrates the slaying of Lycus (l. 814), we have one complete
action as conventional in movement as it is in subject: a familiar
tableau of suppliants, their cruel antagonist, an *agōn* in which the
tormentor is slain by the savior, and a closing hymn in praise of the
hero and the vindicated justice of the gods. This melodramatic
action is shattered by the appearance of Madness and Iris, and the
play, in violation of all probability, careens around to commence a
wholly new action. Utterly unexpected and without causal ground
in the first part of the play, the madness of Heracles and the murder
of his wife and children are simply set down in glaring contrast to
the preceding action. Against theodicity is put the hideous proof of
divine injustice; against the greatness and piety and *aretē* of Heracles
in the first action is placed the terrible reward of heroism in the
second; against the asserted peace and calm and domestic tenderness
which closes the first action is set the utter annihilation of all moral
order in the second. The result is a structure in which two apparently
autonomous actions are jammed savagely against each other in almost total contradiction, with no attempt to minimize or even
modulate the profound formal rift.

That rift is, of course, deliberate; nothing, in fact, has been
omitted which might support the effect of total shock in this reversal. Moreover, even a cursory review of the material which
Euripides used for his tragedy shows how carefully that material
has been ordered to effect, rather than obviate, this dislocation of
structure.

Old tradition told of Hera's persecution of Heracles because of
her jealousy of Zeus's amour with Heracles' mother, Alcmene. It
also told how Heracles, driven mad by Hera, slew his sons and would
also have killed his father, Amphitryon, had not Athene intervened
and knocked the raging hero unconscious with a stone. For the most
part Euripides has retained these traditions, but with this great difference: whereas in the common tradition the great labors of

Heracles were undertaken in penance for the murder of the children, Euripides has transposed the murders to the time just after the completion of the labors, the height of Heracles' career. Because Heracles at the very moment of his fall is at his greatest, the hideousness of Hera's revenge is sharply underscored and its abrupt, tragic senselessness stressed. The dramatist, that is, has ordered his material in such a way as to achieve precisely that dislocation which the play's structure exhibits. Nor is this all. Because Euripides has transposed the labors and the murders, he has been forced to invent a new motive for the labors. This is the motive of filial piety: Heracles undertook his labors in order to win back the country from which Amphitryon had been exiled for the murder of Electryon. Thus at the same time that Euripides freely invents in order to fill the gap caused by the original transposition, he also subtly humanizes his hero in preparation for the conversion which is the heart of the second action.

Tradition also told of Heracles' suicide on Mt. Oeta (cf. Sophocles' *Trachiniae*) and how after death the hero was translated to heaven and given everlasting youth in the person of Hebe. This entire saga is suppressed in the Euripidean version, but the very fact of its suppression informs the *Heracles* throughout, pointing up the direction of the action against what has been excluded. Thus Heracles, far from being deified in Euripides, is humanized[4] as the condition of his heroism. And far from committing suicide, the Euripidean Heracles discovers his greatest nobility in refusing to die and choosing life. If, again in the older tradition, Heracles married Hebe (i.e., youth) and so won everlasting life, in the Euripidean play Hebe is present to the action as nothing more than an impossible anguished reminder of mortal necessity and the haunting image of what in a universe not fatally flawed might have been the reward of human

4. In the humanization of Heracles, Euripides returns to the oldest of all extant Heracles traditions, the Homeric, in which Heracles too had to die. Cf. *Iliad* xviii. 115 ff.: "Not even the great Heracles escaped death, though he was dear to the lord Zeus, the son of Cronus, but the common fate brought him down, and the grievous wrath of Hera." In literature of the historical period this tradition has almost everywhere been eclipsed by the deified Heracles, a version which begins also with Homer (cf. *Odyssey* xi. 601 ff.).

virtue (cf. 637–72). Similarly, the suppression of the deification motif sharpens the courageous endurance of mankind under its necessities in contrast with the happiness of the amoral gods. Deification is replaced by the closest thing to Olympus this world can offer —honored asylum at Athens. For this reason Theseus is introduced as the representative of Athenian humanity to rescue and annex to Athens the greatest Dorian hero.

By deployment of his material Euripides has structured his play into two parallel actions divided by a peripety whose purpose is more to stress the break than to bridge it. If the *Heracles* is broken, the dislocation is at least deliberate, and as such it is clearly consistent with Euripides' practice elsewhere: in the two actions of the *Hecuba*, the double plot of the *Hippolytus*, the episodic *Trojan Women* or *Phoenissae*, the broken *Andromache*, and the dislocated *Electra*. But even more violently than these plays the *Heracles* insists on the irreparable rift in its structure and invites us by its great power to discover what nonetheless makes it one play. It is right that our perception of power in literature should lead us more deeply into the order and disorder created or invoked.

Despite the fact that the first action is entirely free invention, it is important to see how conventional the treatment is. In the shaping of the characters, in their attributes and motives, in the theology and received values to which the action appeals, convention is everywhere visible. Character is essentially static, the action as a whole leached of any really tragic movement. All the emotional stops of a melodramatic situation have been pulled: we move from the despair of the helpless family to the sudden coming of the savior hero to the triumphant final diapason of vindicated divine justice. The characters are only lightly dubbed in, certainly no more so than is necessary to maintain the illusion that these are real people in a situation of unqualified peril. If the action is not quite trite, it is at least customary and predictable, so predictable in fact that it might be regarded as a parody of a standard tragic movement. Certainly no one familiar with Euripides' practice can doubt that the comfortable theodicy which closes the action has been written tongue-in-cheek or is somehow surely riding for a fall. And insensibly the impression of purely tragic power in the second action, although based on an analogous plot, undercuts the first action and exposes its conventionality.

What is true of the first action as a whole is also true of the Heracles of the first action. The traditional *données* which compose his figure have for the most part been carefully preserved; if Heracles is not here the beefeater of comedy or the ruddy sensualist of the *Alcestis*, he is recognizably the familiar culture-hero of Dorian and Boeotian tradition: strong, courageous, noble, self-sufficient, carrying on his back all the aristocratic *aretē* of the moralized tradition of Pindar. Thus the grossnesses or cruelties or philandering which tradition sometimes ascribed to him (cf. again the *Trachiniae*) have been stripped away. In domestic life he is a devoted son, a loyal husband, and a fond father; in civil life he is the just king, the enemy of *hybris*, the champion of the helpless, and the loyal servant of the gods. His civilizing labors on behalf of mankind are accepted as literal truths, and the curious ambiguity in tradition which made Heracles the son of two fathers, Zeus and Amphitryon, is maintained. His heroism is based upon his strength and is essentially outward, but nonetheless valid, or at least valid enough for the muted reality of the first action.

Against this background, the second action breaks with tragic force and striking transformations, showing first the conquering hero, the *kallinikos*, reduced to tears, helpless, dependent, and in love, stripped of that outward strength which until now had exempted him from normal human necessity, and discovering both his common ground with men and a new internalized moral courage. This Heracles is not merely untraditional; he is almost inconceivable in traditional perspective, and he is tragic where the earlier Heracles was merely noble. The point to be insisted upon here is the distance at every point between the two actions. We have here moved a whole world away from the simple virtues and theodicy of the first action, as the new role and courage of the hero undercut everything the play has created up to now. The world of the given, the reality of "things as they are said to be," withers and is replaced, not by a mere contradiction, but by a new tragic myth invoking new values and grounded in a sterner reality. What audience, especially a Greek one, could have recognized in that broken, almost domestic, Heracles fighting back his tears, the familiar and austere culture-hero of received tradition?

We have, then, two savagely different actions, one conventional and the other set in a world where tradition is dumb and conduct uncharted, placed harshly in contrast. The peripety which separates them is the dramatist's means of expressing symbolically the fatal disorder of the moral universe, and also the device by which the heroism of the second action is forced up, through an utter transformation of assumed reality. The whole play exhibits, as though on two plateaus, a *conversion* of reality. A story or legend derived from received beliefs—the world of myth and the corpus of "things as they are said to be"—is suddenly in all of its parts, terms, characters, and the values it invokes *converted* under dramatic pressure to another phase of reality. What we get is something like a dramatic mutation of received reality, and the leap the play makes between the phases or plateaus of its two realities is meant to correspond in force and vividness and apparent unpredictability to mutations in the physical world. It is this violence in the conversion of reality that explains the wrenching dislocation of Euripidean drama from an Aristotelian point of view and the lack of apparent connection between the parts of the play. The play pivots on two seemingly incompatible realities, and if it insists on the greater reality of what has been created over what has been received, it does so, not by denying reality to receive reality, but by subtly displacing it in the transfiguration of its terms.

Thus, point for point in the *Heracles*, each of the terms—the qualities, situation, characters—that was appropriate to the Heracles of tradition is transformed and displaced. If in the first action both Zeus and Amphitryon are the fathers of Heracles, in the second action Amphitryon becomes Heracles' "real" father, not by the fact of conception, but by the greater fact of love, *philia*. In the first action Heracles literally decended to a literal Hades; in the second action this literal descent is transfigured in the refusal to die and the courage which, under an intolerable necessity, perseveres. There is a hint, moreover, that the old Hades of the poets with its Cerberus, Sisyphus, and torments is transformed in the second part into the Hades within, here and now, internalized as Heracles himself declares, "And I am like Ixion, forever chained to a flying wheel." So too the old labors appear to be replaced by the metaphorical sense of the imposed labors of human life and the cost of civilization, while the goddess Hera, who in legend made Heracles mad, passes almost insensibly into a hovering symbol of all those irrational and random necessities which the Greek and the play call *Tyche*, and which we limply translate as "Fortune" or "necessity."

All of these conversions replace and dislodge the reality of the first action by transfiguring it at every point. The first action in the light of the second is neither false nor unreal, but inadequate. Through the force of contrast with its own conversion, it comes to seem obsolete, naïve, or even humdrum, much as fresh conviction formed under *peine forte et dure* insensibly makes the conviction it replaces callow or jejune in comparison. Under the changed light of experience and the pattern it imposes, what was once taken for reality comes to seem illusion at best: true while held as true, but with widened experience, discovered inadequate. What we see is less the contradiction between the two opposed realities than the counterpointed relation of their development, the way in which, under the blow of suffering and insight, one reality is made to yield a further one, each geared to its appropriate experience. We begin with a familiar and conventional world, operating from familiar motives among accepted though outmoded values; by the time the play closes, characters, motives, and values have all been pushed to the very frontiers of reality.

But if in this context of conversion the conventional first action is undercut and dislodged by the tragic second action, the first action also helps to inform the second and to anticipate its discoveries. Thus Heracles' desperation after his madness is paralleled by his family's desperation in the first part; what they say and do there is meant to be applied with full force to his situation later. If courage for them lies in the nobility with which they accept the necessity of death, nobility for Heracles lies in the courage with which he accepts his life as his necessity, for, in Amphitryon's words:

> To persevere, trusting in what hopes he has,
> is courage in a man. The coward despairs [ll. 105–6].

If Amphitryon in the first action possesses a "useless" life (l. 42) by virtue of extreme old age and weakness, Heracles later comes to possess the same "useless" life (l. 1302), and so both meet on the grounds of their common condition. Similarly the chorus speaks of its own necessity, old age, as "a weight more heavy than Aetna's rocks, / hiding in darkness / the light of my eyes" (ll. 639–41); that same darkness, not as age but as grief, lies later on the eyes of Heracles (ll. 1140, 1159, 1198, 1104–5, 1216, 1226ff.), the dark night of his soul. And just as the chorus in the first action finds the hope of its life in poetry and perseveres in the Muses' service, so Theseus uncovers Heracles to the sun and shows him the hope in *philia* which enables him to live. So too when Heracles, self-sufficient and independent, leads his children into the palace before his madness, he draws them behind him like little boats in tow (*epholkidas*); but at the end of the play Heracles, broken, in love and dependent, follows in Theseus' wake to Athens like a little boat in tow (*epholkides*). The same implicit counterpoint between the two actions explains in part, I think, the unqualified villainy of Lycus. Balancing the corruption of human power and brutality (*amathia*) in him, comes the abuse of divine power in Hera—a far more heinous abuse, since divine cruelty is a fortiori worse than human brutality. Beyond this, I suspect, we are intended to see correspondence again in the physical death which Lycus meets at Heracles' hands and the spiritual annihilation of Hera which is the consequence of Heracles' great speech on the gods (ll. 1340–46). But throughout the play, in metaphor, in contrast of whole scenes, in visual imagery, the two actions are paralleled at point after point. Below the level of the violent structural dislocation of the play runs a constant crisscross of reference, comment, and contrast throwing single words or themes into sharp relief in continuous qualification of the whole action. In the perception of this continuous conversion of the play's terms lies the understanding of its movement and unity.

Point by point the deepest motive of the play is to bring Heracles to the place where he shares for the first time common ground with the others, all of whom, like him, are laid under the heavy yoke of necessity but lack that enormous physical strength which has hitherto exempted him. But if he must come to share that yoke with them, if he is reduced to his humanity as the condition of the only heroism that counts, he also comes to know for the first time that other, and redeeming, yoke of love, *philia*, which alone makes necessity endurable. For the *Heracles* is a play which imposes suffering upon men as their tragic condition, but it also discovers a courage equal to that necessity, a courage founded on love. We witness in the play a conversion of heroism whose model is Heracles, and the heart of that conversion lies in the hero's passage in suffering from the outworn courage of outward physical strength to a new internal courage, without exemption now but with the addition of love and perseverance against an intolerable necessity.

Love is the hope, the *elpis*, which permits him to endure, and his discovery of that hope keeps step with his knowledge of anguish. He survives by virtue of love, for love lies close to, if it does not usurp, the instinct for survival. At the close of the play we see Heracles assert the dignity of his grief against the reproaches of a Theseus who, for all his generosity, is still rooted in the old heroism and no longer understands. Having claimed the dignity of his new courage, Heracles can without weakness or loss of tragic stature make plain the wreck of his life and his own dependent helplessness: strong but also weak, in need and in love, a hero at every point.

Heracles comes through suffering, then, to occupy the ground where Megara, Amphitryon, and the chorus stood earlier. Their nobility provides a standard by which to measure his heroism, first challenging it and then being surpassed by it. But nothing in Heracles is diminished because Megara and Amphitryon have set the example he must follow, and know already what he must learn. Their very weakness has set them close to necessity, while Heracles' *aretē* has been so prodigiously developed toward physical strength that nothing short of the greatest moral courage is required for him to survive his necessity. He rises and keeps on rising to his sufferings with an enormous range of spirit that in the end leaves even the un-conventional Theseus far behind him. It is this ability to rise that makes him great as much as the overwhelming anguish of the necessity that confronts him. What counts in the end is not the dis-parity between Heracles' courage and necessity and the courage of the others, but the fact that they all—Megara, Amphitryon, the chorus, and Heracles—meet on the common ground of their condi-tion and discover both courage and hope in the community of weakness and love.

What, finally, are we to make of Hera and that crucial speech of Heracles on the nature of the gods (ll. 1340–46)? That it was Hera who made Heracles mad was, as we have seen, an essential part of Euripides' legendary material. But the consequence of Heracles' speech is apparently to deny that the actions of the gods could in fact be such as they are dramatized to be. Alternatively Heracles appears to deny the reality of the experience out of which he makes the speech in the first place. For to say that "if god is truly god, then he is perfect, / lacking nothing" is clearly to invalidate Hera's claim to divinity, or to deny his own experience of Hera's hatred.

The sentiment is, to be sure, Euripidean, a familiar refusal to be-lieve the old legends which represent the gods as subject to human passions, and a discountenance of the familiar fifth-century notion that immoral conduct could be sanctioned by an appeal to divine conduct as recounted in poetry. But merely because the lines are Euripidean in thought, their effect for the play should not be glozed away as mere inconsistencies or as an undramatic intrusion of the dramatist *in propria persona*. For to say that divine adultery, tyranny, and misconduct are all "the wretched tales of poets" is a direct and unmistakable challenge not only to the Hera of the play, but to the whole Olympian system.

The consequences of Heracles' words for the play are, I suggest, this: that the story of Hera's action as dramatized is true enough, but the Hera who afflicts Heracles as she does thereby renounces any claim to the kind of divinity which Heracles asserts. This conclusion is, I think, supported by Euripides' practice elsewhere and also by the language of the play. Like the *Hippolytus* with Aphrodite and the *Bacchae* with Dionysus, the *Heracles* does two things with Hera: it first dramatizes the legend which contains her action as incredible in a goddess,[5] and then, having shown *and* asserted its incredibility, it converts her into a hovering symbol of all the unknown and unknowable forces which compel Heracles and men to suffer tragically and without cause or sense. As Dionysus is a complex symbol for the forces of life, amoral and necessitous, so Hera comprehends all the principles of peripety and change and random necessity. She is not Hera, but "Hera," a name given her for the want of a name, but loosely what the Greeks meant by *Tyche*, the lady of necessity and reversal. In asserting this "Hera" as the consequence of his own speech, Heracles annihilates the old Olympian Hera as a goddess, but also converts her into that demonic and terribly real power of his own necessity. The tragedy of Heracles is both true and real, but it is no longer the traditional story, nor is Heracles the same man, nor Hera the same goddess. And it is to confirm this conversion that Heracles a few lines later (l. 1357) concludes: "And now, I see, I must serve necessity (*tyche*)." So too in his last reference to Hera he hints at the conversion by significantly juxtaposing both *tyche* and the name of Hera, claiming that "we all have been struck down by one *tyche* of Hera" (l. 1393).[6] And, if this were not enough, the play's overwhelming preoccupation with peripety as theme and as dislocation in structure would confirm the conversion. This, I think, is what we should expect, that the conversion of the old legend of Heracles and his old nobility into a new myth should be accompanied by the conversion of his necessity as well. To alter his old heroism without also altering the source of his suffering would be to cripple the conversion at the crucial point. It would obscure, that is, the fact that Heracles, though broken by necessity, still wins the moral victory over the power that ruins him, earning for himself

5. Cf. ll. 1307–10 where Heracles asks: "Who could offer prayers to such a goddess? Jealous of Zeus for a mortal woman's sake, she has destroyed Hellas' greatest friend, though he was guiltless."

6. Cf. ll. 1314, 1349, 1396, as well as the significant disjunction, "mastered by Hera or by necessity" in Amphitryon's speech at l. 20.

and men in a different sense the victory claimed by Amphitryon over
Zeus earlier:

> And I, mere man, am nobler than you, a great god [l. 342].

He claims a courage more than equal to his condition and can therefore claim the dignity of his grief.

Heracles is no Aristotelian hero, nor is the play an Aristotelian
tragedy; yet the *Heracles* is a great tragedy and Heracles himself a
great tragic hero. The gulf between Euripides and Aristotle on the
issues here is a great and permanent one that deserves to be stressed.
For Aristotle a tragic fall is grounded in a consistent and harmonious
sense of man's responsibility for his nature and his actions: when the
hero falls, he falls for his own failure, and behind the rightness of his
fall, working both pity and fear by the precise and relentless nature
of its operations, stands the order which society and a god-informed
world impose upon the individual. What the law requires the gods
require too, and so the Aristotelian play portrays, like an image of
human life, the individual torn and suffering between his nature and
an objective world-order. In Euripides it is otherwise; here the
suffering of the individual under his necessity may have no such
rightness, or even none at all, as in the *Heracles*. The world-order of
the gods as reflected in "things as they are said to be" is either incredible or an indictment of that order, and if it imposes necessities
unjustly upon a man, the very courage with which he endures makes
him tragic and gives him the moral victory over his own fate.
Similarly with society: for society may be no less corrupt than the
"gods" and as unjust in the necessities it imposes. Euripides, that is,
preserves the disorder of actual experience, measuring its horror
against the unrequited illusion of order which sustains human beings.
His image of tragic humanity is earned less in the conflict between
the individual's nature and the necessities imposed by a higher order
than in the conflict between the individual and his own internalized
necessities. In the *Heracles*, at least, it is the very innocence of the
hero which condemns the "gods" who make him mad; but because
the gods are first rendered incredible and then transformed into a
collective symbol for all the random, senseless operations of neces-

sity in human life, the courage with which the hero meets his fate and asserts a moral order beyond his own experience is just as tragic and just as significant as that of Oedipus.

Date and Circumstances

The *Heracles* is undated, and no attempt to date the play to any one year can be regarded as wholly successful. The most favored date is one close to 424–423. It has been held that the heavy emphasis throughout the play upon old age in connection with military service, particularly the bitter first strophe of the second *stasmion* (ll. 637 ff.), represents a direct personal intrusion of the poet on having reached his sixtieth year (when he would have been exempt from further military service). On such a theory the date of the play would be 424–423. Similarly, the disproportionate debate on the bow (ll. 188 ff.) is interpreted as an overt reference to the Athenian success at Sphakteria in 425—a victory due largely to bowmen—or to the disastrous failure to employ archers in the hoplite defeat at Delium in 424. The reference to Delian maidens (ll. 687 ff.) is taken as a remembrance of the establishment of the quiquennial *Deliades* in Athens in 425.

But no one of these suggestions, nor even their ensemble, can be regarded as decisive. The strongest argument for a later date is one given by stylistic and metrical tests, generally rather accurate for Euripides. These tend to place the play in the group of dramas which directly follow the Archidamian War, or about 418–416.

It is my opinion that the metrical tests are supported in their results by the general political tone of the play, with its sharp emphasis upon factional strife and its concern with the badge of true nobility. Further, the reconciliation between Sparta and Athens which is suggested in Theseus' domiciling of Heracles in Athens would seem to suggest (though it need not) a period in which reconciliation between Athens and Sparta was possible. Such reconciliation was a possibility only, I believe, in the period between the close of the Archidamian War in 421 and the aggressive anti-Spartan policy of Alcibiades which cluminated in the Athenian-Argive defeat at

Mantinea in 418. It is only against such a background as this, when all major parties in the Peloponnesian War were attempting abortive realignments, when peace must have appeared to be at least a remote possibility to contemporaries, that the lines of Megara (ll. 474–79) can be made to yield good sense. If so, the death of the children who embody the peaceful hopes of a united Hellas (ll. 135–37) must mean the renewal of conflict. A renewal of conflict must have seemed the certain consequence of Alcibiades' policies in 418, whereas in the years just previous an alliance between Athens and Sparta must have excited real hopes of an enduring peace.

Text

The basis of this translation is the Oxford text of Gilbert Murray, though it has often been supplemented by others,[1] chiefly the brilliant edition of Leon Parmentier in the Budé series.[2] Upon a few occasions I have also adopted the emendations proposed by Wilamowitz. The notes on the translation are not designed to indicate all departures from the Murray text (nor even to mark the numerous occasions on which I preferred the reading of the manuscripts over modern emendations),[3] but to amplify variations or emendations

1. L. 496: cf. D. S. Robertson, "Euripides, *H.F. 497 ff.*," *C.R.* LII (1938), 50–51.

2. L. 1241: "Then where it touches heaven, I shall strike." I adopt here the emendation of Parmentier and read *kai thenein* for *katthanein*. Since Theseus at l. 1246 asks Heracles what he will do and where his passion sweeps him, and Heracles replies in the following line that he will die, it seems plausible that *katthanein* here is a simple copyist's mistake for the less familiar *kai thenein*. And, as Parmentier remarks, the line as emended pivots on a play with the word *haptēi* in the preceding line (l. 1240). It is also more likely that Theseus in l. 1242 would take *thenein* as a threat against the gods than he would the precise self-directed *katthanein*. See L. Parmentier, *Revue de philologie*, XLIV (1920), 161.

3. L. 1351: *Enkarterēsō thanaton* ("I shall prevail against death"). *Thanaton* is here the reading of the manuscripts and, to some degree, it is supported by the identical phrase at *Andromache* l. 262 (though in each case the contextual meaning is different). Murray, following Wecklein and Wilamowitz, however, has altered *thanaton* to *bioton* (life).
So far as the quality of affirmation is concerned here, however, there is little difference between *thanaton* and *bioton*. Both imply the affirmative decision to bear necessity by living; clarity is unaffected by either reading. Though to prevail against life (in the sense of "persevering") may be more forceful than to prevail against death (in the

whose use appeared to me to bear upon the interpretation of the whole play. Lines which are bracketed indicate probable interpolations.

———

sense of resisting the temptation to die), it seems to me that the imagery of the play is decisive for *thanaton*. In Heracles' words here, that is, we have the metaphorical (but also realistic) equivalent of the mythical descent to Hades and the conquest of death it signifies. Heracles has in his sufferings been to Hades and at death's door; he now wrestles with his death as myth once imagined him as wrestling for Cerberus. And just as the chorus once (ll. 655 ff.) hoped that the noble man might receive a double life as a reward of *aretē*, in this line we see the vindication of *aretē* in the internalized *eugeneia* which conquers death.

CHARACTERS

Amphitryon, father of Heracles

Megara, wife of Heracles

Chorus of old men of Thebes

Lycus, usurper of the throne of Thebes

Heracles

Iris, messenger of the gods

Madness

Messenger

Theseus, king of Athens

For Robert and Renée Preyer
zeugos ge philion

HERACLES

HYPOTHESIS: *Heracles after his marriage with Megara, daughter of Creon, had children by her. . . . Leaving his sons in Thebes, he himself went to Argos to accomplish his labors for Eurystheus. After he had prevailed in all of them, he descended to Hades and passed a long time there and then returned, to the surprise of the living, who had thought him dead. While the Thebans were embroiled in civil strife against Creon the king, a usurper from Euboea by the name of Lycus. . . .*

SCENE: *Before the palace of Heracles at Thebes. In the foreground is the altar of Zeus. On its steps, in the posture of suppliants, sit the aged Amphitryon, Megara, and her three small sons. Amphitryon rises and speaks the prologue.*

Amphitryon
    What mortal lives who has not heard this name—
    Amphitryon of Argos, who shared his wife
    with Zeus? I am he: son of Alcaeus
    Perseus' son, but father of Heracles.
    Here I settled, in this Thebes, where once the earth   5
    was sown with dragonteeth and sprouted men;
    and Ares saved a few that they might people
    Cadmus' city with their children's children.
    From these sown men Creon was descended,
    son of Menoeceus and our late king.
    This lady is Megara, Creon's daughter,
    for whose wedding once all Thebes shrilled   10
    to flutes and songs as she was led, a bride,
    home to his father's halls by Heracles.
    Then my son left home, left Megara and kin,
    hoping to recover the plain of Argos
    and those gigantic walls from which I fled   15
    to Thebes, because I killed Electryon.
    He hoped to win me back my native land

and so alleviate my grief. And therefore,
mastered by Hera or by necessity,
he promised to Eurystheus a vast price
for our return: to civilize the world.   20
When all his other labors had been done,
he undertook the last: descended down
to Hades through the jaws of Taenarus
to hale back up to the light of day
the triple-bodied dog.

                  He has not come back.   25
   Here in Thebes the legend goes that once
a certain Lycus married Dirce, our queen,
and ruled this city with its seven gates
before the twins of Zeus, those "white colts,"
Amphion and Zethus, ruled the land.   30
This Lycus' namesake and descendant,
no native Theban but Euboean-born,
attacked our city, sick with civil war,
murdered Creon and usurped his throne.
And now our marriage-bond with Creon's house   35
has proved in fact to be our greatest ill.
For since my son is gone beneath the earth,
this upstart tyrant, Lycus, plans to kill
the wife and sons of Heracles—and me,
so old and useless, that I scarcely count—   40
blotting murder with more, lest these boys
grown to men, someday revenge their mother's house.
   My son, when he descended to the darkness
underground, left me here, appointing me
both nurse and guardian of his little sons.   45
Now, to keep these heirs of Heracles from death,
their mother and I in supplication
kneeled to Zeus the Savior at this altar,
established by the prowess of my son,
the trophy of his conquering spear
and monument of Minyan victory.   50

Here we sit, in utter destitution,
lacking food, water, and clothing; having no beds
but the bare earth beneath our bodies;
barred from our house, empty of hope.
And of our friends, some prove no friends at all,   55
while those still true are powerless to help.
This is what misfortune means among mankind;
upon no man who wished me well at all,
could I wish this acid test of friends might fall.

Megara

Old man, marshal of our famous Theban arms,   60
who once destroyed the city of the Taphians,
how dark are all the ways of god to man!
Prosperity was my inheritance:
I had a father who could boast of wealth,
who had such power as makes the long spears   65
leap with greed against its proud possessor—
a father, blessed with children, who gave me
in glorious marriage to your Heracles.
But now his glory is gone down in death,
and you and I, old man, shall soon be dead,   70
and with us, these small sons of Heracles
whom I ward and nestle underwing.
First one, then another, bursts in tears,
and asks: "Mother, where has Father gone?
What is he doing? When will he come back?"
Then, too small to understand, they ask again   75
for "Father." I put them off with stories;
but when the hinges creak, they all leap up
to run and throw themselves at their father's feet.
Is there any hope? What chance of rescue
do we have, old man? We look to you.   80
The border is impassable by stealth;
sentries have been set on every road;
all hope that friends might rescue us is gone.

So tell me now if you have any plan,   85
or if you have resigned yourself to death.

Amphitryon

My child, I find it hard in such a case
to give advice offhand without hard thought.
We are weak, and weakness can only wait.

Megara

Wait for worse? Do you love life so much?   90

Amphitryon

I love it even now. I love its hopes.

Megara

And I. But hope is of things possible.

Amphitryon

A cure may come in wearing out the time.

Megara

It is the time between that tortures me.

Amphitryon

Even now, out of our very evils,   95
for you and me a better wind may blow.
My son, your husband, still may come. Be calm;
dry the living springs of tears that fill
your children's eyes. Console them with stories,
those sweet thieves of wretched make-believe.   100
Human misery must somewhere have a stop:
there is no wind that always blows a storm;
great good fortune comes to failure in the end.
All is change; all yields its place and goes;
to persevere, trusting in what hopes he has,   105
is courage in a man. The coward despairs.

(*Enter the Chorus of old men of Thebes. They walk painfully,
leaning upon their staffs.*)

Chorus

STROPHE

Leaning on our staffs we come
to the vaulted halls and the old man's bed,
our song the dirge of the dying swan,   110
ourselves mere words, ghosts that walk
in the visions of night,
trembling with age,
trembling to help.
O children, fatherless sons,
old man and wretched wife   115
who mourn your lord in Hades!

ANTISTROPHE

Do not falter. Drag your weary feet
onward like the colt that, yoked and slow,   120
tugs uphill, on rock, the heavy wain.
    If any man should fall,
    support him with your hands,
    age hold up his years   125
    as once when he was young
    he supported his peers
    in the toils of war
and was no blot on his country's fame.

EPODE

Look how the children's eyes   130
flash forth like their father's!
Misfortune has not left them,
nor has loveliness.
    O Hellas, Hellas,
    losing these boys,   135
    what allies you lose!
No more. Look: I see my country's tyrant,
Lycus, approaching the palace.

(*Enter Lycus with attendants.*)

Lycus

You there,
father of Heracles, and you, his wife: 140
allow me one question. And you must allow it:
I am the power here; I ask what I wish.
How long will you seek to prolong your lives?
What hope have you? What could prevent your death?
Or do you think the father of these boys   145
who lies dead with Hades will still come back?
How shabbily you suffer when you both must die—
you who filled all Hellas with your hollow boasts
that Zeus was partner in your son's conception;
and you, that you were wife of the noblest man!   150
What was so prodigious in your husband's deeds?
Because he killed a hydra in a marsh?
Or the Nemean lion? They were trapped in nets,
not strangled, as he claims, with his bare hands.
Are these your arguments? Because of this,   155
you say, the sons of Heracles should live—
a man who, coward in everything else,
made his reputation fighting beasts,
who never buckled shield upon his arm,
never came near a spear, but held a bow,   160
the coward's weapon, handy to run away?
The bow is no proof of manly courage;
no, your real man stands firm in the ranks
and dares to face the gash the spear may make.

My policy, old man, is not mere cruelty;   165
call it caution. I am well aware
that I killed Creon and usurped his throne.
It does not suit my wishes that these boys
go free to take their grown revenge on me.

Amphitryon

Let Zeus act to guard his interest in his son.   170
For my part, Heracles, I have but words
to prove this man's gross ignorance of you.

I cannot bear that you should be abused.
First for his slander, for such I call it
when you are called a coward, Heracles.   175
I call upon the gods to bear me witness:
that thunder of Zeus, his chariot
in which you rode, stabbing with winged shafts
the breasts of the giant spawn of earth,
and raised the victory-cry with the gods!   180
Go to Pholoë and see the centaurs,
go ask them, those four-legged monsters,
what man they judge to be the bravest,
if not my son, whose courage you call sham.
Go ask Abantian Dirphys which bore you: 185
it will not praise you. You have never done
one brave deed your fatherland could cite.
You sneer at that wise invention, the bow.
Listen to me and learn what wisdom is.
Your spearsman is the slave of his weapons;   190
unless his comrades in the ranks fight well,
then he dies, killed by their cowardice;
and once his spear, his sole defense, is smashed,
he has no means of warding death away.
But the man whose hands know how to aim the bow,   195
holds the one best weapon: a thousand arrows shot,
he still has more to guard himself from death.
He stands far off, shooting at foes who see
only the wound the unseen arrow plows,
while he himself, his body unexposed,   200
lies screened and safe. This is best in war:
to preserve yourself and to hurt your foe
unless he stands secure, beyond your range.
Such are my arguments, squarely opposed
to yours on every point at issue here.
What will you achieve by killing these boys?   205
How have they hurt you? Yet I grant you wise
in one respect: being base yourself,

you fear the children of a noble man.
Still, this goes hard with us, that we must die
to prove your cowardice, a fate which you   210
might better suffer at our better hands,
if the mind of Zeus intended justice here.
But if the sceptre is what you desire,
then let us go as exiles from the land.
But beware of force, lest you suffer it,   215
when god swings round again with veering wind.
    O country of Cadmus, on you too
my reproaches fall! Is this your vigil
for the sons of Heracles? For Heracles,
who single-handed fought your Minyan foe   220
and made Thebes see once more with free men's eyes?
No more can I praise Hellas, nor be still,
finding her so craven toward my son:
with sword, spear, and fire she should have come
to help these boys in gratitude to him,   225
for all his labors clearing land and sea.
Poor children, both Thebes and Hellas fail you.
And so you turn to me, a weak old man,
nothing more now than a jawing of words,
forsaken by that strength I used to have,   230
left only with this trembling husk of age.
But if my youth and strength could come again,
I'd take my spear and bloody your brown hair
until you ran beyond the bounds of Atlas,
trying, coward, to outrun my spear!   235

Chorus
    There is a source of speech in all brave men
    which does not fail, although the tongue be slow.

Lycus
    Go on, rant, pile up your tower of words!
    My actions, not my words, shall answer your abuse.

                              (*Turning to his attendants.*)

Go, men, to Helicon and Parnassus: 240
tell the woodsmen there to chop up oaken logs
and haul them to the city. Then pile your wood
around the altar here on every side,
and let it blaze. Burn them all alive
until they learn the dead man rules no more;   245
that I, and I alone, am the power here.
But you old men, for this defiance,
you shall mourn the sons of Heracles
and each disaster that devours this house,   250
each separate grief, until you learn
you are only slaves; I am the master.

Chorus

O sons of earth, men whom Ares sowed,
teeth he tore from the dragon's foaming jaw,
up, up with these staffs that prop our arms
and batter the skull of this godless man,   255
no Theban, but an alien lording it
over the younger men, to our great shame!

                                            (*To Lycus.*)

Never shall you boast that I am your slave,
never will you reap the harvest of my work,
all I labored for. Go back whence you came;   260
rage there. So long as there is life in me,
you shall not kill the sons of Heracles.
He has not gone *so* deep beneath the earth.
Because you ruined, then usurped, this land,
he who gave it help must go without his due.   265
Am I a meddler, then, because I help
the friend who, being dead, needs help the most?
O right hand, how you ache to hold a spear,
but cannot, want foundering on weakness.
Else, I should have stopped your mouth that calls me slave,   270
and ruled this Thebes, in which you now exult,
with credit. But corrupt with evil schemes

and civil strife, this city lost its mind;
for were it sane, it would not live your slave.

Megara

Old sirs, I thank you. Friends rightly show   275
just indignation on their friends' behalf.
But do not let your rage on our account
involve your ruin too. Amphitryon,
hear what I think for what it may be worth.
I love my children. How not love these boys   280
born of my labors? I am in terror
of their death. And yet how base a thing it is
when a man will struggle with necessity!
We have to die. Then do we have to die
consumed alive, mocked by those we hate?—   285
for me a worse disaster than to die.
Our house and birth demand a better death.
Upon your helm the victor's glory sits,
forbidding that you die a coward's death;
while my husband needs no witnesses to swear   290
he would not want these sons of his to live
by living cowards. Because it hurts his sons,
disgraces break a man of noble birth;
and I must imitate my husband here.
Consider of what stuff your hopes are made;   295
you think your son will come from underground.
Who of all the dead comes home from Hades?
Or do you think you'll mellow *him* with prayers?
No, you must shun a brutal enemy;
yield to noble, understanding men   300
who, met halfway as friends, give mercy freely.
The thought had come to me that prayers might wi
the children's banishment; but this is worse,
to preserve them for a life of beggary.
How does the saying go? Hardly one day   305
do men look kindly on their banished friend.

Dare death with us, which awaits you anyway.
By your great soul, I challenge you, old friend.
The man who sticks it out against his fate
shows spirit, but the spirit of a fool.   310
No man alive can budge necessity.

Chorus

  I could have stopped the mouth of any man
  who threatened you, had I my old strength back.
  But now I am nothing. With you it rests,
  Amphitryon, to avert disaster now.   315

Amphitryon

  Not cowardice, not love of life, keep me
  from death, but my hope to save these children.
  I am in love, it seems, with what cannot be.

                                          (Turning to Lycus.)

  Here, king, here is my throat, ready for your sword;
  murder me, stab me through, hurl me from a cliff,   320
  but, I beg you, grant us both this one boon.
  Murder us before you kill these children;
  spare us from seeing that ghastly sight,
  these boys gasping out their lives, crying
  "Mother!" and "Grandfather!" For the rest,   325
  do your worst. Our hope is gone; we have to die.

Megara

  I beg you, grant me this one last request,
  and so by one act you shall oblige us both.
  Let me adorn my children for their death;
  open those doors which are locked to us   330
  and give them that much share of their father's house.

Lycus

  I grant it. Attendants, undo the bolts!
                  (Attendants slide open the center doors of the palace.)

Go in and dress. I do not begrudge you clothes.
But when your dressing for your death is done,
then I shall give you to the world below.   335

(Exit Lycus.)

Megara

Come, my sons, follow your poor mother's steps
into your father's halls. Other men
possess his wealth; we still possess his name.

(Exit Megara with children.)

Amphitryon

For nothing, then, O Zeus, you shared my wife!
In vain we called you partner in my son!   340
Your love is even less than you pretended;
and I, mere man, am nobler than you, great god.
I did not betray the sons of Heracles.
You knew well enough to creep into my bed
and take what was not yours, what no man gave: 345
what do you know of saving those you love?
You are a callous god or were born unjust!

(Exit Amphitryon to palace.)

Chorus

Strophe 1

First for joy, the victor's song;
then the dirge; sing *ailinos* for Linos!
So Apollo sings, sweeping with golden pick   350
his lyre of lovely voice.
And so I sing of him
who went in darkness underground—
    let him be the son of Zeus,
    let him be Amphitryon's—
of him I sing, a dirge of praise,   355
a crown of song upon his labors.
For of noble deeds the praises are
    the glory of the dead.
First he cleared the grove of Zeus,

and slew the lion in its lair;   360
the tawny hide concealed his back,
oval of those awful jaws
    cowled his golden hair.

ANTISTROPHE 1

Next the centaurs: slaughtered them,
that mountain-ranging savage race,   365
laid them low with poisoned shafts,
with winged arrows slew them all.
Too well the land had known them:
Peneios' lovely rapids,
vast plains, unharvested,
homesteads under Pelion,   370
and the places near Homole,
whence their cavalry rode forth
with weapons carved of pine,
    and tamed all Thessaly.
And next he slew the spotted hind   375
whose antlers grew of golden horn,
that robber-hind, that ravager,
whose horns now gild Oenoë's shrine,
    for Artemis the huntress.

STROPHE 2

Then mounted to his car   380
and mastered with the bit
Diomedes' mares, that knew
no bridle, stabled in blood,
greedy jaws champing flesh,
foul mares that fed on men!   385
And thence crossed over
swirling silver, Hebros' waters,
on and on, performing labors
    for Mycenae's king.
And there by Pelion's headland,

« 295 »

near the waters of Anauros,   390
his shafts brought Cycnus down,
that stranger-slaying monster,
    host of Amphanaia.

ANTISTROPHE 2

Thence among the singing maidens,
western halls' Hesperides.   395
Plucked among the metal leaves
the golden fruit, and slew
the orchard's dragon-guard
whose tail of amber coiled the trunk
untouchably. He passed below the sea   400
and set a calmness in the lives of men
    whose living is the oar.
Under bellied heaven next,
he put his hand as prop:
there in the halls of Atlas,   405
his manliness held up
    heaven's starry halls.

STROPHE 3

He passed the swelling sea of black,
and fought the Amazonian force
foregathered at Maeotis   410
where the many rivers meet.
What town of Hellas missed him
as he mustered friends to fight,
to win the warrior women's
gold-encrusted robes, in quest
for a girdle's deadly quarry?   415
And Hellas won the prize, spoils
of a famous foreign queen,
    which now Mycenae keeps.
He seared each deadly hydra-head   420
of Lerna's thousand-headed hound;

in her venom dipped the shaft
that brought three-bodied Geryon down,
    herdsman of Erytheia.

ANTISTROPHE 3

And many races more he ran,
and won in all the victor's crown,   425
whose harbor now is Hades' tears,
the final labor of them all;
there his life is disembarked
in grief. He comes no more.
His friends have left his house,   430
and Charon's ferry waits
to take his children's lives
the godless, lawless trip of no return.
To your hands your house still turns,
    and you are gone!   435
Could I have my youth once more,
could I shake my spear once more
beside the comrades of my youth,
my courage now would champion
your sons. But youth comes back no more   440
    that blessed me once.

EPODE

Look: I see the children coming now,
wearing the garments of the grave,
sons of Heracles who once was great;
and there, his wife, drawing her sons   445
behind her as she comes; and the old man,
father of Heracles. O pitiful sight!
I cannot hold the tears that break
    from these old eyes.   450

   (*Enter Megara from the palace. She is followed by the children,
                 dressed in the garments of the dead.
                             Last comes Amphitryon.*)

Megara

    Where is the priest with sacrificial knife?
    Where is the killer of our wretched lives?
    Here the victims stand, ready for Hades.
    O my boys, this incongruity of death:
    beneath one yoke, old man, children and mother.   455
    How miserably we die, these children and I!
    Upon these faces now I look my last.
    I gave you birth and brought you up to be
    but mocked and murdered by our enemies.
      How bitterly my hopes for you have failed,   460
    those hopes I founded on your father's words.

                    (*She turns to each child in turn.*)

    To *you* your father would have left all Argos:
    in Eurystheus' halls you would have ruled
    and held the sway over rich Pelasgia.
    It was upon your head he sometimes threw   465
    the skin of tawny lion that he wore.
    You, made king of chariot-loving Thebes,
    would have inherited your mother's lands,
    because you teased them from your father once.
    Sometimes in play, he put in your right hand   470
    that carven club he kept for self-defense.
    To *you*, he would have left Oechalia,
    ravaged once by his far-shooting shafts.
    There are three of you, and with three kingdoms
    your heroic father would have raised you up.   475
    And I had chosen each of you a bride,
    from Athens, Thebes, and Sparta, binding our house
    by marriage, that having such strong anchors down,
    you might in happiness ride out your lives.
    Now all is gone, and fortune, veering round,   480
    gives each of you your death as though a bride,
    and in my tears your bridal shower is,
    while your father's father mourns the feast

that makes you all the sons-in-law of death.
Which shall I take first, which of you the last,   485
to lift you up, take in my arms and kiss?
If only I could gather up my tears,
and like the tawny bee from every flower,
distil to one small nectar all my grief!
O dearest Heracles, if any voice   490
from here reaches to Hades, hear me now!
Your sons, your father, are dying . . . and I,
who was once called blessed because of you.
Help us, come! Come, even as a ghost;
even as a dream, your coming would suffice.
For these are cowards who destroy your sons.   495

Amphitryon

Send your prayers, my child, to the world below,
while I hold out my hands to heaven.
We implore you, Zeus, if still you mean to help,
help us now before it is too late.   500
How often have I called! In vain, my labors.
For death is on us like necessity.
   Our lives, old friends, are but a little while,
so let them run as sweetly as you can,
and give no thought to grief from day to day.
For time is not concerned to keep our hopes,   505
but hurries on its business, and is gone.
You see in me a man who once had fame,
who did great deeds; but fortune in one day
has snatched it from me as though a feather.   510
Great wealth, great reputation! I know no man
with whom they stay. Friends of my youth, farewell.
You look your last on him who loved you well.

          (*Megara suddenly catches sight of Heracles approaching*
                             from a distance.)

Megara

Look, Father! My dearest! Can it be?

Amphitryon

I cannot say. I dare not say, my child.   515

Megara

It *is* he, whom we heard was under earth,
unless some dream comes walking in the light.
A dream? This is no dream my longing makes!
It is *he*, Father, your son, no other!
Run, children, fasten to your father's robes   520
and never let him go! Quick, run! He comes
to rescue us and Zeus comes with him.

> (*Enter Heracles, armed with bow and arrows, his club in
> in his hand. He does not see his family at first,
> but salutes his halls.*)

Heracles

I greet my hearth! I hail my house and halls!
How gladly I behold the light once more
and look on you!   525

> (*He sees his family.*)

                    What is this I see?
my children before the house? with garlands
on their heads? and my wife surrounded
by a crowd of men? my father in tears?
What misfortune makes him cry? I'll go and ask
what disaster now has come upon my house.   530

Megara

O my dearest. . . .

Amphitryon

                    O daylight returning!

Megara

You come, alive, in time to rescue us!

Heracles

Father, what has happened? What does this mean?

« 300 »

Megara

    Murder. Forgive me, Father, if I snatch
    and speak the words that you should rightly say.   535
    I am a woman: anguish hurts me more,
    and my children were being put to death. . . .

Heracles

    Apollo! what a prelude to your tale!

Megara

    My father is dead. My brothers are dead.

Heracles

    What! How did they die? Who killed them?   540

Megara

    Murdered by Lycus, the upstart tyrant.

Heracles

    In revolution? Or civil war?

Megara

    Civil war. Now he rules our seven gates.

Heracles

    But why should you and my father be afraid?

Megara

    He planned to kill us: your sons, father, and me.   545

Heracles

    What had he to fear from my orphaned sons?

Megara

    Lest they take revenge some day for Creon's death.

Heracles

    But why these garments? Why are they dressed for death?

Megara

    It was for our own deaths we put them on.

Heracles

You would have died by violence? O gods! 550

Megara

We had no friends. We heard that you were dead.

Heracles

How did you come to give up hope for me?

Megara

The heralds of Eurystheus proclaimed you dead.

Heracles

Why did you abandon my house and hearth?

Megara

By force. He dragged your father from his bed. 555

Heracles

He had no shame, but so dishonored age?

Megara

Lycus have shame? He knows no such goddess.

Heracles

And were my friends so scarce when I was gone?

Megara

In misfortune, what friend remains a friend?

Heracles

They thought so little of my Minyan wars? 560

Megara

Again I say, misfortune has no friends.

Heracles

Rip from your heads those wreaths of Hades!
Lift your faces to the light; with seeing eyes,
take your sweet reprieve from death and darkness.
And I—a task for my one hand alone— 565

shall go and raze this upstart tyrant's house,
cut off that blaspheming head and give it
to the dogs to paw. All those men of Thebes
who took my goodness and returned me ill—
this bow with which I won the victor's crown   570
shall slaughter them with rain of winged shafts
till all Ismenus chokes upon the corpses
and Dirce's silver waters run with blood.
What should I defend if not my wife and sons
and my old father? Farewell, my labors!   575
for wrongly I preferred you more than these.
They would have died for me, and I should die
in their defense. Or is this bravery,
to do Eurystheus' orders and contend
with lions and hydras, and not to struggle   580
for my children's lives? From this time forth,
call me no more "Heracles the victor."

Chorus

This is right, that a man defend his sons,
his aged father, and his wedded wife.

Amphitryon

My son, it is like you to love your friends   585
and hate your foe. But do not act too fast.

Heracles

How do I act faster than I should?

Amphitryon

The king has henchmen, a mob of needy men
who pass themselves off for men of wealth.
These men, their substance drained away by sloth   590
and spending, have promoted civil strife
and wrecked the state to mulct their neighbors.
You were seen coming here. Beware therefore
lest your enemy be stronger than you guess.

Heracles

   I do not care if all the city saw me!   595
   But seeing a bird in some foreboding place,
   I guessed some trouble had fallen on my house,
   and thus forewarned, I entered secretly.

Amphitryon

   Good. Go now, enter your house and greet your hearth.
   Look on your father's house; let it behold you.   600
   Shortly the king will come to hale us off
   and slaughter us: your wife, your sons, and me.
   Wait here, and everything shall come to hand;
   with safety too. But let the city go,
   my son, until we finish matters here.   605

Heracles

   You advise me well. I will go within.
   I owe first greetings to my household gods
   because they brought me home from sunless caves
   of Kore and Hades. I shall not slight them.

Amphitryon

   Did you really descend to Hades, son?   610

Heracles

   Yes; I brought back the triple-headed dog.

Amphitryon

   You subdued him? or was he the goddess' gift?

Heracles

   Subdued him. Luck was mine: I saw the mysteries.

Amphitryon

   And is the monster at Eurystheus' house?

Heracles

   No, at Hermione, in Demeter's grove.   615

Amphitryon

   Does Eurystheus know of your return above?

Heracles

No, I came here first to learn of you.

Amphitryon

Why did you delay so long underground?

Heracles

To save Theseus from Hades, Father.

Amphitryon

Where is he now? Gone to his native land?   620

Heracles

He went to Athens, rejoicing to be free.

>   (*He turns and addresses his children.*)

Follow your father to the house, my sons,
for this, your going in, shall be more fair
than your coming out. Put your fears away,
and stop those tears that well up in your eyes.   625
And you, dear wife, gather your courage up,
tremble no more, and let my garments go.
I have no wings to fly from those I love.
Look:
They will not let me go, but clutch my clothes
more tightly. How close you came to death!   630

>   (*He sets down his bow and club and takes
>   his children by the hands.*)

Here, I'll take your hands and lead you in my wake,
like a ship that tows its little boats behind,
for I accept this care and service
of my sons. Here all mankind is equal:
rich and poor alike, they love their children.
With wealth distinctions come: some possess it,   635
some do not. All mankind loves its children.

>   (*Exit Heracles with the children, followed
>   by Megara and Amphitryon.*)

Chorus

STROPHE I

Youth I long for always.
But old age lies on my head,
a weight more heavy than Aetna's rocks;
darkness hides   640
the light of my eyes.
Had I the wealth of an Asian king,
or a palace crammed with gold,   645
both would I give for youth,
loveliest in wealth,
in poverty, loveliest.
But old age I loathe: ugly,
murderous. Let the waves take it   650
so it comes no more to the homes
and cities of men! Let the wind
    whirl it away forever!

ANTISTROPHE I

If the gods were wise and understood   655
what human wisdom understands,
second youth would be their gift,
to seal the goodness of a man.
And so, conspicuous of life,
the good would run their race to death   660
and double back to light again.
But evil men should live their lap,
one single life, and run no more.
By such a sign all men would know
the wicked from the good,   665
as when the clouds are broken
and the sailor sees the stars.
But now the gods have put
between the noble and the base
no clear distinction down.   670
And time and age go wheeling on,
    exalting only wealth.

STROPHE 2

Never shall I cease from this,
Muses with the Graces joining,
loveliness in yoke together.   675
I may not live without the Muses.
Let my head be always crowned!
May my old age always sing
of Memory, the Muses' mother,
always shall I sing the crown   680
of Heracles the victor!
So long as these remain—
    Dionysus' gift of wine,
    the lyre of seven strings
    the shrilling of the flute—
never shall I cease to sing,   685
    Muses who made me dance!

ANTISTROPHE 2

Paeans sing the Delian maidens,
a song for Leto's lovely son,
wheeling at the temple gates
the lovely mazes of the dance.   690
So paeans at your gate I raise,
pouring like the dying swan,
from hoary throat a song of praise.
I have a noble theme of song: 695
    He is the son of Zeus!
    But far beyond his birth,
    his courage lifts him up,
whose labors gave this mortal calm,
    who cleared away the beasts.   700

(*Enter Lycus, with attendants. Amphitryon*
emerges from the palace.)

Lycus

None too soon, Amphitryon, have you appeared.
A long time now you've spent in dallying

with your robes and ornaments of death.
Go, call the wife and sons of Heracles
and bid them show themselves before the house.   705
On those terms, I let you clothe yourselves for death.

Amphitryon

King, you persecute in me a wretched man,
and by abusing us, you wrong the dead.
King you may be, but tread more gently here.
Death is your decree, and we accept it   710
as we must. As you decide, then so must we.

Lycus

Where is Megara? Where are the children?

Amphitryon

To chance a guess from here outside, I think . . .

Lycus

Well, what do you think? What makes you think so?

Amphitryon

. . . kneels at the hearth and makes her prayers . . .   715

Lycus

If she asks for life, her prayers are pointless.

Amphitryon

. . . and implores in vain her husband to come.

Lycus

He is not here to help. He will not come.

Amphitryon

Not unless some god restore him to us.

Lycus

Go inside and fetch her from the house.   720

Amphitryon

Then I should be accomplice in her death.

Lycus

    Very well then. Since your scruples forbid,
    I, who lack such petty fears, shall go and fetch
    the mother and her sons. Attend me, guards,
    and help me put good riddance to this chore.   725

             (Exit Lycus, attended by guards, into the palace.)

Amphitryon

    Go, march in to your fate. Someone, I think,
    will see you in. Expect for what you did
    evil in return. How justly, old friends,
    into that net whose meshes hide the sword,
    he goes, the man who would have slaughtered us,   730
    coward that he is! I'll go in and watch
    his body fall. This is sweet: to see your foe
    perish and pay to justice all he owes.

             (Exit Amphitryon into the palace.)

             Strophe 1

Chorus

    Disaster is reversed!
    The tyrant's life turns back to Hades!   735
    Justice flows back! O fate of the gods,
    returning!

    Your time has come. You go now where the price   740
    for outrage on your betters must be paid.

      Joy once more! Overboard with grief!
      The king has come again!
      He has come, of whom I had no hope,   745
      my country's king, come back again!

    Peer within the house, old friends. Let me see
    if what I hope to see is taking place.

Lycus

                            (Within.)

    Help! Help!

Chorus

ANTISTROPHE I

From within the song begins 750
I long to hear. That cry
was prelude to his death:
the tyrant's death is near.

Lycus

O land of Cadmus! Treachery! I die!

Chorus

Die: you would have killed. Show your boldness now 755
as you repay to justice all you owe.

What lying mortal made that fable
that mindless tale
that slander on the blessed?
Who denied the gods are strong?

Old friends, the godless man is dead! 760
The house is silent. Turn to the dances!
Those I love now prosper as I hoped.

STROPHE 2

Let dance and feasting now prevail
throughout this holy town of Thebes!
Joy and mourning change their places, 765
old disaster turns to dancing!
Change now rings my change of song!
The new king runs to death, the old king rules!
Our king runs home from Hades' harbor! 770
He comes again, he comes, my king and hope,
of whom my hope despaired.

ANTISTROPHE 2

The gods of heaven do prevail:
they raise the good and scourge the bad.
Excess of happiness—it drives
men's minds awry; in its train 775

comes on corrupted power.
No man foresees the final stretch of time.
Evil lures him, justice races by,
until he wrecks at last the somber car
    that holds his happiness.   780

STROPHE 3

O Ismenus, come with crowns!
Dance and sing: you gleaming streets
of seven-gated Thebes!
Come, O Dirce, lovely river,
leave your father's waters, bring
the nymphs, Asopus' daughters!   785
Come and sing the famous crown
of Heracles the victor!
O wooded crag of Delphi,   790
O Muses' homes on Helicon!
make my city's walls resound,
echo back the joy of Thebes,
city where the sown men rose
with shields of bronze, where still   795
their children's children dwell,
    a blessed light to Thebes!

ANTISTROPHE 3

O marriage-bed two bridegrooms shared!
One was man; the other, Zeus,
who entered in the bridal bed   800
and with Alcmene lay.
How true, O Zeus, that marriage
proves to be! Your part therein,
against all doubt, is proven true!
For time at last has clearly shown the strength   805
of Heracles the hero.
He made his way from Pluto's halls;
he left the dungeon underground.

He is to me a better king
than that ignoble lord: 810
comparison made plain
in the struggle of the sword,
if justice still finds favor
    among the blessed gods.

> (*A crash of thunder. The figure of Madness, gorgon-faced and*
>   *holding a goad, appears in a black chariot on the roof of*
>   *the palace. On the other side of the roof Iris is seen.*)

Ah! Ah!   815
Is the same terror on us all?
Look, old friends: what phantom hovers on the house?

Fly, fly!
Stir your heavy limbs! Back, away!

Lord Paian, help us! Avert disaster!   820

Iris

Courage, old men. You see there, Madness,
child of night, and me, servant of the gods,
Iris. We bring no harm upon your city.
Against one man alone our war is waged,   825
him whom men call Alcmene's son by Zeus.
Until his bitter labors had been done,
his fate preserved him; nor would father Zeus
let me or Hera do him any harm.
But now Eurystheus' orders have been done,   830
Hera plans, by making him destroy his sons,
to taint him with fresh murder; and I agree.
    Up, then, unmarried child of blackest Night,
rouse up, harden that relentless heart,
send madness on this man, confound his mind   835
and make him kill his sons. Madden his feet;
drive him, goad him, shake out the sails of death
and speed his passage over Acheron,
where he must take his crown of lovely sons.
Let him learn what Hera's anger is,   840

and what is mine. For the gods are nothing,
and men prevail, if this one man escape.

Madness

    I was born of noble birth: my mother
is the Night, and my father, Uranus.
My functions make me loathsome to the gods,   845
nor do I gladly visit men I love.
And I advise both you and Hera now,
lest I see you stumble, to hear me out.
This man against whose house you drive me on
has won great fame on earth and with the gods.   850
He reclaimed the pathless earth and raging sea,
and he alone held up the honors of the gods
when they wilted at the hands of evil men.
I advise you: renounce these wicked plans.

Iris

    Hera's scheme and mine need no advice from you.   855

Madness

    I would place you on the better path: you choose the worse.

Iris

    Hera has not sent you down to show your sanity.

Madness

    O Sun, be my witness: I act against my will.
But since I must perform the service you and Hera ask,
in full cry, like the hound that bays the huntsman,   860
go I will: to the heart of Heracles I run,
more fast, more wild than ocean's groaning breakers go,
than earthquake, or the thunder's agonizing crack!
I shall batter through the roof and leap upon the house!
He shall kill his sons and, killing, shall not know   865
he kills what he begot, until my madness leave him.
    Look: already, head writhing, he leaps the starting-post;
jumps and now stops; his eyeballs bulge, and pupils roll;

his breath comes heaving up, a bull about to charge!
And now he bellows up the horrid fates from hell;   870
he groans and shouts; he dances to the pipes of terror!
Soar to Olympus, Iris, on your honored way,
while I now sink, unseen, to the house of Heracles.

> (*Iris and Madness disappear. As they go, a weird piping of the
> flute begins, now soft, now loud, broken in rhythm,
> pitched insanely, and then suddenly still.*)

Chorus

O city, mourn! Your flower   875
is cut down, the son of Zeus.
O Hellas, mourn! You have lost
your savior! He dances now
to the fatal flutes of madness!

Madness has mounted her car;   880
she goads her team!
she drives for death!
O gorgon of Night, O hiss
of a hundred snakes! O Madness,
whose look makes stones of men!

Instantly, god's fortune is reversed!   885
Instantly, and father murders sons!

Amphitryon
O horror!

(*Within.*)

Chorus
O Zeus, your son has lost his sons!
Vengeance, mad, implacable, exacts
the penalty! Disaster lays him low!   890

Amphitryon
O my house!

Chorus
Now the dance begins! Not here,
the drums! no lovely thyrsos here!

Amphitryon
  O my home!

Chorus
  For blood, she drives, for blood!
  No wine of Dionysus here!   895

Amphitryon
  Fly, children, save yourselves!

Chorus
                      Horrid,
    horrid piping of the flute!
    His sons, he hunts them down!
    Madness through the house,
    madness dancing death!

Amphitryon
  O grief!   900

Chorus
    I grieve for those two,
    for the old man, for the mother
    who bore, who nursed her sons in vain!

    Look, look!
    Whirlwind shakes the house, the roof falls!   905

    Ah! on the roof!
    O daughter of Zeus, what do you do?
    You have brought upon this house
    ruin that reaches to hell,
    as once you ruined Enceladus!
                      (*A messenger appears from the palace.*)

Messenger
  O bodies blanched with age. . . .   910

Chorus
                      Why that cry?

Messenger
  Horror in the house!

Chorus

O my prophetic fears!

Messenger

The children live no more.

Chorus

Ah. . . .

Messenger

Mourn them, grieve them.

Chorus

Cruel murder,
O cruel hands of a father!   915

Messenger

No words could tell what we have seen.

Chorus

How did it happen, how this madness,
children killed by a father's hands?
How did disaster strike, madness
hurled from heaven on this house?   920
How did those pitiful children die?

Messenger

Offerings to Zeus were set before the hearth
to purify the house, for Heracles
had cast the body of the king outside.
There the children stood, in lovely cluster,   925
with Megara and the old man. In holy hush
the basket made the circle of the hearth.
And then, as Heracles reached out his hand
to take the torch and dip it in the water,
he stood stockstill. There he stood, not moving,   930
while the children stared. Suddenly he changed:
his eyes rolled and bulged from their sockets,
and the veins stood out, gorged with blood, and froth
began to trickle down his bearded chin.

Then he spoke, laughing like a maniac: 935
"Why hallow fire, Father, to cleanse the house
before I kill Eurystheus? Why double work,
when at one blow I might complete my task?
I'll go and fetch Eurystheus' head, add it
to that other corpse, then purify my hands.   940
Empty your water out! Drop those baskets!
Someone fetch my bow. Put weapons in my hands:
I march against Mycenae! Let me have
crowbars and picks: the Cyclopes built well,
cramping stone on stone with plumb and mallet,   945
but with my pick I'll rip them down again."
Then he fancied that his chariot stood there;
he made as though to leap its rails, and rode off,
prodding with his hand as though it held a goad.
    Whether to laugh or shudder, we could not tell.   950
We stared at one another. Then one man asked,
"Is the master playing, or is he . . . mad?"
Up and down, throughout the house, he drove,
and riding through the great hall, claimed it was
Nisus' city, though it was, in fact, his house.   955
He threw himself to the floor, and acted out
a feast. He tarried there a while, then said
he was approaching Isthmus' wooded valley.
He unstrapped his buckles and stripped himself bare,
and wrestled with no one; then called for silence   960
and crowned himself the victor of a match
that never was. Then raged against Eurystheus,
and said he'd come to Mycenae. His father
caught him by that muscled hand and said:
"What do you mean, my son? What is this journey   965
that you make? Or has the blood of those you've slain
made you mad?" He thought Eurystheus' father
had come, trembling, to supplicate his hand;
pushed him away, and set his bow and arrows
against his sons. He thought he was killing   970

Eurystheus' children. Trembling with terror,
they rushed here and there; one hid beneath
his mother's robes, one ran to the shadow
of a pillar, and the last crouched like a bird
below the altar. Their mother shrieked:
"You are their father! Will you kill your sons?"   975
And shouts broke from the old man and the slaves.
Around the pillar he pursued his son
in dreadful circles, then caught up with him
and pierced him to the heart. Backward he fell,
dying, and stained the flagstones with his blood.   980
His father shouted in triumph, exulting,
"Here is the first of Eurystheus' youngsters dead;
his death repays me for his father's hate."
He aimed his bow at the second, who crouched
below the altar's base, trying to hide.   985
The boy leaped first, fell at his father's knees
and held his hand up to his father's chin.
"Dearest Father," he cried, "do not murder me.
I am your own son, yours, not Eurystheus'!"
But he stared from stony gorgon eyes,   990
found his son too close to draw the bow,
and brought his club down on that golden head,
and smashed the skull, as though a blacksmith
smiting steel. Now that his second son lay dead,
he rushed to kill the single victim left.   995
But before he drew the bow, the mother
seized her child, ran within and locked the doors.
And, as though these were the Cyclopean walls,
he pried the panels up, ripped out the jambs,
and with one arrow brought down son and wife.   1000
And then he rushed to kill his father too,
but look! a phantom came—or so it seemed to us—
Pallas, with plumed helm, brandishing a spear.
She hurled a rock; it struck him on the chest,
stopped short his murderous rage and knocked him   1005

into sleep. He slumped to the floor and hit
his back against a pillar which had fallen there,
snapped in two pieces when the roof collapsed.

 Delivered from the fear that made us run,   1010
we helped the old man lash him down with ropes 1009
against the pillar, lest when he awakes
still greater grief be added to the rest.
He sleeps now, wretched man, no happy sleep,
killer of his wife and sons. I do not know
one man alive more miserable than this.   1015

         (Exit messenger.)

Chorus

 The hill of Argos had a murder once
Danaus' daughters did, murder's byword,
unbelievable in Hellas!
But murder here has far outrun,
surpassed by far
that ancient crime.   1020

 And Procne's noble son was slain,
murdered by his mother's hands and made,
I say, the Muses' sacrifice.
She had but that one son,
while you, poor wretch, had three,
all murdered by your madness.
What dirge, what song   1025
shall I sing for the dead?
What dance shall I dance for death?

  (The great central doors of the palace slide slowly apart, revealing,
   in the center court, Heracles asleep, bound to a broken pillar.
    The bodies of Megara and the children beside him are
      wheeled on the stage in the eccyclema.)

Ah, look!
Look: the great doors
of the palace slide apart!   1030

Look there!
Look: the children's corpses

beside their wretched father.
How terribly he lies asleep
after his children's slaughter!

Ropes around his body,   1035
knotted cords bind Heracles,
cables lash him down
to the pillars of his house.

Here the old man comes, dragging behind
with heavy steps, mourning in bitterness   1040
like some bird whose unfledged covey is slain.

Amphitryon
  Hush, old men of Cadmus' city,
  and let him sleep. Hush:
  let him forget his grief.

Chorus
  I weep for you, old friend,   1045
  for these boys, and for that head
  that wore the victor's crown.

Amphitryon
  Stand further off: not a sound,
  not a cry. His sleep is deep,
  his sleep is calm. Let him lie.

Chorus
  What murder . . .   1050

Amphitryon
  Hush! Be still: you add but grief.

Chorus
          . . . poured out, piled high!

Amphitryon
  Softly, gently, old friends. Mourn
  in quiet: not a word, not a cry.
  If he awakes and breaks his bonds,   1055

he will destroy us all:
father, city, and his house.

Chorus
I cannot hold my grief.

Amphitryon
Hush:
let me hear his breathing.

Chorus
Does he sleep? 1060

Amphitryon
He sleeps, but sleeps
as dead men do, because he slew his wife
and killed his sons with twanging bow.

Chorus
Grieve then, mourn!

Amphitryon
I mourn, I grieve. 1065

Chorus
Mourn for these dead children.

Amphitryon
Ah. . . .

Chorus
Mourn your son, grieve for him.

Amphitryon
Ah. . . .

Chorus
Old friend. . . .

Amphitryon
Hush, be still:
he stirs and turns! He wakes! Quick,
let me hide myself in darkness here. 1070

Chrous

Courage: darkness lies upon his eyes.

Amphitryon

Take care, take care. My grief is such,
I have no fear to leave the light and die.
But if he murders me who begot him,
he shall add a greater grief to these,   1075
and have on him the curse of father's blood.

Chorus

Best for you it would have been
if you had died that very day
you took revenge on those who slew
the kinsmen of your wife, the day
you sacked the city of the Taphians!   1080

Amphitryon

Run, run, old friends, back from the house,
away! He wakes! Run, run
from his reawakened rage!
He wakes to pile murder on murder,
to dance madness through all Thebes!   1085

Chorus

O Zeus, why have you hated him so much,
your own son? Why launched him on this sea of grief?

Heracles

How now?
I do breathe . . . what I ought to see, I see:
heaven and earth, the gleaming shafts of the sun. . . .   1090
But how strangely my muddled senses swim,
as on a choppy sea . . . my breath comes warm,
torn up unsteadily from heaving lungs. . . .
And look: I sit here, like a ship lashed tight
with cables binding my chest and arms,   1095
moored to a piece of broken masonry;
and there, close beside me, corpses lie . . .

and my bow and arrows littered on the ground,
those faithful former comrades of my arms,
that guarded my chest, and I guarded them. 1100
Have I come back to Hades? Have I run
Eurystheus' race again? Hades? But how?
No, for I see no rock of Sisyphus,
no Pluto, no queen Demeter's sceptre.
I am bewildered. Where could *I* be helpless? 1105
    Help! Is there some friend of mine, near or far,
who could help me in my bewilderment?
For all I took for granted now seems strange. . . .

Amphitryon
    Old friends, shall I approach my affliction?

Chorus
    Go, and I'll go with you, sharing in your grief. 1110

Heracles
    Why do you cry, Father, and hide your eyes?
    Why do you stand off from the son you love?

Amphitryon
    O my son, *my* son, whatever you have done. . . .

Heracles
    What have I done that you should weep for it?

Amphitryon
    Even a god would weep, if he knew it. 1115

Heracles
    A great grief it must be; but you hide it.

Amphitryon
    It is there to see, if you could but see it.

Heracles
    Tell me if you mean my life is not the same.

Amphitryon
    Tell me if you are sane; then I shall speak.

Heracles

O gods, how ominous these questions are!   1120

Amphitryon

I wonder even now if you are not mad. . . .

Heracles

Mad? I cannot remember being mad.

Amphitryon

Friends, shall I loose his ropes? What should I do?

Heracles

Tell me who bound me! Who disgraced me so?

Amphitryon

Your troubles are enough. Let the others go.   1125

Heracles

I say no more. Will you tell me now?

Amphitryon

O Zeus, do you see these deeds Hera has done? ,

Heracles

Is it from *her* hate our sufferings come?

Amphitryon

Let the goddess go. Shoulder your own grief.

Heracles

I am ruined. Your words will be disaster.   1130

> (*Amphitryon removes the shrouds from the children's corpses.*)

Amphitryon

Look. Look at the bodies of your children.

Heracles

Oh horrible! What awful sight is this?

Amphitryon

Your unnatural war against your sons.

Heracles
> War? What war do you mean? Who killed these boys?

Amphitryon
> You and your bow and some god are all guilty.   1135

Heracles
> What! I did it? O Father, herald of evil!

Amphitryon
> You were mad. Your questions asked for grief.

Heracles
> And it was I who murdered wife as well?

Amphitryon
> All this was the work of your hand alone.

Heracles
> O black night of grief which covers me!   1140

Amphitryon
> It was because of that you saw me weep.

Heracles
> Did I ruin all my house in my madness?

Amphitryon
> I know but this: everything you have is grief.

Heracles
> Where did my madness take me? Where did I die?

Amphitryon
> By the altar, as you purified your hands.   1145

Heracles
> Why then am I so sparing of this life,
> born the killer of my dearest sons?
> Let me avenge my children's murder:
> let me hurl myself down from some sheer rock,
> or drive the whetted sword against my side,   1150

or expunge with fire this body's madness
and burn away this guilt which sticks to my life!

(*He glances to the right and sees Theseus approaching.*)

But look: Theseus comes, my friend and kinsman,
intruding on my strategies for death.
And seeing me, the taint of murdered sons   1155
shall enter at the eye of my dearest friend.
What shall I do? Where can this shame be hid?
Oh for wings to fly! to plunge beneath the earth!
Here: let my garments hide my head in darkness,
in shame, in horror of this deed I did,   1160
and so concealed, I'll shelter him from harm,
and keep pollution from the innocent.

(*Enter Theseus, unattended.*)

Theseus

I come, old man, leading the youth of Athens,
bringing alliance to your son; my men
wait under arms by the stream of Asopos.   1165
A rumor came to Erechtheus' city
that Lycus had seized the sceptre of this land
and was engaged in war against your house.
And so, in gratitude to Heracles
who saved me from Hades, I have come,   1170
old man, if you should need a helping hand.

(*He sees the corpses of the children.*)

Ah!
What bodies are these scattered on the ground?
Have I arrived too late, preceded here
by some disaster? Who killed these boys?
That woman lying there, whose wife was she?   1175
Children are not mustered on the field of war:
no, this is some newer sorrow I find here.

Amphitryon

O lord of the olive-bearing hill. . . .

Theseus
Why do you speak in those heavy tones of grief?

Amphitryon
See what grief the gods have given.   1180

Theseus
Whose children are these over whom you mourn?

Amphitryon
O gods, my son begot these boys,
begot them, killed them, his own blood.

Theseus
Unsay those words!

Amphitryon
                              Would that I could!   1185

Theseus
Oh horrible tale!

Amphitryon
                    We are ruined and lost.

Theseus
How did it happen? Tell me how.

Amphitryon
Dead in the blow of madness,
by arrows dipped in the blood
of the hundred-headed hydra. . . .   1190

Theseus
This is Hera's war. Who lies there by the bodies?

Amphitryon
My son, my most unhappy son,
who fought with giant-killing spear
beside the gods at Phlegraia.

Theseus
What mortal man was ever cursed like this?   1195

Amphitryon

    Among all men you would not find,
    greater wretchedness, greater suffering
             than this.

Theseus

    Why does he hide his head beneath his robes?

Amphitryon

    Shame of meeting your eye,
    shame before friends and kin,   1200
    shame for his murdered sons.

Theseus

    I come to share his grief. Uncover him.

Amphitryon

    My son, drop your robe from your eyes,
    show your forehead to the sun.   1205
    A friend has come, a rival weight
    to counterpoise your grief.
    O my son, I impore you,
    by your beard, your knees, your hand,
    by an old man's tears: 1210
    tame that lion of your rage
    that roars you on to death,
    yoking grief to grief.

Theseus

    I call on you, huddled there in misery:
    lift up your head and show your face to friends.   1215
    There is no cloud whose utter blackness
    could conceal in night a sorrow like yours.
    Why wave me off, warning me of blood?
    Are you afraid mere words would pollute me?
    What do I care if your misfortunes fall   1220
    on me? You were my good fortune once:
    you saved me from the dead, brought me back to light.
    I loathe a friend whose gratitude grows old,

a friend who takes his friend's prosperity
but will not voyage with him in his grief.   1225
Rise up; uncover that afflicted head
and look on us. This is courage in a man:
to bear unflinchingly what heaven sends.

(He raises Heracles to his feet and uncovers his head.)

Heracles
Theseus, have you seen this field of fallen sons?

Theseus
I heard. I see the grief to which you point.   1230

Heracles
How could you then uncloak me to the sun?

Theseus
No mortal man can stain what is divine.

Heracles
Away, rash friend! Flee my foul pollution.

Theseus
Where there is love contagion cannot come.

Heracles
I thank you. How right I was to help you once.   1235

Theseus
You saved me then, and now I pity you.

Heracles
A man to be pitied: I slew my children.

Theseus
My tears, my gratitude, I mourn your grief.

Heracles
Have you ever seen more misery than this?

Theseus
Your wretchedness towers up and touches heaven.   1240

Heracles

Then where it touches heaven, I shall strike.

Theseus

What do you think the gods care for your threats?

Heracles

Heaven is proud. And I am proud to heaven.

Theseus

No more: your presumption will be punished.

Heracles

My hold is full: there is no room for more.   1245

Theseus

What will you do? Where does your passion run?

Heracles

To death: to go back whence I came, beneath the earth.

Theseus

These are the words of an ordinary man.

Heracles

Will you, who did not suffer, preach to me?

Theseus

Is this that Heracles who endured so much?   1250

Heracles

Not *so* much. Endurance has an end.

Theseus

Mankind's benefactor, man's greatest friend?

Heracles

What good are men to me? Hera rules.

Theseus

You die so mean a death? Hellas forbids it.

Heracles

Listen: let me tell you what makes a mock   1255
at your advice. Let me show you my life:
a life not worth living now, or ever.
Take my father first, a man who killed
my mother's father and having such a curse,
married Alcmene who gave birth to me.   1260
When a house is built on poor foundations,
then its descendants are the heirs of grief.
Then Zeus—whoever Zeus may be—begot me
for Hera's hatred. Take no offense, old man,
for I count you my father now, not Zeus.   1265
While I was still at suck, she set her snakes
with gorgon eyes to slither in my crib
and strangle me. And when I grew older
and a belt of muscle bound my body—
why recite all those labors I endured?   1270
All those wars I fought, those beasts I slew,
those lions and triple-bodied Typhons,
giants, and four-legged Centaur hordes!
I killed the hydra, that hound whose heads
grew back as soon as lopped. My countless labors done,   1275
I descended down among the sullen dead
to do Eurystheus' bidding and bring to light
the triple-headed hound who guards the gates of hell.
    And now my last worst labor has been done:
I slew my children and crowned my house with grief.   1280
And this is how I stand: I cannot stay
with those I love at Thebes. If I remain,
what temple, what assembly of my friends
will have me? My curse is unapproachable.
Go to Argos then? No, I am banished there.   1285
Settle in some other city then,
where notoriety shall pick me out
to be watched and goaded by bitter gibes—
"Is this the son of Zeus, who killed his wife

and sons? Away with him! Let him die elsewhere."   1290
[To a man who prospers and is blessed,
all change is grief; but the man who lives
akin to trouble minds disaster less.]
But to this pitch of grief my life has come:
the earth itself will groan, forbidding me   1295
to touch the ground, rivers and seas cry out
against my crossing-over, and I am
like Ixion, bound forever to a wheel.
This is the best, that I be seen no more
in Hellas, where I prospered and was great.   1300
Why should I live? What profit have I,
having a life both useless and accursed?
Let the noble wife of Zeus begin the dance,
pounding with her feet Olympus' gleaming floors!
For she accomplished what her heart desired,   1305
and hurled the greatest man of Hellas down
in utter ruin. Who could offer prayers
to such a goddess? Jealous of Zeus
for a mortal woman's sake, she has destroyed
Hellas' greatest friend, though he was guiltless.   1310

Theseus

No other god is implicated here,
except the wife of Zeus. Rightly you judge.
My advice is this: be patient, suffer
what you must, and do not yield to grief.
Fate exempts no man; all men are flawed,
and so the gods, unless the poets lie.   1315
Do not the gods commit adultery?
Have they not cast their fathers into chains,
in pursuit of power? Yet all the same,
despite their crimes, they live upon Olympos.
How dare you then, mortal that you are,   1320
to protest your fate, when the gods do not?
    Obey the law and leave your native Thebes

and follow after me to Pallas' city.
There I shall purify your hands of blood,
give you a home and a share of my wealth. 1325
All those gifts I have because I killed
the Minotaur and saved twice seven youths,
I cede to you. Everywhere throughout my land,
plots of earth have been reserved for me.
These I now assign to you, to bear your name 1330
until you die. And when you go to Hades,
Athens shall raise you up a monument
of stone, and honor you with sacrifice.
And so my city, helping a noble man,
shall win from Hellas a lovely crown of fame. 1335
This thanks and this return I make you now,
who saved me once. For now you need a friend.
[He needs no friends who has the love of gods.
For when god helps a man, he has help enough.]

Heracles

Ah, all this has no bearing on my grief; 1340
but I do not believe the gods commit
adultery, or bind each other in chains.
I never did believe it; I never shall;
nor that one god is tyrant of the rest.
If god is truly god, he is perfect, 1345
lacking nothing. These are poets' wretched lies.
    Even in my misery I asked myself,
would it not be cowardice to die?
The man who cannot bear up under fate
could never face the weapons of a man. 1350
I shall prevail against death. I shall go
to your city. I accept your countless gifts.
For countless were the labors I endured;
never yet have I refused, never yet
have I wept, and never did I think 1355

that I should come to this: tears in my eyes.
But now, I see, I must serve necessity.

And now you see me banished, old man;
you see in me the killer of my sons.
Give them to the grave, give them the tribute   1360
of your tears, for the law forbids me this.
Let them lie there in their mother's arms,
united in their grief, as they were then,
before, in ignorance, I killed them all.
And when the earth conceals their small remains,
live on in this city here, and though it hurt,   1365
compel your soul to bear misfortune with me.

O my sons, the father who gave you life
has slain you all, and never shall you reap
that harvest of my life, all I labored for,
that heritage of fame I toiled to leave you.   1370
You too, poor wife, I killed: unkind return
for having kept the honor of my bed,
for all your weary vigil in my house.

O wretched wife and sons! Wretched father!
In grief I now unyoke myself from you.   1375
O bitter sweetness of this last embrace!

(He turns from his final farewell to his wife and children
and picks up his bow and arrows.)

O my weapons, bitter partners of my life!
What shall I do? Let you go, or keep you,
knocking against my ribs and always saying,
"With us you murdered wife and sons. Wearing us,   1380
you wear your children's killers." Can that be worn?
What could I reply? Yet, naked of these arms,
with which I did the greatest deeds in Hellas,
must I die in shame at my enemies' hands?
No, they must be borne; but in pain I bear them.   1385
Hold with me, Theseus, in one thing more.

Help me take to Argos the monstrous dog,
lest, alone and desolate of sons, I die.
    O land of Cadmus, O people of Thebes,
mourn with me, grieve with me, attend my children   1390
to the grave! And with one voice mourn us all,
the dead and me. For all of us have died,
all struck down by one blow of Hera's hate.

Theseus

Rise up, unfortunate friend. Have done with tears.

Heracles

I cannot rise. My limbs are rooted here.   1395

Theseus

Then necessity breaks even the strong.

Heracles

Oh to be a stone! To feel no grief!

Theseus

Enough. Give your hand to your helping friend.

Heracles

Take care. I may pollute your clothes with blood.

Theseus

Pollute them then. Spare not. I do not care.   1400

Heracles

My sons are dead; now you shall be my son.

Theseus

Place your hand on my shoulder. I shall lead you.

Heracles

A yoke of love, but one of us in grief.
O Father, choose a man like this for friend.

Amphitryon

The land that gave him birth has noble sons.   1405

Heracles
Theseus, turn me back. Let me see my sons.

Theseus
Is this a remedy to ease your grief?

Heracles
I long for it, yearn to embrace my father.

Amphitryon
My arms are waiting. I too desire it.

Theseus
Have you forgotten your labors so far?   1410

Heracles
All those labors I endured were less than these.

Theseus
If someone sees your weakness, he will not praise you.

Heracles
I live: am I so low? You did not think so once.

Theseus
Once, no. But where now is famous Heracles?

Heracles
What were you when you were underground?   1415

Theseus
In courage I was the least of men.

Heracles
Then will you say my grief degrades me now?

Theseus
Forward!

Heracles
          Farewell, father!

Amphitryon
                    Farewell, my son.

Heracles
  Bury my children.

Amphitryon
                  Who will bury me?

Heracles
  I.   1420

Amphitryon
  When will you come?

Heracles
                        When you bury them.

Amphitryon
  How?

Heracles
      I shall have them brought from Thebes to Athens.
Take my children out, take them to their graves,
while I, whose whole house has gone down in grief,
am towed in Theseus' wake like some little boat.
The man who would prefer great wealth or strength   1425
more than love, more than friends, is diseased of soul.

Chorus
  We go in grief, we go in tears,
who lose in you our greatest friend.
    (Theseus and Heracles leave by the left. The chorus goes to the
       right, while Amphitryon slowly follows the eccyclema with
         the bodies of Megara and the children inside the palace.
                The great doors close behind them.)

IPHIGENIA
IN
TAURIS

Translated by

WITTER BYNNER

Introduction by

RICHMOND LATTIMORE

INTRODUCTION TO *IPHIGENIA IN TAURIS*

The Date

THERE is no external evidence for the date of *Iphigenia in Tauris* (it should be *Iphigenia among the Taurians*, but the other title has become regular through use); it has, however, been generally placed between 414 and 410 B.C., and there are good reasons for this. Meter is an excellent guide in dating the plays of Euripides, and metrically this play is similar to *The Trojan Women* (415), *Electra* (413), and *Helen* (412). In structure and plot *Iphigenia* is a romance or romantic comedy, and Euripides at this time seems to have been much interested in the possibilities of this type of play. The plots of *Iphigenia* and *Helen* are in many ways almost identical. In both, a woman who has been miraculously transported to the barbaric ends of the earth (Scythia, Egypt) and there held in honorable captivity is convinced, on the slightest kind of evidence, that the man in the world she loves most (brother, husband), her sole possible deliverer, is dead. Almost immediately she meets this very man and, after some misunderstanding, rushes into his arms in a joyful recognition scene. She then, with female guile (women, to Euripides, are more strategic than men) contrives their escape by working on the simple piety of the barbarian king, whose vengefulness is dispelled by the appearance of divinities (Athene, the Heavenly Twins), and all end at peace in the prospect of a happy future. This similarity might, however, be less striking if we possessed the lost plays of Euripides, since it is clear that he wrote many romantic comedies. *Ion* (possibly 411 B.C.) shares some of these features (supposed death and miraculous transportation, catastrophe barely averted, climax in recognition, happy ending) but is an example of the purer foundling-story. Our tentative date also goes well with the fact that at the end of his career Euripides was much interested in exploring the ramifications of the saga of the House of Atreus

(*Electra*, 413; *Helen*, 412; *Orestes*, about 408; *Iphigenia at Aulis*, posthumous), though the plays do not connect with each other and often conflict in choice of legendary variants.

Iphigenia was probably not produced with *Electra* in 413, since Orestes appears in both plays but with rather different characteristics, and since the predictions at the end of *Electra* ignore the expedition to the Taurians; nor, probably, was it produced with *Helen* in 412, since the dramas are too much alike to have been given together. We must then choose between 414 and 411 (the style is not "late" enough for any posterior date); my own uncertain choice is 414.

The Play

Iphigenia in Tauris was of course presented as a tragedy, but it is not "tragical" like *Medea* or *Hippolytus*. The formulae by which we are accustomed to interpret tragedy—the tragic fault or tragic choice (*hamartia*), the punishment of *hybris* (whatever that means), the irreconcilable conflict of characters, or justified revenge breeding new hatred and wrong—do not apply here and can be blissfully ignored. Euripides is more interested in How than in Why, and even as romantic comedy *Iphigenia* is less seriously problematical, cuts less deep, than *Alcestis* or *Ion*. Note how briskly the murder of Clytemnestra is disposed of, lines 924–27.

But the cheerfulness is serious, and in it I find two dominant ideals. One is the love of Greece. Euripides has been sobered by the horrors of internecine war, and has dropped the narrow, often bellicose pro-Athenian theme, which appears in *Heracleidae* and *Andromache* and *The Suppliants*, in favor of a wider Hellenism. His homesick Greeks find no comfort in even the friendliness of outlanders and long for Greece, all Greece or any of Greece, not merely Athens. The other ideal is friendship, the devoted, disinterested friendship of Admetus, Heracles, and Apollo in *Alcestis,* of Heracles and Theseus in *Heracles*, of Orestes, Pylades, and Electra in *Orestes* (a trio of cutthroats, to be sure, but their love seems to be real), and of the three friends here. Friendship and the love of Greek for Greek may indeed be symbolized for Euripides during this period in those

Dorian twins, Castor and Polydeuces (Pollux) who appear at the end of *Helen* and *Electra*. Polydeuces refused to survive his brother. The twins have no place in this story; yet Euripides goes out of his way to bring them in (l. 272), since they are the prototypes and patrons of those who put all selfishness aside and make the fortunes of their friends their own.

The Translation

The editors asked the distinguished poet Witter Bynner for permission to use his translation originally made in 1915. This translation seemed to them to be in many ways the first modern translation. The present text represents Mr. Bynner's carefully polished revision of a manuscript created under circumstances best recounted by him:

It might be wondered, when what little Greek I had learned at college was forgotten, why and how I came to venture a version in English of a Euripidean play.

In 1914, Isadora Duncan with her six dancers had for some time been bringing Greek figures and friezes to life on the stages of several nations. Almost everyone connected in those days with any of the arts knew Isadora; and when she had been given use of the New Theater near Columbus Circle in New York, later called the Century Theater, we often heard her wish for a "right translation" of a Greek play to produce there. She had removed orchestra seats to make a deep-aproned stage on which she offered almost daily, as public performances, her rehearsals and experiments in dance and drama. Charging dearly for what lower seats were left but only ten cents for a gallery seat, she attracted substantial and ardent audiences to an exciting laboratory unique in American history. After her production of *Oedipus Rex* —the lead well played by her brother, Augustin—she kept begging me to try my hand at a version of *Iphigenia in Tauris*, which, she said from some knowledge or other, "though superbly simple in the original, had never been humanly translated into English, but always with stilted inversions and scholarly heaviness, and the sense subjected to the sound."

She made me try it, the choruses first. Scenes of the play were to follow and be combined into growing length for performance, as fast as I could write them. We had put on the stage all of the choruses, for Margherita Duncan and Helen Freeman, besides the six girls and herself, before someone discovered and reported that by living in the theater's large, luxurious

dressing-rooms Isadora and her group were breaking New York's fire regula-
tions. So the whole experiment ended. But I finished the play, which was
published as a single volume in 1915 and again, as part of my *Book of Plays*,
in 1922. Both times, forgetting that we had omitted certain sections of the
choruses which Isadora had thought too remotely allusive to be understood
or effective, I neglected to restore them for print. They are included, however, in the present volume. I must add that in making the text for Isadora
I relied only on close study of all English versions available. In revising it
through the past two years, I have kept the choruses more or less as they
were, a sort of musical accompaniment to the drama, but have otherwise
written and discarded some seven manuscripts, with the devoted intent
that what I could do for it might become ever simpler, clearer, and worthier
of the humanist who wrote it.

For general accuracy, this new version has had the supervision of Richmond Lattimore, who instigated my endeavor to make it a still more human
play in 1955 than the earlier version seemed to be in 1915. I repeat at this
time the original dedication to my friend Barry Faulkner, the then young
painter who helpfully watched the growth of the first version forty years
ago.

CHARACTERS

Iphigenia

Pylades

Orestes

Temple Maidens

The Herdsman

Soldiers

King Thoas

Athena

IPHIGENIA IN TAURIS

SCENE: *Out of a temple by the seaside in Tauris, down steps leading to a
blood-stained altar seen through its door, comes Iphigenia, the High
Priestess, and stands alone on the stairway above the empty court.*

Iphigenia
 Pelops, the son of Tantalus, by maiming
A chariot, won a bride, who bore him Atreus,
And Atreus had two sons, one Menelaus,
The other Agamemnon, who in turn
By Clytemnestra had a child, and I
Am she, Iphigenia.   5
      People believe
That I was sacrificed by my own father
To Artemis, in the great pursuit of Helen,
Upon an altar near the bay of Aulis,
There where the long deep waves are caught and broken
Hither and thither by the winds, the bay
Where Agamemnon's fleet, his thousand ships 10
From Hellas, waited to avenge on Troy
The wrong done Menelaus through the loss
Of Helen. But a storm came up and still
Another storm and neither sea nor wind   15
Would favor Agamemnon. So he asked
Calchas, the soothsayer, to consult the flame.
And this is what was answered: "Agamemnon,
Captain of Hellas, there can be no way
Of setting your ships free, till the offering
You promised Artemis is given Her.
You had vowed to render Her in sacrifice 20
The loveliest thing each year should bear. You have owed
Long since the loveliness which Clytemnestra
Had borne to you, your daughter, Iphigenia.
Summon your daughter now and keep your word."

They sent Odysseus and his artful tongue
To lure me from my mother by pretending
That I should wed Achilles. When I had come   25
To Aulis, they laid hands on me. The flame
Was lit. The blow would have been struck—I saw
The knife. But Artemis deceived their eyes
With a deer to bleed for me and stole me through
The azure sky. And then She set me down
Here in this town of Tauris, this abode   30
Of savage men ruled by their uncouth king,
Thoas, a horseman headlong as the wind,
Who stationed me High Priestess in Her temple,
And still I serve Her on Her festal days.
Service may seem a holy word. But far   35
From holy are these orders I am bound
To obey, never to question: Her command that I
Must serve to Her the lives of foreigners.
It was a custom long before I came,
An ancient cruel custom. Can She hear me?
My hands prepare the victims. Other hands,
There in the inner temple, spill the blood,   40
Which then is poured upon this altar-stone.

(*She descends the steps into the court.*)

I dreamed last night a deathly dream. Perhaps
The morning will dispel it if I speak it—
I dreamed that I was far beyond the seas.
I seemed to be at home again in Argos,
Asleep among my maidens—when a roll   45
Of thunder shook the ground. I ran outside.
I watched the house. I saw the coping fall,
The cross-beams stir and yield, break and give way,
Then the whole palace plunge from roof to base,
Only one column left upright in all   50
My father's house. But that one stood alive,
A man with bright brown hair and breathing lips.

And then against my will my hand went out,
As it does toward strangers here condemned to die,
And touched his forehead with this fatal water—
And with water of my tears, because I knew
The dream was of Orestes and his end.   55
The pillar of a family is the son.
This water is the certain sign of death.
It could not mean my family next of kin;
Strophius, my uncle, never had a son.
It was my brother whom I touched with tears—   60
For whom I now must pour a funeral-urn,
All I can do for one so far away.

> *(Climbing the steps.)*

Where are the women from Greece the King appointed
To live with me and help me here in the temple?
I wonder where they are. I need their help.   65

The voice of Orestes

Keep a sharp lookout. Somebody may be coming.

Pylades

> *(Entering by the path from the bay.)*

I have looked in both directions and there's no one.

Orestes

> *(Following him and gazing at the temple.)*

Is this the shrine of Artemis we have sailed
So many seas to find since we left Argos?
Is it, O Pylades? Is this the shrine?   70

Pylades

I think it is, Orestes. So do you.

Orestes

And might that stone be stained with blood of Greeks?

Pylades

If ever I saw blood—look, on the edge!

Orestes
> Look, near the roof! Belongings of the dead!

Pylades
> Trophies of foreigners these men have murdered!   75

Orestes
> Careful!
>   O Phoebus, why must Thy oracle
> Bring this on me again, the sight of blood
> Again? Have I not seen enough of blood?
> My mother shed my father's blood, I hers.
> And then the Furies, with their eyes bloody,
> Hunted me, hounded me across the land   80
> Until at last I ran to Thee and begged
> An end of all the cycles of despair
> That sped me, hurled me, maddened me through Hellas.
> The answer was, "Go to the Taurian country   85
> Where Artemis, my sister, has a shrine.
> Find there Her statue which had fallen down
> From Heaven. Then prove yourself a man able
> Enough or fortunate enough to steal it,
> Stalwart enough to face all risk and bring it
> Home to the holy land of Attica."   90
> Although no more was said, I understood
> That this would mean the end of my afflictions.
> And here I am, O Phoebus, far from home
> On a misbegotten shore—doing Thy will.
>   But Pylades, my fellow venturer,   95
> Where can we turn? What man could possibly
> Scale these high walls? Or climb the open stairs
> And not be seen? Or force the brazen locks
> Without whoever is behind them hearing?
> If we are caught, it will be certain death,   100
> Your death as well as mine. Even this waiting,
> Wondering what to do, may cost our lives.
> Enough of it! Enough! Back to the ship!

Pylades

What do we know of flight? How should we dare
To take a course of which our hearts know nothing?
Why should we disobey Apollo's order,   105
Do him dishonor? No, we shall find a way.
Come, let us leave the temple, let us look
For a dark cave to hide in. Not the ship!
By now they must have spied the ship from shore.
They'd be ahead of us, catch us and end us.   110
   Notice the opening between those beams?
It's wide enough. Under the night's dim eye
We could drop through and hoist a wooden statue.
A coward turns away but a brave man's choice   115
Is danger. And by all the Gods, shall we,
Coming this far, now at the end turn back?

Orestes

I should have been the one to say those words.
Yes, let us go and find a hiding-place,
Keep faith with Phoebus and deserve his help.   120
Have we not youth? Youth, with its fill of strength,
Turning away from any task should be ashamed.

(They leave by the path to the shore. A great bell rings.
From the town side the Temple Maidens
assemble in the courtyard.)

A Maiden

Let those who dwell close to these Clashing Rocks
   That guard the Euxine Sea,   125
Keep silence now before Latona's daughter,
Artemis, Goddess of the pointed hills!

(Turning toward the temple as the bell ceases.)

   O Artemis, I come
On consecrated feet into Thy court,
   I hail Thee beautiful   130
As the golden gleaming of Thy colonnades!

A Second Maiden

Thy priestess calls us, she who keeps Thy keys,
    Who left behind, for Thee,
Her land of Hellas, the embattled towers,
The shore of horses, and the quiet fields
    Wherein our fathers lived.   135
And we obey her call to worship Thee
    In this embittered land,
Far from Eurotas and from happiness.

      (*Iphigenia enters from the temple, carrying a heavy golden urn.*)

A Third Maiden

          (*Crossing to Iphigenia and taking it to hold for her.*)

O daughter of the king who gathered ships
    A thousand strong and led
Unnumbered men against high-towering Troy,
We heard your call and we have come to you.
    Why have you summoned us?   140
What makes your cheek so thoughtful and so pale?
    What has your tongue to tell,
That your brow is dark and bowed upon your hands?

Iphigenia

My maidens, listen. Listen while I tell
What I have seen. The Muse has veiled Her face,   145
And I am mourning for a dead kinsman.
Last night in a dream I saw my family's ending,
So grieve for me. I saw my brother dead.   150
The dream was clear. My father's house is fallen,
My race broken and gone, Orestes dead!
So grieve for all of us, for all his people.   155
Fate, in still scourging me, takes from all Argos
My only brother!
             To the vanished dead
I shall now pour an offering, a gift   160
Upon the earth, commingled of the milk

Of mountain-kine and of the wine of Bacchus
And of the honey that the russet bees
Gathered, a soothing gift. This and my heart.   165

                    (*To the Third Maiden.*)

Give me the urn of gold which heavy holds
My tribute to the God of Death.
                              This urn,
Orestes, son of Agamemnon, you   170
Who are lying under the dark earth, I lift
And pour—for you. And may the sweetness reach
And ease your lips. Better I cannot give,
I cannot bring to you braids of my hair
And, crying, lay them down upon your grave.   175
Yet, though from childhood you have thought me dead,
I still can cry—far from my home and you.

A Fourth Maiden

    O Lady, woe is in me for your woe,
        My words are like a song
    Of old which mourners in the far-off East   180
    Chant for the dead, reciting only death,
        A requiem of hell,
    A wail of no returning and no hope,
        Using no note of glory,
    Only the desolation of the grave.   185

The First Maiden

    Mourn for the sons of Atreus, in whose house
        The hearth can never burn.
    Mourn for their bitter heritage, a home
    Which waits the coming of a happy king   190
        But cannot give him welcome.
    Trouble was born forever in their sky
        When Pelops tricked a car
    Of toppling horses out of the race for a bride.

The Third Maiden

Because of a golden lamb which long ago   195
    Beckoned contesting men,
Mischief began to undermine your house.

The Fourth Maiden

Vengeance has made its unappeasèd way
    With every dart of death   200
And visited your family one by one.
    And now with eager hand
Fate is pursuing you. Your turn has come.

Iphigenia

Oh bitter my beginning in the womb
Of her who bore me, from the very night
When she conceived! Appointed by the Fates   205
To suffer in this world, I was a child
Accursed. Yet how she cherished me, her first-born,
And thrilled that I, of all the girls of Argos,   210
Should be a bride upon the way to Troy!
    What had she borne me for and loved me for?—
To be destroyed by my own father's hand,
To come, behind the horses of delight,   215
Not to Achilles—but to grief and horror!
    And now beside this melancholy sea
I live my days—lonely, no love, no friends,
Wife of no man and mother of no child.   220
I know no home. I sing no Argive song
With Argive women to the Queen of Heaven.
I weave upon the whirring loom no tale
Of Pallas routing Titans. . . . Oh, instead,
I face an altar soaked with bloody death.   225
I hear the cry for pity and the moans
Of men—a thing too hideous to be told.
    Yet even that seems little to me now—
Now that a throne is empty and his eyes   230

Are done with weeping, as I wish mine were.
I who have loved him through these lonely years
Shall never see him now but as I left him,
A little baby at his mother's breast—
I who had thought to see him as a king.   235

The Second Maiden

(Pointing.)

That herdsman running, stumbling, from the beach!
    What can have happened there?

(They watch the sea-path.)

A Herdsman

(Entering out of breath.)

O daughter of the house of Agamemnon,
I bring you news!

Iphigenia

                Urgent enough for this
Rough outcry in the temple-yard?   240

The Herdsman

                A ship
From sea has passed through the Symplegades!
And through the fog two fellows waded ashore,
And never was a finer offering
Than these two boys will be for Artemis!
I have been sent to tell you to make ready.   245

Iphigenia

Where are they from?—what country? Could you say?

The Herdsman

From Hellas, but I couldn't say which part.

Iphigenia

What were their names? Perhaps you heard their names?

The Herdsman

One of them called the other Pylades.

Iphigenia

    And the one who spoke?

The Herdsman

                    I didn't hear his name.   250

Iphigenia

    Where were they captured?

The Herdsman

                    Right there on the shore.

Iphigenia

    What were you herdsmen doing on the shore?

The Herdsman

    Washing our cattle there.

Iphigenia

                Tell me again.   255
    How were they captured? This is the first time
    In all the years I have been living here
    That any of you ever brought a Greek
    To be the offering. Never a Greek.

The Herdsman

    Just as we drove our cattle from the woods   260
    To that long hollow where the curving tide
    Has cut away the cliff, where the beach-men rest
    From purple-fishing, one of us ahead
    Came stealing back on tiptoe and he warned us,   265
  "Those are not men but Gods! Behind that rock!
    Not men but Gods!" And then another herdsman
    Caught sight of them, raised up his hands and prayed,
  "Palaemon, born of a Sea-Goddess, Master of Ships,   270
    Protect us, whether these boys be the Twins
    Of Battle, sons and favorites of Zeus,
    Or else be brothers of the Ocean Nymphs,
    Be sons of Nereus, God of Waves like Thee!"

But another jeered at us and laughed out loud,   275
So that I thought the Gods would turn on him.
But he was sure there must have been a wreck,
And these were sailors looking for our cave
To hide in, having heard that strangers here
Are sacrificed. And he persuaded most   280
Of us, and we were thinking what to do,
When one of them ran out around the rock.
Just staring, not at us or anything
That we could see, but at the air and shook
And groaned, ducking his head from side to side
Behind his arms as if he'd gone insane.
And he was calling out, sharp as a hunter,
"Look, Pylades! O look at her! O look!   285
There! There! Surely you see her now!—that Fiend
From Hell! And on her head look at the snakes,
Their mouths wide open, writhing for my blood!
Here comes another one! And look at that one
Up on the cliff, vomiting fire on me,
Lifting my mother's body like a rock
So she can smash it down on me and kill me!   290
Pylades, help me! They are all around me!"
And we could tell, by the way he jerked his head
Whenever a dog barked or a cow mooed,
That if a Fury wasn't chasing him
He thought there was in every sound he heard.

    He might have knocked us flat there in a row,   295
We were so stunned. Instead, drawing his sword,
He lunged into our cattle like a lion,
As if they were the Furies, ripped their sides
With all his might till blood was running down,
Staining the edge. We were just untrained herdsmen   300
Facing expert young swordsmen; but we saw
The cattle wounded and dying and we hunted
For sticks and stones and blew our shells for help
And pretty soon farmers enough had joined us

To fight. Then, as we slowly started forward,   305
His madness left him. I can see him now—
Standing a moment. While I watch he drops
In a heap and foaming at the lips. Once more
We started toward him with our sticks and stones,
But still, his comrade, unafraid of us,   310
Leaned down to wipe the frothy mouth and laid
A piece of linen over the face to shield it—
Till suddenly the fallen man stood up,
Calm and himself again, and faced the rush
Of rocks we heaved at him like breaking waves.   315
We crowded in on him from every side.
He gave one groan as we surrounded him,
Ready to capture him or finish him.
And then we heard his voice ring out and say,   320
"If this is death, let's meet it, Pylades,
Like men! Come on! Together! With our swords!"
    The metal flashed at us. We backed and tricked them
Into the hollow. There, while some of us
Would run for cover, others could throw rocks   325
To draw the swordsmen off and then give way
And let the first lot rally with new armfuls.
And yet we couldn't seem to hit those fellows.
I don't see how it was, with all the stones
We threw at them, that hardly one went straight.
All we could manage was to wear them down   330
By working round each man, aiming our volleys
Just at his sword, which, once he lost his grip,
He was too winded to pick up again.
    And when we took our prisoners to the king,
He told us we should bring them here, and you
Should get them ready for the sacrifice.   335
    Ask Artemis to send us more of them,
More sailor-boys from Greece, send them to Tauris,
And let more men from Hellas pay with blood
After their shouting for your blood at Aulis.

The First Maiden

    This is no ordinary man who has come   340
    From shores of Hellas to an alien shore
        And battles like a God.

Iphigenia

    Go back and bring me the two foreigners.
    I shall be waiting for them when you come.

                        (The Herdsman leaves.)

      Poor heart of mine, which always hitherto
    Has been compassionate, tender toward strangers,   345
    And even yesterday felt a quick pang
    At thought of Greeks who might be lost in Tauris,
    A crushing dream has changed you overnight.
    For since Orestes is no more alive,
    Now, where my heart was, there is only stone.   350
    Strangers who come today, no matter who,
    Will find in me a woman beyond tears.
      Unhappiness, O friends, can harden us
    Toward other sorrow harsher than our own.
      If but some heaven-sent wind, forcing a ship
    Between the Clashing Rocks, might bring me Helen,   355
    The Helen whom I hate, and Menelaus,
    That I might make of them the sacrifice,
    Let a new Aulis expiate the old,
    And vent my vengeance! It was Helen's fault
    And his, that Greek hands lifted me at Aulis
    And led me like a beast where, at the altar,
    My father held the sacrificial knife.   360
    I live it all again. My fingers, groping,
    Go out to him like this and clutch his beard
    And cling about his knees. I cry to him:
  "It is you yourself, yourself, who brought me here,
    You who deceived my maidens and my mother!   365
    They sing my marriage-song at home, they fill
    The house with happiness, while all the time

Here am I dying at my father's hands!
You led me in your chariot to take
Achilles for my lord, but here is death   370
And the taste of blood, not kisses, on my lips!"
    And I had left my home with my white veil
Drawn down. I had not taken in my arms
My brother—dead this day—nor kissed my sister.
I had saved all my kisses and embraces   375
For the man I was to marry. Even then
My heart was homesick and was faint with hope
That I should soon be back again in Argos.
    And now, O dead Orestes, you, as I,
Forfeit your heritage and lose your home.
    And what does Artemis ask of me here?—   380
She who forbids approach by any man
Whose hand is stained with bloodshed or with touch
Of childbirth or of burial, finds him
Unclean and bans him. She so delicate
In all these ways will yet demand the blood
Of human beings on Her altar-stone!
It cannot be. How could Latona bear   385
To Zeus so cruel a daughter? It is not true.
It is as false as tales of Tantalus
Feeding the Gods a child. O Artemis,
These people, being murderers themselves,
Are charging Thee with their own wickedness.   390
No! I will not believe it of a God!

The Second Maiden

    O Clashing Rocks, under whose shadow the dark
        Threat waits, though through this cleft
Io fled safe, in her disguise as heifer
Pursued by the sharp stinging of the gadfly,   395
        Fled beyond Europe's land
And Europe's sea, fled safe but sick at heart,
        Away from home and kin,

Into the alien wilderness of Asia,
What sort of men would leave the holy streams
    Of Dirce, or the reeds   400
Green-growing in Eurotas, to explore
A bitter beach, to dare these ominous rocks
    Where the seas meet in fog,
Where Artemis, among Her colonnades
    Demanding sacrifice,   405
Receives upon her altar human blood?

The Fourth Maiden
Why have they urged the oarsmen of their ship
    To shake the clinging sea
With a great stroke and to accelerate
With rush of rivalry the racing wind?   410
    Was it to sweep the shores
For riches and to vie in bearing home,
    Each to upbuild his house,
The treasures and the trophies of the world?
That glittering hope is immemorial
    And beckons many men   415
To their undoing. Ever insatiate
They sail the sea and look to foreign towns
    To fill their ships with spoil.
But some men never find prosperity,
    For all their voyaging,
While others find it with no voyaging.   420

The Third Maiden
How have they passed the peril of the Rocks
    That Clash and of the coast
Of Phineus heavy with broken waves?   425
I wonder if they sailed across that reach
    Of sea where mariners
Boast to have looked on Ocean's Fifty Daughters
    Under the windowed waves,
Hand in hand dancing, circling round and singing. 430

The Fourth Maiden

   I wonder if their rudder steered them through
      That other reach of sea
   Where the south wind eases and the southwest wind
   Delights a sail and where the isles are white
      With birds that cover them,
   That rise and wheel and then curve back again,
      Where the wings of ocean brood
   And where Achilles races the dark waters.   435

The First Maiden

   My Lady prayed that Fate might hither bring,
      On the way home from Troy,
   The cause of her great misery. Oh, would   440
   That Helen, Helen had been blown ashore,
      That on her fatal head
   For punishment the holy drops might fall
      And that my Lady's knife   445
   Might find in her the fitting sacrifice!

The Second Maiden

   But I have prayed for a deliverer,
      Some mariner from Hellas
   Able to end my grief and set me free.   450
   Ever I go, though only in a dream,
      Back to my father's house.
   And few have greater riches than the joy
      That comes to us in visions,
   In dreams which nobody can take away.   455

The Third Maiden

   Look, there they are! See the two men in chains!
      The herdsman told the truth.
   We must be quiet now for Artemis.

The Second Maiden

   Can hands even from Hellas be so useless   460
      Against this ritual!

The Fourth Maiden

O Artemis, if Tauris in Thy sight
    Win honor by such gift
As never Greece would take, receive this blood!   465

Iphigenia

Once more I must believe that Artemis
Desires this worship, once again I serve Her.

        (To some of the Soldiers, who bring in the two youths.)

  Loosen their hands. For in the temple court,
As in the temple during consecration,
Chains are unhallowed things.

            (To the Temple Maidens, who obey.)

          Enter the temple.   470
Prepare the altar for the sacrifice.

        (Turning to the captives, with Soldiers still by them.)

  I wonder who your mother was, your father,
Whether you have a sister who must lose
Her brothers and lament their bravery.
Fate comes and goes, invisible and mute,   475
And never whispers where Her blow shall fall.
None of us ever sees Her in the dark
Or understands Her cruel mysteries.
Tell me, unfortunate men, where are you from—
You who are far from home and yet must go   480
Farther away from home even than this?

Orestes

But who are you, feeling concern for us?
What could we mean to you that you should care
And make it harder for us with your pity?
What good can come from meeting death with tears?
Only a fool, finding that he must meet it,   485
Wishes to talk about it. If a man
Is sorry for himself, he doubles death:
Is first a coward, then a coward's corpse.

So let a man accept his destiny,
No pity and no tears. The sacrifice
Is customary here. We knew it was.

Iphigenia

One of your names was told me by a herdsman.
May I know which of you is Pylades?

Orestes

He, if it does you any good to know.

Iphigenia

And from what town in Hellas?

Orestes

        Does it matter?

Iphigenia

Brothers?

Orestes

   We are—in everything but birth.

Iphigenia

What is your name?

Orestes

      Call me unfortunate.

Iphigenia

That would be pity's name for you.

Orestes

         Then say
That I am nobody—safe from derision.

Iphigenia

Your name is too important to be told?

Orestes

Come, sacrifice my body, not my name!

Iphigenia

You will not name for me even your town?

490

495

500

505

Orestes

    I am so soon a townsman of no town.

Iphigenia

    Surely it is not much to tell me that.

Orestes

    It is when one can say a town in Argos!

Iphigenia

    Argos? Not Argos? You are not from Argos?

Orestes

    My town, Mycenae, was a lordly place.   510

Iphigenia

    Then what could make you leave it? Were you banished?

Orestes

    In a way banished—banished by myselr.

Iphigenia

    How good it is to see a man from Argos!   515

Orestes

    But not to be one in your company!

Iphigenia

    And let me ask about another town.

Orestes

    But why this questioning?

Iphigenia

                  What is the news
Of that most talked-of town in the whole world?
What is the news of Troy?

Orestes

                  By all the Gods,
I wish that I had never heard its name!

Iphigenia

    But is it true that Troy is overthrown?

Orestes

Its towers lie broken in the dust.   520

Iphigenia

And Helen?
Has Menelaus taken Helen back?

Orestes

Yes, to the sorrow of a noble man.

Iphigenia

She has brought me sorrow too. Where is she now?

Orestes

Gone back with him to Sparta.

Iphigenia

How I hate
The name of Helen! How all Hellas hates it!   525

Orestes

I have my own reason for hating it.

Iphigenia

The Achaeans are safely home, as I have heard?

Orestes

Some of them are. It would take long to tell.

Iphigenia

But tell me all you can while there is time!

Orestes

Then ask me all you can and I will answer.   530

Iphigenia

The soothsayer, Calchas? Is he back from Troy?

Orestes

Mycenae people say that he is dead.

Iphigenia

Praise Artemis! And is Odysseus dead?

Orestes
Not back nor dead, they say. Still wandering.

Iphigenia
Oh how I hope he never reaches home!   535

Orestes
Why wish him worse than he has borne already?

Iphigenia
What of Achilles?

Orestes
                              Dead. The marriage planned
At Aulis never happened.

Iphigenia
                              Those who know
Know well that it was never meant to happen.

Orestes
Knowing so much, are you yourself from Hellas?   540

Iphigenia
I lived in Hellas, many years ago.

Orestes
No wonder you are asking all these questions.

Iphigenia
What of that king they called The Happy King?

Orestes
I know no happy king. Whom do you mean?

Iphigenia
King Agamemnon.

Orestes
                              What can I say of him?   545
Nothing at all of him. No, do not ask me.

Iphigenia
I beg you by the Gods do me that grace.

Orestes
The news is death—his and another death.

Iphigenia
O Agamemnon! O King Agamemnon!

Orestes
Can you be kin to him, you care so much?   550

Iphigenia
Remembering his love of life, his pride!

Orestes
All of it ended by a woman's hand.

Iphigenia
O miserable woman! Poor, poor king!

Orestes
I pray, I beg you, ask me no more questions.

Iphigenia
Only about his queen. Is she alive?   555

Orestes (doggedly)
His queen is dead. Her own son killed her.

Iphigenia
                                        Why?

Orestes
To punish her for murdering his father.

Iphigenia
It was exact of him. I pity him.

Orestes
As well you may, since no God pities him.   560

Iphigenia
Of Agamemnon's children, who is left?

Orestes
Electra—but her husband far from her.

Iphigenia
  The one they sacrificed—what do they say?

Orestes
  Nothing of her, except that she is dead.

Iphigenia
  And he could kill his child—that "happy king!"   565

Orestes
  It was a wicked war for a wicked woman,
  And all the waste that has come from it is wicked.

Iphigenia
  The son of the king? He too is dead in Argos!

Orestes
  Not dead but not in Argos, not in Argos.
                    (*The Temple Maidens return to the court.*)

Iphigenia (*telling them*)
  I dreamt Orestes dead! It was a lie!

Orestes
  Dreams, lies, lies, dreams—nothing but emptiness!   570
  Even the Gods, with all Their name for wisdom,
  Have only dreams and lies and lose Their course,
  Blinded, confused, and ignorant as we.
  The wisest men follow their own direction
  And listen to no prophet guiding them.
  None but the fools believe in oracles,
  Forsaking their own judgment. Those who know,
  Know that such men can only come to grief.   575

The Second Maiden
  Oh who will bring us news whether our kin
      Are living or are dead?

Iphigenia
                                    (*To Orestes.*)

  For years I have had a plan which now might serve
  As much to your advantage as to mine.

« 367 »

Joint undertakings stand a better chance
When they benefit both sides. So tell me this. 580
Would you, if I could win you leave to do so,
Go back to Argos, with a letter from me
Long ready for a friend of mine who lives there?
My words were written down by one who died
A victim here and yet was sorry for me, 585
Blaming his death on Artemis, not me.
No one had come from Hellas till you came,
No Greek who might be spared and take my letter. 590
But you are gentle, you are the very man
To carry it. You know the names of places
And of persons dear to me. And so I ask
Your help and in return could grant your life,
With one condition—that your friend shall pay 595
The price the state exacts for Artemis.

Orestes

Strange lady, you have made a fair proposal
Save in that one respect. What would my life
Be worth to me, gained by forsaking a friend?
I am the captain of this misadventure
And he the loyal shipmate who stayed by me. 600
A sorry ending if he paid the cost
And I rejected my own enterprise!
Your errand shall be done—but not by me.
Give him your confidence, give him your letter.
To you it makes no difference which of us
Carries your message home. To me it would make
No difference when or how my life should finish
If through continuing it, saving it, 605
I brought disaster on a friend and knew
No honor left in me, no faith, no love.
Besides, this man is dear to me, his life
Is even closer to me than my own.

Iphigenia

> Your heart is made of gold. You must have come
> From some great seed, to be so true a friend.   610
> If only the last member of my line
> Be such as you! I have a brother living,
> Though face to face with him, I should not know him.
> As you have chosen then, so let it be.
> Your friend shall take the letter, and you prove   615
> Your loyalty by giving him your life.

Orestes

> Whose hand is it that brings the touch of death?

Iphigenia

> My hand—condemned to it by Artemis.

Orestes

> Your hand is still too young a hand for that.

Iphigenia

> It is the law.   620

Orestes

> That a woman shall stab men?

Iphigenia

> Not that! Oh not the knife! Only the water,
> The marking on the forehead—only the water!

Orestes

> Whose hand then does the deed, uses the knife?

Iphigenia

> Inside the temple—there are men for it.

Orestes

> When I am burnt, what happens to my body?   625

Iphigenia

> They seal the ashes in a rocky gorge.

Orestes

I wish my sister's hand might tend my body.

Iphigenia

Since she is far away and cannot hear you
Or be with you to give these services,
I shall attend to them. I am from Argos.   630
I will do everything that she might do,
Will bring rich robes to be your final clothing
And funeral ornaments to set about you
And yellow oil to pour, cooling and clean,
Upon the embers. I will melt your ashes
In gold that bees collect from mountain-flowers.   635
You shall be pure and sweet.
                                        While I am gone
To find my letter, do not think ill of me.

                                        (*To the Soldiers.*)

Keep careful guard without binding these men.

                (*To herself, pausing as she leaves the court.*)

Oh, if at last my letter should arrive
In Argos and be opened by his own
Beloved hand, a letter never dreamed of,   640
Then he would listen through my opening grave
And hear my living lips cry out to him.

                (*She leaves, passing around the temple.*)

The First Maiden

O you whose head must feel this water's touch,
    My heart goes out to you!   645

Orestes

Have hope for him, instead of pitying me.

The First Maiden

My heart both pities you and hopes for him
    That he may safely reach
His father's country and be happy there.

« 370 »

Pylades
  Could I desert a friend and still be happy?   650

The First Maiden
  Or I help pitying a man who dies?

The Fourth Maiden
  The one who lives will be the one I pity.

The Third Maiden
      Which is the sadder fate?

The Fourth Maiden
  I cannot tell. I watch and cannot tell   655
  Whether to pity you, or you, the more.

Orestes
  What is it, Pylades? What puzzles you?

Pylades
  What do you think it is that puzzles me?

Orestes
  That woman and the way she put her questions.   660
  The sort of questions: the defeat of Troy,
  The Achaeans' homecoming, what happened to Calchas,
  To Achilles, and her being so concerned
  At Agamemnon's death and then inquiring
  About his wife and children. I believe   665
  It true that she herself belongs in Argos
  Or she would never send a letter there
  And care about occurrences in Argos
  As if they flowed within her very veins.

Pylades
  Yes, that is what at first had puzzled me,
  And then I thought it natural enough   670
  That in a place even half civilized
  People should care about the fate of kings.
  But that was not what puzzled me, not that.

Orestes

If we put our heads together, we could surely—

Pylades

How can you wrong me, thinking I would live
And leave you here to die? I came with you.   675
I shall continue with you to the end,
Or I could never show my face again
On an Argive hill or in a Phocian valley
But to be pointed out and rightly spurned
As one who had betrayed a friend. People
Might say worse things than that, the worst   680
An evil mind could think of to enjoy:
That I had wished or even caused your death
To benefit, as husband of your sister,
By my inheritance—to win your throne.
Such thoughts are frightening, but worse my shame
In your imagining that I might leave you.
If you meet knife and flame, then so do I.   685
I am your friend and there's no more to say.

Orestes

How can you be my friend and yet refuse me?
The load I bear can never be laid down—
And would you add to it by lightening yours?
All the contempt you imagine from men's hearts
And tongues, falling on you, would fall on me
In my own heart from my own conduct, if I let   690
The service you have done me bring you harm.
What has Fate left me of my life to cherish
But a good ending? As for you, my comrade,
You have not any right to choose to die.
You have the blessing of your fortunate blood
To make you wish to live. I can but pray
That, by your living, solace may be brought   695
To my ill-fated family. Pylades,
Once home again and with your wife, my sister,

Give me my happiness by having a son
In whom my name shall live, and through your children
Build up once more the house of Agamemnon.
Go back, I say, and make my home your home.
You will be there in Hellas, on the shore
Where Argive horsemen ride. Give me your hand   700
And swear to me that you will build my tomb,
Will set memorials in it and will ask
My sister for a lock of her long hair
To lay with them. Tell her that I was led
Before this altar by a gentle hand,
A woman's hand, a woman born in Argos,   705
And how at last my blood was purified.
   O Pylades, be gentle to my sister!
And so goodbye, my best and closest friend.
When we were boys, we loved sharing our sports.
You rode the hills with me And now in manhood
You are the one who has shared the heartache with me   710
When treacherous Phoebus through his oracle
First lied to me, then tricked me, luring me far
From home, lest watchful eyes in Hellas see
That Gods as well as men break promises.
I trusted Him, with all my faith and will,
Even, at His command, killing my mother,
And in return He has forsaken me.   715

Pylades

   I shall obey your will, though not my own;
Shall build your tomb in Hellas. Your heart knows
That I shall love your sister all my life.
And, close to you in your life, my heart knows
That it shall hold you closer in your death—
If death it be. Gods, in mysterious ways,   720
Never explaining, mask the face of life,
Behind what looks death, disguising life,
And then revealing it.

Orestes
                    The time is gone
When Gods might show that face. For she has come.

Iphigenia
             (*Returning to the temple by the town-path and
                   addressing the Attendants who follow her.*)
    Precede me into the temple and be ready.   725
                    (*The Attendants enter the temple.*)
    Here is my letter, safe within these folds.
    But I have wondered. A man who has been in danger
    When he comes out of it forgets his fears,
    And sometimes he forgets his promises.   730
    Might it not happen that your friend, intent
    Upon his own concerns again, forget
    How very much this letter means to me?

Orestes
    And what would you suggest, to ease your mind?

Iphigenia
    His solemn vow to take this where I say.   735

Orestes
    And will you make a vow balancing his?

Iphigenia
    To do what, or undo what?

Orestes
                    To make sure
    He be allowed to leave this deathly place.

Iphigenia
    How could he keep his vow, unless he leave?   740

Orestes
    What makes you think the king will let him sail?

Iphigenia
  I can persuade the king and will myself
  Go to the ship and see your friend aboard.

Orestes
  Then word the vow as you would have him make it.

Iphigenia
  You promise the delivery of my letter?

Pylades
  I promise the delivery of your letter.   745

Iphigenia
  I promise you the king will let you leave.

Pylades
  In whose name do you swear?

Iphigenia
                              By Artemis,
  Here in Her Temple—and implore Her help.

Pylades
  And I by Zeus Himself, by Heaven's King.

Iphigenia
  And what if you should fail to keep your word?   750

Pylades
  Then may I never again set eyes on Argos.
  And what if you should fail in keeping yours?

Iphigenia
  Then may I never again set foot in Argos.

Pylades
  But we forget one possibility.

Iphigenia
  Which might affect the keeping of your vow?

Pylades

How could I keep my vow if this should happen—   755
If we were wrecked by a storm, torn by a reef,
If we were sunk and everything went down,
And if my life were saved but not the letter.
If that should happen, how could I keep my word?

Iphigenia

In any plan, two ways improve on one.
So I will tell you, slowly, line by line,   760
The contents of my letter, which, if need be,
You are to tell my friend. Then he will know.
For either you will place it in his hand
And the written words will speak to him or else,
If they are lost, your voice will be their echo.   765

Pylades

That is a surer way, for both of us.
So whom am I to find for you in Argos?
What shall I say to him?

Iphigenia

                  Say this to him.
Say to Orestes, son of Agamemnon,
"A greeting comes from one you think is dead."   770
Tell him, "Your sister is not dead at Aulis
But is alive."

Orestes

           Alive? Iphigenia?
Oh, no! Unless the dead come back again!

Iphigenia

You are looking at her now, for I am she.
But let me finish what I ask of him.
"O brother, come and save me from a life
As priestess in a loathsome ritual—   775
Save me from dying in this lonely land."

Orestes

Where am I, Pylades? What am I hearing?

Iphigenia

"Lest memory of me should always haunt you."
The name, you must repeat it, is Orestes.

Orestes

I hear a God!

Iphigenia

You hear only a woman.

Orestes

I hear a woman—and I hear a God!   780
Let me hear more! I hear a miracle!

Iphigenia

Then tell him, "Artemis put out Her hand
And spared my life at Aulis, leaving a deer
To bleed instead." And tell him this, "My father,
Not looking when he struck, believed me dead. 785
Artemis brought me here." The letter ends.

Pylades

No word was ever easier to keep!
Lady, keep yours or not, I keep mine now!   790
I give you this, Orestes, from your sister!

Orestes

How can I look at letters! Let me look—
Oh let me stare at you whom I had lost!
Oh let me touch you with my hands and prove 795
That you are real and hold you close, close!

The Third Maiden

Do not lay hands, whoever you may be,
  Upon a vestment sacred
To Artemis! Do not profane that robe!

Orestes

You are my sister, you are my father's daughter,   800
And nature will not let you turn away
From your own brother given back to you.

Iphigenia

Ah, you would have me think that you are he.
Orestes is not here. He is in Argos.

Orestes

Poor sister, not in Argos! I am here!   805

Iphigenia

You mean Tyndareus was your mother's father?

Orestes

Yes, and my father's grandfather was Pelops.

Iphigenia

What are you saying? How can I believe you?

Orestes

By asking me more questions—about home.

Iphigenia

Say anything—say anything at all.   810

Orestes

Electra used to tell us about Atreus,
About Thyestes, how they came to quarrel.

Iphigenia

The fight they had over the golden lamb!

Orestes

The tapestry you made of it, yourself.

Iphigenia

Are you Orestes? Is it really you?   815

Orestes

Another tapestry you made, of Helios
Changing His course. Have you forgotten that?

Iphigenia
  I can remember every single thread.

Orestes
  And the bath perfumes, a present for your wedding,
  Sent by your mother to Aulis—you remember?

Iphigenia
  I live each bitter moment of that day.

Orestes
  The lock of hair you sent back to your mother?

Iphigenia
  I meant it for my own memorial   820
  To mark a grave where I could never lie.

Orestes
  The keepsake in your room! Do you remember
  The ancient spear, the one Pelops had used
  On Oenomaus, when he won from him
  Hippodamia as a bride from Pisa?   825

Iphigenia
  It is, it is! Orestes! O my brother!
  My home has come to me from far away,
  For you have come, I have you in my arms.   830

Orestes
  And I have you in mine, whom I thought dead.
  No wonder that our eyes are blind with tears,
  Of joy, not sorrow—yet of sorrow too.

Iphigenia
  You were a baby when I sailed away,
  Lifted to watch me, held up by your nurse   835
  To wave goodbye. And now those little arms
  I saw reach out have come to me, grown strong
  To comfort me! How can I tell my joy?
  There is no language sweet enough to tell it.
  There is no joy like this. There never was.   840

Orestes

    And there must never be an end of it.

Iphigenia

    I am bewildered. And I cannot think
    What I should say, my friends. I cannot think
    Of anything but joy—except a fear
    That he might vanish as he came. O Argos!
    My heart is full of my beloved Argos,   845
    Of everybody who belongs to Argos,
    And of my brother born and bred in Argos
    To be a living light honoring Argos!

Orestes

    How could the happiness we both were born for   850
    Become unhappiness?

Iphigenia

                   Unhappiness
    Began for me when my unhappy father
    Lifted a knife and drew it toward my throat.

Orestes

    I was not there, and yet how plain I see you!

Iphigenia

    And do you see what I remember there?   855
    The treachery, the misery, the shame!
    After the trickery, the vanishing
    Of all my dreams! Not to Achilles' arms
    I went, circled with songs, but, shaken with sobs,
    I felt the hot flame from the altar-stone   860
    And the cold water trickled on my head.

Orestes

    O desolate daughter of a desolate father!
    I see his face. I see his haunted face!

Iphigenia

    But why feel pity for the pitiless man
    Who caused all this?   865

Orestes
                    And might have caused today
Your leading your own brother to the grave.

Iphigenia
    Some God prevented. But I came so near,
    My hand so nearly set the final seal,
    That I still shake as though you lay here dead.
    We have seen the beginning of a miracle.   870
    We found each other and my hand was spared
    From signalling your death. How can we now
    Fulfill the miracle, make it complete?
    How can I save you from some other hand
    And speed you safely homeward from this place?   875
    There will be many hands, and many swords,
    For you to face. How could you match them all?
    A giant's task, too much for any man!
    There are no weapons possible but wits,
    And yet I see you stand there dazed as I.   880
    Could you outrun them when they follow you,
    Escape them on an inland wooded trail?
    Or would a dash through breakers be the way?
    Would you be safer trusting to the trail
    Or to the ship? Oh, I can see you losing   885
    Your way on land, risking a thousand deaths.
    The countryside is full of savage men.
    The ship is better, even that sharp cleft
    Between the Clashing Rocks. Yes, risk the sea.   890
    You challenged it, came through it. Having once
    Met it and mastered it, you can again.
    And so let fly your oars. Yes, risk the sea,
    Take to the ship—though who can surely tell
    If God or man shall steer you through the waves   895
    To a safe landing, or if Fate shall grant
    Argos the benison of your return?
    Or me—who knows?—the sweet surprise of mine!

The Third Maiden

    I have heard marvelous tales from story-tellers,   900
        But nothing to compare
    With this event which my own eyes have seen.

Pylades

    Orestes, it was natural and right
    For you and for your sister to compare
    Old memories, but surely it's high time
    We think of nothing else but our escape   905
    From this grim place and how to manage it.
    No man, when Fortune beckons him, should wait
    A single instant. He should follow her.

Orestes

    Meet her halfway, you mean, more than halfway,   910
    Since every God helps him who helps himself.

Iphigenia

    But first—I cannot wait—I have to hear!
    Oh tell me just a word about my sister—
    About Electra! Tell me about Electra!

Orestes

    This is the husband who has made her happy.   915

Iphigenia

    This man? But who. . . .

Orestes

               A Phocian. Strophius' son.

Iphigenia

    Then he is Atreus' grandson! He's our kinsman!

Orestes

    Your cousin—my one friend.

Iphigenia

                Not even born
    When I left home to die.   920

Orestes

He is the son

Of Strophius in old age.

Iphigenia

I welcome you,

My sister's husband.

Orestes

And my more than brother.

Iphigenia

But oh our mother? You have not said why—

Orestes

I said enough—I said she killed our father.   925

Iphigenia

You have not told me why.

Orestes

Then do not ask me.

Iphigenia

May I not ask if you are king of Argos?

Orestes

Not king but exile. Menelaus is king.

Iphigenia

When you most needed him, he drove you out?   930

Orestes

Not he. The Furies—the avenging Fiends.

Iphigenia

Your madness on the beach—it was the Fiends?

Orestes

Anyone seeing me might think it madness.

Iphigenia

Still chasing you because you killed our mother?

Orestes

They try to choke me with my mother's blood!   935

Iphigenia

What brought you here?

Orestes

                              Phoebus—His oracle.

Iphigenia

Why should He choose this place?

Orestes

                                        Oh let me tell
My bitter narrative from end to end.
   After my hand had unforgivably   940
Punished my mother's unforgivable sin,
Down on my head they came, the Avenging Furies,
The nameless Fiends. Then Phoebus ordered me
To Athens that I might explain to Them
In the Tribunal Zeus had sanctified   945
To Ares when she answered ancient charges.
   When I arrived there, none of all my friends
Received me. They avoided me at first
As one unclean. Later they pitied me
And gave me food in the same room with them
But at a separate table where they let   950
My meals be served when theirs were, sent me a cup
When their love-bowl was passed, but then would turn
Away and would not look at me nor speak
To me—because I was a murderer. . . .
I tried to act as though I did not care,   955
But sad and lonely when I thought of her
Whom I had killed, I drank a bitter cup.
   I am told Athenians commemorate
My trial with a Service of the Pitcher,
Everyone drinking his own cup in silence. . . .   960
   While I was facing judgment on that hill,

I on one flagging and across from me
The eldest of the Avengers charging me
With murder, Phoebus rose to my defense.
It was His eloquence that saved my life,   965
Persuading Pallas, in the chair, with votes
Cast evenly for and against me, that she add
Her own vote for me—which acquitted me.

   Some of the Fiends, persuaded, went to found
A cellar temple under the Tribunal.
Others denounced the verdict as unfair   970
And flew at me in such a vicious frenzy
That I ran back for help again from Phoebus,
Faint with despair fell down upon my knees
And swore to starve myself to death unless
The God who had ruined me would rescue me.   975

   Out pealed His voice over the golden tripod,
Bidding me find among the Taurians
Their Artemis of wood carven in Heaven
But fallen on their coast and, stealing it,
Establish it for Grecian worshippers
In Attica.
        Help me to do this thing
And to fulfil His mission. Help me, sister!
Once I have carried home in these two hands   980
The image of the Goddess, I am rid
Of madness! And I urge you with a gift
Of rugged rowers rowing you home to Argos!
O my own sister, for our family's sake,
Help me to save that family and ourselves!
Unless you help me take the image back,   985
This very day our family's name shall die.

The Fourth Maiden
  Some God is visiting ancestral sin
    On the house of Tantalus.

Iphigenia

How I had dreamed, long, long before your coming,
Of you and of my country! How my prayer   990
Joins yours for the renewal of our breed—
Even of his whose hand reached for my blood!
Now that no blood of yours stains my own hand,
I have no anger left, but only hope
That in your life the family name shall live.   995
   But if you leave me, taking Artemis,
When the king sees the empty pedestal,
What can I say? How can my life be saved
Unless, with one quick stroke seizing the image,
We flee together to your leaping deck?   1000
If we succeed, what happiness for me!
But even if I fail, you need not fail.
My life is little. I would gladly die
To earn your safety and your reaching home.
If a man die, a house, a name, is lost.   1005
But if a woman die, what does it matter?

Orestes

It mattered when my mother died! If now
You also were to die because of me—!
Whatever happen, we shall share one fate,
Alive in Greece, or here together dead.   1010
   But by all signs, the Gods are on our side.
If Artemis were not, why should it be
Her Brother's oracle commanding me
To bring Her image back? She wishes it!
Here in Her Temple, in Her very presence,
Has come the omen of my finding you!   1015
Yes, we are being guided by the Gods!

Iphigenia

The king will kill us if we steal the statue.

Orestes

Then why not kill the king?   1020

Iphigenia
Anger the Gods

Again? He has been kind to me.

Orestes
Why not,

To save our lives, take chances with the Gods?

Iphigenia

I like your boldness. But it cannot be.

Orestes

What if you hid me somewhere in the temple?

Iphigenia

To steal out after dark?   1025

Orestes
Since I must steal,

The day for honest men, the night for thieves.

Iphigenia

Guards are on watch inside.

Orestes
How else are we—

Iphigenia

We might—

Orestes
Might what?   1030

Iphigenia
Make use of your misfortune.

Orestes

Women have ways of changing ill to good.

Iphigenia

I shall denounce you as a matricide.

Orestes

Make use of any good you find in that.

Iphigenia

As one unworthy to be sacrificed.   1035

Orestes

I understand—but not how it would serve us.

Iphigenia

You are unclean—cannot be purified—

Orestes

What will that do for us?

Iphigenia

except by deep
Sea-water, beyond stain, off from the shore.

Orestes

Yes, but our mission, you forget the statue—   1040
The reason for our coming here.

Iphigenia

She too,
Having been soiled by your approach, must be
Washed clean, the image too!

Orestes

I see it now.
The inlet where the ship—

Iphigenia

strains at the leash.

Orestes

And you will bring the image there yourself!

Iphigenia

Nobody ever touches it but me.   1045

Orestes

But Pylades? Is he a murderer too?

Iphigenia

He aided you. He also must be cleansed.

Orestes

    A story for the guards—but for the king?

Iphigenia

    In any case I could not keep it from him.
    So he shall hear it and shall be persuaded.

Orestes

    Fifty stout oars are waiting for the word.   1050

Iphigenia

    That is the part of it I leave to you.

Orestes

    I have but one suggestion. Do these women
    Realize how much their loyalty might mean?
    Women know women. Make your plea to them.
    And after that we are in the hands of Heaven.   1055

Iphigenia

    O friends who have been near and dear to me,
    It may depend upon your carefulness
    Whether or not I reach my home and kin.
    A woman knows how much her weakness needs
    The sympathy and help of other women,   1060
    Their understanding and their loyalty.
    I ask you only this, that you say nothing
    Of what has happened here, that you keep silent.
    The stillest tongue can be the truest friend.
    We three must take a hair's-breadth chance between   1065
    Capture and death, deliverance and home.
    But if we do escape, then we shall work
    For your deliverance, for you and you
    To share our happiness at home in Hellas
    And you and you. Holding your hand, I ask you—   1070
    Kissing your cheek. Clasping your knees, I ask you—
    And you I ask by love of your two parents.

                     (*To the Second Maiden.*)

And you by love of the child you left behind.
Who will say yes to me? Who could say no
When it might cost my brother's life and mine?

The First Maiden
Rely on me, dear Lady.

The Second Maiden
                    And on me.   1075

The Third Maiden
We shall do everything we can to help.

The Fourth Maiden
By Zeus we pledge silence and loyalty.

Iphigenia
May Heaven reward the hearts behind those words!

                              (*To Orestes and Pylades.*)
Now for your part—and yours—inside the temple.
The king will soon arrive and will be asking   1080
Whether the strangers have been sacrificed.

                    (*Orestes and Pylades enter the temple.*)
O gallant Goddess, having saved me once
At Aulis from my father's deadly hand,
Save with me now my brother and his friend,
Lest Phoebus be disproved because of Thee
And men forsake His oracle. O come   1085
In gracious might away from this bleak place,
Away from gloom, to the lovely light of Athens.

                              (*She follows into the temple.*)
The First Maiden
O sad-voiced ocean-bird, heard in the foam
    Low by the rocky ledge   1090
Singing a note unhappy hearts can hear,
The song of separation from your mate,
    The moan of separation,

I have no wings to seek like you, but I
    Can sing a song like you, 1095
A song of separation from my mate.

The Second Maiden
  At home in Hellas now my kinsmen gather
    Where Artemis is due
  To bless the new-born from her Cynthian hill
  And soothe the mothers with the cooling palm
    And bay and olive-tree, 1100
  Where once Latona loved the winding streams
    And watched the rounded pools
  White with the song-like motion of the swans. 1105

The Third Maiden
  Alas, the falling tears, the towers fallen,
    The taking of our towns!
  Alas, the clang of bright and angry spears
  Which drove me, captive, to an alien ship, 1110
    Whence I was sold away
  To be an exile here, a handmaiden
    With Agamemnon's daughter,
  Doomed to the bloody rites of Artemis! 1115

The Fourth Maiden
  And at this altar where the sacrifice
    Is not of sheep but men,
  I envy those unhappy from their birth,
  For to be bred and seasoned in misfortune
    Is to be iron to it,
  But there is something in the pang of change 1120
    More than the heart can bear,
  Unhappiness remembering happiness.

The Second Maiden
  Lady, a ship is here to take you home,
    And in the rowers' ears
  Pan shall be sounding all his pointed notes, 1125

Great mountains echoing to His little reed,
    And Phoebus on His lyre
Shall strike profound the seven strings and sing
    To you of Attica,   1130
Shall sing to you of home and lead you there.
Oar after oar shall dip and carry you,
    Lady, away from us,
Oar after oar shall push the empty waves
Wider, wider, leaving us lonely here,
    Leaving us here without you,
And forward over the unceasing bow
    The sail shall faster run,   1135
Ever refilling with the unspent wind.

The First Maiden

Oh to fly swifter than the wingèd sun
    Upon his dazzling track!—
And not to let my golden light be folded   1140
Until I touch my house, my roof, my room,
    From which I used to go
To noble marriages and take my place
    In the bright company,
Give them my hands and circle round and dance   1145
And always try to be the loveliest,
    Under my mother's gaze,
In my unrivalled radiance of attire
And in the motion of my hands and feet,
    While my embroidered veil
I would hold closely round me as I danced
    And bowed and hid my cheek   1150
Under the shadow of my clustering curls.

                (*Enter King Thoas with Soldiers.*)

Thoas

Where is my guardian of the temple gate,
My Grecian girl? Where are the foreigners?
Am I too late to see the sacrifice?
Are the victims' bodies being burnt already?   1155

The Fourth Maiden

She is coming out herself and she will tell you.

(*Iphigenia appears in the temple-door, carrying
the wooden Artemis.*)

Thoas

(*Starting up the stairs.*)

What does this mean, daughter of Agamemnon?
Why have you moved the Goddess from her place?

Iphigenia

O King, stand back—stay back beyond the threshold!

Thoas

But what has happened that would call for this?   1160

Iphigenia

Back from contamination! I am abrupt.

Thoas

Speak bluntly to me. What?

Iphigenia

The offerings
You sent us for the Goddess are impure.

Thoas

How do you know? What makes you think—

Iphigenia

She turned
Away from them. She moved when they came near.   1165

Thoas

Mightn't it be a little bit of earthquake
That moved Her?

Iphigenia

No. She moved of Her own will
And even for a moment shut Her eyes.

« 393 »

Thoas

Because their hands were blood-stained? Was it that?

Iphigenia

It was Her divination of their guilt.

Thoas

You mean they'd killed a Taurian on the beach?   1170

Iphigenia

Their guilt was with them when they came—the crime
Of killing their own kin.

Thoas

What kin?

Iphigenia

Mother
Of one of them—a murder they had planned.

Thoas

O great Apollo, what barbarian
Would do the thing these Greeks have done!

Iphigenia

Greeks once
But now disowned by Greeks, driven from Hellas.   1175

Thoas

Even so, why bring the Goddess out?

Iphigenia

Defiled,
She must be purified, be cleaned again
By the touch of Her own sky.

Thoas

How could you know
What sort of crime these fellows had committed?

Iphigenia

I saw Her turn from them. I asked them why.

Thoas

    You are a Greek, quick-witted, a true Greek.   1180

Iphigenia

    They are Greek too, tried to propitiate me
    With welcome news.

Thoas

              Of Argos?

Iphigenia

                      Of my brother,
  News of Orestes.

Thoas

            Thought they could weaken you.

Iphigenia

    News that my father is alive and prospers.   1185

Thoas

    But you were firm. You didn't let your feelings—

Iphigenia

    What should I feel toward any Greek but hate?

Thoas

    How shall we deal with them?

Iphigenia

                  By temple rules.

Thoas

    Something besides the pitcher and the knife?   1190

Iphigenia

    Complete immersion, for a sin like theirs.

Thoas

    In the bubbling spring? Or is salt water best?

Iphigenia

    The sea is the absorbent of all evil.

Thoas

Artemis says the sea?

Iphigenia

I say the sea.   1195

Thoas

Breakers are handy—just beyond the wall.

Iphigenia

But these especial rites are secret rites.

Thoas

Then choose your place; no one shall trespass on you.

Iphigenia

And I shall have to wash the Goddess too.

Thoas

Can a Goddess be defiled, the same as people?   1200

Iphigenia

Why did I have to bring Her from the temple?

Thoas

You are a pious woman and I thank you.

Iphigenia

Then will you issue orders for me?

Thoas

Name them.

Iphigenia

First have the strangers bound with rope.

Thoas

But why?

Where could they go?

Iphigenia

O King, beware of Greeks!

Thoas

                                      (To his Soldiers.)

Bind them.   1205

Iphigenia

        And have them brought to me.

Thoas

                                 And bring them.

Iphigenia

    But cover both their heads with heavy cloth.

Thoas

    To keep even the Sun from seeing them?

Iphigenia

    Send soldiers with me.

Thoas

                      Take your pick of them.

Iphigenia

    And have a herald tell all Taurians—

Thoas

    To what?

Iphigenia

        To stay indoors till this is done.   1210

Thoas

    One step outdoors and they would be polluted.

Iphigenia

    By matricide!

Thoas

                                (To Attendants.)

        Go tell the herald this.

Iphigenia

    Indoors they stay.

Thoas

My people do concern you!

Iphigenia

The one I am most concerned about—

Thoas

Who? Me?

Iphigenia

Has helpful work to do, inside the temple.   1215

Thoas

To—?

Iphigenia

Purify it with pine smoke from torches.

Thoas

The temple shall be sweet for your return.

Iphigenia

When they come out—

Thoas

What shall I do?

Iphigenia

Hold up

Your sleeve and shield your face.

Thoas

From the contagion.

Iphigenia

And if I seem delayed—

Thoas

How shall I tell?

Iphigenia

Feel no surprise, be patient.

Thoas

You must do,

Carefully, everything the Goddess wants.   1220

Iphigenia

I trust that I can serve Her wish.

Thoas

And mine.

(*The temple doors open for an emerging procession.*)

Iphigenia

And here they come, the strangers in their robes,
And lambs whose blood is used instead of theirs,
And burning torches and the instruments
Needed for purifying them and Her.   1225
  Taurians, turn away from the pollution.
Gate-tenders, open the gates, then wash your hands.
Men who want wives, women who want children,
Avoid contagion, keep away, away!

(*Holding the image high.*)

  O Virgin Goddess, if the waves can wash   1230
And purge the taint from these two murderers
And wash from Thee the tarnishing of blood,
Thy dwelling shall be clean and we be blest! . . .
To Thee and the All-Wise my silent prayer.

(*She signals. The procession moves down the stairs. Carrying
the image, she leads the Soldiers and victims from the foot
of the stairs across the court and out toward the sea.
Thoas enters the temple with Attendants, leaving
in the courtyard only the Temple Maidens.*)

The Second Maiden

Latona bore one day a golden Child,
  Brother of Artemis,   1235
Phoebus, the darling of the vales of Delos—

« 399 »

The First Maiden
    Whose little fingers hovered on the harp
        And pulled at archery.

The Second Maiden
    Up from His birthplace, to Parnassus' top
        The Mother brought Her Boy—   1240

The First Maiden
    Where Dionysus vaults the waterfall.

The Third Maiden
    There, hidden coiling in the leafy laurels,
        A serpent with bright scales   1245
    And blood-red eyes, a creature born of Earth,
    Guarded the cave that held Earth's oracle.
        Phoebus, beholding it, leaped up
    Out of His Mother's arms, a little Child,   1250
        And struck the serpent dead—

The Second Maiden
    And on that day began His prophecies.

The Fourth Maiden
    O Phoebus, having won the golden throne
        And tripod of the truth,
    Out of the very center of the Earth,
    Thou couldst hear wisdom; and Thy voice conveyed,
        Accompanied by all   1255
    The run and ripple of Castalian springs,
        The deepest prophecies
    That ever Earth heard whispered out of Heaven.

The Third Maiden
    But Earth had wished to save the oracle
        For Themis, Her own daughter,   1260
    And so in anger bred a band of dreams
    Which in the night should be oracular
        To men, foretelling truth.   1265

And this impaired the dignity of Phoebus
    And of His prophecies.

The Second Maiden

And the baby God went hurrying to Zeus,   1270
Coaxed with His little hands and begged of Zeus
    To send the dreams away.

The First Maiden

And Zeus was very pleased to have His Son
Come straight to Him with troubles. His great brow   1275
    Decided with a nod
That Phoebus have his prize restored to Him,
    In spite of angry Earth,
His throne, His listening throng, His golden voice . . .

The Fourth Maiden

That throats of night be stricken straightway mute   1280
    And plague mankind no more,
That shapes of night no longer hold their power
To foretell truth in syllables of gloom
    And haunt men's aching hearts—
That men be freed from the prophetic dark
    And every shrouded form
And listen only to the lips of light.

A Soldier

      (Entering headlong on the sea-path, wounded and breathless.)
O temple ministrants and temple guards,
Where is King Thoas? Open all your gates   1285
And call King Thoas out! Summon the king!

The First Maiden

Am I allowed to ask why so much noise?

The Soldier

The two young prisoners have broken free,
With Agamemnon's daughter joining them,   1290
And are taking Artemis aboard their ship!

The Second Maiden

    You have gone mad to dream of such a thing!

The First Maiden

    A likely story! If you want the king,
    He has left the temple. Go and look for him.

The Soldier

    Tell me which way, because I have to find him.   1295

The First Maiden

    I do not know which way.

The Third Maiden

                  None of us noticed.

The Second Maiden

    Go look for him, tell him your crazy story.

The Soldier

    O treacherous women, you're deceiving me,
    You're in the plot yourselves!   1300

The Third Maiden

                 You make no sense.
    What are these men to us? Go try the palace.

The Soldier

    Not till I know what's happening right here.
    Not till the keepers of the inner shrine
    Have answered me! Ho! You inside! Unbar
    The door! Is the king there? Tell him to hurry!   1305
    Tell him a soldier's out here—with bad news!

        (*He beats at the door. The door opens and Thoas appears.*)

Thoas

    Why are you making this ungodly uproar?
    Everyone's in a panic!

The Soldier

These women lied!
They said that you had left, they lied to me,   1310
Tried not to let me find you!

Thoas

What do you mean?
Why should they wish—

The Soldier

That will come later. Listen,
Oh listen first to me, listen to this!
Your Priestess, Iphigenia! She has freed
The prisoners! They've stolen Artemis!   1315
The ocean ceremony was a trick.

Thoas

But why should she be playing tricks on me?

The Soldier

To save Orestes. Yes, I said Orestes!

Thoas

Orestes? What Orestes? Not her brother?

The Soldier

Whom we had brought to you for Artemis.   1320

Thoas

But that's impossible! How can I grasp it?

The Soldier

There isn't time to grasp it! You must say
What's to be done about it! You must order
Galleys to cut ahead of them and catch them!

Thoas

There's no escape for them. Our boats are out there,   1325
So tell me how it happened. Everything.

The Soldier

It was just when we had reached the bend of shore
Hiding their ship that Agamemnon's daughter
Made signs for us to drop the rope which bound
The men, to leave them and fall back. She said   1330
That she was ready to begin the rites
And light the mystic flame to bless the sea.
But when she took the cord and led the boys
Beyond the curve, we had a sudden feeling
Something was wrong. We didn't know what to do.   1335
We heard her voice call high mysterious words
We'd never heard and thought that this must be
The prayer she had to use for cleansing sin.
And then we waited a long time. At last   1340
We were afraid the men had broken loose
And killed her and escaped. And still we waited,
Because you had forbidden us to look,
But we suddenly decided to find out
And hurried to the inlet.   1345
                There we saw
The ship from Hellas swaying near the beach,
And fitted in the tholes were fifty oars
Like feathers in a wing. And the two youths
Were waist-deep by the stern. Sailors held poles
For keeping the bow steady, others hauled   1350
The anchor up. The rest had hands along the ropes
Of a ladder hanging from the rail to help
The Priestess. But we seized her in the water,   1355
Tugged at the ladder, ripped their rudder-oar
Away from them to cripple them and cried
To the fellow facing us, "What kind of man
Are you, stealing our Priestess and our Goddess?"   1360
"I am Orestes, son of Agamemnon,
I am her brother! Now you have the truth!
And she is bound for Greece, out of which land
I lost her long ago—bound home!" We tried

To hold her, tried to drag her from their hands,   1365
Which is the way I came by this and this.
He struck my face, first one side, then the other.
They had no weapons, we had none. We used
Our fists and they their fists, and some their feet
With kicks well-aimed at us from where they stood
Above us—at our heads and hearts. We fought   1370
And fought till we were winded. Then, with bruises
And cuts and blood-filled eyes, we climbed the cliff
And from above we pelted them with rocks.   1375
But the Greek archers had brought up their bows
And with their arrows kept us at a distance.
   Then when a giant wave bore in on them,
Orestes quickly lifted up his sister
Out of the rush of it. Holding her high   1380
On his left shoulder, plunging stride by stride,
He caught a ladder, climbed aboard the ship
And set her safe on deck. And she, she held—
She had it still—the statue out of Heaven,
The image of the Daughter of High Zeus.   1385
   We heard a glad voice ringing through the ship,
"O mariners of Hellas, grip your oars
And clip the sea to foam! O let your arms
Be strong, for we have won, have won, have won
What we set out to win! Soon we shall leave
The jagged Clashing Rocks behind! Pull hard!"
   A shout of joy resounded and the ship   1390
Quivered with dipping oars and shot ahead.
But this was only while the shelter lasted;
For at the harbor-mouth the sharp wind threw her
High on a heavy swell shoreward again.
Her oarsmen rallied, strained, but every time   1395
They made a gain, a great wave drove her back.
Then Agamemnon's daughter stood and prayed:
'Oh save me, Artemis, from this grim place!
Help us all home to Hellas! And forgive

Theft of the image at Thy Brother's bidding!   1400
As He is dear to Thee, so mine to me!"
   The sailors roared their echoes to her prayer,
And bent their bodies and their great bare arms
And shoulders, swinging like the sea,
To the boatswain's cry. But closer to the cliff,   1405
Closer they drew and closer still. And some
Sprang out into the water and began
Trying to fasten hold on the sharp rocks
With ropes. And then our soldiers sent me here
To tell you what has happened. So bring cord   1410
And chains, O King, for if the sea stays rough,
There's not a chance that they can get away.
   Poseidon, Ocean's God, mindful of Troy,
The city which He loved, is punishing   1415
The impious children of her enemies,
And will deliver to the King of Tauris
The son and daughter of the King of Argos—
That daughter who, forgetful now of Aulis,
Betrays the Goddess who was good to her.

The First Maiden

O Lady, Lady! Fate is yielding you   1420
   To Taurian hands again.
You and your brother surely now shall die.

Thoas

Come, citizens, and be uncivilized!
Leap on your horses! Whip them to the beach!
There we can wait until a billow splits
That ship from Hellas. Then go after them!   1425
And hunt them down, every damned dog of them!
Do this for Artemis. And some of you
Go launch my galleys, lest one man of them
Should die untortured! Run them down by sea
And land! Go hurl them from the cliffs!
Oh catch them, crush them, crucify them—kill them!   1430

And as for you, you miserable women,
Count on the punishment which you have earned
By treachery! That punishment can wait—
With this to do. But oh when this is done!

(*Above the confusion appears, with instant dominion,*
Pallas Athena.)

Athena

Quiet, King Thoas! What is all this tumult?   1435
Hold the chase back and listen to Athena.
Hold all your soldiers back. Yes, all of them.
    Apollo sent Orestes to your country
To set him free from the Avenging Furies,
Ordered him, through an oracle, to bring   1440
Iphigenia home again to Argos
And the sacred statue home to Her own land.
You have the story. But there's one addition—
The fact that this Orestes you would hunt
Is gliding on a comfortable sea.
Poseidon made it smooth. I asked Him to.   1445
    Orestes! Gods are heard at any distance.
Though you are far away, you still can hear me.
Do this. Take back your sister and the statue
Safely to Hellas. Pause at God-built Athens.
Then, passing through, continue to the end   1450
Of Attica and find a holy place
Close to Carystus' hill, a place called Halae.
There build a temple. There set up the image,
That men may flock to Her with happy hymns.
Name it for Tauris, to immortalize
Your flight from home, your rescue from the Furies,
Your penitence and your deliverance.   1455
    And let this be the law. When they observe
Her festival, the priest shall hold,
In memory of you, the sharp blade of his knife
Against a human throat and draw one drop   1460
Of blood, then stop—this in no disrespect

But a grave reminder of Her former ways.
   Iphigenia! Steps are cut in rock
At Brauron for a shrine to Artemis.
You shall reside as keeper of the keys there
And at your death you shall be buried there
And honored in your tomb with spotless gifts,   1465
Garments unworn, woven by hands of women
Who honorably died in giving birth.
   These loyal maidens, Thoas, I command you
To send back home.
                Orestes, once I saved you
When I was arbiter on Ares' hill   1470
And broke the tie by voting in your favor.
Now let it be the law that one who earns
An evenly divided verdict wins
His case. Therefore go safely from this land,
O son of Agamemnon. And you, Thoas,
Enjoy the taste of swallowing your wrath.

Thoas

The man who thinks he ever stood a chance   1475
Against the Gods was born a fool. And so
I hold no slightest grievance toward Orestes
Or Iphigenia. They may keep the statue.
There isn't even any dignity
In challenging a God. So off with them.   1480
May Artemis be happy in their land.
   I bid these women also, since I have to,
A pleasant trip to Hellas. Thy word holds
For all my captains too. Call back the galleys!
Here are my spirit—and my spear—bowed down.   1485

Athena

In doing as you must, you learn a law
Binding on Gods as well as upon men.
   O winds of Heaven, speed Orestes home,

And I will guide him on his way to Athens
And will save Thy likeness, Artemis, my Sister.

The First Maiden
   Smooth seas to them and may their journey's end   1490
     Become unending joy!

The Fourth Maiden
   Pallas Athena, let us prove Thy name
   As hallowed upon earth as in high Heaven.

The Third Maiden
     And let us take to heart
   Thy unexpected but so welcome words.   1495

The Second Maiden
     Command us with Thy grace,
  O Conqueror of anger and of fear,
     Award us wiser ways.

The First Maiden
   Undo our troubled guile, crown us with Truth.   1499

HELEN

Translated and with an Introduction by

RICHMOND LATTIMORE

CHARACTERS

Helen

Teucer

Chorus of Greek captive women

Menelaus

Portress

Servant of Menelaus

Theonoë

Theoclymenus

Follower of Theoclymenus

Slave of Theonoë

Castor
Polydeuces
} *as divine*

Because those who are unfamiliar with this play will find that it contains surprises, it is suggested that they read the text first and the introduction afterwards. The introduction is accordingly printed after the play.

HELEN

SCENE: *Egypt, near the Canobic mouth of the Nile and before the gates of the royal house. The tomb of King Proteus is down stage. Helen discovered sitting against the tomb.*

Helen

These are the waters of the Nile, stream of sweet nymphs.
The river, fed with melting of pale snows, and not
with rain, rises to flood the flats of Egypt. Here
Proteus, while yet he lived, was lord over the land,
at home in Pharos, king in Egypt; and his bride   5
was Psamathe, one of the daughters of the deep,
wife once to Aeacus, later sundered from him,
who bore two children to him in the house, a boy
called Theoclymenus (because his father showed
the gods love in his lifetime) and a fine girl they named   10
Ido (her mother's image) when she was a child;
but when she came to nubile age they changed her name
to Theonoë, for she understands all things that are,
all things to be, that divination alone can tell.
Nereus, her forefather, granted her this privilege.   15

Nor is my own country obscure. It is a place
called Sparta, and my father was Tyndareus: though
they tell a story about how Zeus took on himself
the shape of a flying swan, with eagle in pursuit,
and came on wings to Leda my mother, and so won   20
the act of love by treachery. It may be so.
They called me Helen. Let me tell you all the truth
of what has happened to me. The three goddesses came
to remote Ida, and to Paris, for him to judge
their loveliness, and beauty was the cause. These were   25
Hera, the Lady of Cyprus, and the Daughter of Zeus.
But Aphrodite, promising my loveliness

(if what is cursed is ever lovely) to the arms
of Paris, won her way. Idaean Paris left
his herds for Sparta, thinking I was to be his.   30

But Hera, angry that she was not given the prize,
made void the love that might have been for Paris and me
and gave him, not me, but in my likeness fashioning
a breathing image out of the sky's air, bestowed
this on King Priam's son, who thinks he holds me now   35
but holds a vanity which is not I. See, next,
how further counsels of Zeus add to my misery.
He loaded war upon the Hellenic land and on
the unhappy Phrygians, thus to drain our mother earth
of the burden and the multitude of human kind.   40
Also, he would advertise the greatest Hellene prince.
The Phrygians fought for me (except it was not I
but my name only) held against the spears of Greece.
I myself was caught up by Hermes, sheathed away
in films of air, for Zeus had not forgotten me,   45
and set down by him where you see me, in the house
of Proteus, chosen because, most temperate of men,
he could guard my honor safe for Menelaus. So
here am I; but meanwhile my ill-adventured lord
assembled an armament to track me down the trail   50
of my abduction, and assaulted Ilium's towers.
Because of me, beside the waters of Scamander, lives
were lost in numbers; and the ever patient I
am cursed by all and thought to have betrayed my lord
and for the Hellenes lit the flame of a great war.   55

Why do I go on living, then? Yet I have heard
from the god Hermes that I yet shall make my home
in the famous plain of Sparta with my lord, and he
shall know I never went to Ilium, had no thought
of bed with any man. Here, while yet Proteus looked   60
upon this sun we see, I was safe from marriage. Now

that he is dead and hidden in the dark, his son
pursues me for my hand, but I, remembering
my first husband, cling a suppliant here upon
the grave of Proteus, for help to keep my love intact.   65
Thus, though I wear the name of guilt in Greece, yet here
I keep my body uncontaminated by disgrace.

(Enter Teucer, who does not at first see Helen.)

Teucer

What master holds dominion in these lowering halls?
The scope of wall is royal, and the massive pile
bespeaks possession by the Lord of Gold and Death.   70
(seeing Helen) Ah!
O gods, what do I see before me. Do I see
the deadly likeness of that woman who destroyed
all the Achaeans and me? May the gods spurn you for
looking so much like Helen's copy. Were I not   75
footfast on alien ground, with my true-winging shaft
I would have killed you, for looking like the child of Zeus.

Helen

Poor wretch, whoever you are, whatever cause has driven
you here, why must *her* sorrows turn your hate on *me?*

Teucer

I was wrong so to give way to anger more   80
than it became me. Hellas hates the child of Zeus.
Therefore forgive me, lady, for what I have said.

Helen

But who are you? From what country have you journeyed here?

Teucer

Lady, I am one of those Greek unfortunates.

Helen

It is no wonder you hate Helen then. But tell   85
me who you are. Where from? Whose son you should be called.

Teucer

   My name is Teucer, and the father who gave me life
   is Telamon. The land of Salamis nursed my youth.

Helen

   And what has brought you to this valley of the Nile?

Teucer

   I am an exile, driven from my father's land.   90

Helen

   You must be unhappy. Who was it who forced you out?

Teucer

   Telamon, my father. Who could be nearer to my love?

Helen

   But why? Such action means catastrophe for you.

Teucer

   Aias my brother died at Troy. This meant my doom.

Helen

   Surely it was not by your hand he lost his life?   95

Teucer

   His death came when he hurled himself on his own sword.

Helen

   In frenzy? Could a sane man see such an act through?

Teucer

   You have heard of one they call Achilles, Peleus' son.

Helen

   Yes.
   He came once to ask for Helen's hand; so we are told.

Teucer

   He was killed. His armor caused a quarrel among his friends.   100

Helen

   But how could all this have brought Aias any harm?

Teucer
   Someone else won the armor, and he killed himself.

Helen
   But has this suffering of his damaged your life?

Teucer
   Yes, if only because I did not die with him.

Helen
   I see. Tell me, were you at famous Ilium, then?   105

Teucer
   I helped sack it. That act has been my own ruin.

Helen
   And the city has been set afire? It is all gone?

Teucer
   You could no longer tell for sure where the walls stood.

Helen
   Helen, poor wretch! The Phrygians have perished for your sake.

Teucer
   The Achaeans also; for great evil has been done.   110

Helen
   How long is it now since the city was destroyed?

Teucer
   Seven years have almost circled with their crops since then.

Helen
   How much time in addition did you spend at Troy?

Teucer
   Moon after moon, until it came to ten full years.

Helen
   And then you got the woman of Sparta?

Teucer
                                   Yes we did.   115
   Menelaus seized her by the hair and dragged her off.

Helen

Did you see the poor woman, or have you only heard?

Teucer

I saw her with my own eyes, as I see you now.

Helen

Think. Could this be only an impression, caused by God?

Teucer

Speak of some other matter, please. No more of her.   120

Helen

You *do* believe your impression is infallible.

Teucer

These eyes saw her. When the eyes see, the brain sees too.

Helen

So. Then by now Menelaus and his wife are home.

Teucer

They are not in Argos, nor where the Eurotas runs.

Helen

You speak them evil, and, ah, you tell of evil for them.   125

Teucer

The rumor is that he has vanished with his wife.

Helen

Then all the Argives did not cross for home together?

Teucer

They did, but a storm split them and drove them variously.

Helen

Among what waves, where on the open sea?

Teucer

                                                            Just as
they cut across the middle of the Aegean main.   130

Helen

And after this, none knows of Menelaus' return?

Teucer

No one does; and in Greece he is reported dead.

Helen

Then I am undone.
                                Is Thestius' daughter still alive?

Teucer

You mean by this Leda? No, she is dead and gone.

Helen

It could not have been the shame of Helen that caused her death?   135

Teucer

They say so; that she fastened the noose on her fair throat.

Helen

Tyndareus' sons, then; are they alive, or are they not?

Teucer

Dead, not dead. There are two interpretations here.

Helen

Which one prevails? How much sorrow must I endure?

Teucer

Men say that they have been made stars and are divine.   140

Helen

Fair told when thus told; but what is the other account?

Teucer

That for their sister's shame they died by their own hands.
Enough words now. I should not have to suffer twice.
But for the matter of my errand to this house
of kings, it was my wish to see Theonoë   145
the prophetess. Be you my representative
and help me learn from her how I should steer the wings
of my ship with best wind for the sea-girt land

of Cyprus, where Apollo prophesied that I
should found and name New Salamis from my island home.   150

Helen

Sail, friend. Your course will show itself; but you must leave
this country and escape before you have been seen
by the son of Proteus, ruler of this land. He now
has gone with hounds, hopeful of killing beasts of chase.
He slaughters every Greek he lays his hands upon,   155
but why he does this, you must not try to find out,
as I am silent. For how could my speech help you?

Teucer

All you have said was good, my lady, and may the gods
grant you the grace your kindness has deserved. You wear
the bodily shape of Helen, but you have a heart   160
that is not hers. Wide is the difference. May she
die miserably, never see Eurotas' stream
again.
    But may you, lady, always prosper well.

                        (*Exit. Helen is left alone.*)

Helen

Here, with a song of deep wretchedness for the depth of my
    sorrows,
what shall be the strain of my threnody, what singing spirit   165
supplicate in tears, in mourning, in sorrow? Ah me.
You who go winged women in form
young and maiden, daughters of earth,
O Sirens, if you would only come   170
to attend my mourning
with Libyan harp, with pipes,
with lyres, with tears of your own to give
the singing of all my unhappiness.
With passion for passion, sorrow for sorrow,
melody matching
my dirges, given
by Persephone   175

of the dead, she in turn shall be given
in her halls of night the sweet of my sorrow
in consecration
of those who are dead and gone from us.

(Enter the Chorus, singing.)

Chorus

I was down by the shining blue
water, and on the curl of the grass   180
there in the golden glare of the sun
laid out the colored wash
in the bed of the young rushes
to dry. There I heard my lady
and the pitiful sound as she cried out,
the voice of sorrow, lament without lyres,   185
a sharp voice of pain, of mourning
as cries aloud for grief some nymph,
a naiad, caught
in the hills for all her flight, gives voice
to pain, as under the rock hollows
she cries out
on Pan and his captured marriage.   190

Helen

Hear me,
spoil of the savage oar blade,
daughters of Greece, hear;
from Achaea a mariner
came, yes came, and tears on my tears he loaded.   195
The wrecked city of Ilium
is given up to the teeth of fire,
all through me and the deaths I caused,
all for my name of affliction. So
Leda has taken her life within   200
the strangling noose, for the thought of shame
in those sorrows that have been mine.
My lord is lost, he is gone, far driven

over the sea. And the twin-born glory
of the house of my father, Castor   205
and Polydeuces his brother, vanished,
vanished away; the plain where their horses
trampled, their running-field, desolate
down by the reeds of Eurotas   210
where the young men rode and ran.

Chorus

Ah me,
so sorrowful was that destiny,
lady mine, that befell you,
a life better unlived
given to you, yes given, when Zeus blazed in the bright
air, in the snowflash of the swan's   215
wing to beget you upon your mother.
What grief is there you have not known?
What in life have you not lived through?
Your mother is lost and gone:
the twins, beloved children of Zeus,   220
are blessed in fortune no longer. Your eyes
are kept from the sight of your country,
while through the cities of men there goes
the rumor, divine lady, that gives
you up to barbarian lusts. And now   225
your husband, lost on the tossing sea,
is gone from life. You can come no more
to bless the halls of your father, bless
the brazen house of Athene.

Helen

What man of the Phrygians was it
or was it one from Hellenic soil
who cut down the dripping pine timbers   230
fatal to Ilium?
This was the timber that Priam's son
shaped into that accursed ship

which, driven by outland oars, brought him
to the hearth where I lived; he came   235
after my ill-starred beauty,
after my love's capture.
And she, the treacherous goddess,
the murderous queen of Cyprus,
drew death down on the Danaid men
cruel in all her working.   240
Then Hera, goddess of grandeur,
queen of the golden throne, who lies
in the arms of Zeus, sent down to me
Hermes, fleet son of Maia.
I was picking fresh flowers
gathering them into my robe, to take
to Athene there in her brazen house   245
when he caught me away through the bright
air to this unprofitable
country, poor me, made a prize of war
for Priam's sons and the Hellenes
while upon my name
where Simois runs has descended   250
a false fame and a vanity.

Chorus

You have your sorrows, I know it well. But it were best
to bear your life's constraints as lightly as you may.

Helen

Women and friends, what is this destiny on which   255
I am fastened? Was I born a monster among mankind?
[No woman, neither in Greece nor yet in Barbary,
is hatched from the white envelope that contains young birds,
yet thus Leda bore me to Zeus, or so they say.]
And so my life is monstrous, and the things that happen   260
to me, through Hera, or my beauty is to blame.
I wish that like a picture I had been rubbed out
and done again, made plain, without this loveliness,

for so the Greeks would never have been aware of all
those misfortunes that now are mine. So I would keep   265
what was not bad, as now they keep the bad of me.
He who sees from the gods a single strain of luck,
all bad, has a sad lot, but can endure it still.
More complex is the sorrow in which I am involved.
I have done nothing wrong and yet my reputation   270
is bad, and worse than a true evil is it to bear
the burden of faults that are not truly yours. Again,
the gods have torn me from my father's land and made
me live among barbarians. I have no kin
and therefore live a slave although my birth was free.   275
All Barbary is slave except a single man.
There was one anchor to my hope; the thought of how
my husband might come some day and deliver me,
but gone is that hope now, for he is dead and gone.
My mother is dead, I am her murderer. I know   280
that is unfair, but such unfairness I must take.
My daughter, pride of the household and my own pride,
is growing to gray years unmarried. And the sons
of Zeus, or so men call them, the Dioscuri,
no longer live. So all my luck is turned to grief   285
and for all purposes I am dead, yet live in fact.
But worst of all is, if I ever should win home
I must be crushed by scandal, for men think that I
am that Helen whom Menelaus went to Troy
to bring. If my husband were alive, I could be known   290
by him through signs which no one else could recognize.
But this fails now. It cannot be that he lives still.
Why do I go on living then? What course is left?
Shall I choose marriage as my means to get away
from hardship? Live with a barbarian husband? Sit   295
to a rich table? No, for when a hateful lord
lives with a wife, then all the body is hateful too.
Death is best. But to die in some unseemly way?
[When one hangs by the neck, it is ugly

and is thought a bad sight for the slaves to look upon.   300
Death by the knife is noble and has dignity
and the body's change from life to death is a short time.]
Such is the depth of my unhappiness, that while
for other women beauty means their happiness
it is my very beauty that has ruined me.   305

Chorus
  Helen, you should not be so sure that that stranger
  who came, whoever he is, has spoken all the truth.

Helen
  But he said plainly that my husband had been lost.

Chorus
  Many things can be said and yet prove to be false.

Helen
  And much that contradicts the critic may be true.   310

Chorus
  You push yourself to believe the worst and not the best.

Helen
  Yes, I am frightened, and so led by fright to fear.

Chorus
  How does your favor stand with those inside the house?

Helen
  All here are friends, except the man who hunts my love.

Chorus
  Do you know? I think you should . . . leave your place at the
  tomb. . . .   315

Helen
  What advice is it you so hesitantly give?

Chorus
  Go to the house, and ask the daughter of the sea's
  nymph, ask Theonoë, who understands all things,

about your husband, whether he still lives, or if
he is lost from daylight. Then, when you are well informed   320
be happy, or be sorry, as the chance deserves.
Now, when you really know nothing, where is the use
in hurting yourself as you do now? Do what I say.
Give up the shelter of this tomb. Speak with the girl.
Why look further, when in this very house you have   325
a source of knowledge that will tell you all the truth?
I volunteer to go inside the house with you
and help you ask the maiden for her prophecies.
It is right for women to stand by a woman's cause.

Helen

Friends, I accept your argument.   330
Go, then, go inside the house
so that there you may ask
what new trials await me now.

Chorus

I will, nor hesitate. Urge not.

Helen

O pitiful day.   335
Unhappy I, unhappy, oh what
tale of tears shall I be told?

Chorus

Do not be prophetic of grief.
Do not, dear, anticipate sorrow.

Helen

My poor husband, what has happened to him?   340
Do his eyes see the light,
the sun's chariot and four horses, the stars in course,
or among dead men under ground
takes he the long period?   345

Chorus

For the future which is yet
to come, lean to the better hope.

Helen

I call upon you by name, I invoke,
river pale by the washed reeds,
Eurotas; if this tale   350
of my lord's death that has come to me
is true—and where was the story not clear?—
then I will bind my throat
fast in the hanging noose of death,
or with the deadly stroke that cuts
the throat open and bleeding   355
drive the iron with my own hand hard into my body,
a sacrifice to the trinity
of goddesses, and to Priam's son
who held the hollows of Ida
long ago when he tended his herds.

Chorus

From somewhere may defense emerge   360
against evils: the turn of your fortune.

Helen

Ah, Troy, the unhappy,
for things done that were never done
you died, hurt pitifully. The gifts
the Lady of Cyprus gave me brought
showers of tears, showers of blood, pain   365
on pain, tears upon tears, suffering.
Mothers who saw their children die,
maidens who cut their long hair
for kinsmen who were killed beside the waters
of Phrygian Scamander.
Hellas too has cried, has cried   370
aloud in lamentation,
beaten her hands against her head
and with the nails' track of blood
torn her cheeks' softness.

Blessed long ago in Arcadia, maiden Callisto,   375
who shared the bed of Zeus, who were made into
a four-foot beast, how happy was your lot beside
my mother's; for all the bear's shaggy bulk
is made gentle by the soft eyes,
and the metamorphosis took away   380
your sorrows. Artemis drove from her dances
the doe of the golden horns, Titanian daughter of Merops,
for her loveliness. But my body's beauty
ruined the castle of the Dardanians, ruined
all the perished Achaeans.   385

        (Exeunt all into the house. Enter Menelaus, in
                      tattered clothing.)

Menelaus

Ah Pelops, racer of chariots and horses long
ago with Oinomäus in the Pisa field,
how I could wish that, when you were constrained to make
an offering to the gods, you had then left this life
for theirs, before you had sired my father, Atreus;   390
who by his marriage with Aërope begot
Agamemnon and myself, Menelaus, two renowned
brothers; for here I do not boast, yet I believe
we marshalled the greatest of armadas against Troy
although we led them not as tyrants, not by force,   395
but the young men of Greece willingly served with us.
Those who are no more living can be numbered now,
and those who, gratefully escaping from the sea,
brought home again the names of all the dead. But I,
battered and driven over the gray swell of the open   400
sea, have been wandering ever since I stormed the towers
of Ilium, trying to win back to my own land
whereto the gods debar my right of homecoming.
I have now sailed to all the friendless, desolate
approaches of Libya; always, as I make near home,   405
the wind buffets me back again, nor ever fills
favorable my sail to bring me home again.

And now, hapless and shipwrecked, with my friends all lost,
I am driven upon this shore. My ship shattered against
the rocks, and broke up into wreck and flotsam there. 410
Of all the ship's various parts the keel held out,
and on it, by some unexpected chance, I managed
to save myself and Helen, whom I seized from Troy.
What this land is I do not know, nor yet the name
of its people; I was too embarrassed to be seen 415
in public, could not ask, but tried to hide away
my ragged state in shame for my bad luck. For when
a great man falls upon evil chance, the strangeness of it
makes him feel worse than the man accustomed to hard times.
But the need is too much for me, for we have no food 420
nor any clothing for our skin, as you may guess
by the kind of ship's flotsam in which I wrap myself.
The robes and all the shining wraps I had before
are lost at sea with all my treasures. Deep inside
a cave I hid the wife who was the cause of all 425
my evil fortunes, and constrained those friends who still
are left alive, to keep her safe for me. So now
I am here, all by myself, to see if I can raise
some provisions to take to the friends I left behind.
I saw this house with its expanse of masonry 430
and the grand gates as of some fortunate man, and so
came here. Seafarers always hope for charity
from the houses of the rich. Those who themselves are poor
would not be able to help them, though the wish were there.
O-ay! Who is the porter here? Will he come out 435
and take the message of my griefs to those inside?

(Enter Portress, from the house.)

Portress

Who is at the gates? Go away, will you, from the house?
Do not keep standing here before the courtyard doors
and bothering the masters. It will mean your death.
You are a Greek, and Greeks are not allowed in here. 440

Menelaus

Quite so, granny, just as you say, and fair enough.
Very well, I will do what you say, only let me talk.

Portress

Out with you. I have orders, stranger, never to let
anyone come from Greece to stay around this house.

Menelaus

Ah! Keep your hands off me, and stop pushing me. 445

Portress

That is your fault. You are not doing what I say.

Menelaus

Now go inside and take this message to your master.

Portress

I shall smart for it if I take a message from you.

Menelaus

I am a shipwrecked foreigner of high degree.

Portress

Go on then to some other house instead of this. 450

Menelaus

No, I am going in; do as I tell you to.

Portress

I tell you, you are bothersome. We'll throw you out.

Menelaus

Ah, where are all my armies now, which won such fame?

Portress

You may have been a great man at home. You are not one here.

Menelaus

God, what a loss of station, and now undeserved. 455

Portress

Your eyes are wet with tears. Tell me, why are you sad?

Menelaus

　　Thinking of all my happiness in times gone by.

Portress

　　Go then, bestow those tears upon your own people.

Menelaus

　　Tell me first, what is this country, what king's house is this?

Portress

　　This is the house of Proteus; Egypt is the land.　　　　　　　　460

Menelaus

　　Egypt? What an unhappy chance to have sailed here.

Portress

　　What do you find wrong with the glories of the Nile?

Menelaus

　　Nothing wrong. It is my own bad luck that makes me sad.

Portress

　　There are many men who have bad luck, not only you.

Menelaus

　　Is there some master of the house you could name to me?　　　465

Portress

　　This is his tomb you see here. Now his son is king.

Menelaus

　　Where would he be then? In the house, or gone somewhere?

Portress

　　He is not in; and above all else he hates Hellenes.

Menelaus

　　What have we done to him that I should suffer for it?

Portress

　　It is because Zeus' daughter, Helen, is in this house.　　　　470

Menelaus

　　What? What is this you are telling me? Say it again.

Portress

I mean Tyndareus' daughter who lived in Sparta once.

Menelaus

Where did she come from? What is the explanation of this?

Portress

She came from Lacedaemon and made her way here.

Menelaus

When? Has my wife I left in the cave been carried off?   475

Portress

She came, friend, before the Achaeans sailed for Troy.
So go away from here quietly. The state of things
inside is such that all the great house is upside down.
You came at the wrong time, and if my master catches
you, all the hospitality you will find is death.   480
I myself like the Greeks, in spite of those harsh words
I gave you. I was afraid of what the master might do.

(*The Portress goes back into the house and closes the door.*)

Menelaus

What am I to think or make of this? She tells me now
of present difficulties grown from those gone by,
since, while I come bringing my wife, lost once by force,   485
from Troy, and she is guarded for me in the cave,
all the while some other woman with the same name
as my wife has been living in this house. She said
that this one was by birth the child of Zeus. Can it be
there is some man who bears the name of Zeus and lives   490
beside the banks of the Nile? There is one Zeus; in heaven.
And where on earth is Sparta except only where
Eurotas' waters ripple by the lovely reeds?
Tyndareus is a famous name. There is only one.
And where is there another land called Lacedaemon   495
or Troy either? I do not know what to make of it.
I suppose it must be that in the great world a great many
have the same name, men named like other men, cities

like cities, women like women. Nothing to wonder at
in this.

I will not run away for the servant's threats.   500
There is no man whose heart is so uncivilized
that when he has heard my name he will not give me food.
Troy is renowned, and I, who lit the fire of Troy,
Menelaus, am not unknown anywhere in all
the world. I will wait the master of the house. I have   505
a choice of courses. If he is a savage man
I will hide myself and make for where I left the wreck,
but if he gives way and is gentle, I shall ask
for what the present circumstances make me need.
Of all the evils in my distressed plight, this is   510
the worst, that I, myself a king, should have to ask
other kings for sustenance. But so it has to be.
For the saying is not mine, but it was wisely said,
that nothing has more strength than dire necessity.

(*Enter the Chorus and Helen from the house.*)

Chorus

Before I came back I heard from the maid   515
prophetic all she divined for the house
of kings: how Menelaus is not
lost yet nor sunk in the dim,
shining cave of the under-earth,
but still over the sea's surges   520
hard driven he cannot win
to the harbors of his own land,
in hardship, wandering
for want of food, with his friends all gone
all across the wide world he keeps   525
his foot hard for the oarsman's stroke
since ever he sailed from Troy land.

Helen

So, here am I, come back to the shelter of the tomb
once more. I have heard Theonoë's words, and they were good,

and she knows everything. She says my husband lives   530
still in the light and looks upon the day-star; yet
he is driven sailing back and forth along the sea
on endless crossings, hardened by the wanderer's life,
but when his work is ended and over, he will come.
One thing she did not tell me, whether when he comes   535
he will be safe. I carefully did not ask her this,
I was so happy to hear that he is safe so far.
She said also that he was in this country, near
at hand, a shipwrecked castaway with few friends left.
When will you come? And if you come, how dear to me!   540

> (*As she speaks this line, she turns to face Menelaus, whom*
> *she has not seen until now. She gives a little scream.*)

Who is it, who are you? Does this mean I am waylaid
by the machinations of Proteus' godless son? What shall
I do? Not run like a racing filly, like the god's
bacchanal, to the tomb with flying feet? This man
is savage by his look and hunts me for his prey.   545

Menelaus

You, who now race in such an agony of fear
to reach the grave-mound and the uprights where the fires
are burned, stay! Why this flight? Know, when I saw your face
it struck me with amazement and with unbelief.

Helen

We are set upon, my women. This man bars my way   550
to the tomb. His purpose is to catch me, and then give
me over to that tyrant whose embrace I shun.

Menelaus

I am no thief, nor any servant of bad men.

Helen

And yet the clothes that cover you are poor and mean.

Menelaus

Stay your swift feet from running, put aside your fear.   555

Helen

Very well, I will stand, since I have reached my goal.

Menelaus

Who are you? I look, lady, upon your face: whose face?

Helen

And who are you? The same question for both of us.

Menelaus

Never have I seen a form so like another form.

Helen

Oh gods!—it is divine to recognize your own. 560

Menelaus

Are you a Hellene woman or a native here?*

Helen

Hellene. But tell me who you are. I would know too.

Menelaus

You are more like Helen, my lady, than any I know.

Helen

You are like Menelaus, too. What does it mean?

Menelaus

The truth. You have recognized that most unhappy man. 565

Helen

Oh, you are come at long last here to your wife's arms.

Menelaus

Wife? What wife do you mean? Take your hands off my clothes.

Helen

The wife Tyndareus, my own father, gave to you.

Menelaus

O Hecate of the lights, send better dreams than this.

---

* The line is not in the manuscripts of this play. Markland has supplied it from the parody of this scene in Aristophanes' *Thesmophoriazusae*.

Helen

I am no dream of the crossway goddess. You see me.   570

Menelaus

I am only one man and could not have two wives.

Helen

And who might be this other mate whose lord you are?

Menelaus

Whom the cave hides, whom I brought here from the Phrygian
    land.

Helen

I am your wife. There is no other in my place.

Menelaus

Am I in my right senses? Are my eyes at fault?   575

Helen

When you look at me, do you not think you see your wife?

Menelaus

Your body is like her. Certainty fails me.

Helen

                                        Look and see.
What more do you want? And who knows me better than you?

Menelaus

In very truth you are like her. That I will not deny.

Helen

What better teacher shall you have than your own eyes?   580

Menelaus

It is they that fail me, since another is my wife.

Helen

It was an image of me. I never went to Troy.

Menelaus

And what artificer makes bodies live and breathe?

Helen

The air: from which the work of gods shaped you a bride.

Menelaus

And which of the gods made her? This is past all wit.   585

Helen

Hera, to palm on Paris, so he should not have me.

Menelaus

How could you be here and in Troy at the same time?

Helen

My name could be in many places where I was not.

Menelaus

Let me go. I had pain enough when I came here.

Helen

And will you leave me, for that empty shadow's arms?   590

Menelaus

You are like Helen, so, at least, happy farewell.

Helen

Lost, lost! I won my husband, and must lose him still.

Menelaus

I trust my memory of great hardships more than you.

Helen

Ah me, was any woman more wretched ever? They
who stand closest forsake me. I shall never find   595
my way to Greece, land of my fathers, ever again.

> (*Enter Servant of Menelaus. He does not see, or does not notice,*
> *Helen until he has told his story.*)

Servant

Menelaus, I have been wandering all over this land
of barbarians looking for you and find you now
at last. The friends you left behind sent me for you.

Menelaus

What is it? Have the barbarians robbed or plundered you?   600

Servant

A strange thing, stranger in itself than the telling of it.

Menelaus

Tell me. You must bring some surprise, for haste like this.

Servant

I tell you: all your thousand toils were toiled in vain.

Menelaus

This is old weeping for old sorrows. What is new?

Servant

Your wife is gone, swept up and away and out of sight   605
into the hollows of the high air. Sky veils her now.
She left the secret cave where we were keeping her
with only this said to us: "Wretched men of Troy
and all you Achaeans who, day after day, went on
dying for me beside Scamander, by Hera's craft,   610
you thought Paris had Helen, when he never did.
Now I, having kept the duty of destiny, stayed out
the time I had to stay, go back into the sky,
my father. All for nothing Tyndareus' daughter has
heard evil things said of her, who did nothing wrong."   615
    Oh, daughter of Leda, hail! Were you here all this time?
I was in the act of telling him, fool that I was,
how you had left our caverns for the stars and gone
on wings away. I will not let you mock at us
like this again. It was enough hardship that you,   620
your husband, and his helpers gave us there in Troy.

Menelaus

I see it, I see it! All the story that she told
has come out true. O day of my desires, that gave
you back into my arms to take and hold again!

Helen

    Oh, dearest of men to me, Menelaus, time has grown   625
old, but the joy that now is ours is fresh and new.
I have my husband again, all my delight, sweet friends,
my arms circle him now,
beloved, light and a flame in dark that has been so long.

Menelaus

    And I hold you. And we have so much to say about   630
the time between, I do not know where to begin.

Helen

    I am so happy, all my hair is rising
with shivering pleasure, and the tears burst. Husband
and love, I have your body here close in my arms,
happiness, mine again.   635

Menelaus

    O sweetest face, there is nothing left to wish for.
This is my bride, daughter of Zeus and Leda,
she whom the maidens of white horses, girls of your kindred
brought me by candle-light, to bless me, to bless   640
me long ago, but it was a god who took you away
from my house, and drove you
away, where your fate was the stronger.
But evil turned to good brought us together again,
my wife, lost so long. Now may my luck be good.   645

Chorus

    May it be good, surely. All my prayer is as your prayer.
Where there are two, one cannot be wretched, and one not.

Helen

    My friends, dear friends, I will no longer
weep and grieve for the past.
I have my husband, I have him. Long I waited for him,   650
all the years of Troy, waited for him to come.

Menelaus

>You have me, I have you. But the suns of ten thousand days
>were hard to win through to God's gladness here at the end.
>My happiness has its tears in it; but there is more
>sweetness here than the pain. 655

Helen

>What shall I say? Who ever could hope that this would be,
>to have you so unhoped-for here against my breasts?

Menelaus

>Or I to hold you, when I thought you had gone away
>to Idaean Troy and to those pitiful towers.
>In gods' name, tell me how you were taken from my house. 660

Helen

>Ah, a bitter cause that you open here,
>and ah, a bitter story you waken for me.

Menelaus

>Speak. The gods gave this; we must even hear it out.

Helen

>I spit away that story, the story that I must tell.

Menelaus

>Tell it still. There is pleasure in hardships heard about. 665

Helen

>It was not to the bed of a young barbarian man
>borne on the beating of oars,
>borne on the beating of desire for a lawless love.

Menelaus

>No, but what spirit, what destiny robbed home of you?

Helen

>The son of Zeus, of Zeus, my lord, 670
>brought me here to the Nile.

Menelaus

>Strange, strange! Who sent him? There is danger in this tale.

Helen

    I have wept for this, my eyes are wet with tears.
    It was the wife of Zeus destroyed me.

Menelaus

    Hera? What need had she to make it evil for us?   675

Helen

    Ah, there was danger for me in the bathing there and the springs
    where the goddesses made bright
    their bodies; there the judgment was begun.

Menelaus

    And Hera made the judgment mean this evil for you?

Helen

    So she might take away from Paris. . . .

Menelaus

                        How? Speak.   680

Helen

    Me. Cypris had promised him me.

Menelaus

                  Oh, cruel.

Helen

    Cruel, cruel. So I was driven to Egypt.

Menelaus

    She gave him the image in your place. So you tell me.

Helen

    But you in your house, my mother, ah, the sorrows of you,
    the hurt that happened.

Menelaus

                Tell me.   685

Helen

    My mother is gone. Ill starred in marriage for my sake
    and for my shame she caught the noose to her neck.

Menelaus

Ah. But Hermione our daughter, does she live?

Helen

Wedless, childless, my dear, she grieves
for my marriage that was none.   690

Menelaus

Oh, Paris, you sacked my house from top to bottom, and yet
it killed you too, and in their thousands killed
the bronze armored Danaans.

Helen

It was the god who cast me away from my city, from you,
out of the land of my fathers, star-crossed and cursed   695
when I left my house, when I left my bed; but I left them not
for any shameful love.

Chorus

If now for the rest of fortune you are fortunate,
in time to come, it is enough to heal the past.

Servant

Menelaus, let me into your happiness as well.   700
I begin to understand it, but am not yet clear.

Menelaus

Indeed, my father. Share in what we have to say.

Servant

Is she not mistress of sorrows for the men in Troy?

Menelaus

She is not. We were swindled by the gods. We had
our hands upon an idol of the clouds.

Servant

                                    You mean   705
it was for a cloud, for nothing, we did all that work?

Menelaus

The hand of Hera, the hate of the three goddesses.

Servant

    This woman who stands here with us is your real wife?

Menelaus

    Herself. It is I who tell you this. You must believe.   710

Servant

    My daughter, the way of God is complex, he is hard
    for us to predict. He moves the pieces and they come
    somehow into a kind of order. Some have bad luck
    while others, scatheless, meet their evil and go down
    in turn. None can hold fortune still and make it last.   715
    You and your husband have had your turn of trouble now.
    Yours was a story, but he fought with the spear, and all
    his hard fighting was fought for nothing. Now his luck
    has turned, and the highest blessings fall into his hands.
    You never shamed your aged father, never shamed   720
    your divine brothers, nor did what you were rumored to.
    It all comes back to me, your marriage long ago,
    and I remember the torch I carried as I ran
    beside your four-horse chariot, where you, a bride,
    rode from your noble house beside the master here.   725
    He is a poor thing who does not feel as his masters do,
    grieve in their grief, be happy in their happiness.
    I, though I wear the name of lackey, yet aspire
    to be counted in the number of the generous
    slaves, for I do not have the name of liberty   730
    but have the heart. Better this, than for a single man
    to have the double evil of an evil spirit
    and to be named by those about him as a slave.

Menelaus

    Come then, old friend, you who have had your share of work
    in the hard stands beneath the shield and at my side,   735
    share now the blessings of my fortune too, and go
    to take the news back to those friends I left behind
    how you have found our state here, how our luck holds now;
    tell them, too, to wait by the sea-shore, follow from there

the progress of those trials of strength I see in store   740
for me, and if we can steal my wife out of this place
they must see to it that, joining our fortunes all in one,
we get clear of these natives, if we have the strength.

Servant

It shall be done, my lord.

                               Only, now I am sure
how rotten this business of prophets is, how full of lies.   745
There never was any good in burning things on fires
nor in the voices of fowl. It is sheer idiocy
even to think that birds do people any good.
Calchas said nothing about this, he never told
the army when he saw his friends die for a cloud,   750
nor Helenus either, and a city was stormed in vain.
You might say: "No, for God did not wish it that way."
Then why consult the prophets? We should sacrifice
to the gods, ask them for blessings, and let prophecy go.
The art was invented as a bait for making money,   755
but no man ever got rich on magic without work.
The best prophet is common sense, our native wit.

                                         (*Exit.*)

Chorus

My own opinion about prophets marches with
that of this old man. If you have the gods for friends
you have a better thing than prophecy in your house.   760

Helen

So. All has been peaceful here where I have been. But tell
me, my poor husband, how you survived Troy. I know
there is no good in learning, but when you love you feel
a fascination in even the sorrows of those you love.

Menelaus

Your single question, one approach, ask me so much.   765
Why must I tell you how the Aegean wore us out,
of the Euboean wrecking-fires Nauplius set,

of Crete, of the Libyan cities we were driven upon,
of Perseus' eyrie? I could never satisfy
you telling of troubles. Telling would only burden me   770
who am so tired already, and be double pain.

Helen

What you have said was better than my question. Still,
leave out the rest and tell me only this. How long
have you been wandering battered on the waves of the sea?

Menelaus

The years at Troy were ten, and to this add the time   775
I was at sea, where I filled the circles of seven years.

Helen

Too long, unhappy husband, all too long a time
to live through, and survive it, and come here to die.

Menelaus

To die! What will you tell me now? You have broken me.

Helen

Make your escape, get clear of this place with speed, or else   780
you must be killed by the man who is the master here.

Menelaus

What have I done to deserve treatment such as this?

Helen

You have come unlooked-for to prevent my marrying.

Menelaus

You mean someone here is trying to marry my wife?

Helen

He meant to force my favors; and I must endure.   785

Menelaus

In his own private strength, or by some lordship here?

Helen

The man is Proteus' son and master of the land.

Menelaus

Now I understand the puzzle of the portress' speech.

Helen

At what outlandish doors have you been standing now?

Menelaus

These. And like any beggar I was driven away.   790

Helen

You were not asking for charity? Oh, my shame.

Menelaus

The action was that, but I did not call it so.

Helen

It seems, then, you know all about his courting me.

Menelaus

I know; what I do not know is whether you held him off.

Helen

Hear it then: all my love is kept untouched for you.   795

Menelaus

What will make me sure of this? (but how sweet, if true!).

Helen

Do you see where I sat in suffering beside this tomb?

Menelaus

The marks, yes, of your suffering. What was your plan?

Helen

I took a suppliant's place here to escape his bed.

Menelaus

For lack of an altar, or is it a foreign custom here?   800

Helen

It saved me, as well as the gods' temples could have done.

Menelaus

Is there no way for me and my ship to take you home?

Helen

    A sword waits for you, rather than a love-bed with me.

Menelaus

    Thus I would be the most unhappy man alive.

Helen

    Take flight, and do not be ashamed. Escape from here.   805

Menelaus

    And leave you? It was for your sake I captured Troy.

Helen

    But better so than that my love should mean your death.

Menelaus

    Cowardly counsel, unworthy of the siege of Troy.

Helen

    You would kill the king, I suspect. It cannot be done.

Menelaus

    You mean he has a body that no steel can pierce?   810

Helen

    You will see. The bold are helpless without cleverness.

Menelaus

    Shall I then quietly give him my hands to tie?

Helen

    You are desperate. What we need now is strategy.

Menelaus

    I would rather die in action than die passively.

Helen

    There is a single hope for escape, a single way.   815

Menelaus

    What way? Bribery? Daring and force? Or argument?

Helen

    What if the tyrant never learns that you are here?

Menelaus

Who will tell him? He will not know me by himself.

Helen

He has an ally, strong as a god, inside the house.

Menelaus

Has Rumor come and taken a secret place inside?   820

Helen

No, it is his sister, whom they call Theonoë.

Menelaus

The name is ominous, surely. Tell me what she does.

Helen

She knows everything. She will tell her brother you are here.

Menelaus

That would be death. I have no way to lie concealed.

Helen

But if we threw ourselves on her mercy, worked on her?   825

Menelaus

To do what? What is the hope you lead me gently to?

Helen

That she will *not* tell her brother you are in the land.

Menelaus

If we won her over, could we get ourselves out of here?

Helen

With her help, easily. Without her knowledge, no.

Menelaus

Best for woman to approach woman. You do this.   830

Helen

She will not leave until my arms have embraced her knees.

Menelaus

But look now. What if she will not listen to us?

Helen
> You must die, and I be married by force, and sorrowful.

Menelaus
> But treacherous still. By force, you say. Only an excuse.

Helen
> No, then. I have sworn a sacred oath, by your own head.   835

Menelaus
> You mean that you will die and never change your mate?

Helen
> Die by the sword that kills you, and be laid to rest
> beside you.

Menelaus
>   I accept it. Take my hand on this.

Helen
> I take it, swear to forsake the daylight when you die.

Menelaus
> And I swear, when I lose you I shall take my life.   840

Helen
> How, in such death, shall we make men know how we died?

Menelaus
> I will kill you on this grave-mound, then kill myself.
> But come, first we shall dare a great action for your sake
> and for your marriage. If he wants you, let him come.
> I will not shame my glories of the Trojan War   845
> nor take the common blame of Hellas when I come home,
> I who made Thetis lose Achilles, I who looked
> on Telamonian Aias in his suicide
> and saw Nestor made childless. Shall I then not dare
> count death as worth the dying for my lady's sake?   850
> Oh, I must. If there are gods and if they are wise,
> when a man falls high-hearted in the close of war
> they make the earth lie light upon him in the grave,
> but fling the cowards out on the hard stones of earth.

Chorus

 Oh gods, I pray you, let the race of Tantalus   855
 turn fortunate at last, and let their troubles end.

Helen

 Unhappy me! My destiny is luckless still.
 Menelaus, we have no chance left. Theonoë
 the diviner is coming out now, for the house sounds
 to the unbarring of the doors. Run! Only where   860
 to run? What use? Whether or not she is here, she knows
 that you are here. Poor husband, it is ruin now.
 Saved from the savages of Troy, you have come here
 once again to be driven on a savage sword.

    (*Enter Theonoë from the house, attended by women who carry
       torches and a sacred image. Each of her instructions
           is to a single attendant.*)

Theonoë

 Lead the way. Carry torches, let them shine, and bring   865
 the image, gift of the solemn sky, from its inward room
 so we may take and breathe the purity of this air.
 You: if anyone with unhallowed foot has stepped
 and fouled the way, treat it with purifying flame,
 then quench the blaze so I can make my way through. Then   870
 when we have rendered my devotion to the gods
 take the fire back inside to burn upon the hearth.

 Helen, what of my prophecies? Are they not true?
 Here is your husband Menelaus, plain before
 my eyes, with his ships lost, and with your image gone.   875
 Poor man, with what dangers escaped you have come here,
 nor even yet know whether you shall go home or must
 stay here. This very day before the seat of Zeus
 there shall be argument among the gods about
 your case. Hera, who was your enemy before   880
 is now your friend, desires that you go home with Helen
 here, so that Greece may learn how Aphrodite's gift
 to Alexander of a bride was a false gift.

Cypris would wreck your homecoming, so none shall know
the truth of how she bought the name of beauty for   885
false payment, Helen's marriage—which was no real thing.
The decision rests with me, to do as Cypris wills
and tell my brother you are here, destroy you so,
or take the side of Hera, save your life, and hide
your coming from my brother, though his orders were   890
to tell him, when your journey home brought you this way.

Which of you will go tell my brother that this man
is here? Thus will my future be made safe for me.

(*Helen flings herself at the feet of Theonoë.*)

Helen

Maiden, I throw myself as suppliant against
your knees, and kneel in a forlorn posture, for the sake   895
of my own self and for this man. I have found him
at last, and finding him am like to see him die.
Do not then tell your brother that my husband here
has come to my most loving and beloved arms,
but save us, I implore you. You must not betray   900
your duty and your good name for a brother's sake
to buy him wicked pleasures he does not deserve.
God hates violence. He has ordained that all men
fairly possess their property, not seize it. So
the rich man who is wicked must be left in peace.   905
There is the sky, which is all men's together, there
is the world to live in, fill with houses of our own
nor hold another's, nor tear it from his hands by force.
For me it was hard, and yet it was a blessed thing,
that Hermes gave me to your father to keep safe   910
for my husband, who is here and who would have me back.
How can he take me back when he is dead? And how
could your father duly give the living to the dead?
Consider now your father's case, the case of God.
Would the divine power, and would the dead man, wish to see   915
what belongs to another given back, or would they not?

I think they would. You must not give a greater weight
to a wild brother than to an honorable father.
If you, who are a prophetess and lead men through
the ways of God, spoil the just actions of your father   920
and uphold the right of an unrighteous brother, then
knowing the ways of God is a disgraceful thing.
Shame to know past and future, not know right and wrong!
Save me from my misfortunes, from hardships where I
submit. It is an accidental gift of grace.   925
There is no man living but Helen is his hate,
notorious through all Hellas as having betrayed
my husband, to live in the golden houses of the East.
But if I go to Greece and reach Sparta again
and they hear, and see, how it was by the arts of gods   930
that they were ruined, that I never betrayed my loves,
they will restore me to my reputation once
again. My daughter—nobody will take her now—
shall be given by me. I shall escape the shabby life
I lead here, and live on my own money in my own house.   935
If Menelaus lay dead and murdered on the pyre,
I should have loved him from my distance, with my tears.
But he is here, alive. Must he be taken from me?

No maiden, no. I kneel here as your suppliant.
Give me your grace in this, and let your ways be like   940
your upright father's ways, for it is the brightest fame
of children, when they have a father who was good,
if they can match the character that gave them birth.

Chorus

The words you have spoken since we spoke are pitiful
and you have pathos too. Yet still, I long to hear   945
what Menelaus has to argue for his life.

Menelaus

I cannot bring myself to fall before your feet
nor to make my eyes wet with tears. Such abjectness
would be the greatest shame upon the tale of Troy.

Yet I have heard, or read, how even stately men   950
have found it in them to let tears burst from their eyes.
I waive this privilege of honor—if privilege
of honor it is. Courage is better.
                                        Rather, thus:
if you think best to save a man, an outlander,
who asks with right to have his wife given back to him,   955
give her, and save me too. If you do not think it best,
it does not mean new misery for me but the old
continued; and it means you are an evil woman.
But what I think is worthy and right for me to say,
and what will take your heart beyond all else, I shall   960
say here before your father's monument, in grief.

Aged sir, here indwelling in the stony tomb,
give her back to me. What I ask is my own wife
whom Zeus had brought here, so you could keep her safe for me.
I understand now you will never give her back   965
since you are dead. But she must not deign that the invoked
and so much honored father underground shall hear
despiteful speech against him. All is in her hands.

Hades of the downworld, I invoke your aid as well.
You have taken many dead men, fallen before my sword,   970
because of this woman. You are paid your price in full.
Now bring these bodies to life again and yield them back,
or force this maiden to outpass her father's fame
for right dealing, and give me back the bride of my love.
If you Egyptians take my wife away from me,   975
I will tell you what will happen then, as she did not.
For your attention, maiden: we are bound by oath.
First I shall find your brother and we two shall fight.
He will be killed, or I. There is no more to say.
But if he lacks the courage to stand up to me,   980
and tries to starve and snare two suppliants at the tomb,
I have decided to kill her, then thrust the blade
of this two-edged sword into my own heart, upon

the back of this grave mound before us, where the blood
will splash and drip upon the grave. There we shall lie   985
two corpses, side by side, upon the marble tomb,
to shame your father, to hurt you, forevermore.
Your brother will not marry her. Nobody else
will marry her. I shall take her away with me,
away to the dead, if I am not to bring her home.   990

Why do I say this? Turning to woman and to tears
I should be pitied, but I should get nothing done.
Kill me, if you think best. You will not kill your shame.
But better, be persuaded by my arguments;
for so you would be just, and I should have my wife.   995

Chorus

  It is yours to pass judgment on their arguments,
  maiden. Judge then, and judge so all will be well pleased.

Theonoë

  My nature is to deal fairly; so is my wish.
  I have myself to think of, and my father's name
  is not to be defiled. I must not give my brother   1000
  such pleasures as will leave me with my honor gone.
  The sanctity of justice is a powerful thing
  in my own nature. This is Nereus' heritage.
  I have it, Menelaus; I will try to keep
  it always. And, since Hera wishes to help you,   1005
  my vote shall be as Hera votes. And as for Love
  (may Love not be offended!) that means nothing here.
  My aim is to remain a maiden all my life.
  As for reproaches on my father and this tomb,
  the same tale must apply to me. I should do wrong   1010
  not to restore her. For my father, had he lived,
  would have given her back to you, and you to her.
    For all men, in the world below and in the world
  above must pay for acts committed here. The mind
  of those who have died, blown into the immortal air,   1015
  immortally has knowledge, though all life is gone.

I must not strain this matter to great length. I shall
be quiet about your supplication, and shall not
let my good counsels help my brother toward his lust.
Really, I serve him so, though I seem not to do,   1020
if I can make him good, not dissolute any more.
Now it will rest upon yourselves to find a way.
I shall have nothing to do with it, but shall withdraw
and be silent. Begin by praying to the gods, and ask
the Lady of Cyprus to let Helen now come home,   1025
and ask Hera to hold steadfastly that good will
toward you, and toward your husband, which shall save you both.

My father, you are dead, but while I have the strength
your name of goodness shall not change to a vile name.

(Exit, attended.)

Chorus

The unrighteous are never really fortunate.   1030
Our hopes for safety depend upon our doing right.

Helen

We are safe, Menelaus, as far as the maiden is concerned.
Now it is yours to propose measures, so that we
can make a plan between us to escape from here.

Menelaus

Listen then: you have lived some time in this house   1035
and have been familiar with the attendants of the king.

Helen

Yes, but why did you mention it? Does it mean you hope
to accomplish something that will help the two of us?

Menelaus

Would you be able to persuade those who have charge
of the chariots? Would they perhaps give us one?   1040

Helen

I could persuade them. But what course? How shall we run
the plains of this strange land where we do not know our way?

Menelaus

Hopeless, as you say. . . . Come, then, hide me in the house
and I kill the king with my own blade. Shall we do this?

Helen

No. His sister could no longer keep the secret   1045
of your presence here, if it were to mean her brother's death.

Menelaus

But we have no ship in which to make á safe escape.
The ship we had is at the bottom of the sea.

Helen

I know! Even a woman might have one clever thought.
Are you willing, though not dead, to be reported dead?   1050

Menelaus

Unlucky omen. But if it does us any good
I consent. You may say that I am dead, though I am not.

Helen

Then we shall use the pitiful customs of women,
the dirges and cutting of hair to the unhallowed god.

Menelaus

Where is there any help toward our escape in this?   1055
I think there is some trick lurking behind your words.

Helen

Yes. I will say that you have died at sea, and ask
the king to let me bury you in effigy.

Menelaus

Suppose he grants it? Even so, without a ship,
how shall we save our bodies by this funeral?   1060

Helen

I shall ask him for conveyance, so your burial
fineries may be submerged and gathered in the sea's arms.

Menelaus

Well spoken, except for one thing. He will merely say
you must bury him on land. Where, then, is your excuse?

Helen

But I shall tell him that in Greece it is not allowed   1065
to bury ashore those who have met their death at sea.

Menelaus

Right again; so you correct it. Then I too shall sail
in the same boat, and with you let the offerings down.

Helen

By all means, yes, you are to be there. Bring with you
those mariners of yours who escaped from the shipwreck.   1070

Menelaus

Thus once I get possession of the anchored ship
there will be fighting, man to man, sword against sword.

Helen

You shall be in charge of all thenceforward. Only let
the wind blow fair in our sail. Let the ship run!

Menelaus

It shall. The gods will end my troubles now at last.   1075
Who will you say has told you the story of my death?

Helen

You. And you tell him you sailed with Atreus' son, and that
you were the sole survivor, and you saw him die.

Menelaus

This fishing-net of rags I wear upon myself
will be most authentic evidence of my spindrift state.   1080

Helen

It is timely now, though your ship was untimely lost.
The misery of time since might turn now to good.

Menelaus

    Should I then go inside the house with you, or sit
    here and wait quietly for you beside the tomb?

Helen

    Stay here. So, if he uses violence on you   1085
    this tomb, and then your own sword, will be your defense.
    I shall go in the house and cut my curls and change
    the white clothing that I wear for black, and drag
    my nails across my cheek leaving a red furrow there.
    I must. Great hazard. I see two ways the scales can tip.   1090
    I may be caught in treachery, then I must die.
    Or I shall save your life, and we shall both go home.
    O queen and goddess, given to the arms of Zeus,
    Hera. We are two pitiful people. Grant us wind
    from work. We ask, and lift our arms straight toward that sky   1095
    where your home is, among the splendors of the stars.
    And you, whose beauty's cost was my brute marriage, you
    Dione's daughter, Cyprian, oh destroy me not.
    It is enough, that filth you rolled me in before
    when you gave barbarians not my body but my name.   1100
    But if you wish to kill me, let me only die
    in my own country. Why this thirst for evil things?
    Why do you work in passions, lies, devices full
    of treachery, love-magics, murder in the home?
    Were you only temperate, in all else you are found sweet   1105
    to us beyond all other gods. This I confess.

                        (*Exit into the house.*)

Chorus

    To you, who deep forested, choired in the growth
    of singing wood hide nested,
    to you I utter my outcry,
    to you, beyond all other birds sweet in your singing,
    O nightingale of the sorrows   1110
    come, with brown beak shaken,
    to the beat of your melody, come

with song to my sad singing
as I mourn for the hard sorrows
of Helen, for all the suffering,
all the tears of the daughters of Troy   1115
from spears held by Achaeans,
all from the time when with outland oar he swept over
the water-flats, came, came, and his coming was sorrow
in marriage for Priam's people, moving
from Lacedaemon, from you, Helen: Paris, dark lover   1120
brought there by Aphrodite.

And there were many Achaeans who by the spear
and by the stone's smash have died
and are given, in vain, to Hades.
For these, unhappy wives have cut their long hair.
The chambers of their love are left forsaken.   1125
Many Achaeans besides
the man of the single oar drowned
off waterswept Euboea
when he lit his wreck fires, blazed
the false flares, and crashed them to death
on Aegean rocks at Caphereus.   1130
And the harborless mountains of Malea in the storm wind
were death, when he fled from our land, with the prize of his
     outland
glory; prize, no prize, but war,
the Greek cloud shape his ship carried off,   1135
the divine image of Hera.

What is god, what is not god, what is between man
and god, who shall say? Say he has found
the remote way to the absolute,
that he has seen god, and come   1140
back to us, and returned there, and come
back again, reason's feet leaping
the void? Who can hope for such fortune?
Yourself were born, Helen, daughter to Zeus.

Winged in the curves of Leda there   1145
as bird he childed you.
Yet even you were hallooed through Greece
as traitress, faithless, rightless, godless. No man's
thought I can speak of is ever clear.
The word of god only I found unbroken.   1150

                    (*Helen returns and joins Menelaus.*)

Mindless, all of you, who in the strength of spears
and the tearing edge win your valors
by war, thus stupidly trying
to halt the grief of the world.
For if bloody debate shall settle   1155
the issue, never again
shall hate be gone out of the cities of men.
By hate they won the chambers of Priam's city;
they could have solved by reason and words
the quarrel, Helen, for you.   1160
Now these are given to the Death God below.
On the walls the flame, as of Zeus, lightened and fell.
And you, Helen, on your sorrows bear
more hardships still, and more matter for grieving.

                        (*Enter Theoclymenus, from the country,
                                    attended by hunters.*)

Theoclymenus

Tomb of my father, greeting! It was even for such   1165
addresses, Proteus, I caused you to be buried here
at the entrance, and in passing in and out of doors
I, Father, Theoclymenus your son, greet you.

You, my serving men, take the dogs and the hunting-nets
inside the king's palace, put them away.

                                        Now I   1170
have found many hard things to say against myself.
Do we not chastise evildoers with death? And yet
even now they tell me there has been a Greek man seen
who has openly come here but has escaped the guards,

to spy on us, or watching for the chance to steal   1175
Helen away. Let him be caught, and he is dead.
Ah,
I have come too late, it seems. The whole thing has been done
and the daughter of Tyndareus, leaving empty her place
in the tomb's shelter, is carried away out of the land.
Hallo! Unbar all bolts and let the horses out   1180
from their mangers, men, and get the chariots out and ready.
Let it not be for lack of effort that the bride
I would win is stolen secretly from my domain.

No, wait. I see the two that I am after, here
beside the palace still, they have not yet escaped.   1185
Why have you changed from your white clothes, and put on
   black
and wear them? Why have you put the iron to your head
and shorn away the glory of your lovely hair?
And why are your cheeks wet with the fresh tears? For whom
do you weep? Is it compulsion of dreams in the night   1190
that makes you sorrow so, or have you heard from home
some rumor, and the grief of it has wrecked your heart?

Helen

My lord—for now at last I name you in such terms—
my life is ruined. There is nothing left for me.

Theoclymenus

What has happened? What is the disaster that has struck you
   down?   1195

Helen

My Menelaus—how shall I say it? He is dead.

Theocylmenus

I cannot take pleasure in what you tell me, though it is
my fortune. How do you know? Did Theonoë tell you?

Helen

She says so. Also, one who was with him when he died.

Theoclymenus

There is someone here then, with an authentic report?   1200

Helen

Yes, here. May he go where I too desire to go.

Theoclymenus

Who is he? Where is he? Tell me, let me get this clear.

Helen

That man you see there, sitting abject under the tomb.

Theoclymenus

By Apollo! The rags of clothing he is in!

Helen

I think my husband has looked thus. I pity both.   1205

Theoclymenus

Who is this man? Where from? Where did he come ashore?

Helen

He is a Greek, an Achaean who sailed with my husband.

Theoclymenus

What manner of death does he say that Menelaus died?

Helen

The most pitiful; washed down in the running sea.

Theoclymenus

Where in our remote waters was he sailing then?   1210

Helen

He was driven against Libya's harborless cliffs.

Theoclymenus

How was this man his oarsmate, and yet did not die?

Helen

Sometimes the baser have more fortune than their betters.

Theoclymenus

He is here, a castaway. Where did he leave his ship?

Helen

Where I wish he had perished, and Menelaus had not.   1215

Theoclymenus

But Menelaus has perished. In what boat did he come?

Helen

Sailors came on him and picked him up, or so he says.

Theoclymenus

Where is that evil that was brought to Troy instead of you?

Helen

The cloud image? You mean that? Gone into the sky.

Theoclymenus

O Priam, O Troy, how you were brought down in vain!   1220

Helen

I too, with Priam's children, shared this luckless chance.

Theoclymenus

Did he leave your husband unburied? Is he beneath ground?

Helen

Not buried yet. And oh, my grief!

Theoclymenus

Was it for this
you cut away the long curls of your yellow hair?

Helen

He is dear to me. Whoever is with me now is dear.   1225

Theoclymenus

This is real. Sorrow has distracted her to tears.

Helen

It could easily happen that your own sister might die.

Theoclymenus

Oh, no. How?
Will you go on making this tomb your home?

Helen

Why do you make fun of me? Let the dead man be.

Theoclymenus

Yet you showed faith to him when you avoided me.   1230

Helen

That is all past. You may make the wedding arrangements now.

Theoclymenus

It has been long in coming, but I still am glad.

Helen

Do you know what we should do? Let us forget the past.

Theoclymenus

What terms? Grace should be given in return for grace.

Helen

Let us make peace between ourselves. Forgive me all.   1235

Theoclymenus

My quarrel with you is cancelled. Let it go with the wind.

Helen

But by your knees I ask of you, if you are my friend—

Theoclymenus

What is it that your suppliant arms would wrest from me?

Helen

I desire your permission to bury my dead lord.

Theoclymenus

How? Are there graves for the lost? Would you bury a shadow?   1240

Helen

There is a Greek custom for those who die at sea.

Theoclymenus

What is it? Pelops' people are knowing in such things.

Helen

To hold a burial ceremony in empty robes.

Theoclymenus
  Do it, then. Raise a mound on my land, where you wish.

Helen
  It is not thus we bury our drowned mariners. 1245

Theoclymenus
  How, then? I cannot keep up with Greek usages.

Helen
  We take all the dead should be given out to sea.

Theoclymenus
  What shall I give you for your dead, then?

Helen
                              This man knows.
  I am inexperienced. All my luck was good before.

Theoclymenus
  So, friend, you have brought me news that I am glad to hear. 1250

Menelaus
  Not good hearing for me, nor for the dead.

Theoclymenus
                              Tell me,
  how do you bury those who have been drowned at sea?

Menelaus
  As lavishly as a man's substance lets him do.

Theoclymenus
  For this woman's sake tell me without minding the cost.

Menelaus
  First, there must be a blood-victim for the undergods. 1255

Theoclymenus
  What beast? Only tell me, and I will do your will.

Menelaus
  Decide yourself. Whatever you give will satisfy.

Theoclymenus
Among us outlanders, it would be a bull or horse.

Menelaus
Give such then, only give nothing which is malformed.

Theoclymenus
Our herds are rich. We have no lack of good victims.   1260

Menelaus
Coverings are given too for the body, though none is there.

Theoclymenus
That will be done. Is anything else customary?

Menelaus
Brazen armor; for Menelaus loved the spear.

Theoclymenus
What we shall give will be worthy of Pelops' clan.

Menelaus
We need also other fair produce of the earth.   1265

Theoclymenus
What will you do? How will you sink all this in the sea?

Menelaus
A ship must be there, also rowers to man the oars.

Theoclymenus
How far distant is the ship to be from the land?

Menelaus
Out where the breakers can barely be seen from ashore.

Theoclymenus
Tell me, why does Greece keep this custom? For what cause?   1270

Menelaus
So the waves cannot wash pollution back ashore.

Theoclymenus
You shall have a fast-running Phoenician ship, with oars.

Menelaus

That would be excellent. Menelaus would like it so.

Theoclymenus

Do you need her too? Can you not do it by yourself?

Menelaus

A man's mother must do this, or his wife, or children. 1275

Theoclymenus

You mean it is her duty to bury her husband?

Menelaus

It is duty's part not to rob the dead of their due.

Theoclymenus

She may go. A wife kept dutiful is to my own
advantage. Go in, and bring the funeral robes of state.
And if you act so as to please her, I shall send 1280
you from my country with no empty hands, to bear
a good report of me; you shall have clothing, not
this ragged state, and food, enough to bring you home
again; for now I see you are in hard case.

And you, my dear, do not wear yourself away in longing 1285
for the impossible. Menelaus has met his fate,
and your dead husband shall not come to life again.

Menelaus

You see your task, young woman; it is to love and serve
the husband you have, and let the other husband go.
In the circumstances, this is the best that you can do. 1290
But if I come through safe to Hellas, I shall put
an end to former scandals that were said of you.
Only be now the wife that you were meant to be.

Helen

It shall be so. My husband shall have no complaint
of me. You will be there, and you will know the truth. 1295
Come in the house, poor wanderer, you shall have your bath

and a change of clothing. Kindnesses I have for you
shall not be put off. If I give all you should have
from me, in all the better spirit you will do
the things my dearest Menelaus has deserved.   1300

(*Exit Helen, Menelaus, and Theoclymenus inside the house.*)

Chorus

Long ago, the Mountain Mother
of all the gods, on flashing feet,
ran down the wooded clefts
of the hills, crossed stream-waters in spate
and the sea's thunderous surf beat   1305
in wild desire for the lost girl
not to be named, her daughter,
and the cry of her voice keened high to break
through mutter of drums and rattles.
And as the goddess harnessed   1310
wild beasts to draw her chariot
in search of the daughter torn away
from the circling pattern of dance where she
and her maidens moved, storm-footed beside
the mother, Artemis with her bow,   1315
stark eyed, spear-handed Athene
attended. But Zeus, from his high place
in the upper sky shining ordained
a different course to follow.

For when the wandering and the swift
course of the mother was done, the far,   1320
the toilsome, the vain search
for her daughter's treacherous capture,
she crossed the place where the mountain nymphs
keep watch in the snows of Ida,
and there cast the blight of her grief   1325
across the stone and snow of the hill forests.
Earth, green gone from her fields, would give
food no more in the sown lands,

and generations were wasted.
For the flocks she shot out no longer   1330
tender food from the curling leaves.
The cities of men were starving,
the sacrifice to the gods was gone,
no offerings flamed on the altars. She,
turned cruel by grief for her daughter, dried   1335
the springs that gush from deep in the ground,
and there were no jets of bright water.

But now, as those festivals the gods
share with the race of men died out,
Zeus spoke, to soften the ruinous
rages of the Great Mother: 1340
"Go, stately Graces, and go
Muses, to Deio angered
thus for the sake of the maiden.
Change with wild singing the strain of grief
in her, and with choral and dancing."   1345
It was then that the loveliest
of the immortals took the death-
voice of bronze and the skin-strung drums:
Aphrodite. The goddess smiled
and drew into her hands   1350
the deep sounding flute
in delight with its music.

You had no right in this. The flames you lit
in your chambers were without sanction.
You showed, child, no due reverence   1355
for this goddess' sacrifice.
You won the great mother's anger.
The dappled dress in the deer skin
is a great matter, and the ivy wound
green on the sacred hollow reed   1360
has power; so also the shaken,
the high, the whirled course of the wheel

in the air; so also the dances,
the wild hair shaken for Bromius,
the goddess' nightlong vigils.   1365
It is well that by daylight
the moon obscures her.
All your claim was your beauty.

(Enter Helen from the house.)

Helen

Friends, all that happened in the house was favorable.
The daughter of Proteus keeps our secret. Though she knows   1370
my husband is here, and though her brother questioned her,
she told him nothing, rather she told him he was dead
and buried, out of the sunlight. She did this for me.
My lord has gained a capture, fair and fortunate.
He took the armor that is to be sunken in the sea   1375
and fitted the shield-handle upon his powerful arm
and wears it so, with the spear held in his right hand,
as if working to help grace the dead man. Yet still
first he practiced, with the armor on him, for a fight
as one who would raise a monument on a whole world   1380
of outlanders once we embark in the oared boat;
then I took off the wreck-stained clothes he wore, and gave
him new, and made him fine again, and bathed his body
at last in fresh water drawn from the stream.
                                   But see,   1385
this prince, who now thinks that he has a marriage with me
in his hands' reach, is coming from the house. Do me
the favor of silence. We want you on our side. Control
your lips, be kind, and some day, if we ever save
ourselves from here, we shall attempt to save you too.

(Enter Theoclymenus, followed by Menelaus, and leading a
group of serving men who carry the funeral properties.)

Theoclymenus

Men, go on to your work as the stranger told you to   1390
and take with you the funeral offerings to the sea.

Helen, if what I say to you does not seem wrong,
stay here, as I ask you. Your duty to your husband, whether
you go, or stay, will have been done in any case.
I am afraid longing for him will seize you, make   1395
you fling your body down into the tossing sea
stunned with delights remembered from him before. I know
how much, too much, you mourned for him when he was not
    here.

Helen

O my new husband, how can I help holding dear
the memory of my first marriage, all the love   1400
and closeness of it? I have loved him well enough
to die when he died. But what grace would he have known
in death from my death? Only let me go, myself
in person, and give his dead body what it deserves.
So may the gods grant you what I would wish to have   1405
them grant you, and this stranger, who is helping here.
For your kindness now to Menelaus and to me
you shall have me in your house, as wife, to the degree
that you deserve, since all this is in fortune's gift.
Now give your orders to the man who will provide   1410
the ship for our conveyance. For my sake do this.

Theoclymenus

Go then, get ready a Sidonian fifty-oar
galley, have master-rowers aboard, give it to her.

Helen

Is not this man to be in charge of the funeral ship?

Theoclymenus

Certainly. My sailors are hereby ordered to obey him.   1415

Helen

Give the order again so they will be quite clear.

Theoclymenus

Again, and still a third time, if you wish me to.

Helen

    For your good, and for my good in the things I plan.

Theoclymenus

    Now, do not waste yourself with too much weeping.

Helen

                                              No.

    Today will show the quality of my love for you.   1420

Theoclymenus

    Remember, the dead are nothing. This is wasted work.

Helen

    It is matters there of which I speak; and matters here.

Theoclymenus

    You will find me as good a man as Menelaus.

Helen

    I ask no more. I need only the favoring time.

Theoclymenus

    That is in your power, as long as you are kind to me.   1425

Helen

    I shall not need teaching to love those I ought to love.

Theoclymenus

    Shall I go too and see the expedition along?

Helen

    Oh no. My lord, you must not do slave's work for your slaves.

Theoclymenus

    Very well. I shall pass the rituals of the Pelopidae.
    My house needs no lustration, since it was not here   1430
    that Menelaus died. Therefore, one of you go
    and tell my vassals to take the wedding images
    inside my palace. All my country must be loud
    with singing of congratulation and with strains
    of marriage for Helen and me, to bless our state.   1435

Go now, my stranger guest, and give all this to the arms
of the sea, in honor of him who was her husband once,
then make haste back to my house again, and bring my wife,
so that you may be my guest at our wedding feast,
and then go home—or stay and prosper here with me.   1440

                           (Exit into the house.)

Menelaus

O Zeus, renowned as father and wise among the gods,
look down upon us. Grant us surcease from our pain,
and as we grate the shoal-rocks of catastrophe
reach us your hand, touch only with your fingertips
and we are there, triumphant, where we wish to be.   1445
Our past has been our share of troubles, all our share.
I have heard, O gods, much said of you. I have heard good,
and hard things also. I do not deserve bad luck
forever, but to walk with upright stride. Grant me
this one grace. It will make me happy all my life.   1450

              (Helen and Menelaus go out at the side.)

Chorus

Phoenician queen out of Sidon, O
lady of oars swift in the splashing water,
dear mother of oared ships
after whose lead in the dance move
the dolphins, when the open sea   1455
sleeps in stopped winds: may she,
Galaneia, who is called lady of calms,
and the Great Sea's green daughter
so speak: "Set wide the sails on the masts,
leave them free to the salt airs,   1460
but take in your hands the pinewood oars,
mariners, oh mariners,
as you convey Helen home
to kind haven upon the shores of Perseus."
So, Helen, might you find again   1465
the Daughters of the White Horses there by the river,
or before the temple of Pallas

come back at last to the dances
or the revels for Hyacinthus
and the night-long festival   1470
established by Phoebus after
his whirled throw of the discus
in games: for the Laconian land
a day of sacrifices
by ordinance of him, son of Zeus;   1475
come back to the girl you left
in your house, Hermione,
for whose marriage the pine-flares have not shone yet.

Oh, that we might fly in the air
winged high over Libya
where the lines of the migrant   1480
birds, escaping the winter rain,
take their way, following
the authority of their leader's
whistle. And he flying into the rainless, the wheat-burdened flat   1485
places, screams his clear call.
O flying birds with the long throats, who
share the course of the racing clouds,
go to the midmost Pleiades.
Go to Orion of the night,   1490
cry like heralds your message
as you light down on Eurotas,
that Menelaus has taken the town
of Dardanus and will come home.

May you riding down through the bright   1495
air, swift on your horses,
sons of Tyndareus, come
down the stormy courses of your stars' flaring,
oh, dwellers in the sky,
saviors of Helen, come   1500
cross close on the green swell and the dark-skinned back of the
    rollers

and the gray splash of the breaking sea,
bringing from Zeus those winds that blow
sweet airs for the mariners: 1505
and cast away from your sister the shame
spoken, of her barbarian loves,
shame that was hers for punishment
out of the quarrel on Ida, though
she never went to the land of Troy,   1510
not to the towers of Phoebus.

                    (*Enter a servant of Theoclymenus, from the sea.*)

Servant (*shouting*)

  My lord, the worst of news from our house. We have just learned.

                    (*Enter Theoclymenus from the house.*)

  Fresh news, strange news and bad. Hear it from me at once.

Theoclymenus

  What is it?

Servant

  Your work is wasted for a wife who is not
  yours. Helen is gone away, out of our land.   1515

Theoclymenus

  How gone? On wings, or do her feet still tread the earth?

Servant

  Menelaus carried her away. For that was he.
  He came himself, and brought the news of his own death.

Theoclymenus

  This is disgraceful. But still I cannot quite believe.
  What sort of transport carried him away from here?   1520

Servant

  Precisely what you gave your guest. He took your men
  and left you. There you have it in a single word.

Theoclymenus

How? I must understand this, and I cannot yet
credit it that a single arm could overpower
so many sailors, all those who were sent with you.   1525

Servant

After Zeus' daughter left the palace here, and you,
and was escorted to the sea, there as she placed
her tiny feet, she mourned aloud, most cleverly,
for that husband who was by her side, by no means dead.
Now as we came to your shipyards and your arsenal
we hauled down a Sidonian ship of the first class   1530
with fifty rowing benches to accommodate
the oars. And now our various duties were assigned.
One took his place at the mast, another at the bench,
hands on his oar, another had charge of the white sails,   1535
the steersman sat to the tiller and the steering gear.

Now as we were hard at it, there came down to the shore
certain Greek men who had sailed with Menelaus once
and who had been watching for just this. They wore the rags
of shipwreck. Fine-looking men, but in a filthy state.   1540
The son of Atreus saw them as they came, and made
a false pretense of pity for our benefit,
with: "Poor castaways, what ship? It must once have been
Achaean, cracked up now, and so we see you here.
Will you help bury Atreus' fallen son? His wife,   1545
Tyndareus' daughter, buries him in effigy.
This is she." They then let fall some fictitious tears
and took aboard what was to be sunk in the depths
for Menelaus. We had our suspicious here,
and there were words among us, how these newcomers   1550
were very numerous. Nevertheless we held our peace.
We had orders from you and kept them. You had said
your guest was to have full command. That ruined all.
Now all the cargo was light and easily picked up
and stowed inside the ship, except the bull, who stood   1555

and baulked at going up on the steep slanted plank,
but bellowed aloud, and with arched back and head low down
rolled his eyes round the circle past his lowered horns
forbidding all to touch him. Helen's husband raised
his voice, and cried: "Oh, you who captured Ilium,   1560
come, do it the Greek way, can you not? Hoist the bull's
weight on the strength of your young shoulders, heave him in
over the prow. You, draw your sword and prod him on.
For he shall be our sacrifice to the dead man."
They at his order went and laid hands on the bull   1565
and heaved him up and forced him on the rowing deck,
and Menelaus, rubbing its forehead and its skin,
persuaded him, without harness, to go inside the ship.

At last, when all was got aboard and stowed away,
Helen, with dainty steps, put her feet through the rungs   1570
of the ladder, and took possession of the central bench,
with Menelaus, the supposed dead man, by her side,
and left and right along the bulkheads all took place,
man ranked on man in order (but the Greeks had swords
hidden away beneath their garments).
                              Then we all   1575
whitened the water at the bosun's shout of "Row!"
Now when we had reached a point where we were not remote
from the land, nor near it either, then our steersman asked:
"Shall we make further out, my friend, or is this far
enough to suit you? What we do is yours to say."   1580
He said: "This will do." Then, with a sword in his right hand,
crept to the prow, and braced himself to strike the bull,
and where he stood, there were no dead men in his mind,
but as he cut the throat he prayed: "Lord of the sea,
Poseidon in the depth, and you, chaste Nereids,   1585
convey me safe to Nauplia's strand, convey my wife
who left it, but was chaste." And as he spoke, the blood
rained on the water, favoring the stranger's prayer.
One of us said then: "There is treacherous sailing here.

We must make back. You, give the order for right oar, 1590
and you, reverse the rudder." But now Atreus' son
stood from the slaughtered ox and hailed his company:
"Oh, flower of all the land of Greece, why longer wait
to smash these savages, cut them down and throw them off
the ship into the water." Then your bosun called 1595
aloud upon your seamen to resist: "Come on!
Get anything to fight with. Take the end of a spar;
break up a bench and use it, or an unshipped oar,
and smash the heads of these foreigners, who turned on us."
Both sides sprang to their feet then. We laid hands upon 1600
whatever ship's lumber we could find. But they had swords.
The ship ran blood; but there was Helen cheering them
on from the stern: "Where is the glory of Troy? Come on,
show it on these barbarians." Then all fought hard,
and some went down, some kept their feet, but a man down 1605
was a man dead. Menelaus had his armor on
and watched where his companions had the worst of it
and there rallied them, with his sword in his right hand,
so that men, to escape, dived overboard. He swept
the rowing benches clean of your mariners, then went 1610
to the rudder and made the helmsman steer the ship for Greece,
and they got the mast up, and a wind came, favoring him.

They are gone from your country. I myself, escaping death,
let myself into the water where the anchor hung,
and as I was failing, one of the fishermen at his lines 1615
pulled me out and set me ashore so I could bring
this message to you. Man's most valuable trait
is a judicious sense of what not to believe.

(*Exit.*)

Chorus
I never would have thought Menelaus could be here
unknown, my lord, to you and us. Yet so it was. 1620

(*As Theoclymenus speaks the next lines, he starts to rush into the
house but is met at the door by another servant, an attendant
of Theonoë, who struggles to keep him from going in.*)

Theoclymenus

Oh, I have been duped and tricked with women's artful treacheries.
Now my bride has escaped away, and if they could be overhauled
I would make all haste to catch the ship that carries those foreigners.
But at least I can take vengeance on the sister who betrayed
me, who saw Menelaus in my house and did not tell me so.   1625
She shall never again deceive another with her prophecies.

Servant

Hallo, you there, master, where are you going? Is it death you
mean?

Theoclymenus

I am going where justice takes me. Out of my way and stand
aside.

Servant

It is a monstrous thing to rush to. I will not let go my hold.

Theoclymenus

You, a slave, will overpower your master?

Servant

Yes. I mean you well.   1630

Theoclymenus

No good to me, unless you let me go.

Servant

But that I will not do.

Theoclymenus

Let me kill my hateful sister.

Servant

No, not hateful. Dutiful.

Theoclymenus

She betrayed me.

Servant

It was just betrayal. What she did was right.

Theoclymenus
Giving my bride away to others.

Servant
                              Others had more right than you.
Theoclymenus
Who has right over what is mine?

Servant
                              The man her father gave her to.   1635
Theoclymenus
Fortune gave her then to me.

Servant
                              And fate took her away again.
Theoclymenus
You are not to judge what I do.

Servant
                              If I am in the right, I must.
Theoclymenus
Then I am no longer ruler, but am ruled.

Servant
                              For right, not wrong.
Theoclymenus
You desire to die, I think.

Servant
                    Then kill me, but you shall not kill
your sister while I have the power to stop you. Slaves, if they are
    true,   1640
find no glory greater than to perish for their masters' sake.
        (*As Theoclymenus is about to overpower and stab the servant, the
            Dioscuri, Castor and Polydeuces, appear above the palace.*)

Castor
Lord of this land, Theoclymenus, hold hard the rage
that carries you off your true course. We are the twins
called Dioscuri, sons of Zeus, whom Leda once
gave birth to, with that Helen who has fled your house.   1645

That marriage over which you rage was not to be,
nor has the daughter of the divine Nereid done
you wrong, Theonoë your sister, but she kept
the righteous orders of my father and the gods.
It had always been ordained that for the present time   1650
she was to be a dweller in your house. But when
Troy was uptorn from its foundations, and she lent
the gods her name for it, this was no more to be,
for now she must be once more married with her own,
and go home, and live with her husband. Therefore, hold   1655
your hand, nor darken your sword with a sister's blood.
Believe it was in thoughtful care that she did this.
We would have saved our sister long ago, since Zeus
had made us into gods and we had power, except
that we were weaker still than destiny, and less   1660
than all the gods, whose will was that these things should be.

This is for you. Henceforward, let my sister hear.
Sail with your husband, sail on. You shall have fair wind.
We, your twin brothers, guardian divinities,
shall ride the open water and bring you safely home.   1665
And when your life turns its last course and makes an end,
you shall be called, with the two sons of Zeus, divine,
have your libations, and with us be entertained
as honored guests by mortals. Zeus has willed it so.
And where the son of Maia first defined your place   1670
when he caught you up from Sparta on the skyward way,
stealing you, so that Paris might not have you, where
the island stretches to guard Acte, shall your name
be known as *Helen*, meaning Captive, for mankind
hereafter; because you were stolen from your house.   1675
For Menelaus, who has wandered much, the gods
have granted a home upon the island of the blest.
For Heaven never hates the noble in the end.
It is for the nameless multitude that life is hard.

(*The Dioscuri disappear.*)

Theoclymenus

O sons of Leda and of Zeus, I will forego   1680
the quarrel I had with you for your sister's sake.
Nor do I wish to kill my sister now. Then let
Helen go home, if so the gods would have it. Know
that you are born of the same blood from which was born
the best and the most faithful sister in the world.   1685
Go then rejoicing for the great and noble heart
in her. There are not many women such as she.

(Exit. The chorus begin to go off.)

Chorus

Many are the forms of what is unknown.
Much that the gods achieve is surprise.
What we look for does not come to pass;   1690
God finds a way for what none foresaw.
Such was the end of this story.

INTRODUCTION TO *HELEN*

The Legend

THE variant, according to which Helen never went to Troy, is not found here for the first time. Hesiod, in his lost works, apparently told the story of how it was a phantom-image, and not the Spartan queen herself, who was stolen away by Paris and recovered after a long war by Menelaus and the Achaeans. Better known in antiquity was the work of Stesichorus, the sixth-century West-Greek lyricist and successor to Hesiod. He, it seems, had said certain hard things about Helen, and as a result he lost his sight, which returned only after he had composed his Palinode, or Apology, from which we have his lines

> That story is not true.
> You never went away in the benched ships.
> You never reached the citadel of Troy.

"That story" is, of course, the standard version as told by Homer; the corrected version of Stesichorus, as we learn elsewhere, substituted the phantom for Helen herself.

We do not know where Stesichorus (and Hesiod) said that Helen did go, if not to Troy. We might gather from the lines above that she went nowhere at all. But Herodotus, whose work was published in full not much more than a decade (maybe much less) before our play, had told a different story, which he claimed to have heard from the priests of Hephaestus in Memphis, Egypt. According to these, Paris did steal Helen away, but adverse winds forced him ashore on the Egyptian coast. There Proteus, King of Egypt, was deeply shocked to hear of what was going on; he sent Paris about his business, and confiscated Helen, whom he held in safekeeping until her husband should come to claim her. Meanwhile Menelaus and Agamemnon gathered together a Greek armada, sailed to Troy, and demanded Helen. The Trojans protested that they did not have her, she was in Egypt. The Greeks did not believe this. They besieged the city and finally captured it, only to learn that the Trojans had been telling the truth all the time. Menelaus accordingly went to Egypt, collected Helen, and (after disgracing himself and Greece by an illicit sacrifice involving two Egyptian boys) sailed home (Herodotus 2. 112–20).

Euripides, plainly, has combined these two versions, and perhaps drawn on other earlier writers as well. He uses the phantom-image, but has Helen herself supernaturally transported to Egypt. The image has its Homeric precedent in the image Apollo made of Aeneas, for Achaeans and Trojans to fight over, while Aeneas himself was transported away through the air (*Iliad* 5. 443–53, and compare 21. 595–605); so also, in the *Iliad,* Paris, Agenor, and Aeneas once again were divinely spirited away alive, and set down elsewhere; and so, too, in another play, Euripides himself tells how Iphigenia was caught up and transported away to the very ends of the earth, there to live as a lonely Greek princess among barbarians awaiting delivery by means of a long lost relative whom she herself thought was dead.

Despite these precedents, the play which Euripides presented undoubtedly struck most of his audience with a pleasurable thrill of surprise. Although he used the Herodotean variant, he contrived, through the old idol-story, to remove that stain of dishonor which the Egyptian version had re-attached to Helen. And he exploited fully the factor common to both legends: the tragic futility of that utterly unnecessary Trojan War.

Date and Occasion

Helen was produced in 412 B.C., written therefore during the winter which immediately followed the tragic end (tragic for Athens at least) of the great Sicilian expedition. With that defeat there disappeared, once for all, the strange Athenian dream of conquering the entire west. There remained the war at home, where Sparta now held a strong position. But Sparta had seldom, perhaps never, for all these years been pushing the war against Athens with complete conviction; and perfectly patriotic citizens might well hope, and urge, that the fratricidal war be ended, that Athens should save as much out of the wreck as possible, before things got even worse. It was a year later that Aristophanes, in his greatest and funniest peace-play, made a strapping and genial Spartan wench ably second Athenian Lysistrata in her program to save the Greek world, and *Lysistrata* ends with a lyric in Laconian dialect honoring Helen of Sparta. In his play, Euripides too is conciliatory toward Sparta, not only in his kindly treatment of the Spartan hero and heroine, elsewhere maligned (*Andromache, Trojan Women, Orestes*), and his flattering terms in allusion to Sparta, but also in his sweeping condemnation of war, *all* war, under which the war in hand is necessarily subsumed (ll. 1151–57).

Such may be a part of the political motivation, but the times seem to have generated personal and artistic motives as well. The sordid state of the world between 431 and 403 B.C., which has its effect in tragedies like *Hecuba* and *The Trojan Women*, also drove Euripides to escape from his own conscience with a new type of play, which may best be described as romantic comedy. Using the theme of the lost one found, a variation of the foundling story (employed also in such bitter comedies as *Alcestis* and *Ion*) he indulges himself in an illusion of optimism in *Iphigenia in Tauris* and *Helen*.

The Play

What we have, therefore, is a light, elegant romance written not only deftly but with wit. The dominant theme is paradox, illusion, surprise, all to be summed up in the relation of Helen to that other self, the idol who is not, but in some way is, Helen herself. Triumphantly, the heroine emerges with all the attributes Homer gave her—the charm, the wit, the self-importance and self-pity—above all, the inescapable loveliness (featuring, we guess, a most accomplished actor in a ravishing mask and with a voice that fairly demanded an extra allowance of solo lyrics); but adding to all these, in perfect harmony, the virtues of Penelope. To her, enters her minor Odysseus, Menelaus. The plot saves him from the low character he wore in *Andromache* and is to wear again in *Orestes* and *Iphigenia in Aulis*. No doubt his heroic leg may be pulled a little in the scene where the Portress (a manly woman, typical of Egypt, straight out of Herodotus) faces him down; but Euripides saw the pathos in situations where a great man's strength is worn away by circumstance, in this case sheer fatigue and starvation, and the hero in rags and tatters is so standard a Euripidean figure that we should not suspect farce. Better to take this play neither too seriously nor too lightly. It is romance, but not without recognition of realities, even realities new to tragedy. In *Andromeda*, a part of the same set of plays, Euripides dealt with young love, rarely considered worth bothering about in early Greek literature; in *Helen*, he realizes that there can be real, exciting love between two middle-aged people who are married to each other. Doubtless, all these elements are there in the *Odyssey*; nevertheless, what Euripides gives us here is his own, as he saw and experienced it, in the form of one of his most compact and elegant dramas.

HECUBA

Translated and with an Introduction by

WILLIAM ARROWSMITH

INTRODUCTION TO *HECUBA*

Along with Croesus, Oedipus, and Priam, the figure of Hecuba, the *mater dolorosa* of Troy transformed by suffering into the "bitch of Cynossema," survives in classical imagination as a supreme example of the severest degradation the reversal of human fortune can inflict. From Euripides on, through Ovid, medieval literature, and Dante to the "mobled queen" of Hamlet's players, the image persists with extraordinary purity, untampered with, almost unchanged. What Euripides may have taken from his own presumptive source, the lost epic on the sack of Troy by the eighth-century Arctinus of Miletus, we have no way of knowing; but between Euripides and Ovid,[1] very little has been lost, and between Euripides and Dante so little has been lost that the essential experience of the Greek *Hecuba* is still vivid in two compressed tercets of the *Inferno:*[2]

> Ecuba, trista, misera e cattiva,
>> poscia che vide Polìssena morta,
>> e del suo Polidoro in su la riva
>
> del mar si fu la dolorosa accorta,
>> forsennata latrò sì come cane:
>> tanto il dolor le fe' la mente torta.

Whether this persistence of the image derives from the myth or the play hardly matters; but the purity with which it persists argues, I suppose, as much the power of the original play as the authority of Ovid who transcribed it for later literature. Ovid is normally nothing if not fickle with his sources, but in this case he was working with a celebrated play and a myth so standardized in its Euripidean version as to prove intractable. But either through Greek or, via Ovid, through Latin, the Euripidean Hecuba has left to subsequent literatures an authoritative and compelling image of human suffering under the reversal of fortune.

1. *Metamorphoses* xiii. 407 ff.
2. Canto xxx, ll. 16–21: "Hecuba, sad, miserable and captive, after she had seen Polyxena slain, and, forlorn, discerned her Polydorus on the shore of the sea, barked like a dog, out of her senses: to such a degree had the sorrow wrung her soul."

To a large degree this authority was quickened by the high esteem and even popularity which the *Hecuba* enjoyed for more than two thousand years. Admired, much quoted and echoed in antiquity, it became one of the favorite plays of the Byzantine schoolbooks, was translated by Erasmus into Latin, and was finally almost canonized as a model of tragedy by the French classical dramatists. But in the nineteenth century the *Hecuba*, in a peripety as sudden and undeserved as that of its protagonist, fell into a profound disfavor, which has never been withdrawn; indeed, it is still commonly cited by handbooks, those tidy morgues of leached opinion, as one of the feeblest, if not the feeblest, of surviving Greek plays. The cause of this demotion—one which overtook the bulk of Euripides' plays as well—was twofold: first, the persistent misconception, based on too humble or too literal a reading of Aristotle, that Sophoclean structure provides the ideal norm of Greek tragic structure; second, a killing misunderstanding of the political experience of the play and what the logic of political necessity does to the characters. The consequence of the first has been to snarl Euripides' meaning by hopelessly disfiguring his form, while the second has operated to cut off our access to a range and power of experience which Euripides, alone of the Greek tragedians, shares with the twentieth century.

But the *Hecuba*, if it is not a great play, is at least a moving and a powerful one, a taut, bitter little tragedy of the interrelationships between those who hold power and those who suffer it. And, far from lacking unity or formal coherence—though its unity is anything but Aristotelian—it is in fact a tightly constructed tragedy, driving home with great economy and control its central tragic idea. Superficially, the action is episodic; like the *Heracles*, it consists of two separate actions joined together without causal connection. Over both actions—the slaughter of Polyxena by the Greeks and the discovery of the body of Polydorus which leads to Hecuba's atrocious revenge on Polymestor—the figure of the suffering Hecuba loosely presides, giving at least the feel of unity to the various episodes as they occur. Carefully, if not elaborately, her progress, from grief to despair, toward the final atrocity is traced under the rhythm of the descending blows, each one heavier than the last; but the emphasis is not so much on the psychology of the change within Hecuba as the way in which, confronted by her tormentors, she is forced to yield, one by one, her values, her self-respect, and the faith which makes her human. If what she suffers dehumanizes her, Euripides' emphasis is centered at least as much on *what* she suffers, its rationale, its cost, its significance, as on the anguish of the suffering itself. And, for this reason, though Hecuba provides a convenient focus for the play, whose episodes and values converge around her, her figure does not suffice to give the play unity or to make of it a tragedy of character.

Like so many Euripidean plays, the *Hecuba* is not the tragedy of an individual but a group tragedy, its apparently random and disconnected episodes bound together by a single overriding idea, forced up in ever more inclusive complexity by the development of the action. Uniting the *Hecuba*, underlying Hecuba's transformation, and joining persecutors and persecuted alike in a common tragedy is a bleak logic of political necessity, a concern that brings the *Hecuba* close to the *Trojan Women* and Thucydides' Melian Dialogue. Those characters who urge that necessity leaves them no choice are as corrupted by their own logic as those who, like Hecuba and the Chorus, suffer it. Confronted by the fact of power which makes her helpless, Hecuba, like the Melians, can only plead honor, decency, the gods, the moral law (*nomos*); when these appeals fail, what is civilized in her fails with them, and she takes a revenge so hideously brutal that we know, even before Polymestor, himself brutalized by suffering, predicts her transformation into the "bitch of Cynossema," that her humanity has been destroyed. Blow by blow, her hold on her humanity weakens: it is this loss of purchase that explains her sophistic approval of pure persuasion and her appeal to Agamemnon to repay his nights with Cassandra. In the end, she passes beyond the reach of judgment, for no moral judgment is pertinent when the denial of justice has destroyed her human and moral skills alike. At the same time, Hecuba's tormentors are corrupted by their commitment to their own logic: Odysseus involved in private dishonor for public reasons; Agamemnon emptying the meaning of human justice by enforcing justice only when his reputation is threatened.

But there is more to it than that. Necessity—what it is, when it arises, what it entails in action—is not easy to know, especially from the point of view of those who hold power. But just because necessity is hard and because the justification it gives—in politics, in love, in war—is unanswerable, it is the justification most frequently debased. And in the *Hecuba*, which is a tragedy and not a melodrama, it is this difficult and tragic aspect of necessity which interests Euripides. Hecuba is not tormented by the calculating cruelty of two vicious politicians but is a victim of men in the process of corruption by a power whose real necessities they understand no better than their own real motives. For what they do they claim the justification that they cannot act otherwise. In actuality, they do not act from necessity, but the excuse of necessity cloaks their fear. And just as Thucydides, by setting his Melian Dialogue on the strategically unimportant island of Melos, undercuts the Athenian generals' justification of necessity, so Euripides, by introducing Talthybius to pity Hecuba and to describe the soldiers' admiration for Polyxena's courage, undercuts the whole force of Odysseus' and Agamemnon's arguments, all based on the mistaken premise of the insensitivity of the mass to moral considerations. In the disparity between the facts and their arguments justice withers, while the callous shifting of responsibility from those in power to the mass dooms political life by depriving it of either trust or the illusion of moral action.

Within this binding framework of necessity, the characters are presented with severe economy. Hecuba herself is not so much character as an image of character in the process of annihilation. Odysseus is a demagogue by conviction (and hence all the more dangerous), decisive in action, alive to compassion but not to the point of allowing it to affect considerations which, because they are political, he thinks are beyond the reach of morality. Agamemnon, less arrogant than Odysseus, is weak, vacillating for the same reason that Odysseus is decisive, and enormously sensitive to the figure he cuts. But both alike, confident in their crude estimate of their necessities and driven by the same fear, compound the tragedy, forfeiting to their own power their freedom of moral action and as enslaved by their misguided notion of their necessities as Hecuba by her real necessity. Polymestor, alone of the characters in the play, has no necessity; he acts from crude greed and is a stark picture of barbarian viciousness. Opposite him, as virtuous as he is corrupt, stands Polyxena, almost too noble to be true. But Euripides' point is surely that it is only extreme youth and extreme innocence which can afford the illusion of total commitment. Like so many of Euripides' self-sacrificing young heroes, her death, futile in itself, exposes, by the quality of its commitment, the dense ambiguity of the moral atmosphere for those who cannot die.

What, finally, of justice and the gods? To this question the *Hecuba* makes no answer; if the action proves anything, it proves precisely the impossibility of making an answer. In the collision of their powers and necessities and purposes, men and women suffer; their appeals to *nomos* and the gods may be answered or not. Thus, at the close of the play, Polymestor predicts Agamemnon's death in Argos, and so hints at justice from heaven. But it is the very lag between crime and heaven's punishment of it, the apparent carelessness of the gods in the face of human anguish, that indicts any firm answer. Stubbornly, bleakly, rightly, the play refuses to annul the honesty of its experience on behalf of the time-honored theodicy, hinting merely that if there are powers beyond man, their justice is so alien, so slow, so indifferent, as to make impossible even the hope of communication or understanding. But man continues to demand justice and an order with which he can live, and it is the nobility of this demand, maintained against the whole tenor of his experience, in the teeth of the universal indifference and the inconsistency of fortune, that in Euripides makes man tragic. His suffering is limited only by his hope; take away his hope, as Hecuba's was taken, and he forfeits his humanity, destroyed by the hideous gap between his illusion and the intolerable reality.

The Date

The date of the *Hecuba* is uncertain, but the play may be reasonably assigned to the year 425–424. At least line 173 of the play is parodied by Aristophanes in the *Clouds* (423 B.C.) and line 462 refers to the establishment of the Delian Games by the Athenians in

426. The background of the Archidamian War helps to explain the choral emphasis on the tragic waste of war, as well as the concern of the play with the logic of imperial necessity. It is my personal conviction that the *Hecuba* was one of three tragedies for which the extant *Cyclops* was performed as the satyr-play. The connections in theme, treatment, and character are extremely close, especially in the blinding of Polymestor and Polyphemus.

CHARACTERS

Ghost of Polydorus

Hecuba

Chorus of captive Trojan women

Polyxena

Odysseus

Talthybius

Maidservant of Hecuba

Agamemnon

Polymestor, king of Thracian Chersonese

Sons of Polymestor

For Marshall Van Deusen

HECUBA

SCENE: *The shore of the Thracian Chersonese. Pavilioned tents, the quar-*
ters of the Trojan women, stand in the background. The time is
just before dawn. Enter above, ex machina, *the ghost of Poly-*
dorus.

Polydorus
    Back from the pit of the dead, from the somber door
    that opens into hell, where no god goes,
    I have come,
                the ghost of Polydorus,
    son and last surviving heir of Hecuba
    and Priam, king of Troy.
                     My father, fearing
    that Troy might fall to the assembled arms of Hellas,   5
    had me conveyed in secret out of danger
    sending me here to Thrace, to Polymestor,
    who rules this fertile plain of Chersonese
    and curbs with harsh power a nation of horsemen.
    With me my father sent a sum of gold,   10
    intending that, if Troy should someday fall,
    his living sons might be provided for.
    Being the youngest, I was chosen, still too small
    and slight to carry arms or throw a spear.   15
    But as long as Troy's great ramparts stood proud
    and unbreached, so long as our towers held intact
    and Hector, my brother, prospered in the fighting,
    I flourished under the care of my father's friend,
    a green shoot thriving under his watchful eye.   20
    But when Troy fell and Hector died,
    and picks and shovels rooted up our hearth,
    and there, by the altar that Apollo's hands once built,
    Priam fell, butchered by Achilles' son,
    then my father's friend took off his mask,

and moved by nothing more than simple greed,   25
murdered me and threw my body to the sea.
Here, pounded by the surf, my corpse still lies,
carried up and down on the heaving swell of the sea,
unburied and unmourned.
                Disembodied now,
I hover as a wraith over my mother's head,   30
riding for three long days upon the air,
three hopeless days of suffering and fear
since she left Troy and came to Chersonese.
Here on the shore of Thrace, in sullen idleness
beside its ships, the whole Achaean army waits   35
and cannot sail. For Achilles' ghost appeared,
stalking on his tomb, wailing, and stopped the ships
as they stood out for sea on the journey home.
He demanded my sister Polyxena as prize,   40
the blood of the living to sweeten a dead man's grave.
And he shall have her, a prize of honor and a gift
bestowed upon him by his friends. On this day
destiny shall take my sister down to death.
And you, poor Mother, you must see   45
your two last children dead this day,
my sister slaughtered and my unburied body
washed up on shore at the feet of a slave.
These were the favors I asked of the gods below—
to find my mother and be buried by her hands—   50
and they have granted my request.
                    Now I go,
for there below I see my mother coming,
stumbling from Agamemnon's tent, still shaken
by that dream in which she saw my ghost.

    (Enter Hecuba from the tent. At the entrance she crumples to the
           ground, and stretches out her hands to the three or four
                Trojan women who stand beside her in the tent.)

—O Mother,   55

poor majesty, old fallen queen,
shorn of greatness, pride, and everything but life,
which leaves you slavery and bitterness
and lonely age.
            Some god destroys you now,
exacting in your suffering the cost
for having once been happy in this life.

Hecuba

        O helplessness of age!
        Too old, too weak, to stand—
        Help me, women of Troy.   60
        Give this slave those hands
        you offered to her once
        when she was queen of Troy.
        Prop me with your arms   65
        and help these useless
        stumbling legs to walk.

        O star of morning,
            light of Zeus
            shining in the night!
            What apparition rose,
    what shape of terror stalking the darkness?   70

        O goddess Earth,
            womb of dreams
            whose dusky wings
    trouble, like bats, the flickering air!

        Beat back that dream I dreamed,
    that horror that rose in the night, those phantoms of children,
    my son Polydorus in Thrace, Polyxena, my daughter!   75
            Call back that vision of horror!

        O gods who protect this land,
        preserve my son, save him,
        the last surviving anchor of my house,   80

still holding in the snows of Thrace,
still warded by his father's friend!

Disaster I dreamed,
terror on terror!
Never has my heart   85
so shivered with fear!

O Helenus, I need you now,
interpreter of dreams!
Help me, Cassandra,
help me read my dreams!
I saw a little doe, a dappled doe, torn from between my knees,   90
cruelly ripped away, mangled by a wolf with blood-red nails!

And then fresh terror rose:
I saw Achilles' ghost
stalk upon his tomb, howling,
demanding a prize
from the wretched women of Troy.   95

O gods, I implore you,
beat back this dream,
preserve my children!

(*Enter chorus of captive Trojan women.*
They speak individually.)

Chorus
—We come to you in haste,
  Hecuba.

—   We left the tents . . .

—where the lot assigned us.   100

—Slaves, torn from home
  when Troy was burnt and sacked
  by the conquering Greeks!

—We bring you painful news.   105

—We cannot lighten your load.

—We bring you worse to bear.

—Just now, in full assembly,
   the Greek decree came down.

—They voted your daughter must die . . .

—to be slaughtered alive

—on the tomb of Achilles!

—The sails had been unfurled,
   and the fleet stood out to sea,
   when from his tomb Achilles rose,   110
   armor blazing, and held them back,
   crying:
"Ho, Argives, where do you sail,
   leaving my grave unhonored?"   115

—Waves of argument broke loose,
   dividing Greek from Greek.
   If one man spoke for death,
   another spoke against it.

—On your behalf spoke Agamemnon,   120
   lover of your daughter,
   poor, mad Cassandra.

—Then the two sons of Theseus,
   twin shoots of Athens, rose and spoke,
   but both with one intent—   125
   to crown Achilles' grave
   with living blood, asking
   if Cassandra's love meant more
   than the courage of Achilles.

—And so the struggle swayed,   130
   equally poised—

—   Until *he* spoke—
   that hypocrite with honeyed tongue,
   that demagogue Odysseus.
   And in the end he won,
   asking what one slave was worth   135

when laid in the balance
with the honor of Achilles.

—He wouldn't have the dead
descending down to Hades
telling tales of Greek
ingratitude to Greeks
who fell for Hellas
on the foreign field of Troy.   140

—And he is coming here
to tear your daughter from your breast
and wrench her from your arms.

—Go to the temples!

—   Go to the shrines

—Fall at Agamemnon's knees!   145

—Call on heaven's gods!

—Invoke the gods below!

—Unless your prayers prevent her death,
unless your pleas can keep her safe,
then you shall see your child,   150
face downward on the earth
and the stain in the black earth spread
    as the red blood drops
from the gleaming golden chain
that lies broken at her throat.

Hecuba
  O grief!
          What can I say?
  What are the words for loss?   155

  O bitterness of age,
  slavery not to be borne,
  unendurable pain!
  To whom can I turn?   160
  Childless and homeless,

my husband murdered,
my city stained with fire. . . .
Where can I go?
What god in heaven,
what power below
will help me now?
O women of Troy,   165
heralds of evil,
bringers of loss,
this news you bring is my sentence of death.
Why should I live? How live in the light
when its goodness is gone,
when all I have is grief?
Bear me up,
poor stumbling feet,   170
and take me to the tent.

> *(She stumbles painfully to Agamemnon's tent and then
> cries out in terror to Polyxena within.)*

O my child!
   Polyxena,
step from the tent!
Come and hear the news
your wretched mother brings,
this news of horror   175
that touches your life!

> *(Enter from the tent Polyxena, a beautiful young girl.)*

Polyxena
That terror in your voice!
That cry of fear
flushing me forth
like a bird in terror!

Hecuba
O my child! My baby. . . .   180

Polyxena
Again that cry! Why?

Hecuba

    I am afraid for you—

Polyxena

    Tell me the truth, Mother.
    No, I am afraid. Something
    in your face frightens me.   185

Hecuba

    O my child! My child—

Polyxena

    You *must* tell me, Mother.

Hecuba

    A dreadful rumor came.
    Some Greek decree   190
    that touches your life—

Polyxena

    Touches my life how?
    For god's sake, Mother,
    speak!

Hecuba

       —The Greeks,
    in full assembly,
    have decreed your death,
    a living sacrifice   195
    upon Achilles' tomb.

Polyxena

    O my poor mother!
    How I pity you,
    this broken-hearted life
    of pain!
       What god
    could make you suffer so,
    impose such pain,   200
    such grief in one poor life?
    Alive, at least

I might have shared
your slavery with you,
my unhappy youth
with your embittered age.
But now I die,
and you must see my death:—
butchered like a lamb   205
squalling with fright,
and the throat held taut
for the gashing knife,
and the gaping hole
where the breath of life
goes out,
         and sinks
downward into dark
with the unconsolable dead.   210

It is *you* I pity,
Mother.
       For *you* I cry.
Not for myself,
         not for this life
whose suffering is such
I do not care to live,
but call it happiness to die.   215

Coryphaeus
  Look, Hecuba. Odysseus is coming here
  himself. There must be news.

           (*Enter Odysseus, attended by several soldiers.*)

Odysseus
            By now, Hecuba,
  I think you know what decision the army has taken
  and how we voted.
           But let me review the facts.
  By majority vote the Greeks have decreed as follows: 220
  your daughter, Polyxena, must die as a victim

and prize of honor for the grave of Achilles.
The army has delegated me to act as escort.
Achilles' son will supervise the rite
and officiate as priest.

                  There matters rest.
You understand your position? You must not attempt   225
to hold your daughter here by force, nor,
I might add, presume to match your strength with mine.
Remember your weakness and accept this tragic loss
as best you can.

              Nothing you do or say
can change the facts. Under the circumstances,
the logical course is resignation.

Hecuba

                    O gods,
is there no end to this ordeal of suffering,   230
this struggle with despair?

                Why do I live?
I should have died, died long ago.
But Zeus preserved me, saved me, kept me alive
to suffer, each time to suffer worse
than all the grief that went before.

                  Odysseus,
if a slave may put her question to the free—
without intent to hurt or give offense—   235
then let me ask you one brief question now
and hear your answer.

Odysseus

             Ask me your question.
I can spare you the time.

Hecuba

            Do you remember once
how you came to Troy, a spy, in beggar's disguise,   240
smeared with filth, in rags, and tears of blood
were streaming down your beard?

Odysseus

                    I remember

the incident. It left its mark on me.

Hecuba

But Helen penetrated your disguise
and told me who you were? Told *me* alone?

Odysseus

I stood, I remember, in danger of death.

Hecuba

And how humble you were? How you fell at my knees   245
and begged for life?

Odysseus

           And my hand almost froze on your dress.

Hecuba

And you were at my mercy, *my* slave then.
Do you remember what you said?

Odysseus

               Said?

Anything I could. Anything to live.

Hecuba

And I let you have your life? I set you free?

Odysseus

Because of what you did, I live today.   250

Hecuba

Then can you say your treatment now of me
is not contemptible? To take from me
what you confess you took, and in return
do everything you can to do me wrong
and ruin me?

            O gods, spare me the sight   255
of this thankless breed, these politicians
who cringe for favors from a screaming mob

and do not care what harm they do their friends,
providing they can please a crowd!

                 Tell me,
on what feeble grounds can you justify   260
your vote of death?

            Political necessity?
But how? And do your politics require
the shedding of human blood upon a grave,
where custom calls for cattle?

                Or is it vengeance
that Achilles' ghost demands, death for his death,
and exacts of her? But what has she to do
with his revenge? Who ever hurt him less
than this poor girl? If death is what he wants,   265
let Helen die. He went to Troy for *her;*
for *her* he died.

          Or is it merely looks
that you require, some surpassing beauty in a girl
whose dying loveliness might appease the hurt
of this fastidious ghost? Then do not look
for loveliness from us. Look to Helen,
loveliest of lovely women on this earth
by far—lovely Helen, who did him harm   270
far more than we.

          So much by way of answer
to the justice of your case.

           Now, Odysseus,
I present my claim for your consideration,
my just demand for payment of your debt
of life.

    You admit yourself you took my hand;
you knelt at my feet and begged for life.

                 But see—

(*Hecuba kneels at the feet of Odysseus and takes his hand.*)
now I touch you back as you touched me.   275

I kneel before you on the ground and beg
for mercy back:
                    Let her stay with me.
Let her live.
                    Surely there are dead enough
without her death. And everything I lost
lives on in her. This one life   280
redeems the rest. She is my comfort, my Troy,
my staff, my nurse; she guides me on my way.
She is all I have.
                    And you have power,
Odysseus, greatness and power. But clutch them gently,
use them kindly, for power gives no purchase
to the hand, it will not hold, soon perishes,
and greatness goes.
                    I know. I too was great
but I am nothing now. One day   285
cut down my greatness and my pride.
                                But I implore you,
Odysseus, be merciful, take pity on me!
Go to the Greeks. Argue, coax them, convince them
that what they do is wrong. Accuse them of murder!
Tell them we are helpless, we are women,
the same women whom they tore from sanctuary   290
at the altars. But they pitied us, they spared us then.
Plead with them.
                    Read them your law of murder. Tell them how
it applies to slave and free without distinction.
But go.
            Even if your arguments were weak,
if you faltered or forgot your words, it would not matter.
Of themselves that power, that prestige you have
would guarantee success, swelling in your words,
and borrowing from what you are a resonance and force   295
denied to less important men.

Coryphaeus

                                Surely
no man could be so callous or so hard of heart
he could hear this mother's heartbroken cry
and not be touched.

Odysseus

                        Allow me to observe, Hecuba,
that in your hysterics you twist the facts.

                                            First,
I am not, as you fondly suppose, your enemy,   300
and my advice, believe me, was sincerely and kindly meant.
I readily admit, moreover, the extent of my debt—
everything I am today I owe to you.
And in return I stand ready and willing
to honor my debt by saving your life. Indeed,
I have never suggested otherwise.

                                But note:
I said *your* life, not your daughter's life,
a very different matter altogether.
I gave my word that when we captured Troy   305
your daughter should be given to our best soldier
as a prize upon request. That was my promise,
a solemn public commitment which I intend to keep.
Besides, there is a principle at stake
and one, moreover, in whose neglect or breach
governments have fallen and cities come to grief,
because their bravest, their most exceptional men,
received no greater honor than the common run.
And Achilles deserves our honor far more than most,
a great man and a great soldier who died greatly   310
for his country.

                        Tell me, what conduct could be worse
than to give your friend a lifetime of honor and respect
but neglect him when he dies?

                                And what then,
if war should come again and we enlist our citizens

to serve? Would we fight or would we look to our lives,   315
seeing that dead men get no honor?
                              No:
for my lifetime give me nothing more than what I need;
I ask no more. But as regards my grave,
I hope for honor, since honor in the grave
has eternity to run.   320
                    You speak of pity,
but I can talk of pity too. Pity *us*,
pity our old people, those old men and women
no less miserable than yours, the wives and mothers
of all those brave young men who found a grave
in the dust of Troy.
                         Endure; bear your losses,   325
and if you think me wrong to honor courage
in a man, then call me callous.
                          But what of you,
you foreigners who refuse your dead their rights
and break your faith with friends? And then you wonder
that Hellas should prosper while your countries suffer   330
the fates they deserve!

Coryphaeus
                         This is what it means
to be a slave: to be abused and bear it,
compelled by violence to suffer wrong.

Hecuba
                                   O my child,
all my prayers are lost, thrown away   335
on the empty air!
                     So try your powers now.
Implore him, use every skill that pity has,
every voice. Be like the nightingale,
touch him, move him! Fall at his knees,
beg him for life!
                     Even he has children too   340
and may pity them in you.

Polyxena

I see your hand,
Odysseus, hidden in the folds of your robes and your face
averted, lest I try to touch your hand or beard
and beg for life.

Have no fear. You are safe
from me.

I shall not call on Zeus who helps   345
the helpless.

I shall not beg for life.

No:
I go with you because I must, but most
because I wish to die. If I refuse,
I prove myself a coward, in love with life.   350
But why should I live?

I had a father once,
king of Phrygia. And so I started life,
a princess of the blood, nourished on lovely hopes
to be a bride for kings. And suitors came
competing for the honor of my hand, while over the girls
and women of Troy, I stood acknowledged mistress,
courted and envied by all, all but a goddess,   355
though bound by death.

And now I am a slave.
It is that name of slave, so ugly, so strange,
that makes me want to die. Or should I live
to be knocked down to a bidder, sold to a master   360
for cash? Sister of Hector, sister of princes,
doing the work of a drudge, kneading the bread
and scrubbing the floors, compelled to drag out
endless weary days? And the bride of kings,
forced by some low slave from god knows where   365
to share his filthy bed?

Never.
With eyes still free, I now renounce the light
and dedicate myself to death.

Odysseus,
lead me off. For I see nothing in this life
to give me hope, and nothing here at all   370
worth living for.
                    As for you, Mother,
do nothing, say nothing now to hinder me.
Help me instead; help me to die, now,
before I live disgraced.
                              I am a novice   375
to this life of shame, whose yoke I might endure,
but with such pain that I prefer to die
than go on living.

Coryphaeus
                    Nobility of birth
is a stamp and seal, conspicuous and sharp.   380
But true nobility allied to birth
is a greatness and a glory.

Hecuba
                    I am proud of you,
my child, so very proud, but anguish sticks
in this nobility.
                    If your Achilles
must have his victim, Odysseus, if you
have any care for your own honor left,   385
then let her live. Let me take her place
upon the tomb; kill *me*, be merciless
to *me*, not her. For I gave birth to Paris
whose arrows brought Achilles down.

Odysseus
                                        The ghost
demanded this girl's blood, not yours,   390
old woman.

Hecuba
            Then let me die with her at least,
and we shall be a double drink of blood
for earth and this demanding ghost below.

Odysseus

Her death will do. One victim is required,   395
no more.

Hecuba

        I *must* die with her! I *must*!

Odysseus

Must? A strong word, Hecuba. It was my impression
I was the master here.

Hecuba

              I shall stick to her
like ivy to the oak.

Odysseus

               Take my advice, Hecuba.
For your own good, do not.

Hecuba

                 Never, never   400
will I let her go.

Odysseus

             While I, for my part,
refuse to leave her here.

Polyxena

             Mother, listen.
And you, Odysseus, be gentle with a mother's love.
She has reasons for despair.

                 Poor Mother,
do not struggle with those stronger than you.
Is this what you want—to be thrown down in the dust,   405
this poor old body bruised, shouldered away,
hustled off by younger and stronger arms?
They will do it. No, this is not for you.
O Mother, Mother,

             give me your hand,
and put your cheek to mine for one last kiss   410
and then no more. For the last, last time

I look upon this gleaming circle of the sun
and speak the last words I shall ever say.
O Mother, Mother,
                    now I go below—

Hecuba
Leaving me to live, a slave in the light—   415

Polyxena
Unmarried to my death, no wedding-songs for me—

Hecuba
The song of mourning for you, wretchedness for me—

Polyxena
To lie in the dark with Hades, far from you—

Hecuba
O gods, where can I go? Where shall I die?

Polyxena
I was born to freedom and I die a slave.   420

Hecuba
Fifty children I once had, and all are dead.

Polyxena
What message shall I take to Priam and Hector?

Hecuba
Tell them this: I am the queen of sorrow.

Polyxena
O sweet breasts that nourished me!

Hecuba
So wrong, so wrong! So young to die!   425

Polyxena
Farewell, Cassandra! Mother, farewell—

Hecuba
Let others fare well. I never shall.

Polyxena
Goodbye, Polydorus, my brother in Thrace—

Hecuba

    If he lives at all—for all I have is loss.

Polyxena

    He lives. He shall close your dying eyes.   430

Hecuba

    I died of sorrow while I was still alive.

Polyxena

    Shroud my head, Odysseus, and lead me out.
    Even before I die, my cries have broken
    my mother's heart, and she has broken mine.
    O light of day!
                 I still can cry the light   435
    in that little space of life I have to live
    before I die upon Achilles' tomb!

                    (*Odysseus shrouds Polyxena and leads her out.*
                            Hecuba collapses to the ground.)

Hecuba

    I am faint—my legs give way beneath me—
    Polyxena!
             Touch your mother, give me your hand,
    reach me! Do not leave me childless!
                      O gods,   440
    to see there, in her place, Helen of Sparta,
    sister of the sons of Zeus, whose lovely eyes
    made ashes of the happiness of Troy!

Chorus

    O wind of ocean,
    wind that blows on the sea
    and drives the scudding ships,   445
    where are you blowing me?
    Where shall I be slave?
    Where is there home for me?
    There in distant Doris,   450
    in Phthia far away

where men say Apidanus runs,
father of waters,
river whose lovely flowing
fattens the fields?

There in the islands?   455
The salt sea churning, borne on by oars,
to days of mourning in the house,
there where the primal palm
and the bay broke out their leaves
for lovely Leto   460
in honor of her son?
There shall I sing
with the maidens of Delos,
praising Artemis,
the bow and fillets of gold?   465

Or there where Athene drives
her chariot of burnished gold?
There in Athens, yoking
the horses on the goddess' robe,
stitching cloth of saffron
with threads of every color,   470
sewing the Titans there,
killed by stabbing fire,
the thunderbolts of Zeus?

O my children!   475
My father, my mother!
O city, ruined land,
ashes and smoke, wasted,
wilderness of war!
I live, but live a slave,   480
forced to a foreign land,
torn westward out of Asia
to a marriage that is death!

                                  (Enter Talthybius.)

Talthybius

Women of Troy, where can I find Hecuba,   485
your onetime queen?

Coryphaeus

There she lies, Talthybius,
in the dust at your feet, her head buried in her robes.

Talthybius

O Zeus, what can I say?

That you look on man
and care?

Or do we, holding that the gods exist,
deceive ourselves with unsubstantial dreams   490
and lies, while random careless chance and change
alone control the world?

This was the queen
of fabulous Troy. This was once the wife
of Priam the great.

And now, childless, old,   495
enslaved, her home and city wrecked by war,
she lies there on the ground, her proud head
fouled in the dust.

I too am old,
an old man, and life is precious now,
but I would rather die than sink as low
as this poor woman has fallen now.

Rise,
lady. Lift your head to the light; raise
that body blanched with age.   500

Hecuba

Who are you
who will not let me lie? Who disturbs
my wretchedness? Why?

Talthybius

I am Talthybius,
herald of the Greeks, lady. I bring you a message
from Agamemnon.

Hecuba

Have the Greeks decreed my death? 505

Tell me that, and you are welcome, herald.

No other news could please me now.

Talthybius

No, not that.

I come on behalf of the army and the sons of Atreus 510

to bid you bury your daughter. She is dead.

Hecuba

Is that your news, herald?

I cannot die?

You came to tell me *this*?

O gods, my child!

My poor child! Torn from my arms! Dead!

Dead. All my children died with you.

How did you put her to death? With honor and respect, 515

or did you kill her savagely, with cold brutality?

Tell me. Let me hear it all, everything,

no matter how it hurts.

Talthybius

There is a cost

in telling too, a double price of tears,

for I was crying when your daughter died,

and I will cry again while telling you, 520

lady. But listen.

The whole army of the Greeks,

drawn up in ranks, was present at the execution,

waiting and watching while Polyxena was led

by Achilles' son slowly through the center of the camp

and up the tomb. I stood nearby, while behind her

came a troop of soldiers purposely appointed 525

to prevent her struggles.

Then Achilles' son

lifted a golden beaker to pour the offering

of wine to his father's ghost and nodded to me
to call for silence.
             "Quiet, Achaeans!" I shouted,   530
"Silence in the ranks!" and instantly a hush
fell upon the army and he began to pray:
"Great ghost of my father Achilles, receive
this offering I pour to charm your spirit up.   535
Rise and drink this gift we give to you,
this virgin's fresh blood. Be gracious to us:
set free our ships and loose our anchor-ropes.
Grant to us all our day of coming home,
grant us all to come home safe from Troy!"   540
So he prayed, and the army with him.
                   Then,
grasping his sword by its golden hilt, he slipped it
from the sheath, and made a sign to the soldiers
to seize her. But she spoke first:
                 "Wait, you Greeks   545
who sacked my city! Of my own free will I die.
Let no man touch me. I offer my throat
willingly to the sword. I will not flinch.
But let me be free for now. Let me die free.   550
I am of royal blood, and I scorn to die
the death of a slave."
             "Free her!" the army roared,
and Agamemnon ordered his men to let her go.
The instant they released their hold, she grasped her robes
at the shoulder and ripped them open down the sides   555
as far as the waist, exposing her naked breasts,
bare and lovely like a sculptured goddess.   560
Then she sank, kneeling on the ground, and spoke
her most heroic words:
             "Strike, captain.
Here is my breast. Will you stab me there?
Or in the neck? Here is my throat, bared   565
for your blow."

Torn between pity and duty,
Achilles' son stood hesitating, and then
slashed her throat with the edge of his sword. The blood
gushed out, and she fell, dying, to the ground,
but even as she dropped, managed to fall somehow
with grace, modestly hiding what should be hidden   570
from men's eyes.

The execution finished,
the soldiers set to work. Some scattered leaves
upon her corpse, while others brought branches
of pine and heaped her pyre. Those who shirked   575
found themselves abused by the rest.

"You loafers,"
they shouted, "how can you stand there empty-handed,
doing nothing? Where's your present for the girl?
When did you ever see greater courage
than that?"

And now you know it all.

For my part,   580
having seen your daughter die, I count you
of all women the one most blessed in her children
and also the unhappiest.

Coryphaeus

Blow after blow
disaster drops from heaven; suffering shakes
my city and the house of Priam.

Hecuba

O my child,
how shall I deal with this thronging crowd of blows,   585
these terrors, each with its petition, clamoring
for attention? If I try to cope with one,
another shoulders in, and then a third
comes on, distracting, each fresh wave
breeding new successors as it breaks.

But now,
with this last blow I cannot cope at all,

cannot forget your death, cannot stop   590
crying—
        And yet a kind of comfort comes
in knowing how well you died.
                  But how strange it seems.
Even worthless ground, given a gentle push
from heaven, will harvest well, while fertile soil,
starved of what it needs, bears badly.   595
But human nature never seems to change;
evil stays itself, evil to the end,
and goodness good, its nature uncorrupted
by any shock or blow, always the same,
enduring excellence.
              Is it in our blood
or something we acquire? But goodness can be taught,   600
and any man who knows what goodness is
knows evil too, because he judges
from the good.
          But all this is the rambling nothing
of despair.
         Talthybius, go to the Greeks
and tell them this from me: not a hand
is to be laid on my child; make them keep   605
the crowd away.
          For in armies the size of this,
men are prone to violence, sailors undisciplined,
the mob gets out of hand, runs wild, worse
than raging fire, while the man who stands apart
is called a coward.
         (Exit Talthybius. Hecuba turns to a Handmaid.)
        —Take your pitcher, old woman,
fill it with water from the sea and then return.   610
I must give my daughter's body its last bath
before her burial, this wedding which is death.
For she marries Hades, and I must bathe the bride
and lay her out as she deserves.

But how?
I have nothing of my own, nothing precious left.
What then?
                    I'll borrow from my women in the tents   615
those few poor trinkets they managed to pilfer
from their own homes.

                                        (*Exit Handmaid.*)
                    Where is greatness gone?
Where is it now, that stately house, home
where I was happy once? King Priam,
    blessed with children once, in your pride of wealth?   620
And what am I of all I used to be,
mother of sons, mother of princes?
                                        Gone,
all gone, and nothing left.
                    And yet
we boast, are proud, we plume our confidence—
the rich man in his insolence of wealth,
the public man's conceit of office or success—   625
and we are nothing; our ambition, greatness, pride,
all vanity.
                    That man is happiest
who lives from day to day and asks no more,
garnering the simple goodness of a life.

                                (*Hecuba enters the tent.*)
Chorus
    That morning was my fate,
    that hour doom was done,   630
    when Paris felled the tree
    that grew on Ida's height
    and made a ship for sea
    and sailed to Helen's bed—
    loveliest of women   635
    the golden sun has seen.

Grief, and worse than grief,
necessity surrounds us.
One man's folly made
a universal curse, 640
ruin over Simois.
Paris sat as judge
upon three goddesses. 645
His verdict was war.

War, slaughter, and the ruin of my house,
while in her house the Spartan woman mourns,
grieving by the wide Eurotas, 650
and mothers mourn for their sons,
and tear out their snowy hair
and dredge their cheeks with bloody nails. 655

(*The Handmaid rushes in.*)

Handmaid

Where is the queen, women?
Where is Hecuba
whose sufferings outstrip all rival runners?
No one shall take that crown away. 660

Coryphaeus

Speak.
What new sorrow do you bring her? Will this news
of anguish never sleep?

(*Enter other women, carrying on a bier the
shrouded corpse of Polydorus.*)

Handmaid

This is the grief
I bring to Hecuba. Gentle words are hard
to find: the burden I bring is disaster.

(*Enter Hecuba from the tent.*)

Coryphaeus

Look: here she comes now. 665

Handmaid

O my queen,
more wretched, more miserable than I can say.
Now you live no more, the light is gone!

Hecuba

This is mockery, not news. I know it all.   670
But why have you brought Polyxena's body here?
I heard the Greeks were helping with her funeral.

Handmaid

Poor woman, she thinks it is Polyxena.
She does not know the worst.   675

Hecuba

O gods, *no*!
Not my poor mad daughter, Cassandra?

Handmaid

Cassandra is alive. Mourn for this dead boy.
                    (*She strips the shroud from the corpse.*)
Look at this naked corpse we found,
this unexpected horror.   680

Hecuba

It is my son!
Polydorus, warded by my friend in Thrace!
No!

O gods in heaven, let me die!

O my son, my son,
now the awful dirge begins,   685
the fiend, the fury,
singing, wailing in me now,
shrieking madness!

Handmaid

What fury? Is it the curse of Paris you mean?

Hecuba

Horror too sudden to be believed,
unbelievable loss,
blow after blow!   690
And this is all my life:
the mourning endless,
the anguish unending.

Coryphaeus
 In loss and suffering we live our lives.

Hecuba
   O my son, my child,   695
   how were you killed?
   What fate, what hand
   could take your life?

Handmaid
 I do not know. I found his body lying
 on the shore.

Hecuba
     Drowned, his body washed on the sand?   700
 Or was he murdered?

Handmaid
      The surf had washed his body up.

Hecuba
   O gods, my dream!
       I see it now,
   those black wings beating the dark,   705
   brushing over him, touching him,
   dead already, even in my dreams!

Coryphaeus
 Who murdered him? Did your dream show you that?

Hecuba
   Who but our noble friend in Thrace,   710
   where his father sent him out of harm,
   to be safe with our friend in Thrace?

Coryphaeus
 Murdered? Murdered by a friend? Killed for gold?

Hecuba
   Unspeakable, unimaginable crime,
   unbearable!
      Where is friendship now?   715
   O fiend, monster, so pitiless,

to mangle him so, to hack
his sweet flesh with the sword!   720

Coryphaeus
Unhappy Hecuba, most miserable of women
on this earth, how heavily god's anger
falls on you.
           —But look: I see our master,
Agamemnon, coming here.
                       Quickly, friends,   725
withdraw.
                    (*Enter Agamemnon with attendants.*)

Agamemnon
          Why this delay of yours, Hecuba,
in burying your daughter? I received your message
from Talthybius that none of our men should touch her,
and I gave strict orders to that effect.
Hence I found your delay all the more surprising   730
and came to fetch you myself. In any case,
I can report that matters there are well in hand
and proceeding nicely—if a word like "nicely"
has any meaning in this connection.
                   (*He sees the corpse of Polydorus.*)
              Here,
what's that Trojan corpse beside the tents?
I can see from his shroud that he's not a Greek.   735

Hecuba (*aside*)
O gods, what shall I do?
                Throw myself
at his knees and beg for mercy or hold my tongue
and suffer in silence?

Agamemnon
             Why do you turn away,
Hecuba? And what's the meaning of these tears?
What happened here? Who is this man?   740

Hecuba (aside)
  But suppose he treats me with contempt, like a slave,
  and pushes me away? I could not bear it.

Agamemnon
  I am not a prophet, Hecuba. Unless you speak,
  you make it quite impossible for me to help you.

Hecuba (aside)
  And yet I could be wrong. Am I imagining?   745
  He may mean well.

Agamemnon
                    If you have nothing to say,
  Hecuba, very well. I have no wish to hear.

Hecuba (aside)
  But without his help I lose my only chance
  of revenging my children. So why should I hesitate?   750
  Win or lose, he is my only hope.

                              (She falls at Agamemnon's knees.)
  Agamemnon, I implore you, I beg you
  by your beard, your knees, by this conquering hand, help me!

Agamemnon
  What can I do to help you, Hecuba? Your freedom
  is yours for the asking.

Hecuba
                    No, not freedom.   755
  Revenge. Only give me my revenge
  and I'll gladly stay a slave the rest of my life.

Agamemnon
  Revenge? Revenge on whom, Hecuba?

Hecuba
                              My lord,
  not the revenge you think, not that at all.
  Do you see this body here, this naked corpse   760
  for which I mourn?

Agamemnon
I see him very well,
though no one yet has told me who he is.

Hecuba
This was my son. I gave him birth.

Agamemnon
Which son,
poor woman?

Hecuba
Not one of those who died
for Troy.

Agamemnon
You mean you had another son?   765

Hecuba
Another son to die. This was he.

Agamemnon
But where was he living when Troy was taken?

Hecuba
His father sent him away to save his life.

Agamemnon
This was the only son he sent away?
Where did he send him?

Hecuba
Here. To this country
where his body was found.

Agamemnon
He sent him to Polymestor,   770
the king of Thrace?

Hecuba
And with his son he also sent
a sum of fatal gold.

Agamemnon
But how did he die? Who killed him?

Hecuba

                      Who else?
His loving host, our loyal friend in Thrace.

Agamemnon

Then his motive, you think, was the gold?   775

Hecuba

                          Yes.
The instant he heard that Troy had fallen, he killed.

Agamemnon

But where was the body found? Who brought him here?

Hecuba

This old servant here. She found his body
lying on the beach.

Agamemnon

               What was she doing there?
Searching?

Hecuba

         No. She went to fetch water
for Polyxena's burial.

Agamemnon

              He must have killed him first,   780
then thrown his body in the sea.

Hecuba

                  Hacked him, tossed him
to the pounding surf.

Agamemnon

             I pity you, Hecuba.
Your suffering has no end.

Hecuba

             I died
long ago. Nothing can touch me now.

Agamemnon

What woman on this earth was ever cursed   785
like this?

Hecuba
>   There is none but goddess Suffering
> herself.
>   But let me tell you why I kneel
> at your feet. And if my sufferings seem just,
> then I must be content. But if otherwise,
> give me my revenge on that treacherous friend   790
> who flouted every god in heaven and in hell
> to do this brutal murder.
>   At our table
> he was our frequent guest; was counted first
> among our friends, respected, honored by me,
> receiving every kindness that a man could meet—   795
> and then, in cold deliberation, killed
> my son.
>   Murder may have its reasons, its motives,
> but this—to refuse my son a grave, to throw him
> to the sea, unburied!
>   I am a slave, I know,
> and slaves are weak. But the gods are strong, and over them
> there stands some absolute, some moral order   800
> or principle of law more final still.
> Upon this moral law the world depends;
> through it the gods exist; by it we live,
> defining good and evil.
>   Apply that law
> to me. For if you flout it now, and those
> who murder in cold blood or defy the gods
> go unpunished, then human justice withers,   805
> corrupted at its source.
>   Honor my request,
> Agamemnon.
>   Punish this murder.
>   Pity me.
> Be like a painter. Stand back, see me
> in perspective,

see me whole, observe
my wretchedness—
             once a queen, and now
a slave; blessed with children, happy once,   810
now old, childless, utterly alone,
homeless, lost, unhappiest of women
on this earth. . . .

                                        (*Agamemnon turns away.*)

              O gods, you turn away—
what can I do? My only hope is lost.
O this helplessness!
                Why, why
do we make so much of knowledge, struggle so hard   815
to get some little skill not worth the effort?
But persuasion, the only art whose power
is absolute, worth any price we pay,
we totally neglect. And so we fail;
we lose our hopes.
                But as for happiness,
who could look at me and any longer   820
dare to hope:
                I have seen my children die,
and bound to shame I walk this homeless earth,
a slave, and see the smoke that leaps up
over Troy.
            It may be futile now
to urge the claims of love, but let me urge them   825
anyway. At your side sleeps my daughter
Cassandra, once the priestess of Apollo.
What will you give, my lord, for those nights of love?
What thanks for all her tenderness in bed
does she receive from you, and I, in turn,   830
from her?
            Look now at this dead boy,
Cassandra's brother. Revenge him. Be kind to her
by being kind to him.

One word more.   835
If by some magic, some gift of the gods,
I could become all speech—tongues in my arms,
hands that talked, voices speaking, crying
from my hair and feet—then, all together,
as one voice, I would fall and touch your knees,
crying, begging, imploring with a thousand tongues—   840
O master, greatest light of Hellas,
hear me,
              help an old woman,
                                        avenge her!
She is nothing at all, but hear her, help her
even so. Do your duty as a man of honor:
see justice done. Punish this murder.   845

Coryphaeus

How strange in their reversals are our lives.
Necessities define us all, as now,
joining enemies in common cause
and alienating friends.

Agamemnon

                          I pity you deeply,
Hecuba, for the tragic death of this poor boy.   850
And I am touched and stirred by your request.
So far as justice is concerned, god knows,
nothing would please me more than to bring
this murderer to book.

                          But my position
here is delicate. If I give you your revenge,
the army is sure to charge that I connived   855
at the death of the king of Thrace because of my love
for Cassandra. This is my dilemma. The army
thinks of Polymestor as its friend,
this boy as its enemy. You love your son,
but what do your affections matter to the Greeks?   860
Put yourself in my position.

Believe me,
Hecuba, I should like to act on your behalf
and would come instantly to your defense.
But if the army mutters, then I must
be slow.

Hecuba

Then no man on earth is truly free.   865
All are slaves of money or necessity.
Public opinion or fear of prosecution
forces each one, against his conscience,
to conform.

But since your fears make you defer
to the mob, let a slave set you free
from what you fear.

Be my confidant,   870
the silent partner of my plot to kill my son's
murderer. Give me your passive support.
Then if violence breaks out or the Greeks
attempt a rescue, obstruct them covertly
without appearing to act for me.

For the rest,   875
have no fear. I shall manage.

Agamemnon

How?
Poison? Or do you think that shaking hand
could lift a sword and kill? Who would help you?
On whom could you count?

Hecuba

Remember: there are women   880
hidden in these tents.

Agamemnon

You mean our prisoners?

Hecuba

They will help me get revenge.

Agamemnon

But *women?*

Women overpower men?

Hecuba

There is power
in numbers, and cunning makes us strong.

Agamemnon

True,
though I admit to being skeptical of women   885
in a matter like this.

Hecuba

Why?

Women killed
Aegyptus' sons. Women emptied Lemnos
of its males: we murdered every one. And so
it shall be here.

But of that I say no more.
Let this woman have your safe-conduct
through the army.

(*Agamemnon nods. Hecuba turns to the Handmaid.*)
Go to Polymestor
and give him this message:

"Hecuba, once queen of Troy,   890
summons you on business that concerns you both
and requests you bring your sons. They also share
in what she has to say."

(*Exit Handmaid with several attendants.*)
One more favor,
Agamemnon.

Defer my daughter's funeral   895
until my son's body is placed beside her
on the pyre. Let them burn together,
brother and sister joined in a single flame,
their mother's double grief.

Agamemnon

As you wish.
If we could sail, I could not grant this. But now,
until heaven sends us a favoring wind,   900
we must ride at anchor here.

I wish you luck

in your attempt.

The common interests
of states and individuals alike demand
that good and evil receive their just rewards.

> (*Exit Agamemnon, followed by attendants. Hecuba and
> her women withdraw into the tent with the
> body of Polydorus.*)

Chorus

O Ilium! O my country,   905
whose name men speak no more
among unfallen cities!
So dense a cloud of Greeks
came, spear on spear, destroying!
Your crown of towers shorn away,   910
and everywhere the staining fire,
most pitiful. O Ilium,
whose ways I shall not walk again!

At midnight came my doom.
Midnight when the feast is done
and sleep falls sweetly on the eyes.   915
The songs and sacrifice,
the dances, all were done.
My husband lay asleep,
his spear upon the wall,   920
forgetting for a while
the ships drawn up on Ilium's shore.

I was setting my hair
in the soft folds of the net,
gazing at the endless light

deep in the golden mirror,   925
preparing myself for bed,
when tumult broke the air
and shouts and cries
shattered the empty streets:—
Onward, onward, you Greeks!   930
Sack the city of Troy
and see your homes once more!

Dressed only in a gown
like a girl of Sparta,
I left the bed of love
and prayed to Artemis.   935
But no answer came.
I saw my husband lying dead,
and they took me over sea.
Backward I looked at Troy,
but the ship sped on
and Ilium slipped away,   940
and I was dumb with grief.

A curse on Helen,
sister of the sons of Zeus,
and my curse on him,
disastrous Paris   945
whose wedding wasted Troy!
O adulterous marriage!
Helen, fury of ruin!   950
Let the wind blow
and never bring her home!
Let there be no landing
for Helen of Troy!

(*Enter Polymestor, followed by his two young sons and several*
attendants. Throughout his speech, Hecuba refuses to rec-
ognize him, keeping her back turned and her
eyes fixed on the ground.)

Polymestor

Dearest Hecuba, wife of my dear friend,
poor unhappy Priam!

How I pity you,
you and your ruined Troy. And now this latest blow,   955
your daughter's death. . . .

What can we take on trust
in this uncertain life? Happiness, greatness,
pride—nothing is secure, nothing keeps.
The inconsistent gods make chaos of our lives,
pitching us about with such savagery of change
that we, out of our anguish and uncertainty,
may turn to them.

—But how does my sorrow help?   960
Your loss remains.

(*A short silence, while Polymestor waits for Hecuba to recognize him. When she does not, he continues with
mounting embarrassment.*)

But perhaps you are angry with me, Hecuba,
for not coming to you earlier. If so, forgive me.
It just so happened that I was inland, in the mountains
of Thrace, at the time when you arrived. In fact,
I was on the point of coming here myself   965
when your servant arrived and gave me your message.
Needless to say, I lost no time.

Hecuba

Polymestor,
I am so embarrassed by the state in which you see me,
fallen so low since when you saw me last,
I cannot look you in the face.

Forgive it,   970
and do not think me rude, Polymestor.
In any case, habit and custom excuse me,
forbidding that a woman look directly at a man.   975

Polymestor
I quite understand.
                              Now, how can I help you?
You sent for me on some business, I believe?

Hecuba
I have a matter to discuss with you and your sons.
But privately, if possible.
                              Could you ask your men   980
to withdraw?

Polymestor

                                        (*To his bodyguard.*)
              You may leave. There is no danger here.
This woman is my friend and the army of the Greeks
is well disposed.
                    Now, Hecuba, to business.
How can I, your prosperous friend, help you   985
in your time of troubles?

Hecuba
                              One question first.
How is my son Polydorus, your ward?
Is he alive?
              Anything else can wait.

Polymestor
Alive and well. In this respect at least,
you may put your mind at rest.

Hecuba
                              My dearest friend,   990
how like you your kindness is!

Polymestor
                              What else
would give you comfort?

Hecuba
                    Does he still remember his mother?

Polymestor
So much that he wanted to run away
and visit you in secret.

Hecuba

                                    And the gold from Troy?
Is it safe?

Polymestor

                        Quite safe. Locked in my palace   995
under strong guard.

Hecuba

                                    Guard it well, my friend.
Do not let it tempt you.

Polymestor

                                    Have no fears.
What I have of my own is quite enough
to last my life.

Hecuba

                        Do you know why I sent for you
and your sons?

Polymestor

                        Not yet. We are waiting to hear.

Hecuba
You are my friend, a friend for whom I feel   1000
no less love than you have shown to me.
And my business concerns—

Polymestor

                                    Yes? Yes? Go on.

Hecuba
—the ancient vaults, the gold of Priam's house.

Polymestor
I am to pass this information to your son?

Hecuba
In person. I know you for a man of honor.

Polymestor

But why did you ask that my sons be present?   1005

Hecuba

I thought they should know. Something, for instance,
might happen to you.

Polymestor

              A prudent precaution.

I quite agree.

Hecuba

          Do you know where Athene's temple
once stood in Troy?

Polymestor

           The gold is there?

Is there a marker?

Hecuba

           A black rock jutting up   1010
above the ground.

Polymestor

         Is that all?

Hecuba

              No:
my jewels. I smuggled some jewels away from Troy.
Could you keep them for me?

Polymestor

              You have them with you?

Where are they hidden?

Hecuba

           There, inside the tent,
beneath a heap of spoils.

Polymestor

          Inside the tent?   1015

Here, in the Greek camp?

Hecuba

          The women's quarters
are separate from the main camp.

Polymestor

Is it safe?
Are there men around?

Hecuba

No men; only women.
But come inside. We have no time to lose.
Quick.

The Greek army is waiting and eager   1020
to raise their anchors and sail for home.

Then,
when our business here is done, you may go
and take your children where you left my son.

(*Polymestor and his sons, followed by Hecuba,
enter the tent.*)

Coryphaeus
Death is the debt of life. Now your debt falls due:—

Chorus (*individually*)
—As though you stumbled in the surf   1025

—hurled from high ambition down

—trapped, thrashing with terror
in the swirling tow

—   and the water
closing overhead

—   until
you drown.

—   And now you know:

—Life is held on loan.

—The price of life is death.

—Those who take a life—

—repay it with their own.

—Justice and the gods   1030
exact the loan at last.

—Gleam of gold misled you.

—You took the final turn

—where the bitter road veers off

—and runs downhill

—   to death!

—Hands which never held a sword

—shall wrench your twisted life away!

> (*Sudden screams and commotion from inside the tent.*)

Polymestor (*from within*)
  Blind! Blind!
            O light!
                    Light of my eyes!   1035

Coryphaeus
  That scream of anguish! Did you hear that scream?

Polymestor (*from within*)
                                    Help!
  Look out, children!
              Murder!
                      Run! Murder!

Coryphaeus
  New murder, fresh horror in the tent!

> (*More screams and uproar; then a sudden furious batter-
> ing on the walls of the tent.*)

Polymestor (*from within*)
  Run, damn you, run!
                But I'll get you yet!
  I'll batter down this tent with my bare fists!   1040

Chorus (*individually*)
  —Listen to him hammer at the walls!

  —What should we do?

  —   Break down the door

  —Hurry!

  —   Hecuba needs our help!

> (*Hecuba emerges from the tent.*)

Hecuba

Pound away!
                    Go on, batter down the door!
Nothing in this world can ever give you back   1045
the light of your eyes. Nothing.
                                        Never again
shall you see your sons, see them alive.
I have killed your sons, and you are blind!

Coryphaeus

Have you done it? Have you done this thing you say?

Hecuba

Be patient a moment, and then see for yourself.
Watch him as he stumbles and staggers out of the tent—   1050
stone-blind.
                    See the bodies of his sons,
killed by my women and me.
                                        His debt is paid
and I have my revenge.
                                        But hush: here he comes,
raging from the tent. Let me keep out of his reach.
In his fury he will stop at nothing now.   1055

(*Polymestor, blood pouring from his eyes, emerges from the tent
          on all fours. Wildly and blindly he scrambles about like an
                              animal, searching for the women with his hands.*)

Polymestor

Where?
          Where shall I run?
Where shall I stop?
                    Where?
Like a raging beast I go,
running on all fours
to track my quarry down!
Where?
          Where?
                    Here?
                              Where?   1060

Where can I pounce
on those murderous hags of Troy?
Where are you, women?
Where are they hiding,
those bitches of Troy?   1065

O god of the sun,
heal these bleeding eyes!
Give me back the light of my eyes!
Shh.
        The sound of footsteps.   1070
But where?
                Where can I leap?
Gods, to gorge their blood,
to rip the living flesh,
feed like a starving beast,
blood for blood!
                No, no.   1075
Where am I running now?
My children abandoned,
left for Furies to claw,
for savage bitches to gorge,
their mangled bodies thrown
to whiten on the hill!
But where?
                Where shall I run?
Where can I stand at bay?   1080
Run, run, run,
gather robes and run!
Let me run for my lair,
run like a ship,
sails furled, for the shore!
I'll run for my lair
and stand at bay
where my children are!

            (He rushes into the tent and comes out carrying the bodies of
                his children. He lays them down and crouches
                            over them protectively.)

« 543 »

Coryphaeus

Tormented man! Tortured past enduring.   1085
You suffer now as you made others suffer.

Polymestor

Help me, you men of Thrace!
Help!
      Soldiers, horsemen,
help! Come with spears!   1090
Achaeans, help! Help me,
sons of Atreus!
      Help!
          Help!
Hear me, help me, help!
Where are you?
      Help me.
Women have killed my sons.   1095
Murder, dreadful murder!
Butchery! Horror!
Help me!
      Help!
         O gods,
where can I go?
Where can I run?
You gods in heaven,
give me wings to fly!   1100
Let me leap to heaven
where the vaulted stars,
Sirius and Orion,
flare out their fire,
or plunge to Hades
on the blackened flood!   1105

Coryphaeus

Who could reproach this man for wanting to die?
Death is what men want when the anguish of living
is more than they can bear.

      (*Enter Agamemnon, attended by soldiers.*)

Agamemnon
Shouting and screams
of terror brought me here. Ringing Echo,
born of these mountain crags, resounded the cries,   1110
shunting them back and forth throughout the camp,
alarming the men. Unless we knew for a fact
that Troy had fallen to our arms, this uproar
could have caused no little terror or disturbance.

Polymestor
That voice! I know it.
                    —My friend, Agamemnon!
Look, look at me now—

Agamemnon
Oh. Awful sight!   1115
Poor Polymestor! Those blind bleedings eyes,
those dead children. . . . Who did this, Polymestor?
Who killed these boys? Who put out your eyes?
Whoever it was, he must have hated you and your sons
with a savage, ruthless hate.

Polymestor
Hecuba. She did it,   1120
she and the other women. They destroyed me,
they worse than destroyed me.

Agamemnon
You, Hecuba?
Do you admit this hideous, inhuman crime?   1125
Is this atrocity your work?

Polymestor
Hecuba?
Is *she* here?
Where? Tell me where she is,
and I'll claw her to pieces with these bare hands!

Agamemnon
(*Forcibly restraining him.*)
What? Have you lost your mind?

Polymestor

For god's sake,
let me go! Let me rip her limb from limb!

Agamemnon

Stop.

No more of this inhuman savagery now.
Each of you will give his version of the case   1130
and I shall try to judge you both impartially.

Polymestor

Then listen, Agamemnon.

Hecuba had a son
called Polydorus, her youngest. His father Priam,
apprehensive that Troy would shortly be taken,   1135
sent the boy to me to be raised in my own house.
I killed him, and I admit it.

My action, however,
was dictated, as you shall see, by a policy
of wise precaution.

My primary motive was fear,
fear that if this boy, your enemy, survived,
he might someday found a second and resurgent Troy.
Further, when the Greeks heard that Priam's son   1140
was still alive, I feared that they would raise
a second expedition against this new Troy,
in which case these fertile plains of Thrace
would once again be ravaged by war; once again
Troy and her troubles would work her neighbors harm—
those same hardships, my lord, which we in Thrace
have suffered in this war.

Hecuba, however,   1145
somehow hearing that her son was dead or murdered,
lured me here on the pretext of revealing
the secret hiding-place of Priam's gold
in Troy. Then, alleging that we might be overheard,
she led my sons and me, unattended,
into the tent.

Surrounded by Trojan women
on every side, I took my seat on a couch. 1150
The atmosphere seemed one of friendliness.
The women fingered my robes, then lifted the cloth
to inspect it under the light, exclaiming shrilly
over the quality of our Thracian weaving.
Still others stood there admiring my lance 1155
and before I knew it I was stripped of spear
and shield alike.
                    Meanwhile the young mothers
were fussing over my children, jouncing them in their arms
with hugs and kisses and passing them from hand to hand
until they were out of reach.
                    Then, incredibly,
out of that scene of domestic peace, 1160
they suddenly pulled daggers from their robes
and butchered both my sons, while troops of women
rushed to tackle me, seizing my arms and legs
and holding me down. I tried to leap up 1165
but they caught me by the hair and pulled me down.
I fought to free my arms, but they swamped me
and I went down beneath a flood of women,
unable to move a muscle.
                    And then—O gods!—
they crowned their hideous work with worse outrage,
the most inhuman brutal crime of all.
They lifted their brooches and stabbed these bleeding eyes 1170
through and through! Then they ran for cover,
scattering through the tent. I leaped to my feet,
groping along the wall, stalking them down
like a wounded animal hunting a pack of hounds,
staggering blind on all fours, battering 1175
at the wall.
                    This is my reward, Agamemnon,
for my efforts in disposing of your enemies.
What I suffer now I suffer for you.
One word more.

On behalf of all those dead
who learned their hatred of women long ago,
for those who hate them now, for those unborn
who shall live to hate them yet, I now declare   1180
my firm conviction:
                              neither earth nor ocean
produces a creature as savage and monstrous
as woman.
              This is my experience.
I know that this is true.

Coryphaeus

                    Do not presume,
Polymestor, whatever your provocation,
to include all women in this sweeping curse   1185
without distinction.

Hecuba

                    The clear actions of a man,
Agamemnon, should speak louder than any words.
Good words should get their goodness from our lives
and nowhere else; the evil we do should show,
a rottenness that festers in our speech   1190
and what we say, incapable of being glozed
with a film of pretty words.
                              There are men, I know,
sophists who make a science of persuasion,
glozing evil with the slick of loveliness;
but in the end a speciousness will show.
The impostors are punished; not one escapes
his death.
              So much by way of beginning.   1195
Now for him.
              He claims he killed my son
on your behalf, Agamemnon, to spare
you Greeks the horrors of a second war.

                              (*She turns to Polymestor.*)

You liar!
First, what possible friendship could there be
between civilized Greeks and half-savages   1200
like you?
            Clearly none.
                        Then why this zeal
to serve their cause?
                        Are you related to them
or bound by marriage?
                        What *is* your motive then?
Fear, you say, that they might sail for Troy
and burn your crops or ravage your kingdom in passing.
Who could believe that preposterous lie?
                                    No,   1205
if you want the truth, let me tell you why:
it was your greed for gold that killed my son,
sheer greed and nothing more.
                        If not,
what explains your conduct then and now?
Answer me this.
            Why, when Troy still flourished,
when the ramparts ran unbroken about the city,
when Priam was alive and Hector had his day—   1210
why, if you were then so friendly to the Greeks,
did you fail to kill my son or take him prisoner
at least, when you had him at your mercy?
                                    But no.
You waited, biding your time, until our sun
had set, and the smoke announced the sack of Troy.   1215
Then you moved, killing your guest who sat
helpless at your hearth.
                    And what of this,
which shows your crime for what it was?
                                Why,
if you loved the Greeks as much as you assert,
did you miss your chance to present them with the gold—   1220

that gold you claim does not belong to you
but to Agamemnon? But they were desperate then,
long years away from home.

                            But no. Even now
you cannot bear the thought of giving up
the gold, but hoard it for yourself at home.
One point more.

                  If you had done your duty
by my son, raised him and kept him safe,   1225
men would honor and respect you as a noble friend.
For real friendship is shown in times of trouble;
prosperity is full of friends.

                And then,
if someday you had stood in need of help,
my son would have been your friend and treasury.
But killing him you killed your loyal friend;   1230
your gold is worthless now, your sons are dead,
and you are as you are.

                      (*She turns back to Agamemnon.*)
             Agamemnon,
if you acquit this man, you prove yourself
unjust.

          This is a man who betrayed his trust,
who killed against the laws of man and god,
faithless, evil, corrupt.

                Acquit him now   1235
and we shall say the same is true of you.
I say no more.

Coryphaeus

          Well spoken, Hecuba.
Those whose cause is just will never lack
good arguments.

Agamemnon

             It gives me no pleasure   1240
to sit as judge on the miseries of others.

But I should cut a sorry figure in the world
if I allowed this case to come to court
and then refused or failed to give a verdict.
I have no choice.
     Know then, Polymestor,
I find you guilty of murder as charged.
You murdered your ward, killed him in cold blood,
and not, as you assert, for the Greeks or me,
but out of simple greed, to get his gold.   1245
You then construed the facts to fit your case
in court.
    Perhaps you think it a trifling matter
to kill a guest.
     We Greeks call it murder.
How, therefore, could I acquit you now
without losing face among men?
       I could not do it.   1250
You committed a brutal crime; therefore accept
the consequences of your act.

Polymestor
      O gods,
condemned! Defeated by a woman, by a slave!

Hecuba
Condemned for what you did. Justly condemned.

Polymestor
O my children!
     O light, light of my eyes!   1255

Hecuba
It hurts, does it? And what of me? I mourn
my children too.

Polymestor
     Does it give you pleasure
to mock at me?

Hecuba
     I rejoice in my revenge.

Polymestor
Enjoy it now. You shall not enjoy it long.
Hear my prediction.
                    I foretell that you—

Hecuba
Shall be carried on ship across the sea to Hellas?   1260

Polymestor
*—shall drown at sea. You shall climb to the masthead
and fall—*

Hecuba
            Pushed by force?

Polymestor
                            *You shall climb the mast
of your own free will—*

Hecuba
                        Climb the mast? With wings?

Polymestor
—changed to a dog, a bitch with blazing eyes.   1265

Hecuba
How could you know of this transformation?

Polymestor
Because our Thracian prophet, Dionysus,
told me so.

Hecuba
            He neglected, I see, to foretell
your own fate.

Polymestor
            Had he told my future then,
I never would have stumbled in your trap.

Hecuba
Shall I live or die?

Polymestor
                Die. And when you die   1270
your tomb shall be called—

Hecuba

In memory of my change?

Polymestor

—*Cynossema, the bitch's grave, a landmark*
  to sailors.

Hecuba

What do I care how I die?

I have my revenge.

Polymestor

And your daughter Cassandra   1275
  must also die—

Hecuba

I spit your prophecies back.

Use them on yourself.

Polymestor

(Pointing to Agamemnon.)
—killed by this man's wife,
cut down by the bitter keeper of his house.

Hecuba

Clytemnestra? She would never do it.

Polymestor

Then she shall lift the dripping axe once more
and kill her husband too.

Agamemnon

Are you out of your head?

Are you asking for more trouble?

Polymestor

Kill me,   1280
but a bath of blood waits for you in Argos.

Agamemnon

Slaves, carry him off! Drag him away!

(Servants seize Polymestor.)

Polymestor

Have I touched you now?

Agamemnon

Stop him. Gag his mouth.

Polymestor

Gag me. I have spoken.

Agamemnon

Take him away
this instant.

Then throw him on some desert island   1285
since his tongue cannot stop its impudence.

(*Attendants leave with Polymestor.*)
As for you, Hecuba, go now and bury
your two dead children.

The rest of you women,
go and report at once to your masters' tents.
For now the sudden wind sits freshly in our sails.   1290
May heaven grant that our ordeal is done
at last!

May all be well at home in Argos!

(*Exit Agamemnon with remaining attendants. Hecuba and her
women go slowly to the tent, leaving the stage empty except
for the abandoned bodies of Polymestor's sons.
The Chorus files slowly out.*)

Chorus

File to the tents,
file to the harbor.
There we embark
on life as slaves.
Necessity is harsh.   1295
Fate has no reprieve.

ANDROMACHE

Translated and with an Introduction by

JOHN FREDERICK NIMS

INTRODUCTION TO *ANDROMACHE*

Euripides' *Andromache* was written in the first years of the Peloponnesian War, probably between 430 and 424 B.C.; if inspired by a particular Spartan atrocity, the most likely would have been the massacre of the Plataean prisoners in 427. The scholiast reports that the play was not presented at Athens; it may have been performed at Argos (if at all) as part of an Athenian propaganda campaign, or at Epirus, where the young king, educated in Athens, was of the Molossian line acclaimed in the epilogue.

The discontinuity of the plot because of Andromache's disappearance in mid-play has troubled critics; not all have been as candid as D. W. Lucas, for whom the play "falls feebly and mysteriously to pieces. . . . there must be missing clues which would show the play less inept than it seems." (Professor Lucas comes up with a deadpan diagnosis worthy of Euripides himself: the poet, in these difficult days of plague and Spartan incursions, was temporarily out of his head.)

Verrall probably stands alone in defending the plot as such; he assumes (it seems wrongly) that the play is a sequel about a Machiavellian scheme concocted by Menelaus and Orestes. His theory "explains" the apparent breakdown of Menelaus in the presence of Peleus and does away with the time lapse during the chorus (ll. 1009–46), but it depends on effects that only an audience of well-briefed Verrallians could be expected to catch and relate. The breakdown of Menelaus needs no theory to explain it: Euripides' Spartan is a blusterer cowed by any show of vigor. The time lapse (of perhaps a week) is one of several in the extant tragedies; little is gained by pretending it is not there. In the excitement of the performance, who in the audience would be thinking in terms of mileages and time schedules? Who would even notice that the Chorus had been rather casual in informing Peleus of the intended murder of his grandson?

Some have suggested that Euripides, fascinated by character, is indifferent to plot. Once Andromache is out of danger, Euripides dismisses her to concentrate on her lively rival, much as Shakespeare scuttles the Turkish fleet when he has no further need for it.

Still others have found the unity of the play in *dianoia*. In antiquity it was already felt that Euripides often wrote what the poet and not what the plot demanded: Lucan said that "quite without dramatic necessity [Euripides] freely expressed his own opinions." In the words of a twentieth-century observer he "inserts passages suggested as much by the contemporary as by the dramatic situation." For *Andromache*, several key ideas have been proposed: it is about the house of Peleus—unsophisticated northerners undone by a southern alliance; or about the dangers to family life inherent in the practice of slaveholding; or it warns against incautious marriages; or it gives the *aition* of the tomb-worship of Peleus and Thetis; or it records a burning detestation of Sparta and Spartan ways.

Probably a more meaningful approach is that suggested independently by L. H. G. Greenwood and Gunther Zuntz. Euripides, says Greenwood, "is fond of presenting the arguments for or against this or that proposition concerning matters that were the subject of active interest and controversy. . . . he presents these arguments so impartially, and refrains so completely from pronouncing judgement . . . that we really cannot tell what he himself thinks." Zuntz reminds us of the problem of the Euripidean age: How is man to live in a godless world? "Different individuals had different answers, and Euripides gives them all."

It is helpful to keep in mind the philosophical background of the period: the irreconcilable systems of the pre-Socratics had led to the skepticism of the Sophists; if no one way of interpreting reality could be established as the right way, then any way was probably as good as any other. We cannot read long in Euripides before becoming aware of the doctrinal atomism of the age—an age whose values, says Jaeger, were rotten with individualism.

The conviction that standards were what the individual chose to make them was intensified by the war itself. Thucydides (iii. 10) gives a disturbing analysis of how even "words had to change their ordinary meaning and take that which was now given them." This in addition to the moral chaos of the plague of 430 B.C. (cf. ii. 7) which Euripides had lived through not long before he wrote *Andromache*.

It was an age that reminds us in many ways of the similarly disturbed world of the Jacobeans, filled, as Eliot says, with broken fragments of systems. "We have seene the best of our time," Gloucester desponds. "Machinations, hollownesse, treacherie, and all ruinous disorders follow us disquietly to our Graves." Perhaps John Webster has described it most poignantly, with his characters "in a miste" as they face the moment of truth, torn between the religious values of the past and the new self-interest for which Machiavelli was made the lurid figurehead.

In that environment, a restless and passionate temperament might well have been contemptuous of the Aristotelian dramatic formulas —if it could have anticipated them a century in advance. An imitation of an action, without obstreperous episodes or irrational gaps— this, Euripides might have felt, would be no imitation of life as *he* knew it. For the complexities of his vision, an asymmetrical form was just and proper, an objective correlative for the tormented psyche's baroque ado. Euripides (unlike Sophocles) has no *querencia;* his is a restless point of view; and if we, with our more classical habits, stay in one spot to look where he is pointing, we are likely to be left mumbling about the "riddle" of this or that play.

Modern readers may find an enlightening parallel in the work of Picasso, whom they may suspect to be the product of an analogous period: an artist who does not stare flat-footed at his subject and by whom the same face may be painted from quite different coigns of vantage. One celebrated painting shows a lady "nude, dressed, and X-rayed" all at once; it doubles the already multiple image by putting her in front of a mirror. It was with something like this simultaneous point of view that Euripides regarded his subjects; no wonder his portraits too are constructed around an ambiguous axis.

The method is used more brilliantly in the greater plays: in the *Bacchae*, for example, or *Hippolytus*. In *Andromache* the composition is twisted too violently toward propaganda; it has the stridency of caricature. The tone, it has often been observed, is not tragic at all. The events of the play may arouse pity, but they do much to coun-

teract it by arousing the emotion that Aristotle found directly opposed: indignation. Critiques of the play bristle with such phrases
as "the glaring colors of melodrama," "the air of a political pam-
phlet," "the whole tone unheroic," "complete absence of poetic
color," "a painful experience" (for admirers of Sophoclean drama).
In antiquity it was criticized as a conglomeration of comic ingredi-
ents. And yet for the theatergoer there must have been not one dull
or undramatic scene in this "hard and brilliant" play.

The author of *On the Sublime* finds Euripides nearly always among
those writers who use current colloquial diction. In *Andromache*, with
its strongly *ad hoc* bias, colloquial usage seems even more pronounced
than elsewhere; lexicographers find here boldly popular and even
vulgar expressions. In reading what Norwood calls the "utterly unheroic and unpoetical, but vigorous, terse, and idiomatic" dialogue,
we are far from the Olympian resonances of Aeschylus or the nobility of Sophocles, far, in fact, from what the common reader thinks
of as "Greek tragedy."

The text translated here is that of Murray's Oxford edition, with
his line-numbering (which corresponds to the Greek text, not to the
English). I have omitted the bracketed line 7 (probably interpolated
by actors), have disregarded Murray's suggested punctuation for line
1030, and have preferred Musgrave's emendation of line 1190.

CHARACTERS

*Andromache, widow of Hector, allotted at the fall of Troy
to Neoptolemus, son of Achilles*

Slave woman

Chorus of Phthian women

*Hermione, daughter of Menelaus and Helen, wife of Ne-
optolemus*

Menelaus, king of Sparta

Young son of Andromache and Neoptolemus

Peleus, father of Achilles and grandfather of Neoptolemus

Nurse of Hermione

*Orestes, son of Agamemnon and Clytemnestra, formerly be-
trothed to Hermione*

Messenger

The Goddess Thetis

Servants, attendants

ANDROMACHE

SCENE: *The Thessalian plains in Achilles' district of Phthia, near the
city of Pharsalus. Andromache is at the shrine of the goddess
Thetis, placed not far from the dwelling of Neoptolemus.*

Andromache

Thebé my city, Asia's pride, remember
The glory and the gold of that procession
When I arrived at Priam's royal home?
As Hector's wife, soon mother of Hector's son—
Andromache, in the old days oh so lucky,   5
But sunk in misery now, if anyone is.
To have seen with my own eyes Hector my husband
Dead at Achilles' hand! To have seen our son,
Hector's and mine, Astyanax, hurled headlong   10
Down from the highest tower when Troy was taken!
And I—free as I pleased in homes of leisure
Till then—was clapped in servitude, shipped to Greece
As booty for Neoptolemus, wild islander,
His tidbit from the total spoil of Troy.   15
Phthia is my home now, these fields surrounding
The city of Pharsalia. Sea-born Thetis
Lived here with Peleus once in deep seclusion,
Apart from men. The people of Thessaly
Call it the Altar of Thetis for that reason.   20
That roof you see belongs to Achilles' son,
By whose permission Peleus rules Pharsalia:
The young defers to the older while he lives.
Within that house I've given birth to a boy,
Bred to that same Achilles' son, my master.   25
A hard life even at best, but up to now
Hope led me on—the hope this little child
Might prove my strength and shelter against trouble.
Except for her—Hermione from Sparta!   30

Since my lord married her and snubbed a slave-wife,
I'm persecuted cruelly. She's behind it,
Charging I've made her unable to conceive
With secret drugs and dosings, made him hate her.
Charging I want this house all to myself
And mean to crowd her out of it, bed and all—   35
A bed that from the first I never wanted
And now reject for good. The gods are witness
That was a bed I never crept in gladly.
No talking, though, to her. She's out for blood.
And Menelaus her father's working with her.   40
He's in the house this moment, hot from Sparta,
Bent on this very thing. Suspecting the worst,
I've run next door here to the Altar of Thetis
And here I huddle in the hope she'll save me.
For Peleus and his sons are all devotion   45
Toward this memorial of the ocean marriage.
My one and only son, though!—alarmed for his life
I've smuggled him secretly to others' keeping.
The one who served to beget him serves for nothing
In the hour of need—no help at all to his baby.   50
He's off at Delphi making amends to Apollo
For his mad behavior when, the time before,
He clamored the god should pay for killing his father!
He hopes now to plead free of old offenses
And reconcile Apollo for the future.   55

                                    (*Enter Slave woman.*)

Slave woman

My lady—for I'm faithful to that title—
I never used or thought to use another
In your own palace when we lived in Troy.
You always had my love—your husband too
To the very day he died. Well, now there's news   60
I bring in fear and trembling of our masters,
And in sympathy for you. They've black designs,
Menelaus and his daughter. Oh be careful!

Andromache

    Dearest of sister-slaves (for that's our story)

    To one your mistress once, though sadly fallen—   65

    They're planning what? Up to what further mischief?

    What's left to endure but death? Is that their purpose?

Slave woman

    They're aiming at your son, my poor, poor lady;

    The little boy you hid away: his death.

Andromache

    She can't have learned my darling's gone? She can't have!   70

    How could she learn? My heart stopped as you spoke.

Slave woman

    I couldn't tell you how. I heard it first

    From them. But Menelaus is out prowling.

Andromache

    My very heart stopped beating! Poor little baby,

    A pair of buzzards claw at you for carrion.   75

    And his—can I say *father?*—off at Delphi!

Slave woman

    You'd never find yourself in this predicament,

    To my mind, with him present. Now there's no one.

Andromache

    And no report that Peleus means to come?

Slave woman

    Suppose he came, what then? Feeble old man!   80

Andromache

    I've sent for him and sent for him and sent for him.

Slave woman

    Sent whom for him? No friend of yours, be sure.

Andromache

    Ah, so I see! But you—you'd take a message?

Slave woman

    What could I say, being gone from home so long?

Andromache

  Don't tell me you've no bag of tricks. A woman! 85

Slave woman

  She's wary as a watchdog, that Hermione.

Andromache

  Then you—my fine fair-weather friend—refuse?

Slave woman

  That's far from true. You've no need for reproaches.
  I'll do it. What's my life, that I should care
  What happens now? A slave's life, and a woman's. 90

Andromache

  Hurry then; hurry.

                          (*Exit Slave woman.*)

          These same lamentations,
  Sobbings and tears to which my days are given
  I'll now storm heaven with. For nature tempers
  The souls of women so they find a pleasure
  In voicing their afflictions as they come. 95
  I've a wide range of sorrows, not one only:
  My native land destroyed and Hector dead,
  The rigorous fate that shut on me like shackles
  When I awoke—indignity!—to bondage.
  It's vain to say that any man alive 100
  Is in the true sense happy. Wait and ponder
  The manner of his exit from this stage.

                          (*She keens softly.*)

  Paris brought home no bride, no bride but folly and ruin
    To Ilium high on its hill—welcoming Helen to bed.
  She was the cause, O Troy, the Greeks' quick-moving battalions 105
    Out of a thousand ships, took you with fire and sword.
  She was the cause my man, wretched Andromache's Hector,
    Was draggled by Thetis' son from a chariot round about Troy.
  The cause I was driven away from my quiet nook to the seashore,
    There invited to wear slavery's odious yoke. 110

What a torrent of tears on my cheek the day that I left forever
   City and roofs I knew, husband dead in the dust.
Doomed Andromache now! why longer look upon heaven?—
   Only a slave, *her* slave—one who oppresses me so
That here to the goddess' shrine I come, a suppliant clutching,   115
   Melting away, all tears, like water welling on rock.

                        (Enter Chorus of Phthian women.)
Chorus

STROPHE

Lady who, crouched on the ground so long by the chapel of Thetis
   Linger and will not away,
Now, though a Phthian indeed I come to you, woman of Asia,
   To see if I may   120
      Offer a balm for grievances so deep
Embittering you and Hermione too in a spite-ridden, surly,
   Hateful display:
      Over two in a post for one: 125
      The arms of Achilles' son.

ANTISTROPHE

Recognize what you've become and assent to a dismal position:
   Though only a Trojan, you sow
Seeds of unrest with your betters—with nobles from Sparta!
   Far better go
      Away from the Nereid's place of hecatomb.   130
What good to lie quivering here and sadly bedabble your features?
   Their wish is law.
      Necessity's hot on your trail.
      Why struggle to no avail?

STROPHE

Come now, hurry and leave the glorious temple of Thetis.   135
   Consider: only a slave
   Here in a foreign state,
   With no apparent friend.
   Least of all, fate—
      Girl of the gamut of woe.   140

ANTISTROPHE

A sight for compassionate eyes—my heart said—woman of Troy,
   you
  Entered my masters' home.
  Fear keeps me dumb,
  And yet I'm all sorrow.
  But what if Hermione come   145
    And find me in sympathy so?

                            (*Enter Hermione.*)

Hermione
  Wearing tiaras, notice, of pure gold,
  Draped in garments brilliant and luxurious—
  Neither presented to me, I hasten to add,
  From the homes of Achilles or Peleus—here I am.   150
  These weddings gifts are straight from my own Sparta.
  Menelaus gave me these—my father you know—
  With other gifts galore. I'm bound to no one
  And free to speak my mind. As I do now.
  You! you common slave! you soldiers' winnings!   155
  You plan to usurp this house, evicting me!
  Your drugs have made me unlovely to my husband;
  Withered my womb and left it good for nothing.
  This is the sort of thing you Asian women
  Have tricky wits for. But you've met your match.   160
  This sea-girl's home won't help you save your skin
  For all its shrines and altars. Now you've finished!
  Or if any god or mortal interfere
  In your behalf—well, learn to change your tune,
  Eat humble pie and grovel at my knee,   165
  Sweep out the house, *my* house, your fingers sprinkling
  Brook-water from the pails of beaten gold.
  Just where do you think you are? Is Hector here?
  Is Priam with his moneybags? You're in Greece now.
  You! you were even so rotten with desire   170
  You had the gall to cuddle up to the son
  Of the very man who killed your husband, breeding

A butcher's children. Well, that's foreigners for you.
Father and daughter intimate, mother and son,
Sister and brother—murder clears the way   175
In family squabbles. Anything goes. No law.
Don't try those methods here. And it's not decent
Either for one man teaming up two wives.
Clean-living husbands love and honor one,
Gluing affectionate eyes only on her.   180

Chorus

There's a touch of jealousy in the female psyche.
It's inclined to be rather tart where polygamy enters.

Andromache

A sort of disease, youth is. Aggravated
When the young soul's addicted to injustice.   185
I suppose my condition of servitude should daunt me
By censoring free discussion, right as I am.
If I got the better, you'd see I suffered for it.
You high and mighty people can look daggers
Hearing from your inferiors the god's truth.   190
However, I'm one for sticking to my principles.
Speak, pretty miss: for what legitimate reason
Would I keep you from your legitimate marriage?
Troy lords it over Sparta, I suppose,
Or would with a bit of luck? I fancy I'm free?   195
Or trusting in a girl's full-breasted beauty,
A city's strength, a multitude of backers,
I'm planning to dispossess you of your home?
Or so I may have sons instead of you,
Slaves every one, like millstones dragging after me?   200
Or else so someone will exalt my boys
To the very throne itself, if you've no children?
I suppose for Hector's sake the Greeks adore me?
Or thinking I was a nobody in Troy?
It wasn't drugs that made your husband shun you;   205
The plain fact is, you're hardly fit to live with.

There's your witchcraft. It's not beauty but
Fine qualities, my girl, that keep a husband.
When something annoys you, it's always Sparta this
And Sparta that. His Skyros?—never heard of it!   210
You flaunter among paupers! They mention your father?—
He dwarfs Achilles! No wonder your husband flushes.
A woman, even when married to a cad,
Ought to be deferential, not a squabbler.
Suppose you married a king in wintry Thrace   215
Where the custom is one husband in rotation
Take to his bed god knows how many women.
You'd knife them all? And be in a pretty fix
Screaming, "You hussy!" at every wife in sight.
Disgraceful! Well, we women are infected   220
With a worse disease than men, but try to conceal it.
O dearest Hector, for your sake I even
Welcomed your loves, when Cypris sent you fumbling.
I was wet nurse to your bastards many a time
Only to make your life a little easier.   225
And for such conduct he approved and loved me.
But you!—you hardly dare to let your husband
Out in the rain. He might get wet! Your mother
Helen was fond of her man—now wasn't she, dear?
Don't try to outdo her. Sensible children   230
Really ought to avoid the family vices.

Chorus
My lady, as much as you reasonably can,
Come to an understanding with this woman.

Hermione
On your high horse and picking quarrels, eh? Bragging
As if you had a monopoly on virtue?   235

Andromache
You've none at least, one gathers from your talk.

Hermione
We'll never see eye to eye—or so I hope.

Andromache

Young as you are, there's smut enough on your tongue.

Hermione

And on your conscience. Doing your best against me!

Andromache

Still caterwauling your unlucky love!   240

Hermione

I'll not be gagged. Love's all in all to women.

Andromache

And should be: *virtuous* love. The other's foul.

Hermione

Here we don't live by your outlandish standards.

Andromache

Shameful is shameful everywhere, Greece or not Greece.

Hermione

We've a deep thinker here! Not long to live, though.   245

Andromache

You see this statue of Thetis, eyeing you?

Hermione

Despising your country, you mean, for Achilles' murder.

Andromache

All Helen's doing, not ours. Your mother you know.

Hermione

You strike at me where it's tenderest, more and more.

Andromache

I've said my say. You'll get no more out of me.   250

Hermione

One thing. There's still the matter that brought me here.

Andromache

I only say your mind's a twisted thing.

Hermione

Will you or won't you leave this shrine of Thetis?

Andromache

    If you guarantee my life. Otherwise never.

Hermione

    I'll guarantee this: your death. And before my husband comes.   255

Andromache

    Until he comes, I'll not surrender. Never!

Hermione

    I could light a fire, and let you take your chances—

Andromache

    Light up your fire. Don't think the gods are blind, though.

Hermione

    Or tools that tear the flesh—I've ways to get them.

Andromache

    Make all her shrine a shambles. She'll remember.   260

Hermione

    Half-savage creature, all a wild defiance!
    You'd brazen out even death! I'll make you move
    Out of there spryly enough and glad to go.
    I've got the lure for you. Though what it is
    I'll let the event itself disclose, and promptly.   265
    Sit snug and cozy now. But if melted lead
    Had soldered you there, I'd pry you out before
    The son of Achilles comes, your one hope now.

                           (Exit Hermione.)

Andromache

    My one hope now! Some god found antidotes
    Against all poisonous snakes, but—wonder of wonders!—   270
    Against a menace worse than fire or vipers
    No vaccine yet: I mean these vicious women.
    Who knows the trouble we cause the human race!

Chorus

                  STROPHE

    That was the breeding of bitter affliction, when Hermes,
        Son of Zeus, Maia's son,   275

Came to Ida, to the glade
Conducting heaven's lovely team
Of three divine fillies made
All accoutered for passionate war over who was supreme.
   These came to the farmyard   280
And sought the boyish shepherd fond of solitude—
    A hearthfire
  Where but few souls intrude.

ANTISTROPHE

These, when they reached the luxuriant vale, in a mountain pool
  Cooled by springs, shone and bathed—   285
  What a reveling of light!
  And then approaching Priam's son
  With glowing words born of spite
They disputed their suit. Aphrodite prevailed—witching words
  Most sweet to the young judge,   290
  But deadly too, a lewd confusion to destroy
    And throw low
  All the towers of high Troy.

STROPHE

Oh but if only his mother had broken the
  Sorry creature's skull at once
    Before he
  Settled there on Ida's side—
When the marvelous laurel implored, when shrill   295
  Cassandra wild-eyed clamored "Kill
The spreading pollution of Troy, our land!"
And frenzied everywhere to needle, wheedle, warn
  Prominent men
  With: "Destroy the newborn!"   300

ANTISTROPHE

Then on the women of Troy would have fallen no
  Yoke of slavery; lady, you'd
    Have free hand,
  Mistress of a noble home;

Greece would never have shouldered the ten-years' woe
   Or seen the tall young spearmen go   305
To the stagger of war and the ruck round Troy;
Those beds would never lie by absent love undone,
     Parents be made
   Ancient waifs with no son.

(Enter Menelaus with the young son of Andromache.)

Menelaus

   I've fastened on the child you hid away
   In another house behind my daughter's back.   310
   So you thought the goddess' statue would save you
   And his receivers him? But it turned out
   You weren't as cunning as Menelaus here.
   Now either remove yourself and clear the premises
   Or the boy dies for you—a fair exchange.   315
   So think it over. The option's yours: to die
   Yourself or to see the child die for the wicked
   Wrongs you committed against my daughter and me.

Andromache

   Repute! repute! repute! how you've ballooned
   Thousands of good-for-nothings to celebrity!   320
   Men whose glory is come by honestly
   Have all my admiration. But impostors
   Deserve none: luck and humbug's all they are.
   So you're the commander-in-chief of the Greek elite
   That wrested Troy from Priam—you, you piddler!   325
   You, for the mewlings of your darling daughter
   Come snorting so importantly, up in arms
   Against a woman already down, in bondage.
   Troy's story had no role for the likes of you!
   People that seem so glorious are all show;   330
   Underneath they're like anybody else.
   Unless they have money, of course. Oh money's something!
   Well, Menelaus, suppose we thresh this out.
   Assume I lie here dead, thanks to your daughter.

The curse of bloodshed's heavy on her head. 335
A guilt that you share too, at least in the court
Of public opinion. You're involved, no question.
Or assume that I manage somehow to stay alive.
You'll kill my little child? You think the father,
His baby butchered, will stand idly by? 340
At Troy he wasn't commonly thought a coward.
He'll do the right thing now—worthy of Peleus
And of Achilles his father, as you'll find out—
He'll send your daughter packing. With what story
Do you think you'd find her another man? You'd claim 345
Her virtue was simply appalled by such a brute?
Word gets around. Who'd marry her? You'd board her
Single at home till she's a grey-haired witch?
What griefs you'd have if you kept her there, poor man!
Wouldn't you rather she'd time and again be cheated 350
In marital affairs than suffer that way?
There's no use making catastrophes of trifles.
And just because we women are prone to evil,
What's to be gained perverting man to match?
If indeed I've plied your daughter with those potions 355
And made her womb a bungler, as she charges,
I'm ready and willing to submit to trial
(Without invoking sanctuary as now)
Before your assembled kindred, in whose eyes
I'm as guilty as in yours if I made her barren. 360
There—now you know my heart. I'm worried, though,
About your famous weakness. Brawling over
A woman led you to devastate poor Troy.

Chorus

That's quite enough from a female dealing with men.
I'd say your righteousness had gone the limit. 365

Menelaus

Woman, these are admittedly minor matters;
As you say, unworthy of my regime and Greece.

But never forget: whatever one sets his heart on
Gets to be more important than taking Troy.
Being cheated out of marriage now, that matters;   370
That's why my help's enlisted for my daughter.
All other woes a woman bears are minor
But lose her husband!—might as well be dead.
It's right my son-in-law order my slaves about;
Right his be ordered about by any of us.   375
Friends—and I mean real friends—reserve nothing:
The property of one belongs to the other.
Just sitting around and waiting till men came back,
I'd be simple-minded indeed to neglect my interests.
So on your feet; get away from the goddess' shrine.   380
If you decide to die, the boy survives.
If you put your own skin first, he dies instead.
It's one of the two. No other way about it.

Andromache
　Oh, here's a gloomy lottery of life,
　A gloomy choosing. If I win, I lose;   385
　And losing, losing—oh, I'm lost forever!
　You there who make such mountains out of molehills,
　Listen to reason. You're killing me—why? For whom?
　What city did I betray? What child of yours kill?
　Whose home set fire to? I was strong-armed into   390
　A bully's bed. And it's me you kill, not him
　Who caused it all? Oh, you've got everything backwards,
　Punishing the effect, and not the cause.
　All these troubles! O my wretched land,
　What horrors I endure! Why must I bear   395
　A child just to redouble throe on throe?
　I who saw Hector mangled underwheel,
　Who saw our Ilium blindingly afire!   400
　I who came shackled to the Grecian fleet,
　Haled by the hair! And, once I came to Phthia,
　Knew a mock marriage with that murderous brood.

How's living sweet for me? Where should I look—
Toward yesterday's affliction or today's?   405
I had this one son left, light of my life,
And he's to be murdered by such judges now.
Murdered? Oh not to save my scraps of life.
The child has possibilities, if he lives;
And if I let him die, shame come to me.   410
So look, I'm leaving the shrine. I'm in your hands
To mangle, murder, bind, hang by the neck.
O child, the one that bore you moves toward death
And all for you. If you escape that doom
Think of your mother, what a fate she suffered!   415
And covering your father's face with kisses,
Melted in tears, crushing your arms around him,
Describe my ending. All men know their children
Mean more than life. If childless people sneer—
Well, they've less sorrow. But what lonesome luck!   420

Chorus

Her speech rouses my pity. Calamities,
Even a stranger's, call for tears in all.
Menelaus, you ought to arrange some peace between
Your daughter and this woman, instead of crushing her.

Menelaus

Now seize her, men! Lock your arms tight around her.   425
She won't take kindly what I've got to say.
Remember how I bobbled the boy's life
Before your face, to pry you off the shrine
And coax you into my clutches here to die?
You know the facts of the matter—in your case.   430
As for the boy, however—suppose we let
My daughter give the word to kill or not.
And now, get in that house. I'll teach you, slave,
To attempt assault and battery on your betters.

Andromache

Made a fool of! Duped and caught by treachery, treachery!   435

« 575 »

Menelaus

Go tell the world—who cares? I'm not denying it.

Andromache

This passes for high policy back in Sparta?

Menelaus

Also in Troy: being struck at to strike back.

Andromache

And there's no heaven above to punish you?

Menelaus

Heaven I'll handle later. First things first.   440

Andromache

You'll kill this little baby, snatched from my lap?

Menelaus

It's out of my hands. His future's up to my daughter.

Andromache

Then I might as well lament you now, poor darling.

Menelaus

His prospects, it appears, are none too rosy.

Andromache

Where's there a man that doesn't find you odious,   445
You citizens of Sparta, devious schemers,
Masters of falsehood, specialists in evil,
Your minds all warped and putrid, serpentine?
How iniquitous your prosperity in Greece!
Name any foulness and it's yours: assassins;   450
Your palms a tetter of itchiness; your tongues
Off scavenging one way and your minds another.
Damn your Spartan souls! Death's not so much
For me as you seem to feel. I died before
When my poor town in Phrygia was stricken,   455
My glorious husband too, who many a time
Whipped you, a whimpering skipper, back to your ships.
Fine figure of a hero now, you threaten

Death to a woman. Strike! But not before
You and your daughter feel the edge of my tongue.   460
So you think you're really something now in Sparta?
Well, so was I in Troy. If I'm destroyed
You've little cause to gloat. For your time's coming.

(*Exeunt Andromache and child; Menelaus.*)

Chorus

STROPHE

Oh, I'll never approve a double love for any man,   465
  Or children born to juggled wives;
They confuse the home, bringing heavy heartaches.
  I say one man should love and honor one:
    A bride-bed
  Theirs alone till life's done.   470

ANTISTROPHE

Nor in states is it right to see a pair of princes rule:
  One tyrant's better far than two
Who indeed breed woe crowding woe and town strife.   475
  Or when two souls compose a single song,
    The muse fans
  Livid wrath before long.

STROPHE

Or when the hurricane is scudding ship and all,
  In a huddle of colloquy over the wheel, two heads   480
Are worse than one, and a panel of philosophers
  Worse than a petty but positive mind.
  Only one in command: that's the way in the home
  And the way in the state when it must find
    Measures best for mankind.   485

ANTISTROPHE

We've sad example here: the Spartan, daughter of
  Menelaus the general, is running amuck, breathes fire
Against her fellow-wife; her spite destroys the poor
  Trojan. And also her baby I fear.   490

Ungodly, unlawful, unsanctified crime!
But alas! O my queen, there's a day near
   When you'll pay and pay dear.

And indeed I see
The close-huddled pair stumble out of the house   495
Under sentence of death.
O lady so stricken, O woebegone boy
Who die on account of your parent's affairs,
Though never involved,
   Nor to blame in the eyes of the rulers!   500

(Enter Andromache and her son, hands lashed
together; Menelaus.)

Andromache

STROPHE

My hands are helpless; roped so tight,
See, there's blood where the fibers bite.
   Only the grave before me.

Son

Mother, O Mother, I'm here too
   Close to your side, to die with you.   505

Andromache

Hardly lucky this sacrifice,
Phthian counselors.

Son

        Father, do
Hurry and help if you love us.

Andromache

You'll be snuggled, my little lad,   510
Forever close to your mother's breast,
Dust with dust in the underworld—

Son

Mother, what's to become of me?
   What's for us but misery?

Menelaus

    On your way to the grave! You're an enemy brood   515
    From an enemy nest. You two are condemned
    By a separate vote. You, woman, my voice
    Has sentenced to death. And this boy of yours
    By my daughter's doomed. For it's mad indeed
    To let slip through your fingers inveterate foes   520
    When by wiping them out
        You can free your home from its nightmare.

Andromache

                ANTISTROPHE

    Husband, husband, if you could stand
    Here in front of us, spear in hand,
        Son of Priam, to help us.   525

Son

    Dark day! Where's there a song to sing
        Likely to charm away this thing?

Andromache

    Plead with him, kneel at his knees and pray,
    Son, for sympathy.

Son

                Dearest lord,   530
    Don't destroy me! Oh let me go!

Andromache

    Only look at my tear-stained face.
    How I weep, like a marble-cupped
    Flowing spring in a sunless place!

Son

    Poor me! Where is an opening now   535
        Out of trouble? Oh tell me how!

Menelaus

    Why snivel to me? I'm hard as a rock.
    You might as well make your appeal to the sea.

I've a helping hand for kith and kin,
But I'm wasting no favors, boy, on you.   540
When I think of the years of life I lost
To capture Troy and that mother of yours—!
She made your fate;
    You can pay for it six feet under.

Chorus

But look at this: old Peleus approaching   545
As hurriedly as ancient limbs can bring him.

                    (*Enter Peleus, assisted by a servant.*)

Peleus

I'd like to know, from you above all, head-butcher,
What's going on here? What's this? And why's the house
Become a chaos, through your lawless dealing?
Menelaus, stop. Enough felonious haste.   550
(Get me there quicker, fellow. Now's no time
For hanging back, it appears. Rejuvenation,
It's now I could do with a touch of you—now or never.)
First I'd like to put a bit of wind
In this poor woman's sails. By what right   555
Have these men strapped your hands and pushed you off,
You and the boy? Poor sheep, poor little lamb
Bound for the slaughter. All of us away!

Andromache

These, old father, are dragging me and the baby
To our grave, as you can see. What's there to tell?   560
I sent for you, though, begging desperately
Not only once but time and time again.
Surely you must have heard of the ill-feeling
His daughter roused in the house—that murderous woman!
And now from the Altar of Thetis, mother of   565
Your noble son, your own soul's adoration,
They've torn me away by force, without a trial;
Condemned me without waiting for those absent.
For knowing the baby and I were here alone

(Poor blameless innocent) they planned our murder.   570
Now I beg of you, father, crumpled here
Before your knees—for I can't get a finger free
To touch your beloved cheek in supplication—
For god's sake extricate me. Else I die—   575
Not only to my pain but your discredit.

Peleus

Loosen these knots or someone smarts for it!
Free the poor woman's cramped-together hands.

Menelaus

I've as much to say as you—in fact I've more
As far as she's concerned—and I forbid it.   580

Peleus

And by what right? You're master in my house,
Not content with lording it over Spartans?

Melenaus

She was my catch. I brought her back from Troy.

Peleus

Full rights to her passed over to my grandson.

Menelaus

Hasn't he a right to my things? I to his?   585

Peleus

To care for, not to abuse. And not to slaughter.

Menelaus

This woman, at any rate, I'll not return.

Peleus

Suppose I break your head in with this scepter?

Menelaus

Just touch me and you'll see! Only come near me!

Peleus

You call yourself a man, foul-blooded creature?   590
May I ask where you're worthy of that name?
You, who lost your own wife to a Phrygian

For leaving the house unlocked and unattended,
As if you had a decent wife indeed
Instead of the world's worst. No Spartan girl   595
Could ever live clean even if she wanted.
They're always out on the street in scanty outfits,
Making a great display of naked limbs.
In those they race and wrestle with the boys too—
Abominable's the word. It's little wonder   600
Sparta is hardly famous for chaste women.
Ask Helen—she should know. She went gallivanting
Out of her house, pooh-poohing family ties
And skipped the country with a lusty buck.
For such a slut you raised the Greek divisions   605
And led those many thousands against Troy?
You shouldn't have lifted a spear. Just sat and spat once
In her direction, when you knew her nature,
And let her stay away; why, paid to keep her there!
Not you, though. Such a thought never crossed your mind.   610
Instead, you squandered thousands of sweet souls,
Left poor old women childless in their houses,
Left grey-haired fathers weeping their strong sons.
I'm one of those bereaved ones. Bloody murderer!
I hold you accountable for Achilles' death!   615
Oh, *you* returned from Troy without a mark on,
All your pretty armor and regalia
Immaculate as on the day you left!
I warned my grandson, when he courted, never
To marry kin of yours, nor share his home with   620
A filthy woman's litter. They're contagious
With blotches of the mother. (Oh, be careful,
Suitors, to marry a good woman's child!)
Not to speak of your shameless conduct with your brother,
Bidding the fat-head butcher his poor girl!—   625
You, in a panic for your ladylove!
And capturing Troy—I'm on your traces, eh?—
You laid your hands on the woman and didn't kill her.

But casting sheep's eyes on her bosom, you
Unbuckled your sword and puckered up for kisses, 630
Petting that traitorous bitch, you toady of lust!
Then, coming to my grandson's in his absence
You loot his home, commit attempted murder
Atrociously on a poor mother and son
Who'll make you and your daughter rue this day, 635
Born bastard though he is. For don't forget
That poor land often outproduces rich,
And bastards get the upper hand of blue bloods.
Now get your daughter out of here. It's better
To make a poor but honest match than land a 640
No-good wealthy father-in-law. Like you.

Chorus

Out of some little thing, too free a tongue
Can make an outrageous wrangle. Really politic
Men are careful not to embroil their friends.

Menelaus

Well! hearing this, why say the old have sense, 645
Or those the Greeks regarded once as sages?
When you, the famous Peleus, so well born,
And kin to us by marriage, rave away
And blacken us, all for an alien woman.
One that you ought to whip beyond the Nile 650
And beyond the Phasis, crying on me to do so,
Seeing she comes from Asia, where so many
Of the valiant men from Hellas fell and moldered.
Your own son's blood, as well as others', on her.
For Paris, the one that killed your boy Achilles, 655
Was brother to Hector, and she's Hector's wife.
Yet you can bear to enter the same doorway,
Can bring yourself to eat at the same table;
Even let her beget her venomous offspring.
I, looking out for you as well as me, 660
Planned her removal, and you snatch her from me.

Listen (a bit of logic's not amiss):
Suppose my daughter barren, her a spawner,
You'd make her children rulers of this country,
This sacred Phthia? Men of foreign blood   665
Would order Greeks about? You think I'm foolish
Because I hold right's right? And you're the shrewd one?
Another thing: Let's just suppose your daughter
Married some citizen and got such treatment,
You'd sit back mum? I doubt it. Yet for a foreigner   670
You're yelping at your relatives by marriage?
When cheated, wife or husband feels the same.
She doesn't like it. He doesn't like it either,
Finding a frivolous woman in the house.
Yet he can mend things with his good right arm;   675
She has to count on friends' or parents' aid.
What's wrong then in my helping out my own?
You're in your doting days! My generalship,
Which you bring up, is evidence in my favor.
Poor Helen had a time of it, not choosing   680
But chosen by the gods to exalt her country.
For innocent before of arms and battles
Greece grew to manhood then. Experience, travel—
These are an education in themselves.
If coming in the presence of my wife   685
I steeled myself and spared her, I was wise.
(I always deplored, by the way, your killing your brother.)
Well, there's my speech, wise, moderate, not irascible.
If you fly off the handle, a sore throat's
The most you'll get. I find discretion pays.   690

Chorus
    Both of you stop these mad recriminations.
    It's the only thing. Before you go too far.

Peleus
    Too bad the custom here is topsy-turvy.
    When the public sets a war memorial up

Do those who really sweated get the credit?   695
Oh no! Some general wangles the prestige!—
Who, brandishing his one spear among thousands,
Did one man's work, but gets a world of praise.
Those self-important fathers of their country
Think they're above the people. Why they're nothing!   700
The citizen is infinitely wiser,
Gifted with nerve and purpose, anyway.
You were strutters at Troy, you and your brother,
Basking lazily in your high command
And sleek and fat on many another's anguish.   705
I'll show you, though, that Paris, Ida's Paris,
Was a less furious enemy than I am,
Unless you leave this house—my curse upon you!—
You and your childless daughter, that my grandson,
If he's of my blood indeed, will haul by the hair.   710
So the barren creature won't let other women
Have any children until she herself does!
Just because she's a useless reproducer
She means to keep the rest of us from families?
Get back from that woman, slaves. I'd like to see   715
If anyone interferes while I untie her.
Come, straighten up. Although I'm all atremble
I'll unloosen these tightly tangled cords.
You blackguard, look at her mutilated hands!
What did you think you were roping? Bulls? Or lions?   720
You were frightened she'd draw some weapon out and rout you?
Come over here, little boy; scoot under my arms;
Help work your mother loose. I'll bring you up
In Phthia to be a nightmare to these Spartans.
They're touted for cold steel and the hour of battle,   725
We're told. For the rest, a thoroughly inferior breed!

Chorus
Oftener than not the old are uncontrollable;
Their tempers make them difficult to deal with.

Menelaus

It's clear your inclination is toward slander.
However, I'll not resort to force in Phthia.   730
That vulgar sort of thing is quite beneath me.
For now, though—I've just remembered I'm pressed for time—
I must be leaving. There's a—there's a town
Near Sparta, in fact—it used to be quite friendly,
But now makes threatening moves. I'll take steps,   735
And with a little campaigning tranquilize it.
That matter settled to my satisfaction,
I'm coming back. With my son-in-law, man to man,
I'll have a friendly little confabulation.
If he keeps this woman in check, and from now on   740
Behaves as he should, he'll get as good from us.
If he's looking for trouble, trouble's what he'll get.
My meaning's clear: he'll reap just as he sows.
For all your blather I don't care a hoot.
Shrill as you are, you're a feeble shadow in front of me.   745
All you can ever do is talk, talk, talk.

                                        (*Exit Menelaus.*)

Peleus

Go ahead, little boy, here shivering under my arms.
And you, poor woman. You've had a bad voyage, both.
But now at last you've found a quiet haven.

Andromache

O reverence, god be good to you and yours   750
For saving the baby and me in our affliction.
Be careful, though, that on some lonely road
They don't waylay us all and kidnap me,
Seeing you not so young as once, me helpless,
The boy so very little. Be on guard   755
Or, slipping free for now, we'll be seized later.

Peleus

Let's have no womanish tremors any more.
Proceed. Who dares to bother you? He'll be sorry

If he does. For under the gods (and not without
A numerous horse and foot) I'm lord of Phthia.   760
I'm still on my toes and not so old as you think.
If I so much as look hard at that fellow
He'll turn and bolt, along in years as I am.
Stout-hearted oldsters can handle the young all right.
What good are showy muscles to a coward?   765

(*Exeunt Andromache and son; Peleus.*)

Chorus

STROPHE

Best never born, if not of an affluent house,
Of fathers known to fame, with resources to match,
    Then if some appalling disaster befalls, there's   770
      Always a way for the rich.
    For those who are known to be born aristocrats,
Praise and reverence: time can never obscure the estate
    Good men bequeath: their glory (a torch on the tomb)   775
      Has no terminal date.

ANTISTROPHE

Far better not bring home a disgraceful success
Than knock awry all law with a mischievous thrust.   780
    Today's victory flatters the palate of mortals—
      Yes, but tomorrow it must
    Sour, sicken, and turn to an old deep-grown reproach.
This I always have held, to this manner of life I aspire: 785
    May no unjust sway flourish in family affairs
      Or in seat of empire.

EPODE

    White-headed Peleus, I
    Credit that tale: how at the Lapithae wedding   790
      You with the tough centaurs fought
A spectacular fight! Then on the good ship Argo rounded the
      grim cape
    Far beyond those Rolling Rocks few craft escape—

What voyage more storied than yours?   795
  Next you adventured with Heracles to Troy,
Where he, of the true stock of Zeus, hung garlands of carnage.
  Your fame fast bound to Heracles',   800
  You returned to the Greek seas.

                                                        (*Enter Nurse.*)

Nurse

  O my dear women, what a day we've had!
  Sorrow crowding on sorrow is our portion.
  The queen in the house there, poor Hermione
  Left in the lurch by her father, and knowing now   805
  What a heinous thing it was to attempt the murder
  Of Andromache and the youngster, wants to die—
  Afraid of her husband, afraid she'll be ordered out
  Of the house for what she did (think of the scandal!)
  Or killed for threatening lives not hers to take.   810
  Her bodyguard barely managed to restrain her
  From knotting the rope on her neck, then barely managed
  To wrestle the sword from her hand in the nick of time.
  It's clear to her now she acted badly, badly;
  She's all remorse. And I—I'm quite exhausted   815
  Keeping the queen from hanging herself, ladies.
  Won't all of you please go into the palace now
  And plead with her not to destroy herself? New faces
  Have more authority than accustomed ones.

Chorus

  Indeed the clamor of servants in the house   820
  Substantiates your story. It's unlikely,
  Poor thing, she'd keep from seizures of remorse,
  Having done the things she did. Look, wild for death,
  She's broken from her home and her attendants.

                                                    (*Enter Hermione.*)

Hermione

                          STROPHE

  I'll tear out my hair by the roots; these nails   825
  Will furrow my skin!

Nurse

What are you seeking, child? Your beauty's ruin?

Hermione

ANTISTROPHE

Torn from my curls, away, lace veil!   830
Where the wind blows, go!

Nurse

Cover your breast, my darling; pin your garments.

Hermione

STROPHE

If I am bare,
What difference here?
Uncovered, exposed, oh terribly clear
What I plotted against my husband.   835

Nurse

The attempt to kill the other woman rankles?

Hermione

ANTISTROPHE

Now I weep
What I ventured then.
Abominable
In the eyes of men!

Nurse

It's true you went too far. But he'll forgive you.   840

Hermione

Why did you pry the
Sword from my fingers?
Give it back, dear friend. My final hope
Is to strike true once. And why hide the rope?

Nurse

What if I let you die in such distraction?   845

Hermione

Alas my fate!
No flames around?

No rock I can scale
To plunge in the sea? Or on forest ground?
Let the gods of the dead receive me.   850

Nurse

Why carry on so? Divine visitations
Come to all of us, all of us, late or soon.

Hermione

Father, you left me derelict here
Alone by the surf; and no ship near.   855
It kills me; it kills me: I'll not come
Ever again to the bridal room!
Should I supplicate? What shrine's for me?
Should I fall like a slave at a slave's knee?   860
What I'd like to be
Is a black wing leaving the Phthian shore
Or that skiff of fir
The earliest oar
Drove to the end of the ocean.   865

Nurse

Darling, I disapproved of your excesses
When you were in the wrong against the Trojan,
And I disapprove of this irrational panic.
Your husband won't repudiate your marriage
Like this, on the mere complaint of a foreigner.   870
It wasn't you he picked up as a prize
In Troy—a good man's your father, you had dowry
In plenty, and your city's influential
Far more than most. Your father's not forsaken you
As you seem to fear; he'll see you're not rejected.   875
Now please go in; don't make a scene in front
Of the house. It only hurts your reputation
If people see you here outside the palace.

Chorus

Look! Look at this man with the foreign air
Making so hastily in our direction!   880

(Enter Orestes.)

Orestes

Dear ladies, strangers: is this indeed the home
Of Achilles' son? the royal home and palace?

Chorus

It is. If you care to favor us with your name—?

Orestes

I'm the son of Agamemnon and Clytemnestra;
My name's Orestes. And I'm on my way   885
To the oracle at Dodona. Since I'm here
In Phthia, I thought I'd inquire about my cousin,
If she's alive and well, enjoying prosperity—
Hermione from Sparta. For although
She's living far away, she's in our thoughts.   890

Hermione

A port in a storm indeed to this sad sailor,
O Agamemnon's son! Here at your feet
I beg of you, pity the object of your care,
Doing anything but well. My arms, as urgent
As any garlands are, circle your knees.   895

Orestes

Well!
What's this? Am I seeing things, or do I really
Behold Menelaus' child, who should be queen here?

Hermione

Menelaus' child. The only one that Helen
Bore to my father there. Why shouldn't you know?

Orestes

Savior Apollo, from all this deliver us!   900
Whatever's the matter? Who's back of this, god or mortal?

Hermione

It's partly my fault. Partly too my husband's.
Partly some god's. But chaos everywhere.

Orestes

You have no children—so no trouble that way.
What else goes wrong for a woman—except her marriage?   905

Hermione

What else indeed? You've put your finger on it.

Orestes

You mean your husband loves another woman?

Hermione

He's sleeping with Hector's wife, that battle trophy.

Orestes

One man; two loves. No good ever comes of that.

Hermione

That's how it was. I acted in self-defense.   910

Orestes

Scheming against your rival, as women do?

Hermione

I wanted to see her dead. Her and her bastard!

Orestes

Did you see it through? Or did something interfere?

Hermione

Yes—Peleus, with his reverence for riffraff.

Orestes

This deed of blood—was anyone in it with you?   915

Hermione

My father. He came all the way from Sparta.

Orestes

And got the worst of it from the old man?

Hermione

Let's say he respected age. At least, he's left me.

Orestes

I see. And you've good cause to fear your husband.

Hermione

    Naturally. He's within his rights to kill me.   920
    What's there to say? So I beg, by the God of Kindred,
    Take me out of this land, as far as possible
    Or at least to my father's home. The very walls here
    Seem to be howling at me: go! go! go!
    All Phthia hates me. If my husband comes   925
    Home from Apollo's oracle while I'm here
    He'll kill me on foul charges. Or I'll be a slave
    In the bastard-blooming chambers I was queen of.
  "How did you fall so low?" someone may marvel.
    Visits of poisonous women were my downfall.   930
    They made me lose my head by talk like this:
  "So you let that wretched captive, a slave in the house,
    Have rights to your husband, share and share alike?
    If she, in my home, meddled with my marriage
    I swear by Hera that act would be her last!"   935
    And I, attentive to the siren music
    Of these sly, these lewd, these babbling know-it-alls,
    Swelled up like a great fool. Oh why, oh why
    Did I spy on my husband, having all I wanted?
    Money more than enough. Control of the household.   940
    The children I'd have had fully legitimate,
    Hers illegitimate, half slaves to mine.
    Oh, never, never—I can't say this too often—
    Should a man with any sense, having taken a wife,
    Let other women come and buzz around her.   945
    What are they all but teachers of delinquency?
    For one can make a profit by corrupting her;
    Another has fallen and likes company;
    Many love to make trouble—this is why
    Our homes are a sink of evil. Against this   950
    Double-lock your doors and bolt them too.
    For not one wholesome thing has ever come
    From gadabout female callers—only grief.

Chorus

Your tongue's a little free with your own sex.
It's understandable now. But women should   955
Paint womanly vices in more flattering colors.

Orestes

A piece of wise advice (whoever gave it):
In disputations, listen to both sides.
I was fully aware of the uproar in this house,
The struggle between you and Hector's widow,   960
And watched and waited to see if you thought it best
To remain here still, or if the attempted killing
Of the slave had terrified you into fleeing.
I came, though you didn't appeal to me by letter,
On the chance of talking together, as we do,   965
Then seeing you safely away. Though mine by right,
You're living with this man—your father's mischief!
He gave your hand to me before invading
Troy, and then peddled you to your present lord
On condition he be of use in destroying the city.   970
When the son of Achilles returned home
(For I overlooked your father's part) I begged him
To give this marriage up, pleading my fortunes
And the evil genius over me—and considering
It wouldn't be easy to marry outside the family   975
When one had reasons for exile such as I had.
He was highly insulting about my mother's death
And hooted over the scarlet-clotted goblins.
Abject, in view of that family situation,
I was in agony, agony, but I bore it   980
And went away halfheartedly without you.
But now, however, since your luck is changing,
Since you're at this impasse, without resources,
I'll take you away and restore you to your father.
Blood's thicker than water, and when one's in trouble   985
Best to seek out a relative's open arms.

Hermione

    About my marriage it's not for me to decide.
    The whole affair is in my father's hands.
    But help me away from here as quickly as possible.
    My husband might come sooner than we think   990
    And murder me, or old Peleus might get wind of
    My escape and order the horsemen after me.

Orestes

    The old man's no threat; forget him. And never fear
    Achilles' son again—seeing how he scorned me.
    It happens there's a death-trap set for him,   995
    A noose I can't imagine a way out of,
    And all of my contriving. I've said enough now—
    But when it springs, the Delphian rock will know.
    So he called me mother-killer? Well, I'll teach him,
    If my allies at Delphi keep their word,   1000
    To take in marriage women mine by right!
    Black hour for him when he asked Apollo to pay
    For killing his father! No last-minute repentance
    Will keep the god from exacting punishment.
    At Apollo's hand (my imputations helping)   1005
    He'll die—I wouldn't say nicely. And taste my hate!
    Let reprobates expect nothing but havoc
    From heaven above: god stamps on arrogance.

                     (*Exeunt Orestes, Hermione, Nurse.*)

Chorus

STROPHE

Apollo, who made Ilium's hill and its strong walls heaven-high,
Poseidon, with stallions of rain-grey flashing by   1010
    Over the moors of the sea,
    Out of fury you doomed that town—why?
    Child of your art as it was—for   1015
    Ares to wreck, who delights in the spear-hand.
      Ruined! Oh, ruined! You
    Ruined your betrayed land?

ANTISTROPHE

How many war-cars marshalled on the sand-packed riverside,
Proud horses before them! And oh how many men   1020
   Penned in inglorious strife!
  And the monarchs of Troy elate then
  With their fathers are tombed in dark earth.
  Nor on the altars of Troy any fire cries
   "Praise to the bright gods!" and no   1025
  Stirring clouds of myrrh rise.

STROPHE

And Agamemnon's dead by the stroke of his wife;
She too, in the grim-faced round of a death for a death
   At her children's own hand.   1030
The god, the god shaped her name with fatal breath,
Dreaming futurity: her son from Argos marched home,
Agamemnon's in blood, and strode to the inner recess—
   Killed his own dear mother there.   1035
   O Phoebus, divine one, how credit this?

ANTISTROPHE

And mothers, scores on scores, in the markets of Greece
Made stones re-echo shrill with lament for a son,
   Wives were torn from old homes
To serve a strange husband. Not on you alone   1040
Nor on friends of yours came such distressing heartache.
But all Hellas was sick to death, and a horror of blood
    Over Troy's gay-fruited fields   1045
   Rolled like a storm pouring hell's bitter flood.

                          (Enter Peleus.)

Peleus
  Women of Phthia, there's something I must know.
  Tell me the truth. I've heard a vague report
  That Menelaus' girl has left this house
  And gone off who knows where. I've come in haste   1050
  To learn the facts. For when our friends are absent
  The ones at home should keep an eye on things.

Chorus
>You've heard correctly, Peleus. It's not fitting
>For me to hide reverses that I know of.
>The queen's gone from the palace. She's in flight.   1055

Peleus
>Afraid of what? Out with it, the whole story.

Chorus
>Afraid of her husband and her possible exile.

Peleus
>On account of her cutthroat tactics toward the boy?

Chorus
>Exactly. And in terror too of the slave woman.

Peleus
>She left here with her father? Or someone else?   1060

Chorus
>Agamemnon's son escorted her away.

Peleus
>With what design in mind? Meaning to marry her?

Chorus
>Meaning that and worse than that: to kill your grandson.

Peleus
>By treachery? Or in fair fight, man to man?

Chorus
>At Apollo's holy shrine, with a pack of Delphians.   1065

Peleus
>There's danger in that, no question. Will someone go
>Quick as he can to the holy hall of Delphi
>And tell our good friends there what plot's afoot
>Before his enemies get to Achilles' son?
>>   (*Enter Messenger.*)

Messenger
>Oh gloomy news!   1070

I'm under a curse to bring the news I do
To you, old father, and my master's friends.

Peleus

Ah, my clairvoyant heart's all apprehension!

Messenger

You have no grandson, Peleus—hear the worst.
Swords cut him down, so many and so sharp,   1075
In the hands of Delphians and that Mycenaean.

Chorus

What's happening to you there, old man? Don't fall.
Hold yourself up.

Peleus

          My strength is gone. All's over.
My voice is lost. My knees are weak as water.

Messenger

If you meditate revenge for those you loved,
Don't let yourself collapse. But hear what happened.   1080

Peleus

O destiny, at the extreme verge of life
You've brought to bay a pitiful old man!
But tell me how he perished, the one son
Of my one son. I'll hear what no man should.

Messenger

When we arrived in Apollo's famous territory   1085
We spent three entire days, from dawn to dark,
Filling our eyes with all there was to see.
This aroused suspicion, apparently. For the citizens
Gathered in twos and threes, in little huddles.
The son of Agamemnon covered the town   1090
Breathing his slander into every ear:
"Notice that fellow there, who's spying on
Apollo's nooks of bullion, rich donations?
He's back again with the very thing in mind
He had before: to rifle the sanctuary."   1095

This was behind the angry rumor bruited
About the town. The directors and advisers
And other security officers, on their own,
Posted patrols among the colonnades.
But we, however, innocent of this,   1100
With sheep raised on the pastures of Parnassus
Took our places there before the altar,
Attended by our sponsors and the celebrants.
A spokesman put the question: "Now, young man,
What should we ask the god for? What's your mission?"   1105
And he: "I stand here ready to do penance
For my earlier sins against Apollo, charging
He should make payment for my father's death."
It was obvious then Orestes' word prevailed,
Branding my master a liar who really came   1110
Upon some foul design. Reaching the sanctuary
So he could pray to Apollo at the oracle,
We inspected, first, the omens of the fire.
It seems, though, that a heavily armed squad
Lay in ambush in the laurel—Clytemnestra's   1115
Son alone the brains behind this plot.
So my master faced the god and began to implore him,
When they, armed to the teeth, steel sharpened specially,
Lunged at him from behind—he wore no corselet.
But he wheeled around, not seriously hit,   1120
Whipped out his sword, snatched from beside the door
Some votive armor hanging on the pegs there,
Took a stance by the altar, every inch a warrior!
In a ringing voice he challenged the Delphians:
"Why murder one who comes as a good pilgrim?   1125
And what's the accusation I should die for?"
Not one among so many spoke a word,
Only their hands moved, pelting him with rocks.
Battered on all sides by a hail so blinding,
He heaved with rigid arm his covering shield   1130
Here, there, and everywhere, to intercept them.

No use. For many weapons came at once:
Arrows and javelins and unfastened spits,
Meat-cleavers to kill bulls clanged at his feet.
Then you'd have seen a ghastly jig, as the boy   1135
Tried to outtwist them. Men were edging around him,
Pinning him there, not giving him time to breathe,
When he suddenly rushed from the sacrificial stone,
Leaping the leap that Troy knew to its cost,
And burst upon them. They, like little pigeons   1140
Spying a falcon near, convulsed and panicked.
Many fell in the tumult, some of wounds,
Some trampled by their fellows in jammed exits,
While in the holy place unholy shrieking
Thrilled against stone. A moment of respite then—   1145
He stood spectacular in steely splendor,
Till from some deep recess a voice arose
—So weird our very flesh crept—galvanizing
The rout to a show of valor. Achilles' son
Was toppled then, a sharp sword in his ribs   1150
Thrust by a Delphian, who may claim his death
Though abetted by plenty of others. As he slumped,
Who didn't run with cold steel or a boulder
To bruise or mutilate? His handsome body
All desecrated by the berserk blows!   1155
But he lay dead almost touching the altar, so
They dragged him from the frankincense and myrrh.
We hurried the corpse away quick as we could
And now convey him here for you to weep
And wail, poor, poor old man. And so inter.   1160
All this was done by one hailed as a prophet,
Mind you, distinguisher of right and wrong—
And done to a penitent, poor Achilles' boy.
The prophet brooded, like a spiteful man,
Over wrongs done long ago. That's "wisdom" for you?   1165

(*Exit Messenger.*)

Chorus

Oh, but look! the prince, on a litter there,
Brought slowly home from the Delphian land!
Poor stricken youth! And poor old man
Who must welcome the son of Achilles home
Not as you would if you had your wish.   1170
But you've stumbled yourself on a desperate hour,
    One fate swamping the two of you.

(*The body of Neoptolemus is carried in by his attendants.*)

Peleus

STROPHE

Misery! Oh what a horror to gaze upon!
Horror to gather it into my doorway!
This is the end for us, city of Thessaly,   1175
Finished and done for. Never a child again,
Never in this house.
How I'm destroyed by calamities lashing me!
Where's there a friend I can turn to for comforting?   1180
Fingers I loved so! These cheeks! And these lips!
Oh, if only your days had been numbered in Ilium
By the Simois, that far shore.

Chorus

He would have earned appropriate laurels then
In death, old man, and you been far, far luckier.   1185

Peleus

ANTISTROPHE

Marriage, O marriage, you ruined this house of mine!
All of this town you doomed to confusion!
My son, my son,
Oh, but if only that plague of your marriage, that
Home-wrecking, child-wrecking brood of Hermione   1190
Never had noosed you
Tight for the death-blow, child of my child—
Thunder and lightning ought to have blasted her!
Nor, for the archery death to your father, should

Charges of blood have been flung at Apollo,　　　　　1195
　　Divine one, by a mere man.

Chorus

STROPHE

With a cry of despair I mourn for my lost lord!
　　With those rites
　Due the dead I sing this.

Peleus

With a cry of despair I take my disconsolate turn,　　1200
　　An old man
　Weighted down, I weep, weep.

Chorus

God wanted this; god brought this thing about.

Peleus

　　Dearest, you've
　Left all the house a great vacancy.　　　　　　　1205
You've left me alone, desolate and
Without a son, so late in life.

Chorus

Better you died, old man, before your children.

Peleus

Why not wrench away my hair?
Why not batter head and all　　　　　　　　　1210
With savage hands? O city, see!
　　Of both my boys
　This Apollo robbed me!

Chorus

ANTISTROPHE

Luckless old man who saw and felt so much!
　　From now on
　What existence for you?　　　　　　　　　　1215

Peleus

Not a child, not a friend—through unabating pain
　　I'll somehow
　Fumble toward my death-day.

Chorus
>In marriage the gods loved you—all for this?

Peleus
>>Flown away;
>>Gone for good. Oh, how far
>>From those heavenly prospects they offered.   1220

Chorus
>An empty haunter of an empty house.

Peleus
>>City oh no longer mine!
>>Scepter, shatter on the ground!
>>And you, my Nereid, girl of purple grottoes,
>>>How utterly
>>>You behold my ruin.   1225

Chorus
>Look!
>What's stirring around? What prodigy's here
>I somehow sense? Look! Look over there!
>A divinity, girls, on the shimmering air!
>And floating this way over paddock and field
>>Of Phthia, nearer and nearer.   1230

>>>>>>>>>(*Enter Thetis.*)

Thetis
>Because of our marriage, Peleus, long ago,
>I journey here from Nereus' home—your Thetis.
>First I urge you, in these present troubles,
>Not to give way to any inordinate grief.
>Even I, who never should have wept for children,   1235
>Saw the one son I bore you, dear Achilles,
>So fleet of foot—the pride of Greece!—lie dead.
>Hark and approve while I reveal my mission:
>First for the son of Achilles, cold in death here:
>Take him to Delphi; where he fell inter him;
>Let the Delphians read his stone and blush recalling   1240
>The brutal death he met at Orestes' hand.
>Next for the woman won in war, Andromache:

Fate designates, old man, her future in
Molossia, and a marriage there with Helenus.   1245
Her son goes too, the one survivor now
Of your father's line; it's destined his descendants,
King after king, at the summit of prosperity,
Will rule Molossia. Your race and mine
Is not to become extinct as now appears,   1250
Old man; no, neither is Troy's. For the gods keep
An eye on Troy, though passionate Pallas crushed it.
That you may laud our marriage to the skies,
I, a goddess born, a god my father,
Mean to release you from this human dolor   1255
And make you a divinity forever.
There in the house of Nereus, arm in arm,
Goddess with god, we'll live the future out.
And moving dry-shod over the foaming ocean
You'll see your son and mine, dearest Achilles,   1260
Lording it in his island home, on the shore
Of remote Leuké past the Hellespont.
Be off now to the sacred town of Delphi,
Escorting the corpse, and once he's under earth
Come to that grotto in the ancient reef   1265
Cuttlefish love; there take your ease until
I soar from the sea with Nereus' fifty daughters
To choir you home. What fate determines, now
Yours to effect. Great Zeus has spoken so.
And no more lamentation for the fallen.   1270
For every mother's son the gods have posted
A great assessment only death can pay.

Peleus

O royalest of companions, O my queen,
Most welcome, girl of Nereus! All these matters
You've disposed both to your glory and the children's.   1275
Farewell to sorrow at your bidding, goddess.
I'll bury this boy and hurry to Pelion's gorges

Where first I pressed your beauty in these arms.
Did I not say one ought to marry true-hearts   1280
And into honest homes, if one's for virtue?
And never yearn for dishonorable matches
Though there's a world of dowry for the having?
That way the gods are at your side forever.

(Exit Peleus.)

Chorus

Past our telling, the ways of heaven.
The gods accomplish the unforeseen.   1285
What all awaited, fails of achievement;
God arranges what none could dream.
So in the course of our story.

THE
TROJAN
WOMEN

Translated and with an Introduction by

RICHMOND LATTIMORE

INTRODUCTION TO
THE TROJAN WOMEN

In AELIAN'S *Varia historica* (ii. 8), written about the beginning of
the third century A.D., we find the following notice: "In [the first
year of] the ninety-first Olympiad [415 B.C.] . . . Xenocles and
Euripides competed against each other. Xenocles, whoever he may
have been, won the first prize with *Oedipus*, *Lycaon*, *Bacchae*, and
Athamas (a satyr-play). Euripides was second with *Alexander*, *Palamedes*, *The Trojan Women*, and *Sisyphus* (a satyr-play)."

Athens was nominally at peace when Euripides composed this set
of tragedies, of which only *The Trojan Women* is extant; but Athens
had only a few years earlier emerged from an indecisive ten years'
war with Sparta and her allies and was in the spring of 415 weeks
away from launching the great Sicilian Expedition, which touched
off the next war or, more accurately, the next phase of the same war.
This was to end in 404 B.C. with the capitulation of Athens.

During the earlier years of the war Euripides wrote a number of
"patriotic" plays and may have believed or tried to force himself to
believe in the rightness of the Periclean cause and the wickedness of
the enemy. By 415 he had reason to conclude that, at least in the
treatment of captives, neither side was better than the other. A group
of Thebans, working with Plataean traitors, tried to seize Plataea,
failed, surrendered in the belief that their lives would be spared, and
were executed (Thuc. ii. 1–6). Four years later, when Plataea surrendered to the Lacedaemonians and Thebans, the entire garrison
was put to death, the women were sold as slaves, and the city itself
systematically destroyed (Thuc. iii. 68). About the same time the
Athenians suppressed a revolt by the people of Mytilene and other
cities of Lesbos. They voted to kill all grown men and enslave the
women and children but then thought better of it, rescinded the
order just in time, and ended by putting to death *only* rather more
than a thousand men (Thuc. iii. 50). In 421 the Athenians recaptured
Scione, which had revolted, put all grown men to death, and en-

slaved the women and children (Thuc. v. 32). In 417 the Lacedaemonians seized a small town called Hysiae and killed all free persons whom they caught (Thuc. v. 83). The neutral island city of
Melos was invited, in peacetime, to join the Athenian alliance, refused, was besieged in force, and capitulated. The Athenians put all
grown males to death and enslaved the women and children (Thuc.
v. 116). This was in the winter of 416–415, a few months before *The
Trojan Women* was presented. That same winter, the Athenians decided to conquer Sicily (Thuc. vi. 1). This expedition was, like that
against Melos, unprovoked; unlike the Melian aggression, it was
foolhardy, at least obviously very dangerous. It ended in disaster,
and Athens never completely recovered.

The Sicilian venture had been voted and was in preparation when
Euripides presented his trilogy, which, in the manner of Aeschylus,
dealt with three successive episodes in the story of Troy, comple-
mented with a burlesque of satyrs on a kindred theme. The first play
is the story of Paris (Alexander), how it was foretold at his birth
that he must destroy his own city, how the baby was left to die in the
mountains, miraculously rescued (as such babies invariably are), and
at last recognized and restored. The hero of the second story is
Palamedes, the wisest and most inventive of the Achaeans at Troy,
more truly wise than Odysseus, who therefore hated him and treacherously contrived his condemnation and death. While the third
tragedy, our play, ends with the destruction of Troy, the prologue
looks into the future, beyond the end of the action, where the con-
querors are to be wrecked on the home voyage because they have
abused their conquest and turned the gods against them.[1] The plot
of *Sisyphus* is not known, but the Athenian poets were partial to the
scandalous story that Sisyphus, a notorious liar and cheat, seduced
Anticlea and was therefore the true father of Odysseus. This story is
post-Homeric, as is most of the matter of the whole trilogy (Homer
does not mention Palamedes, shows no knowledge of the exposure
of Paris, makes Poseidon the enemy not the protector of Troy, etc.);

---

1. Not only is the parallel of Troy with Melos painfully close, but, with an armada
about to set forth, nothing could have been worse-omened than this dramatic prediction of a great fleet wrecked at sea. Aelian seems outraged that Euripides came second
to Xenocles; I can hardly understand how the Athenians let him present this play at all.

it would go well with the fact that Odysseus, here seen as the unscrupulous politician, is the open villain of *Palamedes* and the villain-behind-the-scenes of *The Trojan Women*.

The effect of current events and policies on *The Trojan Women* is, I think, so obvious that it scarcely needs further elaboration, but I do not believe in the view that the play, loose as it is, is nothing but an outburst, a denunciation of aggressive war and imperialism. The general shapelessness is perhaps permitted partly because the play was one member of a trilogy; no piece which stood by itself could pass with so little dramatic action and such a nihilistic conclusion. The play-long presence of Hecuba on the stage necessitates padding, which is supplied by elaborate rhetorical debates between Hecuba and Cassandra, and Hecuba and Andromache. Out-of-character generalizations bespeak the inspirations of Euripides rather than of his dramatis personae. The trial scene of Helen is a bitter little comedy-within-tragedy, but its juridical refinements defeat themselves and turn preposterous, halting for a time the emotional force of the play. In candor, one can hardly call *The Trojan Women* a good piece of work, but it seems nevertheless to be a great tragedy.

THE TROJAN WOMEN

CHARACTERS

Poseidon

Athene

Hecuba

Talthybius

Cassandra

Andromache

Astyanax

Menelaus

Helen

Chorus of Trojan women

THE TROJAN WOMEN

SCENE: *The action takes place shortly after the capture of Troy. All Trojan men have been killed, or have fled; all women and children are captives. The scene is an open space before the city, which is visible in the background, partly demolished and smoldering. Against the walls are tents, or huts, which temporarily house the captive women. The entrance of the Chorus is made, in two separate groups which subsequently unite, from these buildings, as are those of Cassandra and Helen. The entrances of Talthybius, Andromache, and Menelaus are made from the wings. It is imaginable that the gods are made to appear high up, above the level of the other actors, as if near their own temples on the Citadel. As the play opens, Hecuba is prostrate on the ground (it is understood that she hears nothing of what the gods say).*

(*Enter Poseidon.*)

Poseidon

I am Poseidon. I come from the Aegean depths
of the sea beneath whose waters Nereid choirs evolve
the intricate bright circle of their dancing feet.
For since that day when Phoebus Apollo and I laid down
on Trojan soil the close of these stone walls, drawn true   5
and straight, there has always been affection in my heart
unfading, for these Phrygians and for their city;
which smolders now, fallen before the Argive spears,
ruined, sacked, gutted. Such is Athene's work, and his,
the Parnassian, Epeius of Phocis, architect   10
and builder of the horse that swarmed with inward steel,
that fatal bulk which passed within the battlements,
whose fame hereafter shall be loud among men unborn,
the Wooden Horse, which hid the secret spears within.
Now the gods' groves are desolate, their thrones of power   15
blood-spattered where beside the lift of the altar steps
of Zeus Defender, Priam was cut down and died.

The ships of the Achaeans load with spoils of Troy
now, the piled gold of Phrygia. And the men of Greece
who made this expedition and took the city, stay   20
only for the favoring stern-wind now to greet their wives
and children after ten years' harvests wasted here.

The will of Argive Hera and Athene won
its way against my will. Between them they broke Troy.
So I must leave my altars and great Ilium,   25
since once a city sinks into sad desolation
the gods' state sickens also, and their worship fades.
Scamander's valley echoes to the wail of slaves,
the captive women given to their masters now,
some to Arcadia or the men of Thessaly   30
assigned, or to the lords of Athens, Theseus' strain;
while all the women of Troy yet unassigned are here
beneath the shelter of these walls, chosen to wait
the will of princes, and among them Tyndareus' child
Helen of Sparta, named—with right—a captive slave.   35

Nearby, beside the gates, for any to look upon
who has the heart, she lies face upward, Hecuba
weeping for multitudes her multitude of tears.
Polyxena, one daughter, even now was killed
in secrecy and pain beside Achilles' tomb.   40
Priam is gone, their children dead; one girl is left,
Cassandra, reeling crazed at King Apollo's stroke,
whom Agamemnon, in despite of the gods' will
and all religion, will lead by force to his secret bed.

O city, long ago a happy place, good-bye;   45
good-bye, hewn bastions. Pallas, child of Zeus, did this.
But for her hatred, you might stand strong-founded still.

(Athene enters.)

Athene
August among the gods, O vast divinity,
closest in kinship to the father of all, may one
who quarreled with you in the past make peace, and speak?   50

Poseidon

You may, lady Athene; for the strands of kinship
close drawn work no weak magic to enchant the mind.

Athene

I thank you for your gentleness, and bring you now
questions whose issue touches you and me, my lord.

Poseidon

Is this the annunciation of some new word spoken   55
by Zeus, or any other of the divinities?

Athene

No; but for Troy's sake, on whose ground we stand, I come
to win the favor of your power, and an ally.

Poseidon

You hated Troy once; did you throw your hate away
and change to pity now its walls are black with fire?   60

Athene

Come back to the question. Will you take counsel with me
and help me gladly in all that I would bring to pass?

Poseidon

I will indeed; but tell me what you wish to do.
Are you here for the Achaeans' or the Phrygians' sake?

Athene

For the Trojans, whom I hated this short time since,   65
to make the Achaeans' homecoming a thing of sorrow.

Poseidon

This is a springing change of sympathy. Why must
you hate too hard, and love too hard, your loves and hates?

Athene

Did you not know they outraged my temple, and shamed me?

Poseidon

I know that Ajax dragged Cassandra there by force.   70

Athene

And the Achaeans did nothing. They did not even speak.

Poseidon

    Yet Ilium was taken by your strength alone.

Athene

    True; therefore help me. I would do some evil to them.

Poseidon

    I am ready for anything you ask. What will you do?

Athene

    Make the home voyage a most unhappy coming home.   75

Poseidon

    While they stay here ashore, or out on the deep sea?

Athene

    When they take ship from Ilium and set sail for home
    Zeus will shower down his rainstorms and the weariless beat
    of hail, to make black the bright air with roaring winds.
    He has promised my hand the gift of the blazing thunderbolt   80
    to dash and overwhelm with fire the Achaean ships.
    Yours is your own domain, the Aegaean crossing. Make
    the sea thunder to the tripled wave and spinning surf,
    cram thick the hollow Euboean fold with floating dead;
    so after this Greeks may learn how to use with fear   85
    my sacred places, and respect all gods beside.

Poseidon

    This shall be done, and joyfully. It needs no long
    discourse to tell you. I will shake the Aegaean Sea.
    Myconos' nesses and the swine-back reefs of Delos,
    the Capherean promontories, Scyros, Lemnos   90
    shall take the washed up bodies of men drowned at sea.
    Back to Olympus now, gather the thunderbolts
    from your father's hands, then take your watcher's post, to wait
    the chance, when the Achaean fleet puts out to sea.

    That mortal who sacks fallen cities is a fool,   95
    who gives the temples and the tombs, the hallowed places
    of the dead to desolation. His own turn must come.

(The gods leave the stage. Hecuba seems to waken, and
gets slowly to her feet as she speaks.)

Hecuba

Rise, stricken head, from the dust;
lift up the throat. This is Troy, but Troy
and we, Troy's kings, are perished.   100
Stoop to the changing fortune.
Steer for the crossing and the death-god,
hold not life's prow on the course against
wave beat and accident.
Ah me,   105
what need I further for tears' occasion,
state perished, my sons, and my husband?
O massive pride that my fathers heaped
to magnificence, you meant nothing.
Must I be hushed? Were it better thus?   110
Should I cry a lament?
Unhappy, accursed,
limbs cramped, I lie
backed on earth's stiff bed.
O head, O temples   115
and sides; sweet, to shift,
let the tired spine rest
weight eased by the sides alternate,
against the strain of the tears' song
where the stricken people find music yet   120
in the song undanced of their wretchedness.

You ships' prows, that the fugitive
oars swept back to blessed Ilium
over the sea's blue water
by the placid harbors of Hellas   125
to the flute's grim beat
and the swing of the shrill boat whistles;
you made the crossing, made fast ashore
the Egyptians' skill, the sea cables,
alas, by the coasts of Troy;   130

it was you, ships, that carried the fatal bride
of Menelaus, Castor her brother's shame,
the stain on the Eurotas.
Now she has killed
the sire of the fifty sons,   135
Priam; me, unhappy Hecuba,
she drove on this reef of ruin.

Such state I keep
to sit by the tents of Agamemnon.
I am led captive   140
from my house, an old, unhappy woman,
like my city ruined and pitiful.
Come then, sad wives of the Trojans
whose spears were bronze,
their daughters, brides of disaster,
let us mourn the smoke of Ilium.   145
And I, as among winged birds
the mother, lead out
the clashing cry, the song; not that song
wherein once long ago,
when I held the scepter of Priam,   150
my feet were queens of the choir and led
the proud dance to the gods of Phrygia.

> (*The First Half-chorus comes out of the shelter
> at the back.*)

First Half-chorus
  Hecuba, what are these cries?
  What news now? For through the walls
  I heard your pitiful weeping.   155
  and fear shivered in the breasts
  of the Trojan women, who within
  sob out the day of their slavery.

Hecuba
  My children, the ships of the Argives
  will move today. The hand is at the oar.   160

First Half-chorus

They will? Why? Must I take ship
so soon from the land of my fathers?

Hecuba

I know nothing. I look for disaster.

First Half-chorus

Alas!
Poor women of Troy, torn from your homes,   165
bent to forced hard work.
The Argives push for home.

Hecuba

Oh,
let her not come forth,
not now, my child
Cassandra, driven delirious   170
to shame us before the Argives;
not the mad one, to bring fresh pain to my pain.
Ah no.
Troy, ill-starred Troy, this is the end;
your last sad people leave you now,   175
still alive, and broken.

(The Second Half-chorus comes out of the shelter
at the back.)

Second Half-chorus

Ah me. Shivering, I left the tents
of Agamemnon to listen.
Tell us, our queen. Did the Argive council
decree our death?
Or are the seamen manning the ships now,   180
oars ready for action?

Hecuba

My child, do not fear so. Lighten your heart.
But I go stunned with terror.

« 619 »

Second Half-chorus

Has a herald come from the Danaans yet?
Whose wretched slave shall I be ordained?   185

Hecuba

You are near the lot now.

Second Half-chorus

Alas!
Who will lead me away? An Argive?
To an island home? To Phthiotis?
Unhappy, surely, and far from Troy.

Hecuba

And I,   190
whose wretched slave
shall I be? Where, in my gray age,
a faint drone,
poor image of a corpse,
weak shining among dead men? Shall
I stand and keep guard at their doors,
shall I nurse their children, I who in Troy   195
held state as a princess?

                  (*The two half-choruses now unite to form a
                          single Chorus.*)

Chorus

So pitiful, so pitiful
your shame and your lamentation.
No longer shall I move the shifting pace
of the shuttle at the looms of Ida.   200
I shall look no more on the bodies of my sons.
No more. Shall I be a drudge besides
or be forced to the bed of Greek masters?
Night is a queen, but I curse her.
Must I draw the water of Pirene,   205
a servant at sacred springs?
Might I only be taken to Athens, domain
of Theseus, the bright, the blessed!

Never to the whirl of Eurotas, not Sparta   210
detested, who gave us Helen,
not look with slave's eyes on the scourge
of Troy, Menelaus.

I have heard the rumor
of the hallowed ground by Peneus,   215
bright doorstone of Olympus,
deep burdened in beauty of flower and harvest.
There would I be next after the blessed,
the sacrosanct hold of Theseus.
And they say that the land of Aetna,   220
the Fire God's keep against Punic men,
mother of Sicilian mountains, sounds
in the herald's cry for games' garlands;
and the land washed
by the streaming Ionian Sea,   225
that land watered by the loveliest
of rivers, Crathis, with the red-gold tresses
who draws from the depths of enchanted wells
blessings on a strong people.

See now, from the host of the Danaans   230
the herald, charged with new orders, takes
the speed of his way toward us.
What message? What command? Since we count as slaves
even now in the Dorian kingdom.

(*Talthybius enters, followed by a detail of
armed soldiers.*)

Talthybius
Hecuba, incessantly my ways have led me to Troy   235
as the messenger of all the Achaean armament.
You know me from the old days, my lady; I am sent,
Talthybius, with new messages for you to hear.

Hecuba
It comes, beloved daughters of Troy; the thing I feared.

« 621 »

Talthybius

    You are all given your masters now. Was this your dread?   240

Hecuba

    Ah, yes. Is it Phthia, then? A city of Thessaly?
    Tell me. The land of Cadmus?

Talthybius

    All are allotted separately, each to a man.

Hecuba

    Who is given to whom? Oh, is there any hope
    left for the women of Troy?   245

Talthybius

    I understand. Yet ask not for all, but for each apart.

Hecuba

    Who was given my child? Tell me, who shall be lord
    of my poor abused Cassandra?

Talthybius

    King Agamemnon chose her. She was given to him.

Hecuba

    Slave woman to that Lacedaemonian wife?
    My unhappy child!   250

Talthybius

    No. Rather to be joined with him in the dark bed of love.

Hecuba

    She, Apollo's virgin, blessed in the privilege
    the gold-haired god gave her, a life forever unwed?

Talthybius

    Love's archery and the prophetic maiden struck him hard.   255

Hecuba

    Dash down, my daughter,
    the keys of your consecration,
    break the god's garlands to your throat gathered.

Talthybius

    Is it not high favor to be brought to a king's bed?

Hecuba
　My poor youngest, why did you take her away from me?　　　　260

Talthybius
　You spoke now of Polyxena. Is it not so?

Hecuba
　To whose arms did the lot force her?

Talthybius
　She is given a guardianship, to keep Achilles' tomb.

Hecuba
　To watch, my child? Over a tomb?　　　　265
　Tell me, is this their way,
　some law, friend, established among the Greeks?

Talthybius
　Speak of your child in words of blessing. She feels no pain.

Hecuba
　What did that mean? Does she live in the sunlight still?

Talthybius
　She lives her destiny, and her cares are over now.　　　　270

Hecuba
　The wife of bronze-embattled Hector: tell me of her,
　Andromache the forlorn. What shall she suffer now?

Talthybius
　The son of Achilles chose her. She was given to him.

Hecuba
　And I, my aged strength crutched for support on staves,　　　　275
　whom shall I serve?

Talthybius
　You shall be slave to Odysseus, lord of Ithaca.

Hecuba
　Oh no, no!
　Tear the shorn head,
　rip nails through the folded cheeks.　　　　280

Must I?
To be given as slave to serve that vile, that slippery man,
right's enemy, brute, murderous beast,
that mouth of lies and treachery, that makes void   285
faith in things promised
and that which was beloved turns to hate. Oh, mourn,
daughters of Ilium, weep as one for me.
I am gone, doomed, undone,
O wretched, given   290
the worst lot of all.

Chorus

I know your destiny now, Queen Hecuba. But mine?
What Hellene, what Achaean is my master now?

Talthybius

Men-at-arms, do your duty. Bring Cassandra forth
without delay. Our orders are to deliver her   295
to the general at once. And afterwards we can bring
to the rest of the princes their allotted captive women.
But see! What is that burst of a torch flame inside?
What can it mean? Are the Trojan women setting fire
to their chambers, at point of being torn from their land   300
to sail for Argos? Have they set themselves aflame
in longing for death? I know it is the way of freedom
in times like these to stiffen the neck against disaster.
Open, there, open; let not the fate desired by these,
dreaded by the Achaeans, hurl their wrath on me.   305

Hecuba

You are wrong, there is no fire there. It is my Cassandra
whirled out on running feet in the passion of her frenzy.

(Cassandra, carrying a flaming torch, bursts
from the shelter.)

Cassandra

Lift up, heave up; carry the flame; I bring fire of worship,
torches to the temple.
Io, Hymen, my lord. Hymenaeus.   310

Blessed the bridegroom.
Blessed am I indeed to lie at a king's side,
blessed the bride of Argos.
Hymen, my lord, Hymenaeus.
Yours were the tears, my mother,   315
yours was the lamentation for my father fallen,
for your city so dear beloved,
but mine this marriage, my marriage,
and I shake out the torch-flare,   320
brightness, dazzle,
light for you, Hymenaeus,
Hecate, light for you,
for the bed of virginity as man's custom ordains.

Let your feet dance, rippling the air; let go the chorus,   325
as when my father's
fate went in blessedness.
O sacred circle of dance.
Lead now, Phoebos Apollo; I wear your laurel,
I tend your temple,   330
Hymen, O Hymenaeus.
Dance, Mother, dance, laugh; lead; let your feet
wind in the shifting pattern and follow mine,
keep the sweet step with me,
cry out the name Hymenaeus   335
and the bride's name in the shrill
and the blessed incantation.
O you daughters of Phrygia robed in splendor,
dance for my wedding,
for the lord fate appointed to lie beside me.   340

Chorus
    Can you not, Queen Hecuba, stop this bacchanal before
    her light feet whirl her away into the Argive camp?

Hecuba
    Fire God, in mortal marriages you lift up your torch,
    but here you throw a melancholy light, not seen

through my hopes that went so high in days gone past. O
  child,   345
there was a time I dreamed you would not wed like this,
not at the spear's edge, not under force of Argive arms.
Let me take the light; crazed, passionate, you cannot carry
it straight enough, poor child. Your fate is intemperate
as you are, always. There is no relief for you.   350

*(Attendants come from the shelter. Hecuba gently takes the
torch from Cassandra and gives
it to them to carry away.)*

You Trojan women, take the torch inside, and change
to songs of tears this poor girl's marriage melodies.

Cassandra

O Mother, star my hair with flowers of victory.
I know you would not have it happen thus; and yet
this is a king I marry; then be glad; escort   355
the bride. Oh, thrust her strongly on. If Loxias
is Loxias still, the Achaeans' pride, great Agamemnon
has won a wife more fatal than ever Helen was.
Since I will kill him; and avenge my brothers' blood
and my father's in the desolation of his house.   360
But I leave this in silence and sing not now the ax
to drop against my throat and other throats than mine,
the agony of the mother murdered, brought to pass
from our marriage rites, and Atreus' house made desolate.
I am ridden by God's curse still, yet I will step so far   365
out of my frenzy as to show this city's fate
is blessed beside the Achaeans'. For one woman's sake,
one act of love, these hunted Helen down and threw
thousands of lives away. Their general—clever man—
in the name of a vile woman cut his darling down,   370
gave up for a brother the sweetness of children in his house,
all to bring back that brother's wife, a woman who went
of her free will, not caught in constraint of violence.
The Achaeans came beside Scamander's banks, and died

day after day, though none sought to wrench their land from
    them   375
nor their own towering cities. Those the War God caught
never saw their sons again, nor were they laid to rest
decently in winding sheets by their wives' hands, but lie
buried in alien ground; while all went wrong at home
as the widows perished, and barren couples raised and nursed   380
the children of others, no survivor left to tend
the tombs, and what is left there, with blood sacrificed.
For such success as this congratulate the Greeks.
No, but the shame is better left in silence, for fear
my singing voice become the voice of wretchedness.   385
The Trojans have that glory which is loveliest:
they died for their own country. So the bodies of all
who took the spears were carried home in loving hands,
brought, in the land of their fathers, to the embrace of earth
and buried becomingly as the rite fell due. The rest,   390
those Phrygians who escaped death in battle, day by day
came home to happiness the Achaeans could not know;
their wives, their children. Then was Hector's fate so sad?
You think so. Listen to the truth. He is dead and gone
surely, but with reputation, as a valiant man.   395
How could this be, except for the Achaeans' coming?
Had they held back, none might have known how great he
    was.
The bride of Paris was the daughter of Zeus. Had he
not married her, fame in our house would sleep in silence still.
Though surely the wise man will forever shrink from war,   400
yet if war come, the hero's death will lay a wreath
not lustreless on the city. The coward alone brings shame.
Let no more tears fall, Mother, for our land, nor for
this marriage I make; it is by marriage that I bring
to destruction those whom you and I have hated most.   405

Chorus
    You smile on your disasters. Can it be that you
    some day will illuminate the darkness of this song?

Talthybius

Were it not Apollo who has driven wild your wits
I would make you sorry for sending the princes of our host
on their way home in augury of foul speech like this.   410
Now pride of majesty and wisdom's outward show
have fallen to stature less than what was nothing worth
since he, almighty prince of the assembled Hellenes,
Atreus' son beloved, has stooped—by his own will—
to find his love in a crazed girl. I, a plain man,   415
would not marry this woman or keep her as my slave.
You then, with your wits unhinged by idiocy,
your scolding of Argos and your Trojans glorified
I throw to the winds to scatter them. Come now with me
to the ships, a bride—and such a bride—for Agamemnon.   420

Hecuba, when Laertes' son calls you, be sure
you follow; if what all say who came to Ilium
is true, at the worst you will be a good woman's slave.

Cassandra

That servant is a vile thing. Oh, how can heralds keep
their name of honor? Lackeys for despots be they, or   425
lackeys to the people, all men must despise them still.
You tell me that my mother must be slave in the house
of Odysseus? Where are all Apollo's promises
uttered to me, to my own ears, that Hecuba
should die in Troy? Odysseus I will curse no more,   430
poor wretch, who little dreams of what he must go through
when he will think Troy's pain and mine were golden grace
beside his own luck. Ten years he spent here, and ten
more years will follow before he at last comes home, forlorn
after the terror of the rock and the thin strait,   435
Charybdis; and the mountain striding Cyclops, who eats
men's flesh; the Ligyan witch who changes men to swine,
Circe; the wreck of all his ships on the salt sea,
the lotus passion, the sacred oxen of the Sun

slaughtered, and dead flesh moaning into speech, to make   440
Odysseus listening shiver. Cut the story short:
he will go down to the water of death, and return alive
to reach home and the thousand sorrows waiting there.

Why must I transfix each of Odysseus' labors one by one?
Lead the way quick to the house of death where I shall
    take my mate.   445
Lord of all the sons of Danaus, haughty in your mind of pride,
not by day, but evil in the evil night you shall find your grave
when I lie corpse-cold and naked next my husband's sepulcher,
piled in the ditch for animals to rip and feed on, beaten by
streaming storms of winter, I who wore Apollo's sacraments.   450
Garlands of the god I loved so well, the spirit's dress of pride,
leave me, as I leave those festivals where once I was so gay.
See, I tear your adornments from my skin not yet defiled by
    touch,
throw them to the running winds to scatter, O lord of prophecy,
Where is this general's ship, then? Lead me where I must set my
    feet on board.   455
Wait the wind of favor in the sails; yet when the ship goes out
from this shore, she carries one of the three Furies in my shape.
Land of my ancestors, good-bye; O Mother, weep no more for
    me.
You beneath the ground, my brothers, Priam, father of us all,
I will be with you soon and come triumphant to the dead below,   460
leaving behind me, wrecked, the house of Atreus, which de-
    stroyed our house.

                    (*Cassandra is taken away by Talthybius and his soldiers.*
                                        Hecuba collapses.)
Chorus
    Handmaids of aged Hecuba, can you not see
    how your mistress, powerless to cry out, lies prone? Oh, take
    her hand and help her to her feet, you wretched maids.
    Will you let an aged helpless woman lie so long?   465

Hecuba

No. Let me lie where I have fallen. Kind acts, my maids,
must be unkind, unwanted. All that I endure
and have endured and shall, deserves to strike me down.
O gods! What wretched things to call on—gods!—for help
although the decorous action is to invoke their aid   470
when all our hands lay hold on is unhappiness.
No. It is my pleasure first to tell good fortune's tale,
to cast its count more sadly against disasters now.
I was a princess, who was once a prince's bride,
mother by him of sons pre-eminent, beyond   475
the mere numbers of them, lords of the Phrygian domain,
such sons for pride to point to as no woman of Troy,
no Hellene, none in the outlander's wide world might match.
And then I saw them fall before the spears of Greece,
and cut this hair for them, and laid it on their graves.   480
I mourned their father, Priam. None told me the tale
of his death. I saw it, with these eyes. I stood to watch
his throat cut, next the altar of the protecting god.
I saw my city taken. And the girls I nursed,
choice flowers to wear the pride of any husband's eyes,   485
matured to be dragged by hands of strangers from my arms.
There is no hope left that they will ever see me more,
no hope that I shall ever look on them again.
There is one more stone to key this arch of wretchedness:
I must be carried away to Hellas now, an old   490
slave woman, where all those tasks that wrack old age shall be
given me by my masters. I must work the bolt
that bars their doorway, I whose son was Hector once;
or bake their bread; lay down these withered limbs to sleep
on the bare ground, whose bed was royal once; abuse   495
this skin once delicate the slattern's way, exposed
through robes whose rags will mock my luxury of long since.
Unhappy, O unhappy. And all this came to pass
and shall be, for the way one woman chose a man.
Cassandra, O Daughter, whose excitements were the god's,   500

you have paid for your consecration now; at what a price!
And you, my poor Polyxena, where are you now?
Not here, nor any boy or girl of mine, who were
so many once, is near me in my unhappiness.
And you would lift me from the ground? What hope? What use?   505
Guide these feet long ago so delicate in Troy,
a slave's feet now, to the straw sacks laid on the ground
and the piled stones; let me lay down my head and die
in an exhaustion of tears. Of all who walk in bliss
call not one happy yet, until the man is dead.   510

(Hecuba, after being led to the back of the stage, flings herself
to the ground once more.)

Chorus
    Voice of singing, stay
    with me now, for Ilium's sake;
    take up the burden of tears,
    the song of sorrow;
    the dirge for Troy's death   515
    must be chanted;
    the tale of my captivity
    by the wheeled stride of the four-foot beast of the Argives,
    the horse they left in the gates,
    thin gold at its brows,   520
    inward, the spears' high thunder.
    Our people thronging
    the rock of Troy let go the great cry:
"The war is over! Go down,
    bring back the idol's enchanted wood   525
    to the Maiden of Ilium, Zeus' daughter."
    Who stayed then? Not one girl, not one
    old man, in their houses,
    but singing for happiness
    let the lurking death in.   530

And the generation of Troy
swept solid to the gates

to give the goddess
her pleasure: the colt immortal, unbroken,
the nest of Argive spears,
death for the children of Dardanus   535
sealed in the sleek hill pine chamber.
In the sling of the flax twist shipwise
they berthed the black hull
in the house of Pallas Athene   540
stone paved, washed now in the blood of our people.
Strong, gay work
deep into black night
to the stroke of the Libyan lute
and all Troy singing, and girls'   545
light feet pulsing the air
in the kind dance measures;
indoors, lights everywhere,
torchflares on black
to forbid sleep's onset.   550

I was there also: in the great room
I danced the maiden of the mountains,
Artemis, Zeus' daughter.
When the cry went up, sudden,   555
bloodshot, up and down the city, to stun
the keep of the citadel. Children
reached shivering hands to clutch
at the mother's dress.
War stalked from his hiding place.   560
Pallas did this.
Beside their altars the Trojans
died in their blood. Desolate now,
men murdered, our sleeping rooms gave up
their brides' beauty   565
to breed sons for Greek men,
sorrow for our own country.

*(A wagon comes on the stage. It is heaped with a number of
spoils of war, in the midst of which sits Andromache
holding Astyanax. While the chorus continues
speaking, Hecuba rises once more.)*

Hecuba look, I see her, rapt
to the alien wagon, Andromache,
close to whose beating breast clings   570
the boy Astyanax, Hector's sweet child.
O carried away—to what land?—unhappy woman,
on the wagon floor, with the brazen arms
of Hector, of Troy
captive and heaped beside you,
torn now from Troy, for Achilles' son   575
to hang in the shrines of Phthia.

Andromache
I am in the hands of Greek masters.

Hecuba
Alas!

Andromache
Must the incantation

Hecuba
(ah me!)

Andromache
of my own grief win tears from you?

Hecuba
It must—O Zeus!

Andromache
My own distress?   580

Hecuba
O my children

Andromache
once. No longer.

Hecuba
Lost, lost, Troy our dominion

Andromache
  unhappy

Hecuba
          and my lordly children.

Andromache
  Gone, alas!

Hecuba
              They were mine.

Andromache
  Sorrows only.

Hecuba
                  Sad destiny   585

Andromache
  of our city

Hecuba
          a wreck, and burning.

Andromache
  Come back, O my husband.

Hecuba
  Poor child, you invoke
  a dead man; my son once

Andromache
  my defender.   590

Hecuba
  And you, whose death shamed the Achaeans,

Andromache
  lord of us all once,
  O patriarch, Priam,

Hecuba
  take me to my death now.

Andromache
  Longing for death drives deep;

Hecuba

      O sorrowful, such is our fortune;   595

Andromache
 lost our city

Hecuba

    and our pain lies deep under pain piled over.

Andromache
 We are the hated of God, since once your youngest escaping
 death, brought down Troy's towers in the arms of a worthless
  woman,
 piling at the feet of Pallas the bleeding bodies of our young men
 sprawled, kites' food, while Troy takes up the yoke of captivity. 600

Hecuba
 O my city, my city forlorn

Andromache

     abandoned, I weep this

Hecuba
 miserable last hour

Andromache

    of the house where I bore my children.

Hecuba
 O my sons, this city and your mother are desolate of you.
 Sound of lamentation and sorrow,
 tears on tears shed. Home, farewell, since the dead have forgotten 605
 all sorrows, and weep no longer.

Chorus
 They who are sad find somehow sweetness in tears, the song
 of lamentation and the melancholy Muse.

Andromache
 Hecuba, mother of the man whose spear was death   610
 to the Argives, Hector: do you see what they have done to us?

Hecuba
 I see the work of gods who pile tower-high the pride
 of those who were nothing, and dash present grandeur down.

Andromache

We are carried away, sad spoils, my boy and I; our life
transformed, as the aristocrat becomes the serf.   615

Hecuba

Such is the terror of necessity. I lost
Cassandra, roughly torn from my arms before you came.

Andromache

Another Ajax to haunt your daughter? Some such thing
it must be. Yet you have lost still more than you yet know.

Hecuba

There is no numbering my losses. Infinitely   620
misfortune comes to outrace misfortune known before.

Andromache

Polyxena is dead. They cut your daughter's throat
to pleasure dead Achilles' corpse, above his grave.

Hecuba

O wretched. This was what Talthybius meant, that speech
cryptic, incomprehensible, yet now so clear.   625

Andromache

I saw her die, and left this wagon seat to lay
a robe upon her body and sing the threnody.

Hecuba

Poor child, poor wretched, wretched darling, sacrificed,
but without pity, and in pain, to a dead man.

Andromache

She is dead, and this was death indeed; and yet to die   630
as she did was better than to live as I live now.

Hecuba

Child, no. No life, no light is any kind of death,
since death is nothing, and in life the hopes live still.

Andromache

O Mother, our mother, hear me while I reason through
this matter fairly—might it even hush your grief?   635

Death, I am sure, is like never being born, but death
is better thus by far than to live a life of pain,
since the dead with no perception of evil feel no grief,
while he who was happy once, and then unfortunate,
finds his heart driven far from the old lost happiness.   640
She died; it is as if she never saw the light
of day, for she knows nothing now of what she suffered.
But I, who aimed the arrows of ambition high
at honor, and made them good, see now how far I fall,
I, who in Hector's house worked out all custom that brings   645
discretion's name to women. Blame them or blame them not,
there is one act that swings the scandalous speech their way
beyond all else: to leave the house and walk abroad.
I longed to do it, but put the longing aside, and stayed
always within the inclosure of my own house and court.   650
The witty speech some women cultivate I would
not practice, but kept my honest inward thought, and made
my mind my only and sufficient teacher. I gave
my lord's presence the tribute of hushed lips, and eyes
quietly downcast. I knew when my will must have its way   655
over his, knew also how to give way to him in turn.
Men learned of this; I was talked of in the Achaean camp,
and reputation has destroyed me now. At the choice
of women, Achilles' son picked me from the rest, to be
his wife: a lordly house, yet I shall be a slave.   660
If I dash back the beloved memory of Hector
and open wide my heart to my new lord, I shall be
a traitor to the dead love, and know it; if I cling
faithful to the past, I win my master's hatred. Yet
they say one night of love suffices to dissolve   665
a woman's aversion to share the bed of any man.
I hate and loathe that woman who casts away the once
beloved, and takes another in her arms of love.
Even the young mare torn from her running mate and teamed
with another will not easily wear the yoke. And yet   670
this is a brute and speechless beast of burden, not

like us intelligent, lower far in nature's scale.
Dear Hector, when I had you I had a husband, great
in understanding, rank, wealth, courage: all my wish.
I was a virgin when you took me from the house   675
of my father; I gave you all my maiden love, my first,
and now you are dead, and I must cross the sea, to serve,
prisoner of war, the slave's yoke on my neck, in Greece.
No, Hecuba; can you not see my fate is worse
than hers you grieve, Polyxena's? That one thing left   680
always while life lasts, hope, is not for me. I keep
no secret deception in my heart—sweet though it be
to dream—that I shall ever be happy any more.

Chorus

You stand where I do in misfortune, and while you mourn
your own life, tell me what I, too, am suffering.   685

Hecuba

I have never been inside the hull of a ship, but know
what I know only by hearsay and from painted scenes,
yet think that seamen, while the gale blows moderately,
take pains to spare unnecessary work, and send
one man to the steering oar, another aloft, and crews   690
to pump the bilge from the hold. But when the tempest comes,
and seas wash over the decks they lose their nerve, and let
her go by the run at the waves' will, leaving all to chance.
So I, in this succession of disasters, swamped,
battered by this storm immortally inspired, have lost   695
my lips' control and let them go, say anything
they will. Yet still, beloved child, you must forget
what happened with Hector. Tears will never save you now.
Give your obedience to the new master; let your ways
entice his heart to make him love you. If you do   700
it will be better for all who are close to you. This boy,
my own son's child, might grow to manhood and bring back—
he alone could do it—something of our city's strength.

On some far day the children of your children might
come home, and build. There still may be another Troy.   705

But *we* say this, and others will speak also. See,
here is some runner of the Achaeans come again.
Who is he? What news? What counsel have they taken now?

(*Talthybius enters again with his escort.*)

Talthybius
O wife of Hector, once the bravest man in Troy,
do not hate me. This is the will of the Danaans and   710
the kings. I wish I did not have to give this message.

Andromache
What can this mean, this hint of hateful things to come?

Talthybius
The council has decreed for your son—how can I say this?

Andromache
That he shall serve some other master than I serve?

Talthybius
No man of Achaea shall ever make this boy his slave.   715

Andromache
Must he be left behind in Phrygia, all alone?

Talthybius
Worse; horrible. There is no easy way to tell it.

Andromache
I thank your courtesy—unless your news be really good.

Talthybius
They will kill your son. It is monstrous. Now you know the truth.

Andromache
Oh, this is worse than anything I heard before.   720

Talthybius
Odysseus. He urged it before the Greeks, and got his way.

Andromache
This is too much grief, and more than anyone could bear.

Talthybius

He said a hero's son could not be allowed to live.

Andromache

Even thus may his own sons some day find no mercy.

Talthybius

He must be hurled from the battlements of Troy.

*(He goes toward Andromache, who clings fast
to her child, as if to resist.)*

No, wait!   725
Let it happen this way. It will be wiser in the end.
Do not fight it. Take your grief as you were born to take it,
give up the struggle where your strength is feebleness
with no force anywhere to help. Listen to me!
Your city is gone, your husband. You are in our power.   730
How can one woman hope to struggle against the arms
of Greece? Think, then. Give up the passionate contest.

This
will bring no shame. No man can laugh at your submission.
And please—I request you—hurl no curse at the Achaeans
for fear the army, savage over some reckless word,   735
forbid the child his burial and the dirge of honor.
Be brave, be silent; out of such patience you can hope
the child you leave behind will not lie unburied here,
and that to you the Achaeans will be less unkind.

Andromache

O darling child I loved too well for happiness,   740
your enemies will kill you and leave your mother forlorn.
Your own father's nobility, where others found
protection, means your murder now. The memory
of his valor comes ill-timed for you. O bridal bed,
O marriage rites that brought me home to Hector's house   745
a bride, you were unhappy in the end. I lived
never thinking the baby I had was born for butchery
by Greeks, but for lordship over all Asia's pride of earth.

Poor child, are you crying too? Do you know what they
will do to you? Your fingers clutch my dress. What use,   750
to nestle like a young bird under the mother's wing?
Hector cannot come back, not burst from underground
to save you, that spear of glory caught in the quick hand,
nor Hector's kin, nor any strength of Phrygian arms.
Yours the sick leap head downward from the height, the fall   755
where none have pity, and the spirit smashed out in death.
O last and loveliest embrace of all, O child's
sweet fragrant body. Vanity in the end. I nursed
for nothing the swaddled baby at this mother's breast;
in vain the wrack of the labor pains and the long sickness.   760
Now once again, and never after this, come close
to your mother, lean against my breast and wind your arms
around my neck, and put your lips against my lips.

(She kisses Astyanax and relinquishes him.)

Greeks! Your Greek cleverness is simple barbarity.
Why kill this child, who never did you any harm?   765
O flowering of the house of Tyndareus! Not his,
not God's daughter, never that, but child of many fathers
I say; the daughter of Vindictiveness, of Hate,
of Blood, Death; of all wickedness that swarms on earth.
I cry it aloud: Zeus never was your father, but you   770
were born a pestilence to all Greeks and the world beside.
Accursed; who from those lovely and accursed eyes
brought down to shame and ruin the bright plains of Troy.
Oh, seize him, take him, dash him to death if it must be done;
feed on his flesh if it is your will. These are the gods   775
who damn us to this death, and I have no strength to save
my boy from execution. Cover this wretched face
and throw me into the ship and that sweet bridal bed
I walk to now across the death of my own child.

(Talthybius gently lifts the child out of the wagon, which
leaves the stage, carrying Andromache away.)

Chorus

    Unhappy Troy! For the sweetness in one woman's arms'   780
    embrace, unspeakable, you lost these thousands slain.

Talthybius

    Come, boy, taken from the embrace beloved
    of your mourning mother. Climb the high circle
    of the walls your fathers built. There
    end life. This was the order.   785
    Take him.

                (He hands Astyanax to the guards, who lead him out.)
        I am not the man
    to do this. Some other
    without pity, not as I ashamed,
    should be herald of messages like this.

                                        (He goes out.)

Hecuba

    O child of my own unhappy child,   790
    shall your life be torn from your mother
    and from me? Wicked. Can I help,
    dear child, not only suffer? What help?
    Tear face, beat bosom. This is all
    my power now. O city,   795
    O child, what have we left to suffer?
    Are we not hurled
    down the whole length of disaster?

Chorus

    Telamon, O king in the land where the bees swarm,
    Salamis the surf-pounded isle where you founded your city   800
    to front that hallowed coast where Athene broke
    forth the primeval pale branch of olive,
    wreath of the bright air and a glory on Athens the shining:
    O Telamon, you came in your pride of arms
    with Alcmena's archer   805
    to Ilium, our city, to sack and destroy it
    on that age-old venture.

This was the first flower of Hellenic strength Heracles brought
   in anger
for the horses promised; and by Simois' calm waters   810
checked the surf-wandering oars and made fast the ships' stern
   cables.
From which vessels came out the deadly bow hand,
death to Laomedon, as the scarlet wind of the flames swept over
masonry straight-hewn by the hands of Apollo.   815
This was a desolation of Troy
twice taken; twice in the welter of blood the walls Dardanian
went down before the red spear.

In vain, then, Laomedon's child,   820
you walk in delicate pride
by the golden pitchers
in loveliest servitude
to fill Zeus' wine cups;
while Troy your mother is given to the flame to eat,   825
and the lonely beaches
mourn, as sad birds sing
for the young lost,   830
for the sword hand and the children
and the aged women.
Gone now the shining pools where you bathed,
the fields where you ran
all desolate. And you,
Ganymede, go in grace by the thrones of God   835
with your young, calm smile even now
as Priam's kingdom
falls to the Greek spear.   840

O Love, Love, it was you
in the high halls of Dardanus,
the sky-daughters of melody beside you,
who piled the huge strength of Troy
in towers, the gods' own hands   845
concerned. I speak no more

against Zeus' name.
But the light men love, who shines
through the pale wings of morning,
balestar on this earth now,   850
watched the collapse of tall towers:
Dawn. Her lord was of this land;
she bore his children,
Tithonus, caught away by the golden car
and the starry horses,   855
who made our hopes so high.
For the gods loved Troy once.
Now they have forgotten.

(Menelaus comes on the stage, attended by a detail of
armed soldiers.)

Menelaus

O splendor of sunburst breaking forth this day, whereon   860
I lay my hands once more on Helen, my wife. And yet
it is not, so much as men think, for the woman's sake
I came to Troy, but against that guest proved treacherous,   865
who like a robber carried the woman from my house.
Since the gods have seen to it that *he* paid the penalty,
fallen before the Hellenic spear, his kingdom wrecked,
I come for *her* now, the wife once my own, whose name
I can no longer speak with any happiness,   870
to take her away. In this house of captivity
she is numbered among the other women of Troy, a slave.
And those men whose work with the spear has won her back
gave her to me, to kill, or not to kill, but lead
away to the land of Argos, if such be my pleasure.   875
And such it is; the death of Helen in Troy I will let
pass, have the oars take her by sea ways back to Greek
soil, and there give her over to execution;
blood penalty for friends who are dead in Ilium here.
Go to the house, my followers, and take her out;   880
no, drag her out; lay hands upon that hair so stained

with men's destruction. When the winds blow fair astern
we will take ship again and bring her back to Hellas.

Hecuba

O power, who mount the world, wheel where the world rides,
O mystery of man's knowledge, whosoever you be,   885
Zeus named, nature's necessity or mortal mind,
I call upon you; for you walk the path none hears
yet bring all human action back to right at last.

Menelaus

What can this mean? How strange a way to call on gods.

Hecuba

Kill your wife, Menelaus, and I will bless your name.   890
But keep your eyes away from her. Desire will win.
She looks enchantment, and where she looks homes are set fire;
she captures cities as she captures the eyes of men.
We have had experience, you and I. We know the truth.

> (*Men at arms bring Helen roughly out of the shelter.*
> *She makes no resistance.*)

Helen

Menelaus, your first acts are argument of terror   895
to come. Your lackeys put their hands on me. I am dragged
out of my chambers by brute force. I know you hate
me; I am almost sure. And still there is one question
I would ask you, if I may. What have the Greeks decided
to do with me? Or shall I be allowed to live?   900

Menelaus

You are not strictly condemned, but all the army gave
you into my hands, to kill you for the wrong you did.

Helen

Is it permitted that I argue this, and prove
that my death, if I am put to death, will be unjust?

Menelaus

I did not come to talk with you. I came to kill.   905

Hecuba

No, Menelaus, listen to her. She should not die
unheard. But give me leave to take the opposite case;
the prosecution. There are things that happened in Troy
which you know nothing of, and the long-drawn argument
will mean her death. She never can escape us now.　　　　910

Menelaus

This is a gift of leisure. If she wishes to speak
she may. But it is for your sake, understand, that I give
this privilege I never would have given to her.

Helen

Perhaps it will make no difference if I speak well
or badly, and your hate will not let you answer me.　　　　915
All I can do is to foresee the arguments
you will use in accusation of me, and set against
the force of your charges, charges of my own.

　　　　　　　　　　　　　　　　　　　　First, then!
She mothered the beginning of all this wickedness.
For Paris was her child. And next to her the old king,　　　　920
who would not destroy the infant Alexander, that dream
of the firebrand's agony, has ruined Troy, and me.
This is not all; listen to the rest I have to say.
Alexander was the judge of the goddess trinity.
Pallas Athene would have given him power, to lead　　　　925
the Phrygian arms on Hellas and make it desolate.
All Asia was Hera's promise, and the uttermost zones
of Europe for his lordship, if her way prevailed.
But Aphrodite, picturing my loveliness,
promised it to him, if he would say her beauty surpassed　　　　930
all others. Think what this means, and all the consequence.
Cypris prevailed, and I was won in marriage: all
for Greek advantage. Asia is not your lord; you serve
no tyrant now, nor take the spear in his defense.
Yet Hellas' fortune was my own misfortune. I,　　　　935

sold once for my body's beauty stand accused, who should
for what has been done wear garlands on my head.

I know.

You will say all this is nothing to the immediate charge:
I did run away; I did go secretly from your house.
But when he came to me—call him any name you will: 940
Paris? or Alexander? or the spirit of blood
to haunt this woman?—he came with a goddess at his side;
no weak one. And you—it was criminal—took ship for Crete
and left me there in Sparta in the house, alone.

You see?

I wonder—and·I ask this of myself, not you—   945
why *did* I do it? What made me run away from home
with the stranger, and betray my country and my hearth?
Challenge the goddess then, show your greater strength than
    Zeus'
who has the other gods in his power, and still is slave
to Aphrodite alone. Shall I not be forgiven?   950
Still you might have some show of argument against me.
When Paris was gone to the deep places of death, below
ground, and the immortal practice on my love was gone,
I should have come back to the Argive ships, left Troy.
I did try to do it, and I have witnesses,   955
the towers' gatekeepers and the sentinels on the wall,
who caught me again and again as I let down the rope
from the battlements and tried to slip away to the ground.
For Deiphobus, my second husband: he took me away
by force and kept me his wife against the Phrygians' will.   960

O my husband, can you kill me now and think you kill
in righteousness? I was the bride of force. Before,
I brought their houses to the sorrow of slavery
instead of conquest. Would you be stronger than the gods?
Try, then. But even such ambition is absurd.   965

Chorus

 O Queen of Troy, stand by your children and your country!
 Break down the beguilement of this woman, since she speaks
 well, and has done wickedly. This is dangerous.

Hecuba

 First, to defend the honor of the gods, and show
 that the woman is a scandalous liar. I will not   970
 believe it! Hera and the virgin Pallas Athene
 could never be so silly and empty-headed
 that Hera would sell Argos to the barbarians,
 or Pallas let Athenians be the slaves of Troy.
 They went to Ida in girlish emulation, vain   975
 of their own loveliness? Why? Tell me the reason Hera
 should fall so much in love with the idea of beauty.
 To win some other lord more powerful than Zeus?
 Or has Athene marked some god to be her mate,
 she, whose virginity is a privilege won from Zeus,   980
 who abjures marriage? Do not trick out your own sins
 by calling the gods stupid. No wise man will believe you.
 You claim, and I must smile to hear it, that Aphrodite
 came at my son's side to the house of Menelaus;
 who could have caught up you and your city of Amyclae   985
 and set you in Ilium, moving not from the quiet of heaven.
 Nonsense. My son was handsome beyond all other men.
 You looked at him, and sense went Cyprian at the sight,
 since Aphrodite is nothing but the human lust,
 named rightly, since the word of lust begins the god's name.   990
 You saw him in the barbaric splendor of his robes,
 gorgeous with gold. It made your senses itch. You thought,
 being queen only in Argos, in little luxury,
 that once you got rid of Sparta for the Phrygian city
 where gold streamed everywhere, you could let extravagance   995
 run wild. No longer were Menelaus and his house
 sufficient to your spoiled luxurious appetites.

So much for that. You say my son took you away
by force. What Spartan heard you cry for help? You did
cry out? Or did you? Castor, your brother, was there, a young   1000
man, and his twin not yet caught up among the stars.
Then when you had reached Troy, and the Argives at your heels
came, and the agony of the murderous spears began,
when the reports came in that Menelaus' side
was winning, you would praise him, simply to make my son   1005
unhappy at the strength of his love's challenger,
forgetting your husband when the luck went back to Troy.
You worked hard: not to make yourself a better woman,
but to make sure always to be on the winning side.
You claim you tried to slip away with ropes let down   1010
from the ramparts, and this proves you stayed against your will?
Perhaps. But when were you ever caught in the strangling noose,
caught sharpening a dagger? Which any noble wife
would do, desperate with longing for her lord's return.
Yet over and over again I gave you good advice: 1015
"Make your escape, my daughter; there are other girls
for my sons to marry. I will help you get away
to the ships of the Achaeans. Let the Greeks, and us,
stop fighting." So I argued, but you were not pleased.
Spoiled in the luxury of Alexander's house   1020
you liked foreigners to kiss the ground before your feet.
All that impressed you.
                        And now you dare to come outside,
figure fastidiously arranged, to look upon
the same air as your husband, O abominable
heart, who should walk submissively in rags of robes,   1025
shivering with anxiety, head Scythian-cropped,
your old impudence gone and modesty gained at last
by reason of your sinful life.
                        O Menelaus,
mark this, the end of my argument. Be true to your
high reputation and to Hellas. Grace both, and kill   1030

« 649 »

Helen. Thus make it the custom toward all womankind
hereafter, that the price of adultery is death.

Chorus

Menelaus, keep the ancestral honor of your house.
Punish your wife, and purge away from Greece the stigma
on women. You shall seem great even to your enemies.   1035

Menelaus

All you have said falls into line with my own thought.
This woman left my household for a stranger's bed
of her own free will, and all this talk of Aphrodite
is for pure show. Away, and face the stones of the mob.
Atone for the long labors of the Achaeans in   1040
the brief act of dying, and know your penance for my shame.

(*Helen drops before him and embraces his knees.*)

Helen

No, by your knees! I am not guilty of the mind's
infection, which the gods sent. Do not kill! Have pity!

Hecuba

Be true to the memory of all your friends she murdered.
It is for them and for their children that I plead.   1045

(*Menelaus pushes Helen away.*)

Menelaus

Enough, Hecuba. I am not listening to her now.
I speak to my servants: see that she is taken away
to where the ships are beached. She·will make the voyage home.

Hecuba

But let her not be put in the same ship with you.

Menelaus

What can you mean? That she is heavier than she was?   1050

Hecuba

A man in love once never is out of love again.

Menelaus

Sometimes; when the beloved's heart turns false to him.
Yet it shall be as you wish. She shall not be allowed

in the same ship I sail in. This was well advised.
And once in Argos she must die the vile death earned   1055
by her vile life, and be an example to all women
to live temperately. This is not the easier way;
and yet her execution will tincture with fear
the lust of women even more depraved than she.

(*Helen is led out, Menelaus following.*)

Chorus

Thus, O Zeus, you betrayed all   1060
to the Achaeans: your temple
in Ilium, your misted altar,
the flame of the clotted sacraments,
the smoke of the skying incense,
Pergamum the hallowed,   1065
the ivied ravines of Ida, washed
by the running snow. The utter
peaks that surprise the sun bolts,
shining and primeval place of divinity.   1070

Gone are your sacrifices, the choirs'
glad voices singing to the gods
night long, deep into darkness;
gone the images, gold on wood
laid, the twelves of the sacred moons,   1075
the magic Phrygian number.
Can it be, can it be, my lord, you have forgotten
from your throne high in heaven's
bright air, my city which is ruined
and the flame storm that broke it?   1080

O my dear, my husband,
O wandering ghost
unwashed, unburied; the sea hull must carry me   1085
in the flash of its wings' speed
to Argos, city of horses, where
the stone walls built by giants invade the sky.   1090
The multitudes of our children stand

clinging to the gates and cry through their tears.
And one girl weeps:
"O Mother, the Achaeans take me away
lonely from your eyes
to the black ship
where the oars dip surf   1095
toward Salamis the blessed,
or the peak between two seas
where Pelops' hold
keeps the gates at the Isthmus."

Oh that as Menelaus' ship   1100
makes way through the mid-sea
the bright pronged spear immortal of thunder might smash it
far out in the Aegaean,
as in tears, in bondage to Hellas   1105
I am cut from my country;
as she holds the golden mirror
in her hands, girls' grace,
she, God's daughter.
Let him never come home again, to a room in Laconia 1110
and the hearth of his fathers;
never more to Pitana's streets
and the bronze gates of the Maiden;
since he forgave his shame
and the vile marriage, the sorrows   1115
of great Hellas and the land
watered by Simois.

   (*Talthybius returns. His men carry, laid on the shield of*
           Hector, the body of Astyanax.)

But see!
Now evils multiply in our land.
Behold, O pitiful wives
of the Trojans. This is Astyanax,   1120
dead, dashed without pity from the walls, and borne
by the Danaans, who murdered him.

Talthybius

 Hecuba, one last vessel of Achilles' son
 remains, manned at the oar sweeps now, to carry back
 to the shores of Phthiotis his last spoils of war.   1125
 Neoptolemus himself has put to sea. He heard
 news of old Peleus in difficulty and the land
 invaded by Acastus, son of Pelias.
 Such news put speed above all pleasure of delay.
 So he is gone, and took with him Andromache,   1130
 whose lamentations for her country and farewells
 to Hector's tomb as she departed brought these tears
 crowding into my eyes. And she implored that you
 bury this dead child, your own Hector's son, who died
 flung from the battlements of Troy. She asked as well   1135
 that the bronze-backed shield, terror of the Achaeans once,
 when the boy's father slung its defense across his side,
 be not taken to the hearth of Peleus, nor the room
 where the slain child's Andromache must be a bride
 once more, to waken memories by its sight, but used   1140
 in place of the cedar coffin and stone-chambered tomb
 for the boy's burial. He shall be laid in your arms
 to wrap the body about with winding sheets, and flowers,
 as well as you can, out of that which is left to you.
 Since she is gone. Her master's speed prevented her   1145
 from giving the rites of burial to her little child.

 The rest of us, once the corpse is laid out, and earth
 is piled above it, must raise the mast tree, and go.
 Do therefore quickly everything that you must do.
 There is one labor I myself have spared you. As   1150
 we forded on our way here Scamander's running water,
 I washed the body and made clean the wounds. I go
 now, to break ground and dig the grave for him, that my
 work be made brief, as yours must be, and our tasks end
 together, and the ships be put to sea, for home.   1155

Hecuba

Lay down the circled shield of Hector on the ground:
a hateful thing to look at; it means no love to me.

(*Talthybius and his escort leave. Two soldiers wait.*)

Achaeans! All your strength is in your spears, not in
the mind. What were you afraid of, that it made you kill
this child so savagely? That Troy, which fell, might be   1160
raised from the ground once more? Your strength meant
   nothing, then.
When Hector's spear was fortunate, and numberless
strong hands were there to help him, we were still destroyed.
Now when the city is fallen and the Phrygians slain,
this baby terrified you? I despise the fear   1165
which is pure terror in a mind unreasoning.

O darling child, how wretched was this death. You might
have fallen fighting for your city, grown to man's
age, and married, and with the king's power like a god's,
and died happy, if there is any happiness here.   1170
But no. You grew to where you could see and learn, my child,
yet your mind was not old enough to win advantage
of fortune. How wickedly, poor boy, your fathers' walls,
Apollo's handiwork, have crushed your pitiful head
tended and trimmed to ringlets by your mother's hand,   1175
and the face she kissed once, where the brightness now is blood
shining through the torn bones—too horrible to say more.
O little hands, sweet likenesses of Hector's once,
now you lie broken at the wrists before my feet;
and mouth beloved whose words were once so confident,   1180
you are dead; and all was false, when you would lean across
my bed, and say: "Mother, when you die I will cut
my long hair in your memory, and at your grave
bring companies of boys my age, to sing farewell."
It did not happen; now I, a homeless, childless, old   1185
woman must bury your poor corpse, which is so young.
Alas for all the tendernesses, my nursing care,

and all your slumbers goné. What shall the poet say,
what words will he inscribe upon your monument?
Here lies a little child the Argives killed, because   1190
they were afraid of him. That? The epitaph of Greek shame.
You will not win your father's heritage, except
for this, which is your coffin now: the brazen shield.

O shield, who guarded the strong shape of Hector's arm:
the bravest man of all, who wore you once, is dead.   1195
How sweet the impression of his body on your sling,
and at the true circle of your rim the stain of sweat
where in the grind of his many combats Hector leaned
his chin against you, and the drops fell from his brow!

Take up your work now; bring from what is left some robes   1200
to wrap the tragic dead. The gods will not allow us
to do it right. But let him have what we can give.

That mortal is a fool who, prospering, thinks his life
has any strong foundation; since our fortune's course
of action is the reeling way a madman takes,   1205
and no one person is ever happy all the time.

> (*Hecuba's handmaidens bring out from the shelter a basket of
> robes and ornaments. During the scene which follows,
> the body of Astyanax is being made ready for burial.*)

Chorus

Here are your women, who bring you from the Trojan spoils
such as is left, to deck the corpse for burial.

Hecuba

O child, it is not for victory in riding, won
from boys your age, not archery—in which acts our people   1210
take pride, without driving competition to excess—
that your sire's mother lays upon you now these treasures
from what was yours before; though now the accursed of God,
Helen, has robbed you, she who has destroyed as well
the life in you, and brought to ruin all our house.   1215

Chorus

    My heart,
    you touched my heart, you who were once
    a great lord in my city.

Hecuba

    These Phrygian robes' magnificence you should have worn
    at your marriage to some princess uttermost in pride
    in all the East, I lay upon your body now.   1220
    And you, once so victorious and mother of
    a thousand conquests, Hector's huge beloved shield:
    here is a wreath for you, who die not, yet are dead
    with this body; since it is better far to honor you
    than the armor of Odysseus the wicked and wise.   1225

Chorus

    Ah me.
    Earth takes you, child;
    our tears of sorrow.
    Cry aloud, our mother.

Hecuba

                    Yes.

Chorus

    The dirge of the dead.

Hecuba

                 Ah me.   1230

Chorus

    Evils never to be forgotten.

Hecuba

    I will bind up your wounds with bandages, and be
    your healer: a wretched one, in name alone, no use.
    Among the dead your father will take care of you.

Chorus

    Rip, tear your faces with hands   1235
    that beat like oars.
    Alas.

Hecuba

Dear women. . . .

Chorus

Hecuba, speak to us. We are yours. What did you cry aloud?

Hecuba

The gods meant nothing except to make life hard for me,   1240
and of all cities they chose Troy to hate. In vain
we sacrificed. And yet had not the very hand
of God gripped and crushed this city deep in the ground,
we should have disappeared in darkness, and not given
a theme for music, and the songs of men to come.   1245
You may go now, and hide the dead in his poor tomb;
he has those flowers that are the right of the underworld.
I think it makes small difference to the dead, if they
are buried in the tokens of luxury. All this
is an empty glorification left for those who live.   1250

                    (*The soldiers take up and carry away the body
                                     of Astyanax.*)

Chorus

Sad mother, whose hopes were so huge
for your life. They are broken now.
Born to high blessedness
and a lordly line·
your death was horror.   1255

But see, see
on the high places of Ilium
the torchflares whirling in the hands
of men. For Troy
some ultimate agony.

                    (*Talthybius comes back, with numerous men.*)

Talthybius

I call to the captains who have orders to set fire   1260
to the city of Priam: shield no longer in the hand
the shining flame. Let loose the fire upon it. So

with the citadel of Ilium broken to the ground
we can take leave of Troy, in gladness, and go home.

I speak to you, too, for my orders include this.   1265
Children of Troy, when the lords of the armament sound
the high echoing crash of the trumpet call, then go
to the ships of the Achaeans, to be taken away
from this land. And you, unhappiest and aged woman,
go with them. For Odysseus' men are here, to whom   1270
enslaved the lot exiles you from your native land.

Hecuba
    Ah, wretched me. So this is the unhappy end
    and goal of all the sorrows I have lived. I go
    forth from my country and a city lit with flames.
    Come, aged feet; make one last weary struggle, that I   1275
    may hail my city in its affliction. O Troy, once
    so huge over all Asia in the drawn wind of pride,
    your very name of glory shall be stripped away.
    They are burning you, and us they drag forth from our land
    enslaved. O gods! Do I call upon those gods for help?   1280
    I cried to them before now, and they would not hear.
    Come then, hurl ourselves into the pyre. Best now
    to die in the flaming ruins of our fathers' house!

Talthybius
    Unhappy creature, ecstatic in your sorrows! Men,
    take her, spare not. She is Odysseus' property.   1285
    You have orders to deliver her into his hands.

Hecuba
    O sorrow.
    Cronion, Zeus, lord of Phrygia,
    prince of our house, have you seen
    the dishonor done to the seed of Dardanus?   1290

Chorus
    He has seen, but the great city
    is a city no more, it is gone. There is no Troy.

Hecuba

O sorrow.
Ilium flares.   1295
The chambers of Pergamum take fire,
the citadel and the wall's high places.

Chorus

Our city fallen to the spear
fades as smoke winged in the sky.
halls hot in the swept fire   1300
and the fierce lances.

Hecuba

O soil where my children grew.

Chorus

Alas.

Hecuba

O children, hear me; it is your mother who calls.

Chorus

They are dead you cry to. This is a dirge.

Hecuba

I lean my old body against the earth   1305
and both hands beat the ground.

Chorus

I kneel to the earth, take up
the cry to my own dead,
poor buried husband.

Hecuba

We are taken, dragged away

Chorus

                            a cry of pain, pain   1310

Hecuba

under the slave's roof

Chorus

                    away from my country.

Hecuba

Priam, my Priam. Dead
graveless, forlorn,
you know not what they have done to me.

Chorus

Now dark, holy death   1315
in the brutal butchery closed his eyes.

Hecuba

O gods' house, city beloved

Chorus

alas

Hecuba

you are given the red flame and the spear's iron.

Chorus

You will collapse to the dear ground and be nameless.

Hecuba

Ash as the skyward smoke wing   1320
piled will blot from my sight the house where I lived once.

Chorus

Lost shall be the name on the land,
all gone, perished. Troy, city of sorrow,
is there no longer.

Hecuba

Did you see, did you hear?

Chorus

                            The crash of the citadel.   1325

Hecuba

The earth shook, riven

Chorus

                    to engulf the city.

Hecuba

O
shaking, tremulous limbs,

this is the way. Forward:
into the slave's life.   1330

Chorus

Mourn for the ruined city, then go away
to the ships of the Achaeans.

*(Hecuba is led away, and all go out, leaving
the stage empty.)*

[PRINTED
IN U·S·A]